ISLAM AND S

ISLAM AND STATECRAFT

Religious Soft Power in the Arab Gulf States

Jon Hoffman

I.B. TAURIS
LONDON • NEW YORK • OXFORD • NEW DELHI • SYDNEY

I.B. TAURIS
Bloomsbury Publishing Plc
50 Bedford Square, London, WC1B 3DP, UK
1385 Broadway, New York, NY 10018, USA
29 Earlsfort Terrace, Dublin 2, Ireland

BLOOMSBURY, I.B. TAURIS and the I.B. Tauris logo are trademarks of Bloomsbury Publishing Plc

First published in Great Britain 2025

Copyright © Jon Hoffman, 2025

Jon Hoffman has asserted his rights under the Copyright, Designs and Patents Act, 1988, to be identified as Author of this work.

Cover design: Toby Way
Cover image © Wirestock, Inc./Alamy Stock Photo

All rights reserved. No part of this publication may be reproduced or transmitted in any form or by any means, electronic or mechanical, including photocopying, recording, or any information storage or retrieval system, without prior permission in writing from the publishers.

Bloomsbury Publishing Plc does not have any control over, or responsibility for, any third-party websites referred to or in this book. All internet addresses given in this book were correct at the time of going to press. The author and publisher regret any inconvenience caused if addresses have changed or sites have ceased to exist, but can accept no responsibility for any such changes.

A catalogue record for this book is available from the British Library.

Library of Congress Cataloging-in-Publication Data

Names: Hoffman, Jon, author.
Title: Islam and statecraft: religious soft power in the Arab Gulf states / Jon Hoffman.
Description: London; New York: I.B. Tauris, 2025. | Includes bibliographical references and index.
Identifiers: LCCN 2024026797 (print) | LCCN 2024026798 (ebook) | ISBN 9780755655687 (hardback) | ISBN 9780755655670 (paperback) | ISBN 9780755655694 (epub) | ISBN 9780755655700 (ebook)
Subjects: LCSH: Islam and international relations–Persian Gulf Region. | Soft power (Political science)–Persian Gulf Region. | Persian Gulf Region–Foreign relations.
Classification: LCC DS326 .H64 2025 (print) | LCC DS326 (ebook) | DDC 327.53–dc23/eng/20240823
LC record available at https://lccn.loc.gov/2024026797
LC ebook record available at https://lccn.loc.gov/2024026798

ISBN: HB: 978-0-7556-5568-7
PB: 978-0-7556-5567-0
ePDF: 978-0-7556-5570-0
eBook: 978-0-7556-5569-4

Typeset by Deanta Global Publishing Services, Chennai, India
Printed and bound in Great Britain

To find out more about our authors and books visit www.bloomsbury.com and sign up for our newsletters.

I dedicate this work to all those who have been persecuted in the name of Islam or for being Muslim.

CONTENTS

List of Figures	viii
INTRODUCTION	1
Chapter 1 RELIGION AND FOREIGN POLICY	17
Chapter 2 ISLAM AND STATECRAFT IN THE MIDDLE EAST	45
Chapter 3 SAUDI ARABIA	65
Chapter 4 QATAR	113
Chapter 5 UNITED ARAB EMIRATES (UAE)	151
CONCLUSION	197
Notes	211
References	260
Index	276

FIGURES

1 Religious soft power 9

INTRODUCTION

In 2023, the United Arab Emirates (UAE) debuted the "Abrahamic Family House" in Abu Dhabi. Hailed as a beacon of tolerance and modernity in the Middle East, the complex hosts a Christian church, a Jewish synagogue, and a Muslim mosque in an effort to foster interreligious harmony. In the center is a courtyard for worshipers from all three faiths to congregate in an environment designed to encourage peace and inclusivity. Such government-directed initiatives, marketed as a mechanism to advance peace, tolerance, and moderation, have become increasingly common throughout the Middle East over the past decade, with countries such as Saudi Arabia, Jordan, Morocco, Egypt, and many others launching various international initiatives focused on interfaith dialogue and countering "extremist" religious practices and interpretations.

However, such efforts are regularly paralleled by these same governments relying on religion as a mechanism to divide, repress, and demobilize. Indeed, despite an outward projection of an image rooted in tolerance and moderation, many of these same governments utilize religion to buttress authoritarian rule, limit the freedoms of their peoples, and legitimize their more aggressive policies abroad. For example, the UAE has marshaled religion as a tool of statecraft to prevent efforts toward democratization domestically and regionally. How do we make sense of such stark discrepancies?

The utilization of religion as a tool of international statecraft continues to play a prominent role in the Middle East and globally, with discrepancies—and at times, outright contradictions—between different methods of such usage remaining commonplace. Though the relationship between religion and international relations has received increased scholarly and policy attention over the past several decades, a comprehensive examination of the coupling of religion and state foreign policy remains an underexamined topic. Where this topic has been addressed, most analyses consider how religion constitutes an instrument of soft power for different actors spanning multiple faith traditions. However, though the notion of religion as a mechanism of soft power—popularly referred to as religious soft power—has received increased scholarly attention recently, a comprehensive analysis of the concept and a presentation of an analytical framework capable of conceptualizing the phenomenon remains absent. This study seeks to fill this void.

Why Religious Soft Power?

Religion has been, and continues to be, regularly used by a wide array of state, non-state, and transnational actors in international politics. Examples are everywhere. Religion has been used as a tool to justify imperialism, legitimize transnational terrorism, foster peace and reconciliation, discourage dissent, encourage liberation, and so on. Such usages often have profound ramifications for international politics, impacting state–society relations, engagement between states, and the broader global order. From Christian nationalism in the United States to China's repression of its domestic Muslim community or the Vatican engaging in transnational charity efforts and Russia marshaling religion to justify its military campaign in Ukraine, the relationship between religion and international politics remains a complex and multifaceted phenomenon. However, despite the continued prevalence of religion in international politics, the subject remains considerably underexamined, particularly as it relates to the usage of religion as a mechanism to buttress a state's foreign policy conduct.

The relationship between religion and international politics has steadily received increased scholarly and policy focus over the past several decades. This is despite the fact that religion has traditionally been largely neglected by the dominant theories of international relations (IR). Efforts to reconcile this absence of religion from IR discussions accelerated dramatically following the September 11, 2001, terrorist attacks within the United States and the rise of groups such as *al-Qaeda* and the "Islamic State" (ISIS). Furthermore, questions pertaining to the role of religion in international politics have once again received new impetus as the prevailing "Liberal World Order" dominated by the West—particularly the United States—begins to deteriorate in the face of growing domestic and international challenges.

Yet, despite the increased focus on the relationship between religion and the field of IR, the subject of how religion relates to foreign policy remains considerably underexamined. States regularly utilize religion as a mechanism to buttress their foreign policy conduct. Where the topic of religion and foreign policy has been addressed, most scholarship tends to embrace one of the three major paradigms concerning the relationship between religion and international politics: primordialism, instrumentalism, or constructivism. However, for reasons explained in this study, none of these paradigms in isolation are capable of adequately conceptualizing the myriad competing and often contradictory ways different states utilize religion as a tool of statecraft. Scholarship addressing these relationships remains overwhelmingly concerned with how religion ultimately impacts political outcomes at the international level in a rather linear manner, namely, how religion influences politics.

This study seeks to flip the causal script by examining the ways in which political considerations impact how religion is marshaled as a tool of foreign policy. Instead of religion influencing political outcomes, this analysis examines how politics influences religious outcomes. As will be demonstrated herein, states appropriate and construct religious discourses, doctrines, histories, and symbols primarily according to the particular threats facing political elites at a given time within specific contexts. The specific threats facing political elites in different contexts serve to influence and constrain how religion is coupled with a state's broader foreign policy conduct. So too does the presence or absence of religious resources—or "sacred capital"[1] —influence how states utilize religion to counter such threats. The pool of religious resources available for political elites to mobilize in the service of their strategic interests can considerably influence how religion is ultimately marshaled in the service of the state.

It is the constellation of domestic and foreign threats facing political elites as well as their evolution across time and space and the ability of the state to marshal religious resources at their disposal that most fundamentally shapes the differing ways religion is mobilized as a tool of statecraft. When a domestic threat to regime elites is present, the state must devote resources to combating this internal challenge and preserving the legitimacy of the status quo. If this internal threat is compounded by an interconnected external threat—and if this interrelated threat is perceived by regime leadership as existential in nature—the foreign policy conduct of the state will be centered around combating these intimately tethered threats to political elites. When a domestic threat is absent or at a level perceived as insignificant enough to considerably challenge the authority of regime elites, the state will benefit from a far wider field of maneuverability, given that political elites will have more flexibility to divert their resources to advancing their interests externally without the fear of being challenged internally.

Regime preservation will be far easier to maintain, allowing political elites to shift their focus more toward power projection. The form(s) religion assumes will be influenced by these threat perceptions and the fundamental objectives of political elites to maintain and strengthen their power and influence. Political elites will pick and choose—or, where absent, construct their own—religious narratives, doctrines, jurisprudence, and identities through which to best preserve and advance their own strategic interests.

This analysis uses the concept of religious soft power to establish a new theoretical framework through which the utilization of religion as part of a state's broader foreign policy conduct can be examined. Although the notion of religious soft power has received increased scholarly attention recently, a comprehensive analysis of the concept and the presentation of an analytical framework remain absent. In coupling religious discourse, symbols, doctrines, or jurisprudence with foreign policy objectives, states create religious soft power strategies in order to best advance their strategic imperatives. Religious soft power as a concept is flexible enough to allow for the inclusion of power-based, identity-based, and ideational variables. As will be explained, a state's particular religious soft power strategy—and the causal mechanisms influencing foreign policy decision-making at a given point in time—is inexorably linked to the context within which it is operating and the intended target audience it is seeking to influence.

Why the Middle East?

The Middle East was selected for this study due to the continued widespread prevalence of essentialist and reductionist analytical frameworks examining the relationship between religion and politics in the region. Indeed, the study of the relationship between Islam and politics—including Islam's relationship with the foreign policy conduct of specific states—was for a long period dominated by orientalist assumptions and paradigms that continue to influence certain academic and policy-oriented research. That Islam and the Middle East are both "unique" has permeated academic and policy discourse for decades, as has the notion that Islam—and its relationship with politics across time and space—has remained monolithic.[2] As May Darwich[3] contends, many scholars have long treated the Middle East as too "exceptional" to be theory relevant, subsequently resulting in the region's presentation as a context that defies existing theoretical arguments and approaches in international politics scholarship. Works such as Bernard Lewis's[4] "The Roots of Muslim Rage" and Samuel Huntington's[5] *The Clash of Civilizations* sought to explain all behaviors of Muslims—political, economic, social, and so on—as firmly rooted within an inherently "intolerant" and "hostile" Islamic tradition. Other scholars such as Bolling[6] assert that "the divorce of religion from politics . . . has little standing in the Middle East of today . . . for both good and evil ends, the interaction of religion and politics in the Middle East is a far more powerful force than is the case in any other part of the world." Shadi Hamid,[7] in his book *Islamic Exceptionalism*, succinctly encapsulates the idea that Islam is inherently unique in its relationship with politics: "Islam is, in fact, distinctive in how it relates to politics. Islam is different. This difference has profound implications for the future of the Middle East and, by extension, for the world in which we all live." The supposed exceptionalism of Islam and its relationship with politics have often dominated academic and policy analyses, leading to conclusions that often treat conventional political science tools as inadequate for understanding this relationship.

Debates surrounding Islam's relationship with politics received new impetus following the eruption of the Arab uprisings across the Middle East. This is particularly true for questions addressing the utilization of religion as a tool of statecraft amidst heightened geopolitical competitions following this wave of mass mobilization and the shocks delivered to the regional status quo because of the uprisings. This utilization of Islam by different Middle East states varies widely both between and within cases, often oscillating between both inter- and intra-sectarian argumentation, strict traditionalism and "republicanism," and so on. However, research examining this topic following the uprisings tends to lack a unified framework through which to analyze these evolving dynamics, namely, the differing and often contradicting ways states in the Middle East mobilize religion as part of their broader foreign policy conduct. Many analyses examining the utilization of religion as a tool of statecraft in the Middle East remain overwhelmingly fixated on how Islam influences the foreign policies of different state actors. That Islam, due to its "unique" or "exceptional" relationship with politics, drives political outcomes at the international level in the Middle East is a myth this research seeks to counter by demonstrating how the political considerations of ruling elites—specifically, the intersection of domestic and foreign threats—influence and constrain the kinds of religious soft power strategies adopted by states in the region. In order to properly conceptualize the dramatic variation often present both between and within cases, a new framework is needed, one that is capable of analyzing the differing and often contradictory ways religion is utilized by state actors as a tool of statecraft.

Toward a New Framework

The coupling of religion and state foreign policy conduct can assume a myriad of different—and often competing—forms. The utilization of religion as a tool of statecraft differs not only between states but often internally as well, depending on the specific contexts within which the state is operating at any particular time. These different initiatives pursued by the state mobilizing religion as a tool of soft power— referred to herein as religious soft power strategies—vary considerably both between and within cases.

These strategies can be top-down or bottom-up in nature; particularistic or pluralistic in scope and vision; proactive or reactive; designed to preserve the status quo or encourage a more revisionist, or even liberating, vision; directed internally toward one's own faith community or externally toward other faith communities; or designed to legitimize or delegitimize specific actors and/or policies. Some religious soft power strategies rely on deeply rooted communal identities, while others seek to construct new identities. Some emphasize strict traditionalism and adherence to a particular established orthodoxy and orthopraxy, while others are more "progressive" in orientation, challenging such entrenched approaches. Religion can assume a more subtle, complementary role in statecraft, or it can assume a more central and, in some cases, dominant position in a state's conduct abroad. Or, as is quite common, states often pursue an amalgamation of different—even competing/contradicting—strategies according to the specific context within which they are operating, the target audience they are seeking to influence, and the religious resources at their disposal.

What explains the variation in the ways religion is utilized as a tool of statecraft? What explains the variation between the religious soft power strategies pursued by different states as well as the variation between strategies pursued by the same state actor? This research probes the causal mechanisms behind this variation and seeks to establish a more comprehensive theoretical framework of religious soft power and the causal factors that influence a state's religious soft power strategy. It does so by bridging the two dominant paradigms—instrumentalism and constructivism—that have come to dominate the literature on the relationship between religion and international politics. Since these paradigms are concerned with a more high-level examination of the relationship between religion and international politics without a thorough discussion of causality, it remains necessary to analyze the actual primary causal mechanisms driving a state's foreign policy conduct, the coupling of religion with such conduct, and how we can account for variation both between and within observed religious soft power strategies.

There are four primary plausible causal mechanisms within these two broader paradigms that will be examined here, though it is recognized that there may be other mechanisms at work in addition to the preliminary few: (1) foreign (external) threat perceptions, (2) foreign (external) *and* domestic (internal) threat perceptions, (3) identity, and (4) ideology. These causal mechanisms should not be viewed as mutually exclusive and are often interconnected. The first two causal mechanisms are located underneath the instrumentalist umbrella, while the second two are located underneath the constructivist umbrella.

This research uses three in-depth case studies to develop and test the theoretical framework of religious soft power. Case studies are "an in-depth study of a single unit (a relatively bounded phenomenon) where the scholar's aim is to elucidate features of a larger class of similar phenomena."[8] They are particularly effective for developing, testing, and challenging theoretical frameworks due to their emphasis on "thick description" and ability to examine the microfoundations of causality when observing specific phenomena. Case study analysis is most appropriate for this study to uncover the causal process behind variations in the ways religion is utilized as a tool of statecraft by different states.

To gather such diagnostic evidence most efficiently, this research utilizes both process-tracing and cross-case comparison. Process-tracing dives internally into cases and traces the causal chain between the proposed causal mechanisms (independent variables [IVs]) and the observed phenomena (dependent variables [DVs]). Process-tracing probes for the causal mechanisms linking causes and outcomes together by "unpacking the constituent parts of the causal process."[9] In other words, process-tracing documents the unfolding of events over time to establish the causal chain—"the multistage causal process"— linking the IV and DV.[10] By establishing the microfoundations of causality and documenting the causal sequence leading to the outcome of interest, process-tracing is used to "establish the validity of trends and relationships within complex cases that are explored in considerable detail."[11]

However, since process-tracing is a tool of within-case analysis, it must be coupled with cross-case comparison to generalize more broadly about causal processes. This is essential for the wider applicability of the theoretical framework of religious soft power developed herein. Therefore, this research conducts a cross-case analysis of the religious soft power strategies implemented by these states to make these broader generalizations and draw better inference regarding the relationship between religion and state foreign policy conduct in a more generalized sense. This combination of within-case and cross-case analyses is critical: the strongest means of drawing causal inference from case studies is the combination of both within-case and cross-case analyses.[12] It is this combination of process-tracing (to establish the causal chain) and cross-case comparison (to gauge the applicability of these specific cases to a larger population of cases) that generates a strong and transferable theory.[13] The intensive internal examination of these three cases combined with in-depth cross-analysis of my cases provides the best methodology through which to investigate both within- and across-unit variation found in the dependent variable.

The three cases selected for this analysis—Saudi Arabia, Qatar, and the UAE—were chosen for several reasons. First, these cases were chosen in accordance with what is referred to as the "method of difference" or a "most similar systems design."[14] Here, cases are selected that are as similar as possible, except with regard to the phenomenon under observation, in order to keep constant as many other variables as possible. These three cases are strikingly similar in most areas besides the variable under consideration—similar autocratic monarchial governments, adherence to conservative forms of Sunni Islam, culture, geographic location, rentier economies powered by expatriate workers, and so on—allowing for the control of various other causal mechanisms possibly of relevance when conducting this cross-case comparison.

Second, these cases were selected because they represent the full spectrum of variation of religious soft power strategies pursued by Middle East states following the Arab uprisings. The religious soft power strategies pursued by Saudi Arabia, Qatar, and the UAE varied considerably not only between one another but also internally, with these states often utilizing religion as a tool of statecraft in different, often contradicting, ways according to the specific context within which they were operating, the target audience(s) they sought to influence, and the specific religious resources they possessed.

Political elites inside Saudi Arabia viewed the Arab uprisings primarily as an existential threat and mobilized religion mainly as a mechanism to help preserve the prevailing status quo internally and across the broader Middle East. Saudi Arabia engaged in a delicate balancing act following the uprisings, whereby it enforced a top-down, statist conceptualization of Islam rooted in strict traditionalism designed primarily to demobilize internally and in contexts where Riyadh's allies were challenged while simultaneously projecting an image to the West rooted in "tolerance" and "moderation." However, when presented with an opportunity to undermine their adversaries, Islam was quickly reshuffled to legitimize mobilization against Riyadh's enemies.

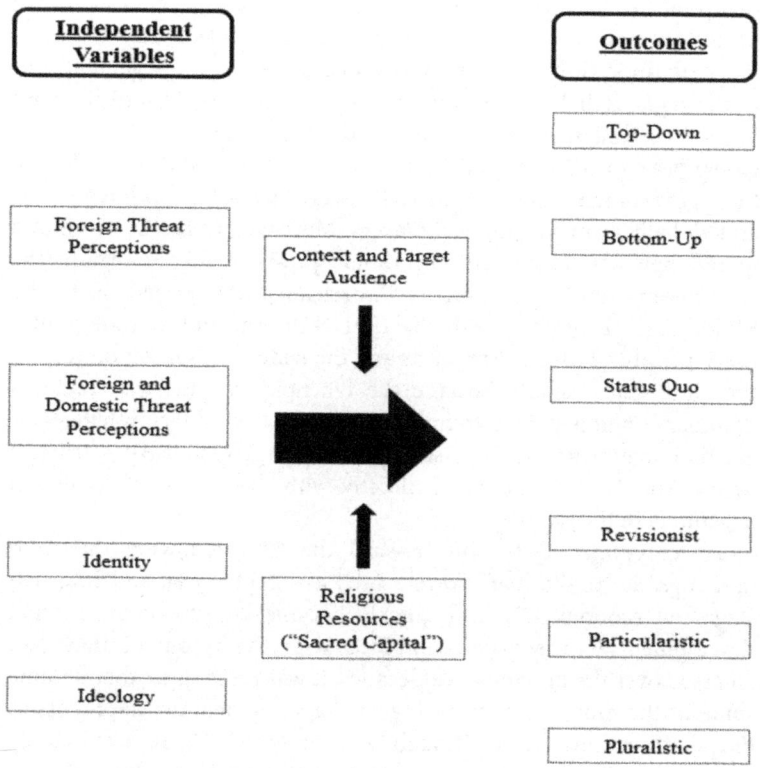

Figure 1 Religious soft power

On the other hand, Qatar, facing no considerable domestic threat to the authority or legitimacy of the ruling Al-Thani family, viewed the uprisings primarily as a strategic opportunity and mobilized religion as part of Doha's efforts to capitalize on the wave of mass mobilization that swept throughout the region. Doha embraced a bottom-up, community-oriented, and "republican" conceptualization of Islam abroad designed primarily to legitimize popular mobilization against (certain) established authorities. However, Islam was marshaled as a tool of demobilization in contexts where the ruling Al-Thani family had an interest in the preservation of the status quo.

The UAE viewed the uprisings primarily as an existential threat and mobilized religion in the effort to crush these popular movements while simultaneously asserting the Emirates as a major regional powerbroker. The UAE marshaled a statist, top-down "neo-traditionalist" Islam that reaffirmed the ultimate and unquestionable authority of the state and that projected an image to the West depicting the Emirates as a source of "moderation" and "stability" within the Middle East.

These three Gulf countries were chosen due to a more general shift in the regional balance of power in the Middle East toward the Gulf in recent decades. As oil production in the Gulf skyrocketed and the global price of the commodity steeply increased, so did the coffers of these governments, allowing them to assert themselves both regionally and globally as major political players. Moreover, as the United States increasingly established its hegemonic presence in the region, the Gulf became the foundation for American power projection in the Middle East. Beginning with the 1991 Gulf War and extending after the September 11 terrorist attacks and the wider "global war on terror," the Gulf states rapidly became the lynchpin of American regional dominance and benefited tremendously from US military, intelligence, and diplomatic support. The rise of the Gulf as a geopolitical powerhouse in the Middle East coincided directly with the advent of American hegemony in the region.

Power continued to shift toward the Gulf following the Arab uprisings, as "traditional" powers such as Egypt, Syria, and Iraq had stagnated economically and quickly became consumed by internal developments.[15] Therefore, combined with the resources they had amassed over the previous two decades, it was these states that became some of the most active in trying to shape regional developments in the post-uprisings period. Though Qatar and the UAE are considerably smaller than Saudi Arabia and may not traditionally be thought of as major regional powers, this has changed considerably over the past several decades given the dramatic shift of the political, economic, and geostrategic center of gravity in the Middle East toward the Gulf. For example, like Saudi Arabia, Qatar and the UAE are involved in almost every geopolitical fault line spanning the greater Middle East and North Africa, and they—like Riyadh—are at the forefront of the region's shift toward multipolarity.

Additionally, these Gulf states were selected due to the intimate relationship that exists between Islam and politics in these monarchies and the fact that Islam has regularly been mobilized as a tool of religious soft power to advance the strategic interests of these governments. At the same time as this power shift to the Gulf, there was also a shift away from Arab nationalism toward more overt expressions of Islamism. Religion emerged as a lucrative currency used by political elites in the Gulf to advance their interests at home and abroad. As Courtney Freer[16] details,

> Perhaps in the Gulf more than in any other region in the Middle East, Islam carries substantial political weight ... [Gulf states] invest large sums into Islamic causes to appear as pious rulers and thus to enhance their legitimacy, transforming religion into a potent political force. Islam thus has not only proven successful in strengthening government legitimacy, but also has provided a strong basis for political movements.

The methods selected for this study are not without their own limitations. In using process-tracing and cross-case comparison to examine the religious soft power strategies of Saudi Arabia, Qatar, and the UAE, this analysis has utilized a top-down approach, examining religious soft power from the perspective of the religious "producer." It remains to be seen how such strategies are viewed bottom-up from the perspective of the religious "consumer." In other words, how effective are these strategies in influencing their target audiences?

In terms of data, this project draws heavily upon both formal works of jurisprudence and doctrine as well as more informal discourse (sermons, lectures, public statements, etc.) drawing upon Islamic narratives, symbols, histories, and so forth, used by the institutions of these states (i.e., the clerical establishments) as well as *ulema* connected to the leaders of these polities. Clerical networks—specifically the relationship between religious organizations, institutions, and individuals and state authorities throughout the Middle East—will also be examined.

Religious Soft Power: Saudi Arabia, Qatar, and the United Arab Emirates

This analysis is concerned with establishing a theoretical framework of religious soft power to more holistically and systematically examine how religion is mobilized as a tool of contemporary statecraft and the causal processes behind variation both between and within cases. It seeks to uncover how religious texts, narratives, histories, and symbols are mobilized as a tool of statecraft to counter perceived domestic or foreign adversaries, attempts to construct and project a particular state identity, and efforts to construct and promote particular religio-political visions. Looking specifically at the Middle East following the Arab Uprisings, this framework is applied to the cases of Saudi Arabia, Qatar, and the UAE to elucidate how the underlying causal mechanisms addressed herein ultimately drive such variation. The investigation herein will trace ten years—from 2010 to 2020—and how Islam was coupled with the foreign policy conduct of these three states during this critical period in the Middle East history in order to generalize more broadly about the use of religion as a tool of statecraft.

The religious soft power strategies of Saudi Arabia, Qatar, and the UAE are a complex amalgamation of material, identity-based, and ideational variables. Of the four causal mechanisms considered in the analysis, the presence or absence of a perceived domestic threat to regime authority—coupled with an intimately interconnected presence of external threats—had the greatest causal impact on the religious soft power strategies adopted by Saudi Arabia, Qatar, and the UAE. Deciphering how to respond to specific threats facing political elites within these three countries was the first step of regime calculus from which Riyadh, Doha, and Abu Dhabi encountered the Arab uprisings. It represented the starting point from which Saudi, Qatari, and Emirati religious soft power would emerge as a coherent strategy to protect the authority and legitimacy of political elites within these three cases and project their influence abroad. The need for political elites to be strategically flexible to counter such threats is why these religious soft power strategies often differed dramatically between different contexts.

In short, the variation observed both between and within the religious soft power strategies of Saudi Arabia, Qatar, and the UAE is primarily the result of how political elites within these three countries maneuvered in the face of a diverse and evolving matrix of perceived threats following the Arab uprisings. These strategies involve the construction of specific religious narratives, identities, histories, and ideologies for the advancement of what are inherently political objectives, namely, the imperatives of regime preservation and power projection.

Outline of the Book

This book begins by first building a new theoretical framework for examining the relationship between religion and foreign policy in the contemporary world. Despite the increased focus on the relationship between religion and the field of IR, the subject of how religion relates to foreign policy remains underexamined. This chapter examines the three dominant paradigmatic approaches to understanding the relationship between religion and international politics: primordialism, instrumentalism, and constructivism. As will be demonstrated, instrumentalism and constructivism have emerged as the two dominant approaches, while primordialism has been rightly criticized for being too essentialist and, at times, outright prejudiced. After addressing the underlying causal mechanism within these two paradigms and explaining the need to bridge them conceptually, this analysis uses the concept of religious soft power to establish a new framework through which the utilization of religion as part of a state's broader foreign policy conduct can be examined.

Chapter 2 addresses the question of how Islam relates to international politics and the foreign policies of specific states, particularly following the 2011 Arab uprisings. As explained throughout the chapter, the coupling of Islam and state foreign policy conduct is neither purely instrumentalist nor constructivist in nature, but rather an interconnected combination of the two, best examined through the lens of religious soft power as formulated in the previous chapter. The framework of religious soft power developed in Chapter 1 is applied to literatures examining the relationship between Islam and politics. Looking specifically at state actors following the Arab uprisings, religious soft power as a framework best encapsulates the varied ways in which governments have appropriated and/or constructed narratives, jurisprudence, and doctrines rooted in Islam to buttress their foreign policy conduct.

Chapters 3–5 address the three case studies examined in this book. Beginning first with Saudi Arabia, Chapter 3 investigates the evolution of Riyadh's utilization of religion as a tool of soft power following the

Arab uprisings. The relationship between Islam and the Saudi state—a union which has historically served as the legitimizing foundation of the ruling Al-Saud family—is imperative to this discussion. Religion remains a critical resource used by Riyadh to advance its vast portfolio of interests at home and abroad. Material interests, ideology, and identity are all essential components comprising Saudi Arabia's religious soft power strategies. Saudi religious soft power remains a top-down initiative designed to buttress the authority of the regime while delegitimizing opposition and competing conceptualizations of the relationship between religion and politics. The eruption of the Arab uprisings represented an existential threat to Al-Saud. The threat faced by Riyadh was interrelated in nature: the uprisings threatened the regime at home and the broader authoritarian status quo in the Middle East and had the potential to transform the regional balance of power which they have traditionally benefited from. Additionally, critical to the evolution of Saudi religious soft power has been the rise to power of Crown Prince Mohammed bin Salman (MbS). Though MbS has been depicted as pursuing a fundamental "break" from Saudi Arabia's historic relationship with religion, it will be shown instead that religion is being remolded and recast toward MbS' desire to consolidate absolute power in the Kingdom.

Next, Chapter 4 examines the case of Qatar, namely, how Doha's strategy of religious soft power following the Arab uprisings was considerably different than the other two cases addressed in this book. Lacking a formally institutionalized religious establishment, Doha's approach has relied upon individuals, organizations, and networks associated with mainstream political Islamists, primarily the Muslim Brotherhood and its various regional affiliates. Facing no considerable political threat at home, the Arab uprisings were viewed by Doha as a strategic opportunity to expand its own influence across the Middle East and must be situated within the context of a broader turn in Qatari foreign policy in the post-1995 period. In the wake of the uprisings, Qatar assumed a more activist, society-oriented approach in support of the revolutions in Tunisia, Egypt, Libya, and Syria. The absence of a significant domestic political threat was critical for the calculus of the Al-Thani monarchy, allowing them to be almost entirely outward oriented during this period in support of these mass movements for change. However, this calculus did not extend to calls for fundamental change to the status quo within the Gulf region itself. In both Bahrain and Yemen, Qatar—an authoritarian government itself—preferred to operate underneath the GCC umbrella to preserve the status quo in these contexts. While Qatar's strategy was considerably successful during the uprisings and their immediate aftermath, the success of counterrevolutionary actors throughout and the intense crackdown on political Islamist movements have served to limit Doha's room to maneuver.

Chapter 5 investigates how the UAE responded to the Arab uprisings by first mobilizing hard power assets, then later assembling the resources needed for an effective religious soft power strategy during the second, counterrevolutionary phase of the Arab uprisings, beginning in earnest in 2013. This strategy was rooted in ongoing efforts within the Emirates to subordinate Islam to state authority and longstanding hostility toward Islamism among Abu Dhabi's leadership since the 1990s. The increased utilization of religion as a tool of statecraft by the UAE must be situated within the broader context of a turn in Emirati foreign policy toward greater assertiveness abroad. The UAE and its instruments of religious soft power have sought to portray the Emirates as a moderate, tolerant, and progressive country within the Middle East. Abu Dhabi has also sought to champion itself—primarily toward a Western audience—as a source of stability within a region wrecked by revolutionary upheaval, civil wars, and transnational terrorism. In doing so, the UAE has embraced a statist, top-down conceptualization of Islam that renders religion subservient to the state while mobilizing "moderate Islam" as a central pillar of their state-branding efforts. Moreover, Mohammed bin Zayed (MbZ), the architect of this strategy, has molded religion within the Emirates in such a way that buttresses his own authority and places his policies above questioning. The continued rise of MbZ has corresponded with the increased securitization of Emirati policies both at home and abroad.

Finally, this book concludes by bringing together common patterns and themes as well as diverging trends across the three cases addressed. Also discussed are the relevant scholarly and policy-oriented implications of this study, in addition to areas of future research that can build upon the theoretical framework produced herein.

Chapter 1

RELIGION AND FOREIGN POLICY

Religion has traditionally been largely neglected by the dominant theories of international relations (IR). As Markus Fischer[1] argues, this is primarily because the major paradigms of IR—with some exceptions—primarily follow a logic of Enlightenment rationalism. Such a rationalist, utility-maximizing approach privileges the pursuit of security, material well-being, and self-interest over ideational concerns. Classical realism, Neorealism, Liberalism, Liberal Institutionalism, and Marxism adhere to this rationalist approach. Constructivism, on the other hand, is more open to considering the role of religion due to its emphasis on ideas, culture, norms, and so on. As opposed to the more material focus of other theories, this approach is more interested in the construction of the identities and interests of actors, rather than taking them as given, arguing that material interests "cannot be understood apart from the cultural or ideological discourses that endow them with concrete meaning in the minds of the agents."[2] Since ideas construct "both identities and interests,"[3] the building blocks of international reality are ideational as well as material[4] and are socially constructed as opposed to the result of some unseen force.[5] Though most of the canonical constructivist literature says little to nothing about religion, the importance it ascribes to ideational and identity-based variables provides an initial framework for examining the significance of religion for international politics.

Jeffrey Haynes[6] explains that "International Relations has long seen the international as a demonstrably secular one. The fundamental norms of international relations were enshrined in the Treaty [Peace] of Westphalia (1648)—particularly the notion of state restraint in religious matters, and the general privatization of the latter, implying political marginalization." However, the post–Cold War era has witnessed a resurgence of literature focusing on the relationship between religion and IR.[7] The main purpose of these studies was to gauge the applicability and utility of existing IR theories in understanding the relationship between religion and international politics. This endeavor expanded dramatically following the September 11, 2001, terrorist attacks within the United States, and the rise of groups such as *al-Qaeda* and ISIS, as academics, journalists, and lay individuals scrambled to try and comprehend the religious motivations behind what many perceived as a hostile Islamic tradition that governed the actions and policies of Muslims and Muslim states.

The question of the role of religion in international politics has once again received new impetus as the prevailing "Liberal World Order" dominated by the West—particularly the United States—has begun to deteriorate in the face of growing domestic and international challenges. As Mandaville and Hamid[8] argue, it is becoming more important to "pay attention to the increased salience of culture, religion, and ideas in the context of an emerging post-liberal world order." As we increasingly enter what Amitav Acharya[9] refers to as a "multiplex world order"—a global order in which there is a multiplicity of important international actors (states, transnational corporations, transnational social movements, transnational terrorist organizations, etc.), as well as increased cultural, ideological, and political diversity among these important actors—being able to properly conceptualize the relationship between ideational variables (such as religion) and international politics will remain of paramount importance.

Despite the increased focus on the relationship between religion and the field of IR, the subject of how religion relates to foreign policy remains underexamined. Most studies addressing this relationship are concerned with how religion ultimately impacts political outcomes at the international level in a rather linear manner. Fox and Sandler[10] summarize this view succinctly when arguing that there are two primary ways religion can impact international politics: either via how particular belief systems influence the behaviors of policymakers or how widely held religious beliefs among a state's populace can serve as a constraining force on foreign policy decision-makers. They assert that "religion's greatest influence on the international system is through its significant influence on domestic politics. It is a motivating force that guides many policy makers." Likewise, Jeffrey Haynes[11] emphasizes how religion can impact international politics in two ways. First is through religious actors directly influencing the thought processes of foreign policy decision-makers and encouraging them to "adopt policies which are favored by the religious entity." Second, non-state religious actors that "regularly cross country borders in pursuit of their goals" can also impact how states act in the global sphere.

Missing here is the role of the states themselves and regime-driven uses of religion as a mechanism to advance their own interests. Of concern for this analysis are the varying ways in which states, specifically political elites, have incorporated religion into their broader foreign policy conduct to advance their own strategic imperatives. Foreign policy conduct refers to "the sum of external relations conducted by an independent actor (usually a state) in international relations."[12] Foreign policy is situated at the nexus of the international and the domestic—a "two-level," "dual," or "nested" game[13]—and foreign policy analysis "needs to be multilevel and multifaceted in order to confront the complicated sources and nature of foreign policy."[14] In order to determine how religion is used by the state as a strategic instrument, it is first necessary to examine the competing paradigms concerning the relationship between religion and international statecraft more broadly in order to then contrast the possible causal explanations offered concerning the link between religion and a particular state's foreign policy conduct more generally. In other words, it is necessary to first examine the *raison d'etre* for the use of religion in a state's foreign policy conduct to begin with and then zoom in to consider the main drivers of a state's foreign policy and how religion fits into this equation.

Broadly speaking, there are three dominant paradigmatic approaches to understanding the relationship between religion and international politics: primordialism, instrumentalism, and constructivism.[15] As will be demonstrated, instrumentalism and constructivism have emerged as the two dominant approaches as primordialism has been rightly criticized for being too essentialist and, at times, outright prejudiced. This being the case, it is then necessary to examine more specifically the primary causal mechanisms at work within these two respective camps that can explain the relationship between religion and foreign policy decision-making. Within the instrumentalist camp, these are (1) strictly foreign (external) threat perceptions and (2) foreign (external) *and* domestic (internal) threat perceptions. Within the constructivist camp, these are (1) identity and (2) ideology.

To bridge these paradigms and their underlying causal mechanisms, this analysis uses the concept of religious soft power to establish a new theoretical framework through which the utilization of religion as part of a state's broader foreign policy conduct can be examined. Although the notion of religious soft power has received increased scholarly attention recently, a comprehensive analysis of the concept and presentation of an analytical framework remains absent. This study seeks to fill this void. In coupling religious discourse, symbols, doctrines, or jurisprudence with foreign policy objectives, states create religious soft power strategies to best advance their strategic imperatives. Religious soft power as a concept is flexible enough to allow for the inclusion of power-based, identity-based, and ideational variables. As will be explained, a state's particular religious soft power strategy—and the causal mechanisms influencing foreign policy decision-making at a given point in time— is inexorably linked to the context within which it is operating, the intended target audience they are seeking to influence, and the religious resources they possess. The remainder of this chapter is dedicated to reviewing these competing paradigms and causal explanations, demonstrating how the concept of religious soft power can serve as a powerful conceptual bridge between them.

A War of Paradigms

Primordialism

The primordialist camp ascribes to religious actors a set of fixed theological beliefs whose political actions are the direct result of the actors' inflexible religious doctrines.[16] In other words, the primordialist camp "treats religion as an ever-present guide to individual and communal behavior."[17] In short, primordialists perceive religious political actors as driven by doctrine and dedicated to creating a political order modeled after their own divine outlook.[18] With shared religious tradition as the common denominator for these "communities of believers," those who fall outside of this tradition are sharply distinguished as "others" (nonbelievers, infidels, etc.). This distinction between believers and nonbelievers is critical to the primordialist approach and results in conceptualizing the world as strictly divided along these cultural lines. As such, the primordialist camp assumes that an inherent tension exists between religious traditions, which can range from cynicism to outright hostility.

When religion becomes the main source of a ruler's or country's identity, it impacts how that state interacts with other states. According to the primordialist approach, religiously similar states are more likely to cooperate due to their shared beliefs, values, and identities.[19] Conversely, there is more chance for friction between religiously dissimilar states due to ideational divergence, different values, and contrasting priorities.[20] Therefore, such a view purports that the degree of cooperation between states that share the same religious tradition should be greater than between those that adhere to different traditions. The primordialist understanding of religious identity is therefore based on "deeply rooted historical animosities between identity-based groups or on supposedly intrinsic qualities of a given religious identity, ideology, or community."[21]

With little room for the possibility of political change—due to the inherent adherence to inflexible religious doctrines—studies that adopt the primordialist explanation tend to focus almost exclusively on interreligious conflict or religiously inspired fundamentalism. Examples of such primordialist thinking span academia and journalism.[22] Huntington posits that with the end of the Cold War era, conflicts between different "civilizations," which he defines as "the highest cultural grouping of people and the broadest level of cultural identity people have short of what distinguishes humans from other species. It is defined by both common language, history, religion, customs, institutions and by the subjective self-identification of people."[23] Although religion is mentioned in conjunction with other factors such as language, history, etc., most of the civilizations Huntington lists—Western, Sino-Confucian, Japanese, Islamic, Hindu, Slavic-Orthodox, Latin American, and "possibly" African—include religion in their definition.[24] Therefore, in essence, Huntington's "clash of civilizations" may be described, largely, as a clash of religious identities.[25]

The primordialist approach suffers from numerous shortcomings. First, the approach assumes that religious communities are fixed, cohesive entities with shared, monolithic interests. The communities that comprise different religious traditions are incredibly diverse, as demonstrated by the various sects within major religious traditions such as Christianity, Islam, and Judaism. Moreover, the primordialist approach takes these religious communities as a "given," and does not address different conceptual debates surrounding these various diverse traditions. For example, the questions surrounding "what is Islam?"—how we are supposed to conceptualize and measure/analyze it—is heavily debated within the field of Islamic studies.[26] Assuming that there is such thing as a cohesive "Islamic civilization" (i.e., that the "Muslimness" of these countries/peoples somehow binds them together culturally or politically) is problematic. Scholars such as Cemil Aydin have detailed how the idea of assembling such a "Muslim world" based solely on the adherence of the majority of the population to Islam—which glances over the various historical, political, and cultural nuances of each of the different countries and communities that comprise it—is largely a product of Western imperialism and colonialism.[27] Such cultural essentialism masks the nuances within these highly diverse communities.

A further shortcoming of the primordialist approach is its overly deterministic framework. The primordialist camp presents no causal claim as to what explains the absence of tensions or cooperation between different religious traditions at different periods throughout history, nor does it explain the often-bitter religious infighting that takes place within these confessional communities. Furthermore, the assumption that religious actors adhere to "inflexible" religious doctrines denies the adherents of these traditions the agency whereby they are free to interpret these doctrines for themselves and subsequently act upon their respective exegesis. Finally, in assuming that these actors privilege religious belief/identity and subsequently act exclusively upon them, the primordialist approach neglects other possible motivating factors behind the use of religion in foreign policy conduct, such as the pursuit of material interests.

Instrumentalism

The dominant camp concerning the relationship between religion and foreign policy is the instrumentalist camp. Instrumentalism "rejects the view that differences in religion are real causes of political conflict," and instead emphasizes how religion is "used as a tool by self-interested elites" via manipulation of the masses to improve their strategic advantage.[28] In the instrumentalist view, religion is used "as a means to enhance something considered more 'real' and of higher significance."[29] In other words, this strategic manipulation of religion is for inherently political/material objectives, rather than ideational objectives: "it does not assume the exceptionalism of any identity or ideology, but only its utility to political actors—it is founded on the assumption that political elites seek to maximize payoffs for themselves, whether in terms of political survival, regime security, or victory in war."[30] This view of religion as a "political tool" by elites emphasizes how religious values, symbols, and rhetoric are used to advance personal political objectives, primarily the desire to remain in power. Therefore, "for the instrumentalist approach, religion is a political weapon, part of the arsenal of political elites (and counter-elites), that can be turned on or off based on political calculations regarding its utility and associated risk."[31]

The instrumentalist camp remains the dominant camp concerning the relationship between religion and international politics. As Markus Fischer[32] argues, this is primarily because the major paradigms of

IR—with some exceptions—primarily follow a logic of Enlightenment rationalism. Such a rationalist, utility-maximizing approach privileges the pursuit of security, material well-being, and self-interest over ideational concerns. Classical realism, Neorealism, Liberalism, and Marxism adhere to this rationalist approach and assume that the pursuit for material self-interest and security will dominate ideational concerns either outright or if the two come into conflict.[33]

Finding historical cases where purported ideational commitments such as religion were abrogated by strategic concerns is not difficult to come across and is often pointed to by proponents of the instrumentalist camp when framing their arguments. Some contemporary examples include the United States' funding of the *mujahideen* fighters in Afghanistan against the Soviet Union, the United States' relationship with Wahhabi Saudi Arabia, the growing partnership between the GCC countries and Israel (and the normalization of relations between Tel Aviv, the UAE, and Bahrain), and Iran's support for Sunni insurgents in Afghanistan to undermine US efforts there, among others.

Other studies employing the instrumentalist approach tend to focus specifically on how elites exploit religious symbols, identity, and rhetoric to manipulate the masses in the efforts to advance their own strategic interests. Religion has been strategically manipulated for elite interests in conflict settings such as the Sri Lankan civil war against the Tamil Tigers,[34] the Chechen secession wars of the 1990s,[35] the Iran–Iraq war,[36] the ethnic wars in the Caucasus and southeastern Europe,[37] the Syrian civil war,[38] and numerous other contexts. The invoking of real or imagined internal or external threats can also serve to unite a fractured ruling coalition or country around an embattled ruling regime.[39] Much work has also been done on the instrumentalist approach to religious sectarian politics, whereby elites strategically exploit sectarian divisions to divide the masses and buttress their own authority/legitimacy.[40] Similarly, instrumentalists have focused a great amount of attention on how religious political parties will strategically either abandon or "moderate" elements of their ideological doctrines to compete in elections.[41]

Despite its popularity, the instrumentalist approach too suffers from noticeable shortcomings. A purely instrumentalist approach—which emphasizes the primacy of material interests over ideational interests and views the latter solely as a means to achieve the former—glances over the fact that ideology is often necessary in order to mobilize, divide, or otherwise manipulate the masses in the first place. As Stein[42] argues, "it is difficult to reconcile instrumentalism's focus on material factors with its recognition that religious discourses are often necessary to mobilize the masses." In other words, the fact that the success of mass manipulation relies on the utilization of ideology and serves as such a useful means to leaders "implies that cultural concerns can rouse thousands of if not millions of people to political action," and therefore, religious and ethnic concerns must be perceived as an end by some element of the populace.[43] Therefore, if ideology is irrelevant, what explains the often massive and costly production—and the incessant use—of religious ideologies and narratives by elites in these contexts? If the strategic manipulation of religion is such a lucrative strategy, then the idea that religious ideology gains traction among the masses must imply that they view religious objectives as more than just a means toward a different, material, end.

The second criticism of the instrumentalist camp concerns the problematic way in which it views religious ideologies, specifically the fact that it interprets them as unitary and their evolution as unidirectional and unintentional. The approach fails to "explain the mechanism of ideological change or account for variation in the adoption or rejection of a [religious] ideology by the same political actors."[44] In other words, although the instrumentalist approach recognizes that elites strategically manipulate religion for their own purposes, it inherently views them as restricted to the confines of religious ideologies already available because it takes them "as exogenous and does not account for change in the content of ideology and activation of certain ideological attributes over time."[45]

Due to this limitation, the instrumentalist camp fails to account for how elites can strategically construct religious narratives, identities, and doctrines to meet their desired objectives, nor does it explain why elites adopt a particular ideology at a particular time (discussed more below). Connected with this critique is the underlying idea that elites are able to maintain exclusive control over the use of religion. As Fischer explains, leaders can lose control over the manipulation of religion, whereby the masses demand that elites pursue and advance the ideology that was originally intended by these leaders to only serve as the means to a more self-interested and strategic end.[46] Since the instrumentalist camp perceives religion as exogenous and unitary and does not provide an explanation as to how leaders can strategically construct their own religious doctrines and narratives, elites can quickly become prisoners of the very ideology they sought to manipulate.

Constructivism

The final camp is the constructivist camp. This group posits that the world is socially constructed and that it cannot be understood through reference to only material forces, but that it consists of both material and ideational factors.[47] In other words, the constructivist approach is more interested in the construction of the identities and interests of actors, rather than taking them as a given, and how they impact foreign policy conduct.[48] According to this logic, material interests "cannot be understood apart from the cultural or ideological discourses that endow them with concrete meaning in the minds of the agents."[49] Since ideas construct "both identities and interests,"[50] the building blocks of international reality are ideational as well as material[51] and are socially constructed as opposed to the result of some unseen force. [52]In short, "the fundamental idea of constructivism is that seemingly tangible factors, which appear to shape behavior in 'materialist' paradigms of world politics—interest, power, or international anarchy—are not exogenous," but are socially constructed concepts people come to ascribe certain meanings to.[53]

While, on the surface, the constructivist and primordialist approaches appear to be similar considering their emphasis on identity-based and ideational factors in driving actors' perceptions and actions, there is a significant difference in that constructivism provides an element of dynamism to the more static and determinist primordialist perspective: the importance of specific identity-based or ideational factors (such as religion) is not fixed throughout time and maintains the ability to transform.[54]

The social construction of identity and its ramifications for foreign policy conduct is a central tenet of the constructivist approach. As constructivists like Ted Hopf argue, "the identity of a state implies its preferences and consequent actions."[55] Such identities are derived and constructed from one's culture,[56] which includes religion. As Warner and Walker[57] argue, when religion is embedded in a particular country's national identity, religion should be expected to help shape how that country defines its foreign policy interests. Religion can also have an impact on foreign policy conduct by influencing the belief system or worldview of a particular policymaker and helping shape how they identify global problems, allies, enemies, and so on, and how they assess national interests.[58]

Under the constructivist approach, religion can also play a crucial role in the construction of legitimacy. Legitimacy can be defined as "the normative belief by an actor that a rule or institution ought to be obeyed."[59] Religion can play a central role in lending legitimacy to governments as well as specific policies: "to convince another that your policy preference is legitimate is to convince them that you are correct, perhaps even morally correct, and that they should support your policies and the actions based on those policies, or at least not oppose them."[60]

Constructivist studies emphasize how ideational and identity-based factors can have a significant impact on the foreign policy conduct of a particular state. Looking at the Middle East, Michael Barnett and Shibley Telhami[61] argue that common identity, rather than the notion of a shared threat, best explains alliance patterns in the region. Peter Hene[62] explains that "cultural-symbolic" instruments of power are one of the various tools states can use to organize international action. Similarly, Bassel Salloukh[63] contends that threats to identity are just as important as material threats to governments within the region. Likewise, Mark Haas[64] asserts that it is not simply power that defines the international system, but identity also plays a role in the way that states define friends and foes: states may "eschew alliances ... because they dislike and fear the ideological stance of a potential ally." Courtney Freer[65] notes the salience of these ideational factors in the foreign policy conduct on Middle East states, arguing that "foreign policy has been used to promote ideology" throughout the region.

The constructivist camp is not without its limitations. Although it allows for the influence of religion as an ideology and an identity, it still views foreign policy decision-makers as constrained by these very factors. Daniel Nexon[66] argues that "actors operating within a particular set of religious frameworks have a limited number of scripts, rhetorical commonplaces, and styles of reasoning available to them ... religious beliefs, experiences, and frameworks draw boundaries, however blurred, around what constitutes acceptable arguments and warrants."[67] Fox and Sandal[68] proffer a similar argument, suggesting that religious beliefs and worldviews influence international politics via the "constraints placed on policymakers by widely held religious beliefs among their constituents ... it may be unwise for policymakers to take an action that runs counter to some belief, moral, or value that is cherished by their constituents ... to do so could easily undermine the legitimacy of the regime and its rulers."

However, this approach does not account for how actors can strategically construct their own doctrines or identities to serve their strategic imperatives. In other words, the approach is primarily concerned with how ideology can influence or drive political interests but neglects how political interests can influence or drive changes in ideology.[69] Moreover, the constructivist approach offers no causal explanation as to why—in many cases throughout history—identity and ideology have been sidelined in the foreign policy conduct of different states, many of whom have pursued seemingly contradictory policies. Finally, the constructivist approach does not provide adequate explanation of how two states that adhere to the same ideology or possess the same religious identity can diverge dramatically in their foreign policies and view the other as a serious threat despite these identity-based and ideational similarities.

A Bridging of Paradigms

The three paradigms listed above are limited in their explanatory ability when viewed in isolation. However, when you bridge instrumentalism and constructivism, it provides you with a powerful lens through which to analyze how elites construct religious narratives and doctrines to serve their self-interests. Such a combined paradigm allows for the analysis of instrumentally constructed religious narratives, doctrines, identities, histories, and so on. This approach focuses not solely on how religion drives political outcomes, but on how politics can drive religious outcomes: elites strategically construct and appropriate religious narratives, doctrines, jurisprudence, identities, and so on according to the strategic context within which they are operating. In short, political considerations do not invalidate religion's importance, but the opposite: political considerations greatly influence shape and the ways in which religion manifests itself publicly and how a state harnesses this resource as a tool of statecraft.

The work by Mohammad Ayatollahi Tabaar[70] represents one of the first efforts to bridge the instrumentalist and constructivist camps, arguing that it is imperative to examine the construction of religious narratives and doctrines for instrumentalist purposes. He explains that religious narratives can change rapidly, change frequently, and change dramatically in accordance with elites' threat perceptions. Political behavior that many experts interpret as an outcome of ideology, he argues, should rather be examined as a cause of that specific ideology. As opposed to viewing these actors—regardless of the time and space— as confined by particular theological, jurisprudential, or ideational limitations, we must conceive of them as rational actors capable of crafting different discourses and doctrines for political purposes. In other words, religious ideology is ultimately what elites make of it, and ideologies themselves can change—as can the selective appropriation of different ideologies—in response to the strategic opportunities available to different actors. What we must do is flip the causal script, examining how political considerations influence religious outcomes.

Such a bridged approach does not privilege one paradigm over the other, but rather recognizes the interconnected nature between power-driven instrumentalist variables and the salience of ideational and identity-based constructivist variables. The bridging of these two paradigms allows for each of their respective weaknesses addressed above to be compensated for by the other. Although Tabaar's work is foundational in that it recognizes the need to bridge instrumentalism and constructivism, there remains a need for a conceptual framework capable of incorporating both paradigms and recognizing the causal mechanisms at work within them. Religious soft power can provide such a framework, but it is first necessary to examine the causal processes that drive foreign policy decision-making within these two paradigms.

Causal Mechanisms

Since the three dominant paradigms addressed above are concerned with a more high-level examination of the relationship between religion and international politics without a thorough discussion of causality, it remains necessary to analyze the actual primary causal mechanisms driving a state's foreign policy conduct and how religion fits into the equation. Four primary plausible causal mechanisms will be examined here, though it is recognized that there may be additional mechanisms at work in addition to the preliminary few: (1) foreign (external) threat perceptions, (2) foreign (external) *and* domestic (internal) threat perceptions, (3) identity, and (4) ideology. These causal mechanisms should not be viewed as mutually exclusive and are often interconnected. The first two causal mechanisms are located underneath the instrumentalist umbrella, while the second two are located underneath the constructivist umbrella. These four causal mechanisms are often the primary determinants of variation observed both between and within cases.

The presence or absence of a considerable perceived foreign or domestic threat greatly influences whether political elites must focus on countering external stimuli, must devote considerable resources to countering challenges to their own authority at home, or both. The presence of a perceived foreign threat but the absence of a perceived domestic threat allows political elites to focus primarily on the former without having to be concerned with preserving their own authority at home. Conversely, the presence of both a perceived foreign and a domestic threat means elites must devote resources to both. The relative share of resources devoted to the countering of each depends in large part on the intensity of these respective threats. So too does the shape and form of the response taken by the state to these threats vary according to the nature of the threat faced. The questions of "from where?" and "how?" political elites are challenged will considerably influence how religion is ultimately mobilized as a tool of statecraft.

The coupling of religion and foreign policy will also be influenced by the particular state identity—or "brand"—the state wishes to project to both internal and external audiences. Indeed, the constructed image states seek to project to different domestic, regional, or international audiences will have considerable bearing on how religion is marshaled in service of such efforts. Context and target audience are critical here: states often seek to construct and project different identities/images to different audiences and often move between such constructed images as they move between contexts. Context and target audience therefore considerably influence the differing ways religious symbols, histories, narratives, and so forth, are molded in accordance with the desired "brand" projected by the state.

Finally, ideological concerns, specifically pertaining to the supported and constructed religio-political visions embraced by political elites, will also significantly impact how religion is integrated into the foreign policy conduct of different states. Particularly important here is how political elites in a country believe religion should relate to state authority as well as the broader relationship between state and society. The efforts of different states to spread their own visions or counter those in competition with their own are commonplace. Again, context and target audience are critical here, with different religio-political visions often constructed and deployed according to the specific environment within which the state is operating at any given time.

Foreign (External) Threat Perceptions

This causal mechanism adopts a systemic approach in attempting to explain variation in foreign policy behavior and stresses structure over agency. A systemic theory is one that "envisions states as unitary and purposive actors that consider what other states will or might do when they choose foreign policies."[71] Such an approach "gives primacy to external/systemic factors in the explanation of foreign policy behavior and orientation, emphasizing the determining role of the world context on foreign policy."[72] Therefore, changes in foreign policy orientation and behavior are a direct result of changes in the international political or economic structure. Such an approach considers the state as a "black box" in the sense that its internal characteristics are not relevant to its foreign policy conduct: what matters is the organization of the international system and the subsequent ordering of states according to its structure. In short, policy is driven by the international context, not the domestic context, and is the result of interactions between, not within, states.

The most famous proponent of the structuralist approach is Kenneth Waltz, who emphasized the structural constraints of the international system and how the balance of power dictates how states act. Waltz explains that a systemic theory is one that explains "how the organization of a realm acts as a constraining and disposing force on the interacting units within it."[73] Such organizing structure established a set of constraining conditions within which all units are subjugated. Due to the anarchic nature of the international system and the lack of overarching authority with the ability to enforce rules and/or compliance, states then act to secure their own interests by maximizing (balancing) their own power against the relative power of their competitors (other states).[74] In other words, it is the relative distribution of power in the international system—and a state's subsequent position within this system—that determines its rivals as well as its foreign policies.[75] According to such systemic approaches, continuity of a state's foreign policies is more likely than change, since change can come only as a result of a shift in that state's position in the system (increase or decrease in relative power).

Much work has been done to both critique and improve upon Waltz's balance-of-power theory. The most prominent (and relevant for this analysis) is Stephen Walt's balance-of-threat theory. Instead of relative power differentials determining friend from foe in the international system (as is argued in Kenneth Walt's balance-of-power theory), Stephen Walt argues that states balance against threats rather than against power alone.[76] A threat can be defined as "a situation in which one agent or group has either the capability or the intention to inflict a negative consequence on another agent or group."[77] According to Walt, the factors that affect the level of threat that a particular state may pose include aggregate power, geographic proximity, offensive power, and aggressive intentions.[78] Therefore, external threats can be the result of perception as opposed to simply raw aggregate or relative power.

Where foreign threat perceptions play a causal role, we should expect to see states formulating foreign policies that are driven by external stimuli. Religion would be molded into a tool to buttress a state's efforts against a particular perceived foreign adversary. Additionally, religion could be used as a legitimizing mechanism for one's own policies and a delegitimizing mechanism for the policies pursued by rivals. Likewise, religion may also be used to mobilize one's own forces or allied actors against the perceived foreign threat. The form such utilization assumes will be influenced by the nature of the perceived foreign threat a particular state is attempting to counter. This can include struggles for regional hegemony, clashes between status quo and revisionist actors, competition for foreign patronage, and so on. Important too is whether this external competition involves actors of different religious traditions or if this is an internal clash within a single faith. If the latter, is this a struggle between different sectarian actors or is the competition intra-sect? Such a systemic-level state use of religion would entail religious narratives, symbols, doctrines, and so on being directed externally to counter a perceived threat.

Foreign (External) and Domestic (Internal) Threat Perceptions ("Two-Level Game")

The leaders of a state stand at the intersection of both domestic and foreign policies—what Robert Putnam refers to as a "two-level game."[79] Domestic pressures have often outweighed external threat perceptions when governmental elites are crafting foreign policy. As previously stated, foreign policy is situated at the nexus of the international and the domestic, and foreign policy analysis "needs to be multilevel and multifaceted in order to confront the complicated sources and nature of foreign policy."[80] This means that leaders must be viewed as "coping simultaneously with the pressures and constraints of their own domestic political systems as well as with those of the international environment."[81] As Moravcsik[82] argues, "states represent some subset of domestic society, on the basis of whose interests state officials define state preferences and act purposively in world politics." Jack Snyder[83] proffers a similar argument, stating that "recent exponents of realism in international relations have been wrong in looking exclusively to states as the irreducible atoms whose power and interests are to be assessed . . . domestic pressures often outweigh international ones in the calculations of national leaders." The implication of such arguments is that international politics is driven not solely by systemic structures but also by domestic factors.[84] State interests and policies are formulated and conditioned not solely by external stimuli but by those individuals/groups that control the reins of power.

Such an approach seeks to open the "black box," that is, the state, to understand foreign policy decision-making. Those who focus on the role of domestic/internal factors "focus on the effects of the individual characteristics of leaders and decision-makers, on decision-making processes, governmental and political structures, pressure groups, classes, national history, and so on."[85] Domestic/internal approaches have been used to explain the absence of war between democratic states (so-called democratic peace theory);[86] how national leaders have, at times, aggressively manipulated a foreign policy in order to expand one's base of support at home and/or hedge against domestic opposition;[87] how public opinion can constrain the ability of a national leader to act abroad;[88] how policy behavior is a reflection of the preferences of dominant groups or actors who struggle against other groups or actors in order to influence the policy-making process;[89] and so on.

Of particular importance for this analysis is how political elites use foreign policy to retain their own grasp on power domestically and hedge against internal rivals. This is particularly true of the authoritarian states of the Middle East, where the domestic legitimacy of ruling elites is constantly being challenged. There are three primary internal threats these regime elites face: "1) division within the leadership itself, 2) organized groups operating within (or having access to) state and party institutions, and 3) mass-level activity in the wider political environment."[90] The third primary threat listed here—mass-level activity in the wider political environment—is precisely what autocratic rulers in the Middle East faced during the 2011 Arab uprisings: a wave of mass mobilizations that called for an end to the status quo. During this period—and the roughly 10 years following it—the primary objective of these governments has been regime preservation, which often resulted in these elites pursuing foreign policies designed to balance against domestic opposition to guarantee their own political survival.

Such a foreign policy—where regime elites balance against both external and internal threats—is recognized as a commonplace strategy. Writing specifically about "third world" states, Steven David[91] argues that the leadership of these countries engage in what he calls omnibalancing. A strategy designed to counter *all* threats—not just internal or external—omnibalancing "asserts that realism must be broadened to examine internal threats in addition to focusing on external threats and capabilities (that is, structural arguments) and that the leader of the state rather than the state itself should be used as the unit of analysis."[92] Omnibalancing "assumes that the most powerful determinant of alignment is the drive of third world leaders to ensure their political and physical survival."[93] Building off David's theory of omnibalancing—and keeping the ruling regime as the unit of analysis— Richard Harknett and Jeffrey Vandenberg[94] emphasize that states must also, at times, face external and internal threats that reinforce one another. Referred to by the authors as *interrelated* threats, the authors argue that states must engage in what they call omnialignment to deal with internal and external threats that feed off of one another.[95]

Where foreign and domestic threat perceptions play a causal role, we should expect to see states formulating foreign policies that are designed to counter perceived adversaries at both the international and domestic levels. The presence or absence of a perceived domestic threat is critical: whether a state is constrained domestically due to an internal challenge to their own authority will considerably influence the allocation of resources and how they respond to different internal and external stimuli. Indeed, the presence or absence of a domestic threat will determine whether external stimuli are filtered through the lens of a pressing domestic challenge. In such contexts where a perceived domestic threat is present, religion can be used to justify certain repressive measures taken by the regime domestically and can also serve as a demobilizing mechanism discouraging dissent and opposition.

In the presence of both domestic and foreign threats, religion would thus be mobilized by the ruling elites in the service of preserving its own power domestically—particularly against those who seek to challenge the regime's authority or monopoly on power—as well as advancing the state's power vis-à-vis external opponents. Countering transnational actors that seek to co-opt or influence a state's domestic population in service of challenging the ruling regime would also fall into this category. Religion would thus serve as a mechanism to legitimize the policies of the ruling elite at both the domestic and international levels. Where a perceived internal threat is absent, ruling elites would be free of these domestic concerns and could focus their efforts on primarily external matters without having to fear the usurpation of their own authority at home.

Identity

The third plausible causal mechanism in attempting to explain foreign policy orientation and decision-making is identity. Identity refers to "a mental construct that both describes and prescribes how an actor should think, feel, evaluate, and ultimately behave."[96] In other words, an identity is "the mechanism that provides individuals with a sense of self and the means for comprehending the relationship of the self to the external environment."[97] The identity-based approach stresses that the interests of the state—or the ruling elite—are not determined solely by material interests but also by their preexisting notions of identity. As Finnemore[98] states, "interests are not just out there waiting to be discovered," but rather are shaped through social construction and identities.

These identities are the foundation of interest formation and how one views the interests of others.[99] Hopf[100] explains that identities "strongly imply a particular set of interests or preferences" and "offer each state an understanding of other states, its nature, motives, interests, probable actions, attitudes, and role in any given political context." Likewise, Jervis[101] argues that identities often serve as the pretext for distinctive views of the world and other actors within it. Identities are shaped by specific historical, cultural, political, and social contexts. Such approaches have served to challenge the dominant paradigms where they assume interests are shaped by purely material motivations (whether they be domestic or external in nature). Given that identities are rooted in a particular existing schema about how an individual or a group relates to the broader environment, it is argued that such modes of self-classification are relatively stable and resistant to change. As Chafetz et al. argue, international actors change their conceptualizations of their own identity only reluctantly due to the inherent need for predictability and consistency—which leads to identity formation in the first place.[102]

In the realm of foreign policy, identity-based approaches have been used to explain alliance formation/patterns;[103] how a shared sense of democratic/liberal identity serves to contribute to so-called democratic peace;[104] how macro-level "civilizational" identities will supposedly replace the rivalries of the Cold War era and usher in a new "clash of civilizations";[105] and so on. Notions of identity are also often central to the process of state formation and development. The construction of "invented traditions" by the state to unify its population or legitimize governmental authority often involves the rewriting and depoliticization of certain historical processes and/or memories as a form of repressive erasure to eliminate challenges to temporal authority in the present.[106]

Identity-based approaches have also focused on how states have often constructed their own conceptualizations regarding their respective "role" within the international system. This is commonly referred to as role theory. Holsti[107] defines a state's "role" as "the image of the appropriate orientations or functions of their state toward, or in, the external environment." Similarly, Stephen Walker[108] argues that "role identity theory . . . suggests how and why roles are selected when cues from others are conflicting, ambiguous, or absent." Political elites and communities often go to great lengths to "develop powerful myths and institutions designed to enhance and defend their roles and to foster citizen identification with those roles."[109] Such state "roles" imply an identity and define "orientations towards neighbors (friend or enemy), towards great powers (threat or patron), and towards the state system (revisionist or status quo)."[110]

Identity-based approaches also seek to explain how states come to view others as rivals/enemies due to a conflict of identity and how this impacts their respective foreign policies. The construction of collective identities serves to sort actors into either "us" or "them" categories. Using what they call construction of threat theory, Rousseau and Garcia-Retamero[111] argue that

> the perception of threat is a function of the line drawn between the in-group and the out-group . . . the higher the level of shared identity between the self and the other, the less threatening the other will appear . . . .in the extreme case in which the other and the self are members of the same in-group, the other will not be seen as a threat regardless of the particular balance of power.

Shared identity will increase the willingness of two states to cooperate, whereas differing identities will increase the perception of threat. For example, Peter Henne[112] argues that state appeals to shared religious values or shared religiosity are a powerful supplemental tool to "build friendly coalitions or break apart rival ones." According to Henne, "religious appeals can persuade a targeted regime of the proposed international coalition's value, increasing the likelihood they will join."

Additionally, another critical element of identity-based approaches to foreign policy includes the notion of "nation branding," which refers to the ways in which a country seeks to project an image of itself to the broader international community. This effort to construct a specific image is critical due to how perceptions regarding reputation play a central role when attempting to attract desired economic and political attention, investment, and so forth.[113] Such a "brand" encompasses "a complex bundle of images, meanings, associations, and experiences in the minds of people."[114] Risen[115] explains that "just as companies have learned to 'live the brand,' countries should consider their reputations carefully . . . .in the interconnected world, that's what statecraft is all about." The desire of the state to construct a favorable image of itself onto the international community's "cognitive map" is of utmost importance in a globalized world.

Where identity plays a causal role, we should expect to see foreign policy decision-making influenced by the constructed identity advanced by ruling elites both at home and abroad. Such efforts to instill a particular identity domestically and project a particular image (i.e., "brand") to the broader international community while assuming a specific "role" within the world will considerably impact state foreign policy. Preservation of one's identity—or the carving out of a distinctive identity—in relation to other identities would be an important factor influencing foreign policy decision-making. Context and target audience are critical here: states often construct and project different— and at times, contradicting—identities to different audiences when operating in different contexts.

Regarding religion, this causal mechanism emphasizes the sense of a particular religious identity and how the state seeks to preserve and project a specific desired image. Whether such efforts are directed toward one's own faith community or other religious communities often influences the shape and form of these constructed images. These "brands" can assume different forms, as a state may wish to project an image of being "moderate" and "liberal" or "traditional" and "conservative"; advance an image that they are a strong upholder of a particular religious identity against hostile "others"; or present themselves as a "vanguard" that seeks to spread a particular religious vision. Such identities are often pitted against other competing images, while at times different actors compete for being the "legitimate" representative of the same identity/image.

Ideology

The final causal mechanism under consideration herein is ideology. Such an approach considers how ideology/beliefs are central to how foreign policy decision-makers process new information and how it is incorporated into their preexisting belief systems. This approach is concerned with how such ideas shape behavior. Ideology refers to "widely shared and comprehensive theories about how the world does and should work."[116] Ideologies are "values and principles of a specific kind, distinguished by being both political in character (unlike, say, moralities) and universal in scope (unlike, say, identities)."[117] Keohane and Goldstein[118] explain that "actions taken by human beings depend on the substantive quality of available ideas, since such ideas help clarify principles and conceptions of causal relationships, and to coordinate individual behavior." Because ideologies are both descriptive and prescriptive, "they powerfully shape both the world that we apprehend, and the world that we desire."[119] In other words, such predispositions often serve to contextualize events according to a particular (existing) cognitive makeup.

Ideology can influence foreign policy decision-making both directly and indirectly via both individually held beliefs, and all-embracing, "big I" ideologies. Beginning with the former, personally held ideological dispositions by foreign policy decision-makers can shape policy by influencing the way in which they approach various issues or other states. The ways in which these leaders view the world and others can have a significant impact on their policy selections. The ideological positions of a state's populace can also impact foreign policy by acting as a restraining force on leadership: if the citizenry of a particular state holds strong ideological convictions toward some issue, it could be unwise for rulers to trample such beliefs by implementing foreign policies that blatantly contradict or challenge such ideologies.

On the other hand, all-embracing, "big I" ideologies such as liberalism, communism, Islamism, Fascism, Nazism, and so on, serve to unite peoples of different nations in (sometimes opposing) worldviews.[120] Much work has been done to show how "big I" ideologies have shaped international politics and the foreign policies of particular states: Michael Hunt[121] has shown how ideology has consistently guided US foreign policy; Jian Chen[122] argues that ideology has dramatically shaped China's domestic and foreign policies; Hal Brands[123] and Matthew Kroenig[124] have argued that the conflict between the competing ideologies of liberalism and authoritarianism have been central to international politics writ large; and so on. Such states often engage in what Lawrence Rubin[125] refers to as "ideational balancing," which is when a regime "aims to mitigate the domestic political threat from a projected transnational ideology."

An ideological approach "holds that states' foreign policies vary according to the content of their belief systems rather than their political and economic systems."[126] At the collective level, the state is "the most effective vehicle and resource for the propagation and implementation of an ideology that it embodies."[127] A concept frequently focused on concerning the relationship between ideology and foreign policy is the notion of an "ideological state." Such a state "seeks to bring about internal changes in other states that it has already achieved in its own domestic sphere."[128] In other words, ideological states seek the power to spread their own domestic system, define security in terms of the expansion of their domestic system, and define threats in terms of the expansion of their adversary's domestic system.[129] Ideology is often central to the process of state formation and development for such entities. Such an approach conceptualizes threats not in the geopolitical sense, but rather the geoideological sense: ideological differences between nations serve to heighten threat perceptions.[130]

Looking back through history, it is not difficult to find such states that seem to fit the mold of an ideological state: the Soviet Union sought the promulgation of a communist system of governance; the United States has sought the advancement of a liberal democratic system of governance; Iran has sought to spread its idea of "Islamic revolution" throughout the Middle East; Saudi Arabia has sought to spread Wahhabism throughout the Middle East; and so forth. However, whether the advancement of such ideologies represents an end in and of themselves or rather simply a means to a more material, self-interest-based end remains a serious point of contention. Meibauer[131] argues that ideas are "deliberative tools wielded instrumentally and strategically" be elites in their efforts to achieve their strategic self-interests. Similarly, Levi[132] argues that while it is true that some behavior may result directly from an ideological value, values and beliefs do not normally represent ends of behavior. He proffers that "statesmen act in order to satisfy interests, not to make ideology function."[133]

It is important to note here the conceptual differentiation between ideology and identity and how they are two distinct causal mechanisms. Though identities and ideologies often complement and can be subsumed by one another, they are—at their core—distinct. As explained above, identity here is concerned with how one defines oneself in relation to others, whereas ideology here refers to a belief system (an idea) often rooted in doctrine. Ideology refers to "those systems of political thinking, loose or rigid, deliberate or unintended, through which individuals and groups construct an understanding of the political world they, or those preoccupying their thoughts, inhabit, and then act on that understanding."[134] In other words, ideology can be thought of as a particular "set of political beliefs that promotes a particular way of understanding the world."[135]

Where ideology plays a causal role, we should expect to see states formulating foreign policies that promote a particular constructed political vision. Those who profess alternative or hostile visions would be perceived as a threat, and the strategies pursued by the state would be designed to hedge against these threats. The foreign policies pursued by the state would be designed to undermine the legitimacy of competing ideologies while buttressing their own. In the context of religion, the ideology causal mechanism emphasizes the advancement of particular religio-political visions. In other words, the ideology causal mechanism here implies the advancement of a specific constructed religio-political doctrine or jurisprudential formulation regarding the relationship between religion and political authority. Imperative for some ruling elites is establishing a monopoly on what constitutes "legitimate" religious practice and interpretation—what I refer to herein as "hermeneutical hegemony."

By controlling the contours of what constitutes "legitimate" religious practice and interpretation, ruling elites seek to influence whether religion is a mobilizing and "liberating" or demobilizing and "stabilizing" force, a source of regime legitimacy or subservient to political authority, and so on. This often results in competitions between contrasting religio-political visions and struggles between different actors laying claim to the same vision. Such religio-political visions are often constructed specifically to promote the authority of ruling elites while delegitimizing adversaries and calls for change to the status quo.

Religious Soft Power

Religious soft power is the theoretical framework capable of bridging the instrumentalist and constructivist camps while allowing for the equal coupling of all four causal mechanisms, giving each its own respective weight according to specific context and target audience. Soft power refers to "the ability to get what you want through attraction rather than coercion or payments" and "arises from the attractiveness of a country's culture, political ideals, and policies."[136] Such an approach is more designed to win "hearts and minds" via cooptation as opposed to coercing someone into submission. As Nye[137] explains, competing soft powers are really competitions for "attractiveness, legitimacy, and credibility." Indeed, "if a state can make its power seem legitimate in the eyes of others, it will encounter less resistance to its wishes."[138]

Nye does not discuss religion at length in his analysis, briefly noting that "for centuries, organized religious movements have possessed soft power."[139] Soft power as a phenomenon is more difficult to measure and conceptualize than hard power—number of troops, tanks, missiles, and so on. Despite this, observers can focus on tangible outcomes and manifestations of soft power—namely, how states mobilize narratives, ideas, norms, culture, and so on as part of their foreign policy conduct.

Religious traditions certainly possess the ability to attract and legitimize. The use of religion by different actors as a form of soft power represents a more particularized form of Nye's original concept, which will be referred to here as religious soft power. Religious soft power is concerned specifically with how governments appropriate narratives, symbols, or doctrines rooted in religion to buttress their foreign policy conduct. Religious soft power is empirically operationalized as a regime's utilization of informal religious discourse, symbols, or narratives, as well as the formal use of religious jurisprudence or doctrine, when seeking to influence/co-opt a specific target audience. These symbols, narratives, doctrines, and so on are coupled with tangible policies pursued by the state to buttress and legitimize them. In other words, both the informal and formal elements of religious soft power are used to legitimize one's own policies while often delegitimizing those of others. Religious soft power is not a passive resource: it is a tool deliberately and actively utilized by states to advance their strategic prerogatives.

Some of the first literature on religious soft power dealt specifically with transnational religious actors and the influence of these ideologies or movements across national borders.[140] Other works have highlighted how if religious actors are able to "get the ear" of foreign policy decision-makers, "the former may become able to influence foreign policy outcomes through the exercise of religious soft power."[141] In other words, certain religious groups or actors can seek to influence the foreign policy process by "encouraging policy makers to incorporate religious beliefs, norms, and values into foreign policy."[142]

Yet, by focusing so heavily on transnational religious movements/organizations or the ways in which religious actors influence foreign policy while remaining relatively autonomous actors, the early literature on religious soft power tended to neglect a central element of the broader phenomenon of religious soft power: the role of the state. As a result, more recent scholarship has sought to bring the state "back in" to discussions pertaining to religious soft power. This is because, as Kristin Diwan[143] argues, states are "competing within a game of established players including both state and non-state actors," such as religious establishments, independent clerics, transnational religious movements, and competitor states. In the effort to recognize the critical importance of the state to discussions of religious soft power, Mandaville and Hamid[144] turn to questions of how state actors seek to "harness the power of religious symbols and authority in the service of geopolitical objectives." Far from being passive actors, states have their own interests and can seek to harness the power of religion in order to advance their own objectives.

In the effort to bring the state "back in," Mandaville's[145] recent edited volume *The Geopolitics of Religious Soft Power* compiles a series of case studies examining government appeals to religion as a tool of foreign policy. Whether as a tool of coalition building, a legitimizing mechanism, a source of identity, or a tool of (de)mobilization, religion represents a lucrative resource for state actors. Government outreach to religious communities and leadership, dissemination of religious propaganda, and state-sponsored religious educational initiatives are all examples of how the state can co-opt religion to expand its own influence. Such efforts extend beyond any particular country or religious tradition and vary based on context, target audience, and the specific resources available to different states.

Religious soft power is often influenced by the presence or absence of what Bettiza[146] refers to as "sacred capital." He explains that "certain states are endowed with significant religious resources by virtue of hosting the historical, cultural, and institutional centers of major faith traditions and communities with global reach."[147] States such as Italy, Saudi Arabia, and Israel, for example, possess considerable "sacred capital" within the religions of Christianity, Islam, and Judaism (respectively) due to the presence of holy sites and widely recognized religious authorities. A successful religious soft power is influenced whether a country maintains sufficient religious resources—what he refers to as "sacred capital"—that can be effectively mobilized by the state in service of their objectives. In other words, does the particular state in question possess the institutions, scholars/officials, holy sites, and so on to reach the necessary audiences it ultimately seeks to influence? The presence of such resources is critical for an effective religious soft power strategy: like how the projection of hard power depends on the presence of tangible economic and religious resources, so too does religious soft power rely on the presence of tangible religious resources—that is, sacred capital— that can be marshaled in service of the state.

This utilization of religious language, narratives, doctrine, and symbols in the service of foreign policy objectives is also heavily dependent on context-specific messaging to best influence the target audience. Indeed, "because power is a relationship, by definition it implies some context."[148] The varying types of religious soft power strategies wielded by the state will differ according to the target audience whom the state is attempting to influence. Religious soft power can be used as a source of identification, a way of spreading a particular worldview, a tool for legitimization or delegitimization, a mechanism of mobilization or demobilization, a way to co-opt or exclude, and so on. This utilization of religion can be used for more instrumentalist and power-oriented objectives such as countering perceived foreign or domestic threats or in a more constructivist manner designed to advance a particular sense of state identity or ideology.

These strategies can be bottom-up or top-down in nature or a combination of the two. They can be directed at both international and domestic audiences, co-religionists, or those outside of one's tradition or toward non-state actors who seek to challenge the state's attempted monopolization of religious discourse. These strategies can be particularistic or pluralistic in scope and vision; proactive or reactive; designed to preserve the status quo or encourage a more revisionist, or even liberating, vision; and so on. Some emphasize strict traditionalism and adherence to established orthodoxy and orthopraxy, while others are more "liberal" and "progressive" in orientation, challenging such entrenched approaches. Religion can assume a more subtle, complementary role in statecraft, or it can assume a more central and, in some cases, perhaps dominant position in a state's conduct abroad. The state will therefore appropriate and/or construct the needed religious lexicon, jurisprudence, or even doctrine according to the specific target audience the state is ultimately seeking to influence and the context within which it is operating.

The framework of religious soft power effectively builds a conceptual bridge between the instrumentalist and constructivist camps and the four primary causal mechanisms within them. Religious soft power is interested in how elites construct religious narratives and doctrines to serve their self-interests. This combined paradigm allows for the analysis of instrumentally constructed religious narratives, doctrines, identities, jurisprudence, histories, and so on. Such an approach flips the causal arrow by shifting attention toward how political considerations can drive religious outcomes: elites strategically construct and appropriate religious narratives, doctrines, identities, and so on according to the strategic context within which they are operating. Religious soft power is flexible enough as a concept to acknowledge the variation between different cases—that is, how different states incorporate religion into their foreign policy conduct in different ways—but also the variation within cases and how different (and sometimes, contradictory) religious narratives, jurisprudence, or doctrines can be used by the same state actor in different contexts. In other words, the framework of religious soft power is capable of examining the different strategies employed by state A compared to state B, but also the variation within how state A and state B themselves utilize different religious narratives, jurisprudence, or doctrines in differing ways according to context and desired target audience.

Conclusion

Although the relationship between religion and theories of IR has garnered renewed focus in the past few decades, the subject of how religion relates to foreign policy continues to be underexamined. Existing paradigms exploring the relationship between religion and foreign policy remain limited in their explanatory power when viewed in isolation. Additionally, these paradigms remain focused on a high level of abstraction and often neglect causal processes. By bridging instrumentalism and constructivism while also bringing the subject of causality into the equation, the theoretical framework of religious soft power provides a powerful new conceptual lens through which to examine the coupling of religion with foreign policy. Religious soft power does not inherently privilege one paradigm or causal mechanism above another but is rather a flexible framework that recognizes their interconnected nature while acknowledging the importance of context. In a world where power-based and ideational/identity-based variables often intermix and reinforce and influence one another, religious soft power emerges as a framework capable of accounting for the intricate relationship between religion and international politics in the modern era.

Chapter 2

ISLAM AND STATECRAFT IN THE MIDDLE EAST

The question of how Islam relates to international politics and the foreign policies of specific states has spurred a plethora of academic and policy-oriented analyses over the past several decades. Many scholars have long treated the Middle East as too "exceptional" to be theory relevant, subsequently resulting in the region being presented as a context that defies existing theoretical arguments and approaches.[1] For a long time, scholarship on this topic—and Islam and Muslims more generally—was firmly rooted in essentialist, orientalist, and primordialist assumptions.[2] Scholars such as Bernard Lewis[3] and Samuel Huntington[4] sought to explain all behaviors of Muslims—political, economic, social, and so on—as firmly rooted within an inherently "intolerant" and "hostile" Islamic tradition. Huntington,[5] for example, spoke of an "Islamic resurgence" following the end of the Cold War and how Islam is destined to clash with other "civilizations" and will continue to serve as a "source of instability in the world."

Though such assumptions and frameworks persist today in certain academic and policy circles, they have largely been discredited as far too essentialist, deterministic, and often outright prejudiced. Scholarship by those such as Cemil Aydin[6] has been critical in the efforts to dispel such myths and reductionisms, detailing how the idea that the "Muslimness" of certain countries or peoples somehow binds them together—while ignoring the various historical, political, and cultural nuances of each of the different countries and peoples that comprise the Islamic community—is largely a product of Western imperialism and colonialism. Indeed, questions and arguments surrounding how we are supposed to conceptualize, measure, and analyze the diverse and varied tradition that is "Islam" remain greatly debated within the field of Islamic studies, and such overly deterministic frameworks mask these nuances.[7]

With the primordialist approach largely discredited, scholarship today dealing with the subject of how Islam relates to international politics typically finds itself located within one of two paradigms: instrumentalism or constructivism. As was explained in the previous chapter, the instrumentalist paradigm emphasizes how religion is wielded strategically by elites as a mechanism to advance political and material objectives, while the constructivist paradigm considers religion as central to the identity and ideological disposition of states and peoples. However, each of these paradigms suffers from its own respective shortcomings. A purely instrumentalist approach neglects the salience of identity-based and ideational variables, while a purely constructivist approach forsakes how strategic and power-based interests often supersede and drive notions of identity or particular ideologies. These limitations can be overcome by bridging instrumentalism and constructivism. As will be shown, the coupling of Islam and state foreign policy conduct is neither purely instrumentalist nor constructivist in nature, but rather an interconnected combination of the two. The framework that allows for this bridging of paradigms—religious soft power—is thus the primary conceptual lens utilized in this analysis.

Critical to understanding state usage of religion as a mechanism of soft power and this relationship between Islam and international politics is how Islam relates to the modern nation-state and the subject of Islamic religious authority in the contemporary world. This study is concerned with the Middle East and the struggle for Sunni religious authority in the post-2011 Arab uprisings context, particularly the role of the state and how different ruling regimes sought to couple Islam with their foreign policy conduct. Even before the uprisings, Islam had often been mobilized by governments in the Middle East as an instrument to help counter perceived domestic or foreign threats; as a "branding" tool and sense of identity; and as an ideological mechanism used for legitimization or delegitimization, mobilization or demobilization, and so on.

This analysis focuses specifically on the relationship between Islam and state foreign policy conduct following the 2011 Arab uprisings. The wave of mass mobilization that swept through the Middle East and North Africa in 2011 and its aftermath had dramatic ramifications for the relationship between Islam and politics at both the state and international levels. The Arab uprisings represented an existential threat to rulers throughout the region and the broader authoritarian status quo, demonstrating how domestic and international contexts are intimately interconnected. Additionally, the uprisings highlighted how the state operates within a broader matrix of other actors at the sub-state, non-state, and transnational levels, which can all serve to influence the foreign policy decision-making process and challenge the state's attempted monopoly on religion.

A comprehensive framework for examining the relationship between Islam and foreign policy—capable of accounting for the great deal of variation across and within various contexts and cases and how political considerations often drive religious outcomes—remains absent. This study seeks to apply the theoretical framework of religious soft power developed in Chapter 1 to debates surrounding the relationship between Islam and politics, particularly within the period following the Arab uprisings. By bridging the instrumentalist and constructivist paradigms—and the underlying causal mechanisms within them—religious soft power emerges as a powerful framework through which to examine the eclecticism that underpins the relationship between Islam and international politics in the contemporary Middle East.

This chapter begins by first addressing the relationship between Islam, the modern nation-state, and international politics following the 2011 Arab uprisings. This discussion provides the context for then examining the ways in which Islam has been coupled with the foreign policy conduct of various Middle East states after the eruption of the uprisings. Finally, the framework developed in Chapter 1 is then presented as the most efficient and comprehensive analytical framework capable of accounting for the considerable variation that exists between and within cases concerning the strategic utilization of Islamic narratives, jurisprudence, and doctrines by state actors as a tool of statecraft.

Islam, the State, and International Politics

Both historically and doctrinally, Islam is a varied and diverse tradition. When discussing Islam, Piscatori[8] argues that scholars must first ask "whose Islam and when?" Esposito[9] expands on the diversity of Islam, explaining that "while we commonly speak of 'Islam,' many Islams or interpretations of Islam exist. The images and realities of Islam and of Muslims are multiple and diverse: religiously, culturally, economically, and politically." With such a rich heritage, "Muslims are faced with a large volume of conflicting views of Islamic requirements."[10] Debates within Islam regarding governance and legitimate authority have always been more political than religious in nature due to the fact that the Quran did not specify a particular form of government.[11] The imposition of the sovereign nation-state system within the Middle East during the early twentieth century had a tremendous impact on Islamic jurisprudence and the Muslim community, greatly exacerbating these debates. As

Piscatori and Saikal[12] explain, "the lack of a present Caliph and Imam [the latter a reference to Shi'a theology] has posed a pressing theological as well as pragmatic quandary: who rightly wields communal authority in their absence?" In other words, who now "rightfully" speaks for Islam, given that there is no centralized religious—or now, political—authority?

Questions regarding religious authority are inexorably linked to those pertaining to political authority: "whoever can legitimately claim religious authority has an opportunity to shape the extent of the politicization and 'objectification' of religion."[13] Yildirim[14] argues that there are two distinct features of Islam that set it apart from other faith traditions: "the centrality of the text and the absence of a centralized hierarchical religious structure." The battle over who has the rightful authority to interpret these texts—what I refer to as hermeneutical hegemony—therefore has considerable political ramifications.

Religious authority and control over its interpretation are powerful political resources. This struggle for religious authority has been compounded by globalization. Massive flows of people, information, and new technologies have dramatically revolutionized the market of religious ideas and voices. More Muslims today have "direct access to the primary sources of religious authority" and can "put forward their own views on Islam before a mass audience."[15] The growth of television, the internet, social media, and other platforms has connected the global Muslim community in a way that was never possible before. This has helped lead to what Nathan Brown[16] refers to as "the democratization of shari'a-based discourse and the debates over the relationship between the Islamic shari'a and political authority." In such a globalized context, there has naturally been tensions and competition between various sub-state, state, non-state, and transnational actors vying for the status of "legitimate" religious authority.

The state is not a religiously neutral actor: "as state control grew, religion became more tightly controlled, contained, and subservient."[17] However, it does not operate in a vacuum and must compete with alternative claims to religious—or political—authority from other sub-state, state, non-state, or transnational actors. Over the past few decades, particularly following the 9/11 terrorist attacks perpetrated by *al-Qaeda*, scholarship focusing on Islam and international politics tended to be dominated primarily by the growth of transnational actors and movements. However, by focusing so heavily on transnational religious actors/movements, the literature during this period tended to neglect a central element: the role of the state. As a result, more recent scholarship has sought to bring the state "back in," recognizing it itself is an actor with its own interests. The state is critical because it "defines what roles religion can play in politics, economics, society, culture, etc., and continuously upholds and makes changes, if necessary, in those defined roles."[18] Indeed, the modern state has played a central role in redefining and politicizing Islam.[19]

The state today is increasingly asserting itself in the religious sphere, attempting to assert greater hegemony over Islamic discourse and interpretation. It is critical here to differentiate between what Brown[20] refers to as "state Islam" and "regime Islam." The former refers to "religion as it is expressed in official structures and bureaucracies, from mosque oversight to official fatwas," while regime Islam refers to "religious interpretations designed to buttress current policies, chosen ideologies—or even just the rulers themselves."[21] Though tensions often exist between these two despite the regime desiring a "state Islam" that remains concomitant with their own interests, there has been an increased push by embattled rulers to merge them, especially following the 2011 Arab uprisings.

The Arab uprisings represented an existential threat to the political, economic, and military elites in the region who have sought to uphold the illiberal status quo that has dominated the Middle East for decades. The wave of mass mobilization that swept the region in 2011 dealt incredible damage to the domestic legitimacy of the authoritarian old guard of the Middle East, with almost every country in the region witnessing some form of protest calling for political, economic, and/ or social change. Chalcraft[22] explains that the Arab uprisings shook the status quo by bringing to the forefront widespread democratic aspirations and by politicizing a new generation of youth activists pursuing political and economic liberalization. Fear among the region's ruling elites intensified as mass mobilization deposed dictators in Tunisia, Egypt, Libya, and Yemen; seriously challenged government control in Syria and Bahrain (resulting in direct external intervention to save these regimes); and spurred widespread calls for change in Saudi Arabia, the UAE, Morocco, and other states.

A significant outcome of the Arab uprisings was the rise to power and increased prominence of political Islamists in the wake of this mobilization, despite these actors not having led the uprisings. Mainstream Islamists—specifically, the Muslim Brotherhood (MB) and its regional offshoots—rose to power peacefully in both Tunisia and Egypt in 2011 (as well as in Morocco, albeit in a monarchical system); voiced calls for change in numerous other states including Saudi Arabia and the UAE; and some took up arms in Syria, Libya, and Yemen following the descent of these countries into civil war. Salafi political parties also made significant electoral gains in places such as Egypt. Radical Islamists—particularly the "Islamic State" (ISIS), *al-Qaeda*, and various splinter/affiliated organizations—were able to take advantage of state disintegration in places such as Syria, Libya, and Yemen and project their own influence throughout the region, culminating in the declaration of an "Islamic caliphate" by ISIS in 2014 after the group conquered large swaths of territory in Iraq and Syria.

Both mainstream and radical Islamist movements seriously undermined the authority and legitimacy of the authoritarian old guard, ushering in a contest for "hermeneutical hegemony" (i.e., rightful authority over religious interpretation and propagation) between these various state, non-state, and transnational actors. However, different Islamist movements undermined state authority in different ways. Radical Islamist movements denounced regional governments as apostates and puppets of the West, emphasizing the need to engage in armed conflict against them. Mainstream Islamists decried these regimes for preventing democracy, denying their people basic human rights, and constructing economic systems built upon systemic inequality and cronyism.

The rise of these Islamist actors set off an intense battle for religious authority and seriously jeopardized the legitimacy of state-controlled Islamic institutions throughout the region. Although radical Islamists tend to receive the majority of attention in media and policy circles within the West, mainstream Islamists such as the Muslim Brotherhood are viewed by the majority of autocratic states in the Middle East as a more substantial threat to their rule than extremist organizations due to the ability of these mainstream groups to peacefully mobilize large numbers of people around notions of democracy and human rights against the status quo. Such mainstream movements and organizations have increasingly embodied what is often referred to as "post-Islamism," an endeavor to "fuse religiosity and rights, faith and freedom, Islam and liberty" and "turn the underlying principles of Islamism on their head by emphasizing rights instead of duties, plurality in place of a single authoritative voice, historicity rather than fixed scriptures, and the future instead of the past."[23]

The rise of these popular movements against established state authorities accentuated an intra-Sunni divide between what Fadel[24] refers to as "traditionalist" and "republican" conceptions of religion and political authority. Traditionalist political theology in Sunnism "urges obedience and loyalty to the government in power on the pragmatic argument that stability is preferable to revolution, instability, and lawlessness."[25] Such an approach stresses the illegitimacy of rebellion (*khuruj*) or challenging the authority of rulers as a source of *fitna* (internal communal strife) while privileging the upholding of "order," forbidding such actions except in very rare circumstances, namely, if they openly disavow Islam. The development of this political theology occurred alongside the strengthening of state authority and the formation of an "*ulema*-state alliance," culminating in a more centralized "Sunni creed" that discouraged new interpretations of Islam and emphasized obedience.[26] This new state-imposed orthodoxy entrenched an "exclusive and hegemonic theology,"[27] which was consolidated over generations and led to the gradual establishment of a more statist Islam that stressed obedience to established authorities.

This "statist" conceptualization is juxtaposed with an alternative strand of "republican" Islamic political theology that stands in opposition to this sort of blind obedience. Such a perspective emphasizes how state authority within Islam was meant to be a guarantor of freedoms and respectful toward intellectual eclecticism while upholding the pillars of the Islamic tradition. Religious scholars such as Khaled Abou El-Fadl detest demands by rulers for unquestionable authority. Abou El-Fadl[28] argues that "all the prophets of God, without exception, were a voice for the dispossessed against the empowered . . . Islam is, heart and soul, a rebellion against injustice, oppression, despotism, and suffering." According to this approach, Islam was meant to be a liberating force: "the very purpose of Islam is to rebel. The purpose of the prophecies of Abraham, Moses, and Jesus was to rebel against the classism, racism, elitism, and unfair institutions of human society."[29]

During the Arab uprisings, many sought to put these ideas into action, thereby challenging centuries of state-promoted orthodoxy. This led to the creation of a new body of Islamic jurisprudence known as the "jurisprudence of revolution" (*fiqh al-thawra*), which sought to "provide legal guidance on peaceful rebellion under contemporary conditions, addressing itself to a twenty-first century world order shaped by new internet media and post–Cold War international human rights conventions."[30] These new works of jurisprudence—which lacked a clear precedent in Islamic jurisprudential history—were developed to support mass non-violent protests (i.e., revolution) against established authorities in the contemporary world to push for the pursuit of liberty, freedom, and justice.[31] The works of *fiqh al-thawra* were designed to provide a "third way" between armed rebellion against the state and absolute authority to the ruler, namely, how to challenge contemporary autocrats when democratic processes are either absent or a façade. The uprisings deepened the divide between those stressing "traditionalist" views regarding the ultimate authority of the state/rulers versus adherents to a more "republican" vision of Islam and political ordering around principles of justice and accountability.

Despite the initial successes of mainstream Islamist movements and a burgeoning of new religio-political thought, these advances were swiftly curtailed during what Adam Hanieh[32] terms the "second phase" of the Arab uprisings. Though several actors had worked to stifle calls for change from the very beginning of the uprisings, this "second phase" was initiated in full force following the 2013 military coup in Egypt that deposed the democratically elected President Mohamed Morsi and installed General Abdel Fattah El-Sisi as Cairo's new leader. A counterrevolutionary axis of Arab states—led by Saudi Arabia, the UAE, and post-2013 Egypt—now drove to forcefully return the region to the pre-uprisings status quo (discussed further below). They mobilized state religious institutions, figures, and networks to use Islam in a counterrevolutionary manner designed to forcefully merge state and regime Islam to further the interests of the ruling elite. This counteroffensive sought to eradicate mainstream Islamist movements while isolating and hedging against state actors in the region—particularly Qatar and Turkey—who often supported such movements, seeking to leverage their longstanding relationships with such organizations and figures to advance their own strategic interests (discussed further below). Mainstream Islamists across the Middle East now find themselves brutally repressed, internally fractured, and fallen from power.[33] The Middle East has witnessed an authoritarian resurgence and a strengthening of personalistic rule designed to "shatter existing institutional conventions seen as undermining their desired level of autonomy."[34] It is within this context that many regimes throughout the region have sought to establish sole authority on religious discourse and interpretation.

Islam and Foreign Policy

Governments across the Middle East, including nominally "secular" states, often couch their foreign policies within an Islamic lexicon as a means of legitimization or delegitimization, mobilization or demobilization, and so on. Traditional approaches to the relationship between Islam and state foreign policy conduct tend to be rather linear in their analysis, focusing on how religion influences or directs political outcomes. One of the first comprehensive investigations into the relationship between Islam, foreign policy, and the modern state in the contemporary Middle East was Ahmed Dawisha's[35] edited volume *Islam and Foreign Policy*. The contributors to Dawisha's volume were primarily concerned with advancing specific cultural/religious causes behind foreign policy outcomes. Dawisha[36] argues that Islam "does not prescribe the separation of religion from politics," and therefore, "devout Muslims argue that Islam is a complete social, political, legal, and cultural system." While this is debated, it embodies the approach adopted by Dawisha and the contributors to his volume: that there is little to no disjunction between religion and politics within Islam; therefore, it has a direct influence on foreign policy decision-making. Many studies since Dawisha's volume continue to build off of this framework, exploring how Islam directly influences policy formulation and guides decision-making in various Muslim countries[37], with some suggesting the need to move toward a new framework of "Islamic geopolitics."[38]

These perspectives—many rooted in primordialist assumptions— have been criticized for their more essentialist and deterministic frameworks. Thus, most scholarship today examining the relationship between Islam and foreign policy is rooted in either of the remaining two paradigms: constructivism or instrumentalism. Constructivist approaches to Islam and foreign policy are commonplace: from Sunni-Shi'a sectarianism to pan-Islamism, Salafi-jihadism, intra-Sunni and intra-Shi'a competitions for authority, and so on. Approaches using identity-based or ideational variables as their focal point in attempting to explain regional foreign policies are commonplace.[39] For example, Salloukh[40] emphasizes how regimes within the region seek to balance against "identity threats" and asserts that "transnational sectarian identities have reemerged as a potent power resource shaping regime foreign policy and alliance choices." Rubin[41] makes a similar claim, arguing that Middle East states often engage in "ideational balancing," whereby a regime "aims to mitigate the domestic political threat from a projected transnational ideology." Others such as Warren,[42] explore how religious figures or movements can impact foreign policy decision-makers by more indirect means, such as influencing their religio-political visions. The common underlying assertion of such approaches is that religious ideology or identity influences/dictates political outcomes.

While constructivist approaches to Islam and foreign policy have yielded critical research, they often neglect the strategic utilization of religion by Middle East governments and the great deal of variation—and at times, outright contradictions—in the policies pursued by these actors. Instrumentalism privileges power-based variables and emphasizes how strategic interests dominate identity-based or ideational concerns. Though identities and ideologies are often mobilized by Middle East states, scholars such as Stephen Walt[43] argue this is done in order to advance more material interests in an environment shaped by intense competitions for power. Looking at sectarianism in the region, Gengler[44] argues that the rise of sectarian sentiments, rhetoric, and policies across the region should be viewed as regime-driven and instrumentalist in nature, ultimately representing a broader effort to advance material state interests. Addressing alliances, Ryan[45] argues that the primary driver of alignment in the Middle East remains power-driven calculations—not necessarily shared identity or ideology—designed to balance against external, internal, and transnational threats to regime security. Cavatorta[46] summarizes such an instrumentalist view of the Middle East quite succinctly, stating,

> In the current context, regional regimes do not really defend any ideological position and are simply interested in their own survival, which generally equate with the survival of ruling elites. While ideological rhetorical devices are employed constantly, they have very little to no credibility . . . they are just employed as a façade to disguise the real objective, which is the perpetuation of the elites in power.

It is not difficult to find examples where identities or ideologies have been sidelined in the Middle East in the pursuit of strategic interests: the alignment between Shi'a Iran and Hamas; the intense rivalry between co-sectarian Sunni states such as Saudi Arabia, Egypt, and the UAE versus Qatar and Turkey; various normalization deals between several Arab states and Israel; and so on. Such examples demonstrate how easily ideologies or identities can be abrogated when they come into conflict with regime interests. However, instrumentalism remains limited due to its tendency to view Islam as "representing nothing more than a form of rhetoric used to justify policies the real motivation of which lies elsewhere," thereby eliminating any causal role of identity-based or ideational variables.[47] Though material interests often drive the strategic utilization of Islam across the Middle East, a wholesale neglect of ideology or identities masks why states feel it is necessary to mobilize such discourses, ideas, or senses of identity to buttress their foreign policies if they are indeed so easily discarded as farcical.

Given the limitations of each paradigm in isolation, it is therefore necessary to bridge them. States across the Middle East continue to rely on the appropriation and construction of specific Islamic narratives, histories, symbols, identities, jurisprudence, and doctrines to advance the strategic interests of political elites. Islam is used by an array of different actors as a mechanism to simultaneously advance power-based, identity-based, and ideational objectives which often complement and reinforce one another, demonstrating the interconnected relationship between the instrumentalist and constructivist paradigms. Islamic narratives, works of jurisprudence, or doctrines are selectively appropriated—or constructed—to complement the strategic interests of the state. The salience of particular ideologies or identities waxes and wanes according to context, but the driving impetus remains the same: the advancement of elite interests. Hence, the way the state strategically incorporates Islam into its foreign policy conduct and the particular character it assumes depends on the environment within which it is operating at any given time. In short, the ways in which the state incorporates Islam as a tool of foreign policy and the specific Islamic narratives, works of jurisprudence, and doctrines commandeered or constructed by the ruling regime in the pursuit of its strategic interests are context-dependent.

The period following the 2011 Arab uprisings best encapsulates these nuances and the need to bridge the instrumentalist and constructivist paradigms for a more holistic understanding of the relationship between Islam and foreign policy. The uprisings fundamentally altered state–society relations in the Middle East as well as the regional balance of power, initiating several simultaneous and interwoven competitions for dominance over the region's political, economic, religious, and security landscapes. With traditional regional powers such as Egypt, Syria, and Iraq consumed by internal developments, it was the Gulf countries, Turkey, Israel, and Iran, that emerged as the dominant competing players. The virtual collapse of states such as Syria, Libya, and Yemen resulted in intense proxy conflicts that continue to this day. As the United States sought to maintain its regional dominance, it increasingly relied on the Gulf as the main springboard for American force projection and influencing developments within the broader Middle East.

The direct threats to the old order posed by the uprisings were unique because they were interrelated, challenging not only the domestic authority of various individual rulers but also the broader regional order.[48] As Kristian Ulrichsen[49] details, "the outbreak of the Arab Spring in 2011 and regional responses to the broader political upheaval . . . gave urgency to the porous relationship between internal and external security." Governments across the Middle East feared their own people mobilizing against their rule, inspired or aided by those abroad, as well as the rise to power of regional groups connected with oppositionists at home. Moreover, they feared that their adversaries would benefit from the collapse of longstanding autocrats by taking advantage of the resulting vacuum. Placating ruling elites against these interrelated threats has become a primary driver of regime decision-making.[50]

Every development in the region came to be viewed through the lens of a zero-sum competition for power: whether out of a desire to spread one's own power or a defensive interest in preventing rivals from doing the same, almost every regime found itself drawn into the regional civil wars and power games in some shape or form. As Marc Lynch[51] highlights, many of these interventions and proxy efforts have failed, resulting in powers being trapped by the classic competitive logic of the security dilemma: they are unable to win, yet unable to leave for fear of the advancement of their rivals.

Religious identities and ideologies proved central to these competitions for power. More than a mere instrumentalization of religion or deployment of rhetorical devices, states went to great lengths to mobilize Islamic discourses, jurisprudence, and/or doctrines to buttress their foreign policies. Many regime-supported or sponsored religious figures and institutions engaged in extensive efforts to debate and provide justifications for the policies pursued by the state. They drew from the long and varied histories of Islamic political, jurisprudential, and doctrinal development as a means of legitimization or delegitimization, mobilization or demobilization, and so on, according to the specific context within which they were operating. If there was a lack of a clear precedent in the diverse political, jurisprudential, or doctrinal histories of Islam in support of their desired political outcomes, these figures or institutions would often manipulate or construct new interpretations or legal rulings in this battle for hermeneutical hegemony.

It is worth highlighting some of the most intense theaters of regional competition in the post-2011 period to demonstrate how Islam has been marshaled as a tool of foreign policy. The first such theater involves the dramatic rise in state weaponization of sectarian discourses, identities, and ideologies following the uprisings. Indeed, the period following the Arab uprisings witnessed an intensification of what Hashemi and Postel[52] refer to as "sectarianization," a process "shaped by political actors operating within specific contexts, pursuing political goals that involve popular mobilization around particular (religious) identity markers." This utilization of sectarianism should not be viewed as due to some immutable "struggle for the soul of Islam" between Sunnism and Shi'ism or the embodiment of ancient hatreds, as has been suggested by some reductionist scholarship.[53] Instead, sectarianism should be viewed as strategically deployed and manipulated in response to specific contexts and political circumstances.

Heightened geopolitical competition was critical to this explosion of sectarianization. The weaponization of sectarianism for geopolitical purposes—often referred to as geosectarianism[54]—was most profound in the struggle for regional hegemony between Saudi Arabia and Iran. This competition is not an inherently religious struggle between "Sunni Saudi Arabia" and "Shi'a Iran."

Both Riyadh and Tehran saw the uprisings as an opportunity to advance their own respective positions while weakening the other.[55] Sectarianism was marshaled as a political tool by these regimes as they engaged in a series of proxy conflicts throughout the region, taking various forms according to the context within which these states were operating. For example, Saudi Arabia utilized sectarianism as a means of revolution and mobilization against Bashar Al-Assad in Syria but also exploited it as a tool of counterrevolution in Bahrain to save the Al-Khalifa monarchy. Likewise, though Iran sought to present itself as a "vanguard" of Shi'as throughout the region, such a depiction obscures how the Imamite conceptualization of Shi'ism promoted by Tehran often discriminated and even demonized Alawites and Zaydis in the past, whom they now embraced as their brethren in Syria and Yemen, respectively. The form(s) religious sectarianism assumes in the Saudi–Iran rivalry is context-dependent and centered on concerns regarding power and influence.

Though sectarianism often receives a disproportionate amount of scholarly and policy attention—often due to internalized stereotypes and reductionisms prevalent in the West—a strict sectarian lens of religio-political conflict in the Middle East following the Arab uprisings masks the intense competition that occurred between Sunni states and how Islam was marshaled in different ways as part of these conflicts. In fact, these feuds between various Sunni states were arguably more impactful and expansive than regional struggles incorporating sectarianism, for these contests were not dependent upon the presence of religious demographic divisions like sectarian conflicts are. Though these contests were primarily political in nature—centered around the preservation of regime authority, power projection, and the undermining of adversaries—religious discourses, identities, and ideologies played a critical role in these regional divides. These feuding Sunni states can be broadly categorized into two groups. The first consists of Saudi Arabia, the UAE, and post-2013 Egypt, while the second consists of Turkey and Qatar.

Beginning with the latter, both Ankara and Doha viewed the overthrow of certain longstanding autocrats as a way to increase their own political networks and influence.[56] Seeking greater independence in their foreign policy decision-making, Qatar and Turkey sought to capitalize on several of the region's revolutions by supporting Islamist groups—primarily the Muslim Brotherhood and its various regional offshoots—who, with earlier electoral successes, appeared to be key new players shaping the region's future. Both Ankara and Doha were able to build upon their historic connections and relationships with such organizations and figures, providing safe havens for religious ideologues to promote a more bottom-up, "republican"—and, at times, populist—Islamism abroad that sought to legitimize mobilization against certain autocrats. State support for Islamism would develop into a "defining issue within a new regional geopolitical axis."[57]

However, support for these Islamist groups and figures should not be interpreted as a wholesale embrace of revolutionary regional revisionism by Qatar and Turkey in the pursuit of democracy. Qatar remains an autocratic government, while Turkey has witnessed intense democratic backsliding in the past two decades. Furthermore, Doha stood against the revolution in Bahrain that sought to topple the Al-Khalifa monarchy, while Ankara fiercely repressed Kurdish efforts toward self-determination. Context determined whether these states embraced more activist or counterrevolutionary positions. Instead of seeking to fundamentally upend the regional order, Qatar and Turkey sought to advance their relative positions by supporting regime change in certain contexts where they stood to benefit and discouraging regime change in contexts where they preferred the status quo.

In contrast to Qatar and Turkey, a counterrevolutionary axis consisting of Saudi Arabia, the UAE, and post-2013 Egypt sought to mobilize Islam as a mechanism to delegitimize the regional uprisings. In order to maintain a monopoly on religious discourse and interpretation, these actors constructed/promoted a quietist interpretation of Islam that sought to affirm the authority of the state. As Amasha[58] argues, this axis focused their domestic Islamic institutions on "delegitimizing political activism, promoting obedience to rulers, advocating the Islamic legitimacy of the modern state, and prioritizing peace over justice." The struggle between the promotion of this statist, top-down Islam versus the more bottom-up and "republican" political theology supported by the Brotherhood and its backers would usher in an intense competition for hermeneutical hegemony within Sunnism. Invested primarily in the preservation of the status quo, the Saudi–UAE–Egypt axis sought to crush political Islamists and isolate those who supported such movements. The support allotted by Qatar and Turkey for the Muslim Brotherhood and its offshoots was one of the primary reasons for the deterioration of relations between these two camps of states, including the land, air, and naval blockade of Qatar spearheaded by the Saudi–UAE–Egypt axis in 2017. Gregory Gause[59] explains that a central element underlying this conflict was "very different understandings of how political Islam should relate to the state among the Sunni powers of the Middle East." The conflict between these two groups of states would go on to infect almost the entire region, from the Levant to the Maghreb, the Gulf, and even their relations with the international community. However, Saudi Arabia would use Islam as a mobilizing mechanism against the regime of Bashar Al-Assad in Syria, breaking from the statist/quietist religio-political theology promoted at home and elsewhere in the region. Once again, context ultimately determined the way in which Islam was coupled with statecraft.

Related to this intra-Sunni competition for religious authority are fights over what constitutes "terrorism" and the promotion of so-called "moderate Islam" by various regimes in the Middle East. In the post-9/11 period, the "terrorism" label has served as a strategic mechanism wielded by governments across the world, designed to delegitimize opposition—whether religious or more secular in nature—to their authority or allies under the guise of protecting national security. This has especially been the case in the Middle East. Maria Josua[60] explains that the region witnessed two main waves of anti-terrorism legislation: one following the attacks of September 11, 2001, and one following the 2011 Arab uprisings. The language of such legislation was always designed in a vague manner to be capable of targeting almost any challenge to the status quo. Intended to criminalize dissent, such "anti-terror" campaigns were presented to the West as efforts to combat extremism. A central objective of several governments in the region post-2011 has been the utilization of such legislation to delegitimize mainstream Islamist activism, equating it with the religio-political theology of groups such as ISIS and *al-Qaeda*. This is due to the threat such movements posed to the authority and legitimacy of various regional autocrats. In order to combat such threats, Saudi Arabia, the UAE, Egypt (post-coup), and others designated the Muslim Brotherhood, several of its affiliates, and various other mainstream Islamist organizations as terrorist organizations, pressing the United States to do the same.[61] The Saudi–UAE–Egypt axis also charged Qatar with "supporting terrorism" over its relationship with the Brotherhood when they launched the blockades in 2017. In such an environment, statist Islam is mobilized as a counterbalance to such threats, denouncing all alternative manifestations of Islam or Islamism as "terrorism."

Unlike these "terrorists," numerous governments across the Middle East have gone to great lengths to portray themselves as dedicated to so-called "moderate Islam." Such a constructed dichotomy serves to divide Muslims into arbitrary categories of "good" or "bad."[62] The Islam practiced and promoted by the autocratic regimes in the Middle East is presented to the West as "good" and "moderate" and is designed to depict these governments as the best—perhaps the only—partners capable of working with the West to combat "bad" and "extreme" Islam. By placing blame for such "radicalism" entirely on alternative readings of Islam, these governments are simultaneously able to deflect attention away from how their authoritarian policies contribute to extremism while also repressing any they deem a threat to their own rule under the guise of preventing terrorism. Such efforts to point the finger at Islam often fit comfortably with Islamophobic tendencies within Western academic and policy circles, reinforcing the constructed notion that these regimes are the only actors capable of preventing an "Islamist takeover."

In the efforts to brand themselves as "moderate," these regimes have also adopted the strategic manipulation of interfaith "tolerance" via efforts such as the courting of influential Christian and Jewish organizations or figures. The so-called "Abraham Accords" brokered between Israel and a series of Arab states under the Trump administration is evidence of such efforts, namely, how governments seek to use such initiatives to "garner outside powers' investment in ruling families' security in the face of both external threats to state sovereignty and internal demands for democracy and respect for human rights."[63]

Though much attention has been allotted here to how various Middle East governments strategically utilize Islam in their relations with the West, it would be a mistake to not recognize how religion plays an important role in the region's relationship with other international actors, such as Russia and China. A reflection of an ongoing transition to global multipolarity, Moscow and Beijing have both increased their political, economic, and security footprints in the Middle East.[64] Religion has come to complement these relationships, and there has been a dramatic increase in direct outreach regarding political Islam between Russia, China, and several Middle East countries following the 2011 Arab uprisings.[65] Russia and China are both home to sizeable Muslim populations, many of whom have historic links and interests in the Middle East and were forcefully incorporated via imperial expansion. Moscow and Beijing fear the exporting of political Islamism—both mainstream and radical—from the region and the challenges such ideologies can present to their authority over these contested areas. Both Russian president Vladimir Putin and Chinese president Xi Jinping view the Muslim communities in their countries as a national security threat that needs to be contained, and they share the mutual objectives of the Saudi–UAE–Egypt axis to construct a state-controlled Islamic discourse favorable to their regimes.

As Russian and Chinese interests in the Middle East continue to grow, so does their stake in the prevailing status quo. Islamist actors—whether mainstream or radical—who seek to upend the political order in the Middle East are viewed as anathema to the expanding regional interests of Moscow and Beijing. This engagement also serves to advance the interests of the Saudi–UAE–Egypt axis: increased engagement with Moscow and Beijing serves to further their efforts to establish a global hegemony over Islamic discourse in the post-uprising era and gain the backing of other global powers for sidelining their adversaries. Though the United States remains the unmatched hegemon in the Middle East and the upholder of the prevailing political and security order, the increased presence of Russia and China and the return of global multipolarity will continue to impact how regional states project particular Islamic narratives and images to the international community.

Religious Soft Power and the "Politics of Islam"

As the previous sections have demonstrated, the nature of the relationship between Islam and international politics is highly fluid. A wide array of actors—be they sub-state, state, non-state, or transnational—frequently appropriate, de-appropriate, and re-appropriate a variety of often conflicting principles, "from liberalism and authoritarianism to secularism, 'fundamentalism,' anti-Americanism, capitalism, socialism, nationalism, etc."[66] These discourses, ideas, and identities shift according to the strategic environment within which these actors are situated. Frederic Volpi[67] provides one of the best overviews of this diversity and variation surrounding the relationship between Islam and politics today, and it is worth quoting him at length:

> The relationship between Islam and the state in the Middle East and North Africa hardly ever involves a fixed and well-defined set of discourses or practices. Instead, it is an open-ended, ongoing debate about the meaning of Islamic religiosity for individuals and communities, and about its political implications for institutionalized governance. It would be misguided to assume that a generic concern with reviving the "fundamentals" of Islam strictly constrains what actors inspired by the Islamic creed could do in a modernizing (or postmodern) societal order and international system. New and old Islamist actors are continuously repositioning themselves—tactically, strategically, and substantively—vis-à-vis other ideas and practices in the political and religious fields. There is a never-ending re-examination of what it means to follow the fundamentals of Islam, even when actors claim that the text speaks for itself or that no new interpretation is needed anymore. In its turn, this process generates a repeated re-articulation of what Islam means for and demands of the state.

Due to this wide variation and ability of different actors to appropriate and/or construct religious narratives, symbols, jurisprudence, or doctrines in accordance with their respective interests in a particular context, Mohammad Ayatollahi Tabaar[68] introduced a new way to conceptualize the ever-evolving relationship between Islam and politics, referred to as the "politics of Islam." Tabaar[69] argues that there is no such thing as "political Islam" as the field has traditionally understood it, but rather "politics of Islam," which should be conceptualized as "the complex, variable appropriation and application of a rich, religious tradition to serve the ever-changing political imperatives of those who vie for power." As opposed to viewing such actors as confined by specific theological, jurisprudential, or doctrinal limitations, they should instead be conceived of as rational actors capable of appropriating or constructing religious discourses and ideas for strategic purposes and in response to other actors.

2. Islam and Statecraft in the Middle East 63

The framework of religious soft power developed in Chapter 1 is holistic and comprehensive enough to account for the great deal of variation that comprises the "politics of Islam" within the contemporary Middle East at the international level. Religious soft power bridges the instrumentalist and constructivist camps while allowing for the equal coupling of all four primary causal mechanisms within them, giving each its own respective weight according to specific context and target audience. Religious soft power is flexible enough as a concept to acknowledge variation between different cases—that is, how different states incorporate Islam into their foreign policy conduct in different ways—but also variation within cases and how different— and sometimes contradictory—Islamic narratives, jurisprudence, or doctrines can be used by the same state actor in different contexts. Such a framework is also capable of accounting for the fluidity of Islam's long and varied political and jurisprudential history and how state actors seek to harness elements of these histories for their own strategic benefit.

Religious soft power is also capable of accounting for the flexibility of Islam's long and varied political and jurisprudential history, demonstrating how different actors are therefore capable of selecting from a very diverse and ever-evolving tradition to support their desired conceptualizations regarding religion and political ordering, religious authority and legitimacy, and so on. Given that Islam and Islamism have always "had within them multiple and sometimes contradictory strands of thought and action," a conceptual approach rooted in a framework as encompassing as religious soft power allows us to better incorporate the "many, and often quite disparate, trajectories of contemporary Muslim politics."[70]

Looking specifically at state actors following the 2011 Arab uprisings, religious soft power as a framework best encapsulates the varied ways in which governments have appropriated and/or constructed narratives, jurisprudence, and doctrines rooted in Islam as a means to buttress their foreign policy conduct and advance the strategic interests of political elites. This is done both to legitimize one's own policies and buttress one's authority as well as to undermine and delegitimize one's adversaries.

The usage of Islam as a mechanism of religious soft power is empirically operationalized as a regime's utilization of informal Islamic discourse, symbols, or narratives, as well as the formal use of Islamic jurisprudence or doctrine when seeking to influence/co-opt a specific target audience. Context and target audience are critical: these religious soft power strategies can be directed toward fellow Muslims or segments of the international community, can be top-down or bottom-up in nature, and so on. Furthermore, context and target audience also influence the form such religious soft power strategies take, such as whether they emphasize quietist or activist political theologies, are sectarian or non-sectarian, are designed to legitimize or delegitimize, are meant to mobilize or demobilize, and so on. Also important is the pool of religious resources—or "sacred capital"[71]—available for the state to mobilize in the service of their strategic interests. The objective(s) of the state within any particular context—such as countering domestic or foreign threats, projecting an image or a "brand" to particular segments of the international community, or promoting a particular religio-political vision—will determine how Islam is ultimately integrated with statecraft.

Applying the Framework of Religious Soft Power in the Middle East

This research conducts three in-depth case studies using the theoretical framework of religious soft power to explore how Islam has been utilized as a tool of statecraft following the Arab uprisings. The three selected case studies—Saudi Arabia, Qatar, and the UAE—represent the full variation of religious soft power strategies pursued by state actors in the post-uprisings period. However, since the strategies employed by each of these countries are not monolithic in nature—they change according to context and audience—it is also necessary to examine the variation *within* the strategies employed by each respective state. In other words, different strategies of religious soft power were adopted by these actors according to the specific context they encountered and the audience they were ultimately trying to influence. Therefore, this project is concerned with both the inter-variation and intra-variation of the religious soft power strategies deployed by Qatar, Saudi Arabia, and the UAE following the Arab uprisings. Additionally, these three cases serve as microcosms of the fluid and varied relationship between Islam, the state, and international politics in the contemporary Middle East. The investigation herein will trace 10 years—from 2010 to 2020—and how Islam was coupled with the foreign policy conduct of these three states during this critical period in Middle East history.

Chapter 3

SAUDI ARABIA

Saudi Arabia's utilization of religious soft power evolved considerably in the period following the Arab uprisings. So too has the relationship between Islam and the Saudi state, a union which has historically served as the legitimizing foundation of the ruling Al-Saud family. Challenged by the Arab uprisings at home and abroad, Riyadh adapted its religious soft power strategies to conform with the context within which the state was operating. Material interests such as regime preservation and power projection were intimately tethered to ideological and identity-based concerns facing the Kingdom.

This chapter examines the ways in which inherently political considerations influenced how religion was marshaled as a tool of statecraft by Riyadh following the Arab uprisings. In order to counter what they perceived as an existential threat to their own authority and legitimacy, political elites in Saudi Arabia appropriated and constructed religious discourses, doctrines, histories, and symbols in order to most effectively combat the diverse and evolving matrix of threats they encountered following the uprisings. They did so primarily by embracing a top-down, heavily traditionalist conceptualization of Islam that sought to delegitimize challenges to the prevailing status quo inside Saudi Arabia and across the wider Middle East. However, when presented with the opportunity to push back against their chief strategic rival (Iran) in Syria and Yemen, religion was instead marshaled as a legitimizing and mobilizing mechanism to justify Riyadh's assertive foreign policies in these contexts. The need of political elites in Riyadh to be strategically flexible to counter such threats is the reason why Saudi religious soft power strategies often differed dramatically between different contexts and when involving different target audiences.

This chapter begins by first detailing the interconnectedness between religion and Saudi state history and how this relationship evolved over time, leading up to the Arab uprisings. The next section details the interrelated nature of the threats facing the Saudi regime as a result of the uprisings and how domestic, regional, and international developments were intimately connected. Also addressed here is how the regime responded to these threats and mobilized religion to advance its interests within varying contexts. Addressed next is the rise to power of Crown Prince Mohammed bin Salman (MbS) and how he has sought to recast the role of religion as the domestic, regional, and international challenges facing Saudi Arabia have evolved. Finally, this chapter concludes by connecting the themes and patterns that have comprised Saudi religious soft power post-2010.

Islam in Saudi Arabia

Islam has been integral to the creation, history, and overall ethos of the Saudi state. As Lacroix[1] explains, "in almost all countries in the Muslim world, Islamism arose and developed outside the state. The converse was true of Saudi Arabia: from the beginning, Islamism was integrated into official institutions." The current (third) Saudi state was established in 1932 by Abdulaziz bin Abdul Rahman Al-Saud, commonly referred to as Ibn Saud. The third iteration of the Saudi state grew from the foundations of the first Saudi state, an initiative that began in 1744 when Mohammed bin Saud joined in alliance with the conservative religious scholar Muhammad Ibn Abd Al-Wahhab to establish a new political and religious order in the Arabian Peninsula. Al-Wahhab sought to cleanse Islam of corrupting influences and practices, ultimately returning the religion to what he considered "pure" monotheism. He embraced a strict textual literalism and "rejected any attempt to interpret the divine law from a historical, contextual perspective," treating much of Islamic history as "a corruption of the true and authentic Islam."[2]

However, he and his acolytes lacked the political and military resources to bring about their vision. Al-Saud, then the emir of Diriyah, sought to expand his authority and bring vast portions of the Arabian Peninsula under his rule. Yet, he needed a unifying and legitimizing mechanism for such a military campaign. A union was proposed whereby Al-Wahhab and his family—the Al-Sheikh—would provide religious justification for Al-Saud's military campaign and temporal authority, and the latter would allow the Al-Sheikh to enforce their religious vision within the conquered areas. This rough division of powers between the Al-Saud and the Al-Sheikh would serve as the foundation of the third and current Saudi state established in 1932.

At its core, the Saudi state was a joint political-religious project. As Mandaville[3] explains, "the legitimacy of the Saudi state . . . rests on the twin pillars of the royal family and the support they receive from the ulema. We can thus speak of something like a 'contract' between the palace and the ulema, whereby the latter provides for the legitimacy of the former so long as the royal family upholds the shariah, while the crown ensures a privileged institutional position for the religious scholars." This project relied on a religious nationalism rooted in narratives depicting Saudi Arabia as a purified Islamic utopia. Instead of viewing themselves as part of a "Saudi nation," the architects of this project constructed a national ethos rooted in the idea of an "Islamic nation."[4] The theological doctrine of Al-Wahhab—popularly referred to as Wahhabism outside of Saudi Arabia—had a profound impact on the development of the Saudi state. At its core, Wahhabism mirrors Salafism and emphasizes political quietism and strict obedience to established authority. Rebellion and revolt are strictly forbidden and denounced as sources of turmoil and communal strife (*fitna*), and allegiance to those in power is stressed as paramount. Additionally, in its efforts to return Islam to its "pure" form, Wahhabism views as heretical the practices and traditions of other religious communities within Islam such as Sufis and the Shi'a, resulting in the regular demonization of such groups. This religio-political vision has represented the foundation of the modern Saudi state and the authority/legitimacy of the Al-Saud monarchy.

The central role of religion in the state's founding and the historical development of a native clerical class sets Saudi Arabia apart from the other cases discussed in this book. Indeed, from its founding, Saudi Arabia has institutionalized Islam into the state apparatus. However, a number of Islamic scholars in Saudi Arabia exist outside of this formal institutionalization. Broadly speaking, Ismail[5] explains that the Saudi ulema can be divided into two categories: establishment and non-establishment. Establishment ulema refers to scholars within the state bureaucracy and on government payroll as a formal element of the religio-political establishment, while non-establishment ulema refers to religious scholars independent from the state who have, at times, voiced criticisms toward the monarchy.[6] Representing the institutionalization of religion, establishment ulema include the office of the Grand Mufti, the Council of Senior Scholars, the Ministry of Islamic Affairs, Dawah, and Guidance, and other formal elements of the state. Not formally affiliated with the state yet still profoundly prominent and influential, the leading non-establishment clerical body in Saudi Arabia is the *sahwa al-islamiyyah* (Islamic awakening) movement. Typically referred to simply as the "sahwa," this organization represents a hybrid mix of Wahhabi Islamic theology and the political ideology of the Muslim Brotherhood. As will be discussed, the relationship between the state and these non-establishment *ulema* has ebbed and flowed historically according to changing political circumstances.

For decades, Saudi Arabia has devoted considerable resources toward promoting this conservative vision of Islam abroad. From the funding of universities, charities, mosques, and so on, Saudi proselytization of an ultra-conservative form of Islam has truly been global in form. Though support for Islam and global Muslim causes was an important aspect of Saudi foreign policy from an early stage, Islam became an integral part of Saudi diplomacy beginning in the late 1950s and early 1960s as the regional balance of power began to shift. Under King Faisal bin Abdulaziz Al-Saud, Islam became a central pillar of the Kingdom's response to rising pan-Arabism throughout the region spearheaded by Egypt's Gamal Abdel Nasser, which at the time was Riyadh's primary regional adversary. This "Arab Cold War" between Nasser's pan-Arab socialism and Faisal's pan-Islamism rapidly engulfed the entire region.

Domestic influences within Saudi Arabia also played a central role in the spread of religion abroad: "many within the Kingdom's religious establishment viewed the global propagation of Islam as a religious obligation deeply intertwined with Saudi Arabia's role as home to Islam's two holiest sites."[7] Under King Faisal, Saudi Arabia erected numerous parastatal organizations designed to use pan-Islamism abroad as a counterweight to pan-Arabism, such as the Organization of Islamic Cooperation (OIC), the Muslim World League (MWL), along with various Islamic charities and media platforms. During this time, Faisal instructed religious scholars to condemn pan-Arab socialism and its leaders while championing Saudi Arabia as a vanguard of Islamic causes.

Throughout this "Arab Cold War," Saudi Arabia relied heavily on Islamist professionals fleeing crackdowns in places such as Egypt who sought refuge in the Kingdom. Indeed, the backdrop to the formation of the sahwa within Saudi Arabia was the increased repression of the Muslim Brotherhood and its offshoots at the hands of secular nationalist regimes in countries such as Egypt, Syria, and Iraq. Pascal Menoret[8] notes, "numerous Egyptian, Syrian, and Iraqi Muslim Brothers fled to Saudi Arabia from the 1950s to the 1970s to escape the nationalist crackdown on Islamic activism." A significant number of these individuals were trained professionals and intellectuals, finding positions within the Saudi education system, including in both secondary schools and universities. These Brotherhood members "affected the educational system not only as teachers but also by acting as a major force in reconfiguring it and redefining its curricula."[9] It was during this time that the sahwa were able to significantly increase their presence and influence throughout Saudi society as the state actively encouraged Islamism as an identity and ideological force.

During this period, in its effort to combat pan-Arabism, Saudi Arabia found itself aligned with the efforts of the United States at the height of the Cold War with the Soviet Union and was additionally boosted by a windfall of oil profits. Indeed, Saudi Arabia would emerge as a critical partner for the United States as part of Washington's efforts to establish its hegemony in the region, a relationship that would witness several "shocks" in the coming decades but nevertheless remained. The United States viewed Saudi Arabia's promotion of religion as a strategic bulwark against the growing power of socialist and communist movements in the region. Islam was viewed by the United States as a "powerful anti-communist belief system" capable of "luring Muslim youth away from radical socialist and communist trends, in addition to what was defined as subversive Arab nationalism with its anti-imperialist rhetoric."[10] Cooperation between Saudi Arabia and the United States culminated in their joint support for the *jihad* in Afghanistan during the 1980s against the Soviet-aligned government. Both Saudi Arabia and the United States supported the Afghan *mujahideen* monetarily and with weapons, while Riyadh also contributed ideologically to the endeavor by legitimizing and encouraging the fight against the communists. Krithika Varagur[11] succinctly describes this movement as a "perfect midcentury storm," whereby "the Wahhabi clerics' goals to spread their version of Islam, the Kingdom's new oil wealth, its ambitious foreign policy to create solidarity amongst Muslim peoples, and global geopolitical alignments all came together."

Saudi Arabia's embrace of religion as a tool of foreign policy would again be reinvigorated in 1979, following the Iranian Revolution and seizure of the Grand Mosque in Mecca by a group of rebels led by Juhayman Al-Otaybi. With the establishment of the Islamic Republic of Iran and its vows to export its revolution, Saudi Arabia felt challenged in its efforts to present itself as leader of the Muslim world. Moreover, Riyadh feared the emergence of a government born out of a popular Islamic revolution as well as the empowerment of marginalized Shi'a within its own borders and in countries such as Bahrain. The subsequent geopolitical struggle between Iran and Saudi Arabia that emerged would be compounded by each side seeking to mobilize religion in its own favor. At home, the seizure of the Grand Mosque in Mecca directly challenged the religious credentials of the regime. Al-Otaybi, a Sunni, and his group of rebels argued that the Al-Saud had lost their religious and political legitimacy because of corruption and their imitations of the West. The seizure of the Grand Mosque in Mecca was so significant because it represented the most open and blatant attack against the religious authority of the monarchy, striking at the heart of where the Al-Saud sought to derive its legitimacy. By challenging the religious fervor of the monarchy so directly, the Al-Saud were determined to buttress their Islamic credentials by seeking to establish themselves as the leader of the global Muslim community through widespread proselytization.

Seeking to bolster their religious authority against new domestic and foreign challenges, Riyadh intensified its usage of Islam as a political instrument at both home and abroad. King Fahd bin Abdulaziz Al-Saud would even replace the title of "His Majesty" with the title of "Custodian of the Two Holy Mosques" in 1986, which has been used ever since.

The next shock delivered to the Saudi monarchy was Iraq's invasion of Kuwait in 1990. Fearing that Saddam Hussein would continue his push into Saudi Arabia, Riyadh turned to the United States for assistance, which led to thousands of US military personnel being stationed in the country. This decision by the Al-Saud to rely on the West to defeat Saddam and protect Saudi Arabia led to serious criticism leveled against the regime by different sectors of Saudi society, despite the monarchy marshaling the official religious establishment to legitimize its decision. One center of criticism came from individuals such as Osama bin Laden and other returning fighters from the Afghan *jihad*, who argued that the Al-Saud should allow them to confront Saddam and defend Saudi Arabia. Bin Laden himself proposed this idea to the monarchy and viewed the presence of non-Muslim troops in Arabia as a serious violation of Islam and the sanctity of the Muslim holy sites Mecca and Medina. After being turned away by the monarchy, bin Laden became very critical of the Saudi government, denouncing the Al-Saud as corrupt, un-Islamic, and puppets of the West. Bin Laden would later go into exile, and the Saudi government would strip him of his citizenship in 1994.

The other center of criticism against the Al-Saud came from individuals associated with the sahwa movement. This represented the first time the sahwa translated its influence across Saudi society into tangible mobilization. The sahwa protested the decision by the Al-Saud to rely on American support to defeat Saddam in Kuwait. The sahwa protested by criticizing the regime directly, arguing that "the Al-Saud have abused religion by turning it into a tool of power."[12] The period of mobilization from 1991 to 1994—termed the "Sahwa Insurrection" (*intifadat al-sahwa*)—witnessed inflammatory sermons by sahwa clerics denouncing the American presence as the stigma of a moral and political failure of the Saudi "system" as well as petitions signed by members of the intellectual and religious elite within the Kingdom demanding radical reforms, street protests, and the incarceration of several hundred oppositionists.[13] This seminal event represented the first instance of modern, mainstream Islamic activism against the Saudi state. As a result of the "Sahwa Insurrection," the regime cracked down hard against the organizing and supporting clerics as well as protesters, with hundreds, perhaps thousands, being arrested. While the Sahwa Insurrection failed in its goal of catalyzing meaningful reform, it served to further entrench the sahwa movement within the public sphere.

The terrorist attacks of September 11, 2001, in the United States would deliver the next shock to Saudi Arabia and its relationship with Islam. Osama bin Laden and his newly formed organization *al-Qaeda al-Jihad* declared war against the West and its partners in the Middle East, whom they cast as puppets of the West who have abandoned religion. The organization would expand its operations, striking Saudi Arabia directly, establishing a separate branch for the Arabian Peninsula, and boasting a number of Saudi nationals in its ranks. *Al-Qaeda's* regional and international campaign of terrorism—coupled with its expansion of affiliates across the Middle East—rapidly brought Saudi Arabia's support for conservative Islamism at home and abroad under global scrutiny. After the 9/11 terrorist attacks, "Saudi Arabia was put under international pressure that criticized its transnational Wahhabi links, its promotion of an uncompromising religious ideology, and its sponsorship of radical religious education worldwide."[14]

Additionally, surrounding the 9/11 attacks were the deaths of two of the most respected and influential figures in the Saudi religious establishment, Sheikh Abd al-Aziz Ibn Baz and Muhammad Ibn Al-Uthaymeen. These two individuals were essential to the Saudi regime for their ability to lend religious legitimacy to the state. Facing the threat posed by radical Salafi-jihadists and lacking the charisma and legitimizing power of Ibn Baz and Ibn Al-Uthaymeen, the Saudi state turned to the clerics of the sahwa in the hopes of combating such extreme ideologies. This shift from repression to cooptation was signaled by the pardoning of sahwa ulema, including Salman Al-Awdah, Safar Al-Hawali, and Nasir Al-Umar, all of whom were released from prison and were expected to "not engage in any political activities" while also denouncing violence in the name of religion.[15] At this time, the sahwa movement had undergone numerous transformations. The term "sahwa" now best represents an umbrella for those who constitute a fusion of Wahhabi theology and the political activism of the Muslim Brotherhood and those who have their roots in the sahwa movement and advocate for reform.

By the end of the first decade of the twentieth century, the Al-Saud's religious legitimacy was being challenged by both radical and mainstream Islamist movements. In order to combat such challenges, the regime began efforts to centralize and consolidate strict state authority over religion by declaring in 2010 that only ulema directly affiliated with the state—those that comprised the Council of Senior Scholars—were permitted to issue religious rulings (*fatawa*).[16] A mechanism designed to buttress state authority and control over religion, this decree has not always been enforced equally throughout Saudi society, with ulema not affiliated with the Council of Senior Scholars often issuing religious edicts that are in support of regime policies. Instead, this move has largely been used to silence those who speak against regime policies. As will be shown below, the eruption of the Arab uprisings would present serious challenges to the Al-Saud's efforts to centralize and consolidate the monarchy's control over the religious sphere due to the challenges posed by mainstream Islamists in particular.

Saudi Arabia, Islam, and the Arab Uprisings

The eruption of the Arab uprisings represented an existential threat to the Al-Saud, facing the presence of both internal and external perceived threats. The threat faced by Riyadh was interrelated in nature: the uprisings threatened the regime at home and the broader authoritarian status quo in the Middle East, and had the potential to transform the regional balance of power which they have traditionally benefited from. These threats compounded one another, making domestic security intimately connected with broader regional developments. From the very beginning, the Kingdom sought to quell the tide of popular mobilization and preserve the pre-uprisings status quo. However, this disdain for popular mobilization was not applied to all contexts equally, with Riyadh encouraging the revolution against Bashar Al-Assad in Syria, who remains allied with Saudi Arabia's chief geopolitical rival, Iran. Additionally, the Al-Saud have continued to rely on religion as a legitimizing and mobilizing mechanism for their ongoing military campaign in neighboring Yemen.

The first part of this section details this interrelated threat and how domestic opposition within Saudi Arabia intersected with the wider revolutionary wave sweeping the region, compounding Riyadh's threat perceptions both internally and externally. Next, the response of the regime to such developments is discussed, primarily how Riyadh mobilized religion as a tool of counterrevolution at home and abroad, where the Al-Saud had a vested interest in the sustainment of the status quo and, conversely, as a tool of mobilization where they sought to alter the regional balance of power in their favor. Adapting to events as they unfolded, the monarchy strategically molded religion as a tool of soft power according to the specific context within which they were operating and the intended audience of their messaging.

Interrelated Threats

The Arab uprisings presented a host of perceived internal and external threats to political elites within Saudi Arabia. Domestically, the Al-Saud faced opposition from a broad spectrum of Saudi society, including mainstream Sunni Islamists, youth, and the marginalized Shi'a community in eastern Saudi Arabia. Religion was mobilized domestically to discourage and delegitimize dissent while justifying the government's repressive policies to squash this opposition. Intimately connected to these domestic concerns was the broader threat posed by the uprisings to the regional authoritarian order upon which Saudi Arabia has historically depended. The Al-Saud feared that the successful emergence of a popular democratic paradigm within the Middle East would undermine their own legitimacy and inspire opposition against the monarchy. To combat this, Saudi Arabia mobilized religion as a mechanism of counterrevolution in order to preserve the status quo.

Coupled with these concerns were fears regarding external adversaries benefiting strategically from the vacuums that would emerge following the overthrow of different longstanding autocrats across the region. The regional balance of power—historically tilted in Riyadh's favor—was jeopardized by more revisionist actors seeking to advance their own strategic imperatives. Of particular concern for Saudi Arabia was its ongoing struggle for regional hegemony with Iran as well as an increasingly assertive Qatar, which sought greater independence in its foreign policy by supporting elements of the uprisings and political Islamists in a direct affront to the strategy adopted by Riyadh.

Beginning first with domestic threats to the Al-Saud at the time of the Arab uprisings, those influenced and associated with the sahwa constituted the public body most capable of challenging the Al-Saud via peaceful opposition. Instead of a formal organization or group, Lacroix[17] argues that the sahwa at the time of the uprisings is best thought of as the "new sahwa" and "neo-sahwis," who are a product of the organization's mobilization and educational system but do not necessarily label themselves as "sahwa." Toby Matthiesen[18] explains that the sahwa now represents "an umbrella term for a group that was heavily influenced by Muslim Brotherhood networks in the kingdom and fused Brotherhood [political] ideology with local Wahhabi tradition." Ideologically, the discourse established by the "new" or "neo" sahwis sought to "deconstruct the religious foundations of [Saudi] authoritarian rule" by reinterpreting Islamic texts and aiming to "create a modern state based on representation, accountability, and freedom."[19] In other words, these "new" or "neo" sahwis proffered an alternative and competing religio-political vision to the one that has historically underpinned the Al-Saud monarchy as their source of "legitimacy." Leading the emerging discontent within the Saudi state during this period would be veteran Islamists associated with the sahwa such as Salman Al-Awdah, Abdullah Al-Hamid, Suleiman Al-Rushoudi, and Muhammad Al-Ahmari, as well as many younger activists inspired by the regional uprisings. This generational diversity represented a dangerous challenge to the Al-Saud.

Protests soon emerged within Saudi Arabia following the regional wave of mobilization: street demonstrations, sit-ins at symbolic places such as the Ministry of Interior, prisons, governorates, or branches of the government-sponsored human-rights association. Petitions and other writings were the primary language of opposition. Of particular interest are those penned and endorsed by high-profile individuals and their widespread dissemination through social-media platforms. The "National Reform Declaration" released in February 2011 argued that

> The revolutions of Tunisia and Egypt, and their aftermath of crises and changing political discourse in many Arab countries, have created circumstances in which we need to reevaluate our situation and do our best to reform before it is too late. . . . The status quo is full of risks and causes for concern. We are witnessing with the rest of the Saudi people the decline of our country's regional role, the stagnation of the government, the deterioration in the efficiency of the management, the prevalence of corruption and nepotism,

fanaticism, and the increasingly widening gap between the state and society, especially the new generation of youth. This could lead to disastrous consequences on the country and the people, and it is something we cannot accept for our homeland and our children. Addressing this situation requires a serious review and an immediate adoption of large-scale reforms by both the state and society, focusing on fixing the fundamental flaws in our political system, and leading the country to a well-grounded constitutional monarchy.[20]

Taking aim directly at the Al-Saud, the petition calls for the separation of government into three distinct branches (executive, legislative, and judicial), the protection of human rights and the rights of expression, the release of political prisoners, the right to form political and professional associations, the creation of a constitutional monarchy, and other reforms to the country's political, social, economic, and judicial structures. Another petition, "Towards a State of Rights and Institutions," echoed the language of the National Reform Declaration and called for "radical, serious, and rapid reform," urging the monarchy to listen to the demands of its people, especially the youth.[21] The petition, addressed directly to "The Custodian of the Two Holy Mosques," was signed by several prominent veteran activists of the sahwa such as Salman Al-Awdah, Sulieman Al-Rushoudi, Muhammad Al-Ahmari, and Abdullah Al-Maliki.

Another petition, "Demands of the Saudi Youth for the Future of the Nation," is unique from the others.[22] It originated from unknown youth activists, claiming that the young men and women of Saudi Arabia "refuse to continue to be wasted resource surrounded by neglect, unemployment, financial and administrative corruption, forgery, and silence." The petition presented fourteen reforms to the monarchy, arguing that these needed changes "can only be achieved in a democratic atmosphere." Also crucial during this period was the creation, despite the legal ban, of the Kingdom's first political party, the Islamic Umma Party. One of the party's founders, Abdul Aziz Mohammed Al-Wohaibi, stated: "we think the royal family is not the only one who has the right to be a leader of the country . . . we should treat the royal family like any other group . . . no special treatment."[23]

More than any other individual during this period, Sheikh Salman Al-Awdah has arguably emerged as the vanguard. A veteran of the sahwa movement and one of the most popular religious figures in Saudi Arabia, Al-Awdah sought to blend "Islamic theological concepts with a sociopolitical analysis of current conditions of oppression and marginalization. . . . thus creating a hybrid discourse that has the potential of appealing to a wide audience of young Saudis searching for a language to articulate political change."[24] Al-Awdah's praise for peaceful protest is articulated in his 2012 book *Questions of Revolution* (*as'ilat al-thawra*), which has since been banned in Saudi Arabia.[25] In his book, Al-Awdah distances revolution via peaceful protests from traditionalist Islamic rulings on revolutions, which denounce the phenomenon as a source of chaos and fitna. Incorporating Western scholarship on revolutions by scholars such as Marx, Popper, and Fanon, Al-Awdah criticizes the notion of blind, absolute obedience to established authorities as supported by the Al-Saud, arguing that the pact between the ruler and ruled is akin to a contractual obligation that must be entered into willingly and freely and upheld by both parties.

Al-Awdah argues that "repression, injustice, corruption, backwardness, and poverty" are the factors that motivate revolution. He criticizes the idea of "theocracy," arguing that "this was never part of Islamic thought, nor was it practiced in Islamic history except in the new Shi'a theory of *wilayat al-faqih* [the Shi'a religio-political theory practiced in Iran] . . . In Islam, religious scholars are not legislators. They monopolize neither power nor politics." Al-Awdah points toward democracy as "infinitely better than all types of dictatorship" and as a system capable of acknowledging its mistakes and taking measures to rectify them. Concerning the compatibility between Islam and democracy, he explains:

> democracy is based on general agreement and contractual arrangements that endorse Arab identity and Islam, ensures justice and equal opportunities for all, guarantees the separation of authorities, enshrines general freedoms and adopts the choices of the people through their civil institutions and independent channels of expression.

Al-Awdah was also vocal in several other ways. Following the eruption of protests in Egypt, he traveled to Tahrir Square in Cairo alongside Yusuf Al-Qaradawi. When Hosni Mubarak was overthrown, Al-Awdah congratulated the Egyptian people, saying, "congratulations from the heart on the success of the revolution of the great youth of Egypt. Tonight, Egypt was born with a new spirit, and the defenseless people triumphed over their tormentors."[26] Later, Al-Awdah expressed his satisfaction with the election of Muslim Brotherhood candidate Mohamed Morsi, hailing it as "a new beginning and a glorious historic day."[27] Additionally, in 2013, Al-Awdah issued "An Open Letter to the Saudi People," in which he denounced the suppression of peaceful protests: "If revolutions are suppressed, they turn into armed action, and if they are ignored they expand and spread. The solution is in wise decisions and in being timely, to avert any spark of violence."[28]

Several internal developments made this new form of opposition possible. First, as previously mentioned, social media—particularly Facebook and Twitter—provided activists new avenues through which to reach different social groups. Another key development is the universal focus on the plight of political prisoners, an issue that transcends the ideological divide. Furthermore, the plight of political prisoners is also an issue for which there exists a core group who are easy to mobilize—the prisoners' relatives—as was demonstrated during the 2013 "Burayda sit-in," when 176 people were arrested for protesting extended political sentences without trials.[29] However, the most significant development is arguably the combined efforts of Islamists and more liberal-minded actors in their pursuit of reforms. As Al-Rasheed[30] argues, the reformers' petitions proved that, while ideological divisions may persist, both non-Islamists and reformist Islamists were concerned with fundamental questions about the future of Saudi Arabia and "called into question the widely accepted view that the two camps never agree on a common set of demands."

This fusion of Islam and modern political concepts, coupled with the demonstrated ability of individuals such as Al-Awdah to work with actors of different ideological views, represented an existential threat to the authority and legitimacy of the ruling Al-Saud.

The Al-Saud also faced challenges from their historically marginalized Shi'a community. Saudi Arabia is home to a sizable Shi'a population comprising between 10 and 15 percent of the population. The majority of Shi'a in Saudi Arabia reside in the Kingdom's Eastern Province, where the majority of Saudi oil reserves are located. Shi'a in Saudi Arabia have suffered a long history of discrimination and marginalization and are often depicted as an "Iranian fifth column." Sectarianism remains a prominent element of Saudi religious soft power and was also strategically utilized by the regime in the period following the uprisings.

The instrumentalization of sectarian identities and ideologies has long been a staple of Saudi Arabia's efforts to combat perceived internal and external threats while also using such particularistic ideologies to form a sense of united identity among Sunnis while defending against the efforts of various Shi'a actors to do the same.

Saudi Arabia has a long history of politicized anti-Shi'ism.[31] The dominance of Wahhabism within Saudi Arabia lends itself to this sectarianization. Wahhabism is known for its denunciation of Shi'a Islamic theology and practices as illegitimate. Indeed, Saudi Arabia is the epicenter of doctrinal anti-Shi'ism.[32] In 1927, a fatwa issued by Saudi ulema denounced the Shi'a as kafir (unbelievers), which is a theme that continues to be repeated by many religious clerics in Saudi Arabia today.[33] Religious clerics associated with the Council of Senior Scholars—the country's highest religious body—continue to propagate anti-Shi'a rhetoric, with one member stating, "they [the Shi'a] are not our brothers . . . they are the brothers of Satan."[34] The Shi'a are often demonized by Saudi religious officials via pejorative terms such as *rafidha* (rejectionists) and *mushrikeen* (polytheists and those who ascribe partners to God). In Saudi Arabia, sectarianism involves "not only politicizing religious differences, but also creating a rift between the majority Sunnis and the Shi'a minority. At the political level, the rift means that Sunnis and Shi'a are unable to create joint platforms for political mobilization."[35]

The eruption of the Arab uprisings inspired some Saudi Shi'a to openly voice their grievances toward Riyadh in what was interpreted by the state as a direct challenge to its authority. Protests emerged in the Eastern province, particularly in towns such as Safwa and Qatif. They demanded the release of political prisoners—many of whom had been detained since earlier protests that were staged in 2009—expressed their desires for greater representation in the Saudi government and criticized Riyadh's intervention in Bahrain to crush the protests against the ruling Al-Khalifa monarchy. Many, such as the Shi'a cleric Tawfiq Al-'Amir, who called for the establishment of a constitutional monarchy in Saudi Arabia, were immediately imprisoned.[36] Facebook pages focusing specifically on the Eastern Province began to emerge, some calling for sit-ins and expressing their demands for an end to discrimination against the Shi'a community.[37] In 2012, a small coalition of Shi'a opposition groups and youth activist groups announced the "Coalition for Freedom and Justice," focused primarily on the advancement of democracy and human rights. One of the most outspoken individuals within the Saudi Shi'a community was Sheikh Nimr Al-Nimr, an influential cleric who has a long history of confrontation with the Saudi state over the mistreatment of its Shi'a community and someone who has repeatedly been labeled by the state as an agent of Iran.[38] On October 7, 2011, Sheikh Al-Nimr delivered a lengthy speech addressing the marginalization of the Shi'a community and calling for change:

For the past 100 years, we [the Saudi Shi'a community] have been subjected to oppression, injustice, fear, and intimidation . . . A few months ago, the flame of honor was sparked in the spirits of the youth. The torch of freedom was lit. The people took to the streets, demanding reform, honor, and freedom . . . They [the Saudi regime] say that we are acting "at the behest of a foreign country." They use that false pretext. By 'foreign country' they mean Iran, of course . . . We have no ties with Iran or any other country. We are connected to our values, and we will defend them, even if your media continues with its distortions . . . We have the determination to resist your injustice, and we will not surrender . . . We submit to the authority of Allah, His Messenger, and his family, and that's it. We do not submit to the authority of a ruler. Never. No ruler, whoever he may be, has authority over us. [Political] power does not grant a ruler legitimate authority. The legitimacy of authority emanates from Allah. Authority is bestowed by Allah, and He does not bestow it upon the unjust. We are not loyal to other countries or authorities, nor are we loyal to this country. What is this country? The regime that oppresses me? The regime that steals my money, sheds my blood, and violates my honor? What does a country mean? The regime? The ruling clan? The soil? I don't know what a country means. Loyalty is only to Allah. We have declared, and we will reiterate, that our loyalty is to Allah, not to the Saud clan.[39]

Sheikh Al-Nimr also expressed his anger over the military intervention led by Saudi Arabia into Bahrain to crush the protests against the Al-Khalifa monarchy. Showing solidarity with the protesters, he stated:

We will continue to express even stronger solidarity with Bahrain. It is our own kin in Bahrain. Even if the Saudi army and the Peninsula Shield forces had not intervened, it still would have been our duty to stand by the people of Bahrain, our kin, let alone when the Saudi army takes part in the oppression, the killing, the violation of women's honor, and the plundering of money.[40]

The protests among the Shi'a in the Eastern Province were largely unable to mobilize a considerable number of protesters out into the streets in a manner that would considerably challenge the state. Critical too was the silence of Sunni Islamist leaders within Saudi Arabia during this time—despite efforts by Shi'a activists to adopt inclusive slogans—demonstrating the difficulty of creating broad base cross-sectarian opposition in Saudi Arabia's securitized political environment.

These domestic developments within Saudi Arabia were intimately connected with the broader revolutionary wave sweeping the Middle East. The overthrow of Zine El-Abidine Ben Ali in Tunisia, Hosni Mubarak in Egypt, Muammar Gaddafi in Libya (with the help of NATO), and Ali Abdullah Saleh in Yemen shook the region. These successful overthrows were coupled with strong protest movements challenging regime authority in places such as Bahrain, Syria, and elsewhere. Later, the devolution of Libya and Syria into intense civil wars and proxy conflicts, the Saudi-led expedition in Bahrain to crush the uprising, and the Saudi-UAE military intervention in Yemen in 2015 would plunge the region into further turmoil while fueling the feeling of an existential threat felt among Riyadh's leadership.

The early successes of mainstream Islamist groups—specifically the Muslim Brotherhood and various regional affiliates—in many of the vacuums that emerged following the overthrow of different rulers were of grave concern to Riyadh. This is due primarily to the fact that the Brotherhood represents an alternative, competing, religio-political vision than the one embraced by Saudi Arabia and that has traditionally served as the legitimizing foundation of the Al-Saud's rule. The Brotherhood's embrace of a "bottom-up," societal Islamization directly contrasts with the Saudi state's "top-down," imposed control over Islamic practice and interpretation. Indeed, "Saudi Arabia's attitude toward the Muslim Brotherhood is informed by a fear that Islamic government in other nations could threaten its political and religious claim to leadership of the Muslim world based on the fact that it is home to Mecca and Medina, Islam's two holiest cities, its puritan interpretation of Islamic dogma, and its self-image as a nation ruled on the basis of Islamic law with the Quran as its constitution."[41] Worse, the ability of these groups to come to power peacefully via elections also challenged the type of highly authoritarian religio-political system adopted by Saudi Arabia. Riyadh feared this normative challenge to its own legitimacy and that the successes of such groups would inspire and embolden Saudi Islamists to challenge the authority and legitimacy of the Al-Saud. Moreover, Saudi Arabia found itself in direct conflict with states that supported such movements. In particular, Saudi Arabia and Qatar were on opposing sides in numerous different regional theaters (Egypt, Libya, and Syria in particular) due to the latter's support for the Brotherhood and providing its leaders with a platform, the Aljazeera news channel, to spread their message (discussed further in the next chapter).

Of particular concern for Saudi Arabia was Egypt. When mass mobilization erupted in Egypt, the most populous Arab nation, it sent shockwaves throughout the region, particularly within the Gulf. The possibility of the Egyptian Muslim Brotherhood, the country's most organized opposition and the founding branch of the movement, coming to power was especially worrisome for Saudi Arabia. As Matthiesen[42] explains, "the fear that a newly empowered Egypt, particularly one championing a rival ideology such as that espoused by the Muslim Brotherhood, could once again emerge and challenge Saudi-GCC dominance in the region" played a critical role in the overall threat calculus of the Saudi government. Not only could a Muslim Brotherhood–dominated Egypt shift the state's foreign policy in a direction more supportive of other regional oppositionist movements and Brotherhood branches, but it would also represent a dangerous new regional paradigm: a popularly elected government in the heart of the Arab world led by an Islamist movement with a contrasting conceptualization of a Sunni political order directly at odds with the one held by Saudi Arabia.

It is for these reasons that Saudi Arabia staunchly supported Mubarak as he tried to withstand the protests. Just days before Mubarak's fall, the late King Abdullah of Saudi Arabia openly took the side of the regime: "the Kingdom of Saudi Arabia and its people and government declares [sic] it stands with all its resources with the government of Egypt ... No Arab or Muslim can tolerate any meddling in the security and stability of Arab and Muslim Egypt by those who infiltrated the people in the name of freedom or expression, exploiting it to inject their destructive hatred."[43] After Mubarak's overthrow and the successful election of Muslim Brotherhood candidate Mohamed Morsi, Saudi Arabia would partner with the Egyptian military to overthrow Morsi via a military coup in 2013 (discussed more below).

As the Syrian uprising devolved into a long, protracted civil and proxy war, the meteoric rise and expansion of the Islamic State (ISIS) also impacted Saudi decision-making during this period. ISIS boasted many Saudi recruits and quickly metastasized across the region, claiming affiliates in Libya, Yemen, Egypt, Afghanistan, and even Saudi Arabia.[44] For Abu Bakr Al-Baghdadi, the self-pronounced "caliph" of this new Islamic state, Saudi Arabia represented the "head of the snake" plaguing the Middle East and the Islamic umma.[45] ISIS sought to present itself as the "true guardian" of Wahhabism, and many of the group's publications drew directly from the works of Al-Wahhab.[46] Abu Bakr Al-Baghdadi called directly for attacks against the Al-Saud in Saudi Arabia, which he referred to as the "serpent's head."[47] The group would go on to carry out a series of attacks across Saudi Arabia, targeting the country's Shi'a minority as well as Saudi security forces, while claiming to represent the true legacy of Al-Wahhab that had been distorted by the Al-Saud.

The Al-Saud quickly found themselves challenged from all corners: domestically and internationally; from mainstream and radical Islamist movements; from youth activists to veteran activists; from Sunnis and Shi'as.

The Regime Responds: Religion in the Service of Political Elites

With regime security jeopardized by these interconnected threats, one of Riyadh's main tools to counter such challenges was the mobilization of the religious establishment to delegitimize calls for protests at home and throughout the region while affirming the legitimacy of the Saudi state as both a political and religious authority that is to be obeyed. Central to Riyadh's response to the Arab uprisings was the preservation of the existing religio-political vision that has underpinned the Kingdom for decades. Relying on traditionalist discourse that urges obedience to established authority and sectarian polemics, Islam was marshaled primarily as a demobilizing mechanism to preserve the prevailing status quo. By utilizing Islam to delegitimize protests and expressions of dissent, Saudi authorities sought to frame these events not only as politically and legally prohibited but also as religiously prohibited.

The uprisings were denounced by the Kingdom's Grand Mufti Abdulaziz bin Abdullah Al-Sheikh as "planned and organized by the enemies of the umma," designed to "strike the *umma* and destroy its religion, values, and morals."[48] He released a lengthy statement prohibiting demonstrations, arguing that they directly contradicted Islamic law and risked sowing and inciting fitna :

> Praise be to Allah, Lord of the worlds. Greetings and peace be upon His honest servant and Messenger and upon his family and companions. . . . It is necessary for the scholars to make statement in times of strife and crises, the like of what is happening these days in various parts of the world. The Council of Senior Scholars prays to Allah Almighty for all Muslims, rulers and ruled alike to maintain

the safety, stability and loyalty to the truth. The Council praises Allah Almighty for what He has bestowed upon the Kingdom of Saudi Arabia with unity of words and action on the basis of the book of Allah and tradition of the messenger, under the wise leadership of legitimate allegiance. May Allah prolong its success and correct it constantly. May Allah guard for us this blessing and complete it. Protection of the community is of the greatest principles of Islam. It is the great of what Allah commanded in His Holy Book and condemned whoever abandoned it. . . . It has been the great blessing of Allah upon citizens of this country, rulers and ruled alike, that He honored them with the service to two noble shrines which, by praise and grace of Allah, receive full care of the government of the Kingdom of Saudi Arabia. . . . The Kingdom has won a special priority in the Islamic world because of this service for it is direction of the worship for Muslim and land of the two shrines. Muslims come from all directions to perform the pilgrimage in the season of Hajj and whole year for Umrah and visiting. The Council of Senior Scholars, with the blessing of loyalty to guidance of the book and tradition and under wise leadership, hereby call all people to utilize all means that increase the cohesion, strengthen intimacy, and warn against all means contrary to this. Taking this opportunity, the Council affirms the necessity of mutual advice, understanding and cooperation in righteousness and piety, and in prohibition of evil and hostility. It warns against injustice, oppression, and despise of the truth, as it warns also from deviated intellectual trends and partisanship. This nation in this country is one group committed to tradition of the pious Salaf and their followers and to the footsteps of Imams in the past and present . . . Therefore, the council hereby reaffirms that only the reform and council that has its legitimacy is that which may bring welfare and avert the evil, whereas it is illegal to issue statements and take signatures for the purposes of intimidation and inciting the strife. That is contrary to what Allah Almighty commanded in His words. . . . Since the Kingdom of Saudi Arabia is based on the Qur'an, Sunnah, the pledge of allegiance, and the necessity of unity and loyalty, then reform should not be by demonstrations and other means and methods that give rise to unrest and divide the community. This is what is affirmed by scholars of this country in the past and present to prohibit these methods and warn against them. The Council affirms prohibition of the demonstrations in this country and the legal method which realizes the welfare without causing destruction rests on the mutual advice. It is what practiced by the Prophet (peace be upon him) and followed by his companions and their followers.[49]

This official statement was buttressed by sermons pre-written by regime clerics denouncing the protests as well as official and quasi-official state media spreading this narrative.[50] Saudi's interior minister addressed the nation while building on this narrative, stating that "regulations in the kingdom forbid categorically all sorts of demonstrations, marches and sit-ins, as they contradict Islamic Sharia law and the values and traditions of Saudi society," while also adding that Saudi police and security services are "authorized by law to take all measures needed against those who try to break the law."[51] New laws were also introduced during this period, such as King Abdullah's amendment to the 2000 Press and Publications Law, prohibiting the publishing of anything that "contradicts rulings of the Islamic Sharia or regulations in force," anything that "calls for disturbing the country's security, or its public order, or services foreign interests that contradict national interests," anything that "causes sectarianism or that spreads divisions between citizens" or "damages public affairs in the country," as well as anything that violates the "reputation, dignity, or the slander or libel" of the Grand Mufti, members of the Council of Senior Scholars, or any other government official or government institution.[52] Coupled with this religious response to the uprisings was the increase of material benefits deployed by the rentier state in the hopes of quelling unease. In February and March 2011, King Abdullah announced two economic packages targeting the poor and the youth, amounting to a total of around $130 billion.[53]

In addition to these efforts designed to quell mobilization at home, Saudi Arabia also helped lead the regional counterrevolution to return the Middle East to the pre-uprisings status quo. This was most evident in Egypt, where Riyadh was one of the principal supporters of the 2013 military coup that overthrew the democratically elected government of MB-affiliated Mohamed Morsi and installed General Abdel Fattah El-Sisi. Immediately following the coup, Saudi Arabia pledged $5 billion in aid to the new government while also increasing its funding to Egypt's Al-Azhar University in an attempt to help promulgate an alternative Islamic narrative and balance against the Muslim Brotherhood.[54] Saudi's King Abdullah also publicly expressed his support for the Egyptian military's fight against "terrorism" in the aftermath of the 2013 Rabaa Massacre in which an estimated 1,000 people were killed by the regime.[55] Later, following Cairo, Riyadh formally labeled the

Muslim Brotherhood—and therefore the sahwa, who are equated as synonymous with the Brotherhood by the regime—as a terrorist organization in 2014, putting the organization on par with groups such as *al-Qaeda* and ISIS.[56] The designation was deliberately wide-ranging, including "all groups that resemble those in the list, in ideology, word, or action."[57] In essence, the Al-Saud was designating the religio-political vision of the Muslim Brotherhood—and likeminded groups, whether within Saudi Arabia or abroad—to be synonymous with terrorism and punishable accordingly.

Saudi support for the counterrevolution in Egypt was quickly denounced by Sunni Islamists associated with the sahwa at home. Sahwa-affiliated persons within Saudi Arabia were outraged at the forceful removal of Morsi (and Saudi support for El-Sisi), prompting a new wave of criticism. Numerous sahwa-affiliated clerics came out to publicly denounce the coup. Nasir Al-Umar argued that it is "forbidden to rebel against a Muslim ruler" and that the coup was an example of "sedition" that has ignited *fitna* in Egypt.[58] Additionally, 34 sheikhs came together to condemn Egypt's salafi Al-Nour party for siding with the coup and harming "the interests of Islam and Muslims inside and outside of Egypt."[59] Later, in an interview with *The New York Times*, Salman Al-Awdah directly criticized the Kingdom and its Gulf allies, arguing that

> The Gulf governments are fighting Arab democracy, because they fear it will come here... look what they have done in Egypt—sending billions of dollars right after the coup last summer. This is a Gulf project, not an Egyptian project. And the Saudi government is losing its friends. If it continues on this path, it will lose its own people and invite disaster.[60]

Saudi Arabia's efforts to lead the regional counterrevolution brought Riyadh into direct conflict with not only protest movements but also the states that supported them. As mentioned above, Saudi Arabia found itself pitted against Qatar in various theaters throughout the region due to the latter's support for political Islamist movements in certain contexts. Saudi Arabia came to view Qatar as a threat to its own interests due to Doha's support for elements of the uprisings, specifically political Islamists (discussed more in the following chapter). Riyadh and its allies sought to isolate Qatar by withdrawing their ambassadors from Doha in 2014. It would be later revealed that a secret agreement—leaked to the press in 2017—was signed between Qatar and its Gulf neighbors based on the commitment to avoid "interference in the internal affairs of other Gulf nations"; stopping support for "antagonistic media"; and ending financial and political support for "deviant" groups, specifically referencing the Muslim Brotherhood.[61] Another agreement dated 2014 "specifically mentions the signatories' commitment to support Egypt's stability, including preventing Aljazeera [mentioned by name] from being used as a platform for groups or figures challenging the Egyptian government."[62] Saudi Arabia and its allies cited Qatar's failure to adhere to the stipulations in the two aforementioned agreements upon withdrawing their officials, which would also serve as the foundation for the 2017 blockades of Qatar (addressed below).

Riyadh's response to the uprisings was also influenced by the rise and rapid expansion of ISIS. The emergence of ISIS represented a unique challenge to the Al-Saud: unlike the Muslim Brotherhood, who challenged Saudi leadership with an alternative, competing religio-political vision, ISIS attempted to lay claim to being "true" representatives of the original vision established by Al-Wahhab, challenging the Al-Saud for authority within this religio-political vision. The Saudi Grand Mufti denounced ISIS as "the number one enemy of Islam" and sought to distance Saudi Arabia from being associated with such extremist thought while also joining the international military coalition against the group.[63] The Council of Senior Scholars argued that ISIS was crafted by "hidden hands" meant to "distort the true Islamic religion."[64] Other establishment scholars, such as Abd al-Latif Al-Sheikh, argued that ISIS was "conceived and developed in the womb of the Muslim Brotherhood" and that it serves a "foreign agenda."[65] Though the emergence of the group and its campaign of international terror represented its own unique threat to Saudi Arabia, it also provided Riyadh with the ability to denounce all opposition under the broad brushstroke of "fighting terrorism." New terrorism laws were enacted in 2014, stipulating that any action can ultimately be characterized as terrorism if it undermines "state or society" while simultaneously allowing state security services to raid homes and track both telephone calls and online activities. The law classifies terrorism as follows:

> Any act carried out by an offender in furtherance of an individual or collective project, directly or indirectly, intended to disturb the public order of the state, or to shake the security of society, or the stability of the state, or to expose its national unity to danger, or to suspend the basic law of governance or some of its articles, or to insult the reputation of the state or its position, or to inflict damage

upon one of its public utilities or its natural resources, or to attempt to force a governmental authority to carry out or prevent it from carrying out an action, or to threaten to carry out acts that lead to the named purposes or incites [these acts].[66]

Such laws sought to delegitimize any opposition to the state or its policies while solidifying government control over religious practice and discourse. As will be shown below, such sweeping anti-terror legislation would serve as the pretext for a series of arrests and state executions across the country under the new leadership of Crown Prince Mohammed bin Salman (MbS).

Another central pillar of the regime's response to the Arab uprisings was the strategic mobilization of religious sectarianism. In the period following the Arab uprisings, Saudi Arabia has continued to wield religious sectarianism as part of its arsenal of religious soft power. This was done to counter various perceived threats both domestically and abroad, namely, challenges from Saudi's marginalized domestic Shi'a community and geopolitical competition with Iran. Sectarianism was utilized by Saudi Arabia as an instrument of both counterrevolution and mobilization, depending on context. Both internally and externally, Saudi Arabia has sought to present itself as the leader of the Sunni Islamic community and a "bulwark" against what it describes as an expansionist and subversive Shi'a Iran. Ideologically, Saudi Arabia has often sought to depict Shi'ism as both "deviant" and "illegitimate," while accusing Shi'a communities across the region of being beholden to authorities in Iran.

At home, sectarianism was used as a tool of counterrevolution to legitimize regime repression. Despite the lack of imminent danger to regime authority protests among the country's Shi'a elicited, the Saudi government still met these initiatives with a strong reaction. Denounced as a Shi'a and Iranian conspiracy, these calls for change were blasted by the Saudi Ministry of Interior, which tried to cast the protesters as "instigators of sedition, discord, and unrest" and who were acting "at the behest of a foreign country seeking to undermine the security and stability of the homeland in blatant interference in national sovereignty."[67] Saudi cleric Sheikh Nasir Al-Barrak blasted the call for protests by the Shi'a, stating, "as for our country, may Allah protect it . . . [it] has enemies at home and enemies abroad, and the greatest goal for them is to uproot its goodness, and to melt the country so that it can be like other countries in terms of lawlessness."[68] In 2014, the state moved against Sheikh Al-Nimr, sentencing him to death for being disloyal to the ruling family, inciting violence, and foreign meddling.[69] He was later executed by the state in 2016, alongside 46 other individuals, resulting in protests in Iraq, Iran, Saudi Arabia's Eastern Province, and elsewhere.[70] Following his execution, the Saudi embassy in Tehran was sacked, which resulted in Saudi Arabia and Iran severing diplomatic ties. State repression directed at the Shi'a community has continued, with 33 Shi'a activists—including religious clerics such as Sheikh Mohammed Al-Attiyah—being executed in 2019 and another 41 Saudi Shi'a individuals being executed in 2022.[71]

Sectarianism has also been critical to Saudi Arabian foreign policy abroad after the Arab uprisings in places such as Bahrain, Syria, and Yemen. Saudi weaponization of sectarianism—as a mechanism of both identity and ideology—has been compounded by their zero-sum regional geopolitical competition with Iran. Beginning with the 1979 revolution in Iran and compounded by events such as the collapse of Iraq due to the 2003 US invasion, the growth of *al-Qaeda* and later ISIS, and the Arab uprisings, this competition for regional hegemony between Riyadh and Tehran has regularly involved the weaponization of sectarianism for geopolitical purposes. This sectarianized geopolitical struggle for dominance has come to overlay events throughout the region in places such as Syria, Iraq, Lebanon, Bahrain, Yemen, and elsewhere. Saudi Arabia regularly denounces Shi'a political activism and demands for greater rights and representation by Shi'a communities as Iranian conspiracies designed to foment unrest. The growth of television, the internet, and social media has allowed for the rapid deployment of politicized sectarianism by these actors, often exacerbating communal and geopolitical tensions.[72]

Bahrain witnessed mass mobilization against the ruling Sunni Al-Khalifa monarchy in 2011, who rule over a majority Shi'a population that has historically been marginalized and suppressed by the regime. Though a number of Sunnis also participated in the protests against the monarchy in its beginning, sectarianism was immediately weaponized by the regime as a tool of counterrevolution in order to hedge against cross-sect opposition at home.[73] The Al-Khalifa stoked fear within the Sunni community of a Shi'a-Iranian takeover and a reversal of the benefits they reap from the current status quo of minority rule. The protests were met with fierce repression, and the Al-Khalifa relied on this anti-Shi'a and anti-Iran messaging to justify their actions and gain support from allies abroad. Bahrain's King Hamad bin Isa Al-Khalifa denounced the protests as "an external plot" that has been "fomented for 20 to 30 years" in an attempt by enemies of the state to bring down the monarchy.[74]

The Al-Khalifa, long allied with Riyadh, was aided directly by Saudi Arabia and the UAE in their project of counterrevolution. On March 15, 2011, approximately 1,000 Saudi troops, 500 UAE police officers, and a small contingent of Qatari police officers crossed the King Fahd Causeway into Bahrain to help quell the uprising. The six countries of the Gulf Cooperation Council (GCC) issued a joint statement accusing Iran of interfering in the domestic affairs of Gulf countries.[75] The commander of the dispatched force, Mutlaq Bin Salem Al-Azima, likewise expressed that the purpose of troops being sent to Bahrain was to aid Manama against foreign interference, undoubtedly referring to Iran.[76] Leading the charge, Saudi Arabia has a vested interest in sustaining the status quo within Bahrain. Riyadh fears the empowerment of the Shi'a majority in Bahrain would spill over into Saudi's Eastern Province and inspire them to challenge the Saudi monarchy (examples of such expressions of solidarity between Saudi Shi'a and the protesters in Bahrain can be seen above). Saudi Arabia also views the preservation of the status quo in Bahrain through the lens of its zero-sum competition with Iran. Finally, Saudi Arabia and the other GCC monarchies have a strong interest in preventing the emergence of political liberalization and/or democratization in Manama, which would challenge the broader authoritarian status quo that prevails in the Gulf.

Taking aim at the protesters, Saudi religious clerics embraced the state narrative that sought to portray the protesters as agents of Iran. In a televised phone interview, Saudi Sheikh Abdullah Al-Salafi decried the protests in Bahrain as part of a broader malign initiative by Iran and the Shi'a in the region, arguing that Kuwait may well be next.[77] He claimed that Shi'a are loyal only to Iran and called on other Saudi ulema to educate the public about Shi'a evilness and treachery. Following the Saudi-led intervention to support the Al-Khalifa, Saudi Grand Mufti Abdulaziz bin Abdullah Al-Sheikh accused Iran of interfering in the domestic affairs of GCC countries, claiming that the "Safavids" are known for their "hatred toward Islam and Sunnis."[78] Others such as Sheikh Yusuf al-Ahmad criticized the Al-Khalifa for not dealing with the protesters more strongly.[79] The Organization of Islamic Cooperation (OIC)—an international organization based in and led by Saudi Arabia—addressed the protests in Bahrain, denouncing "Iran's interference in the internal affairs of the [Gulf] states of the region and other member states (including Bahrain, Yemen, Syria, and Somalia) and its continued support for terrorism."[80] The OIC later praised Bahrain's leadership for advancing and consolidating human rights in the country.[81]

Critical too was the reaction of Sunni Islamists within Saudi Arabia to the events in Bahrain. The efforts of Riyadh and Manama to quell the Bahraini uprising were largely supported by Sunni Islamists within Saudi Arabia. Indeed, despite their tensions with the Al-Saud over competing religio-political visions, Sunni Islamists in Saudi Arabia converged with the monarchy when it came to matters of sectarian divisions both internally and externally. The League of Muslim Scholars, which included several Sahwa-connected clerics, described the protests in Bahrain as an example of "sectarian strife," warning of a "Safavid" (i.e. Iranian) tide in the country while praising the Saudi-led military efforts to crush the uprising.[82] They argued that the events taking place in Bahrain were very different from what had transpired in Egypt or Tunisia:

> The events of the Kingdom of Bahrain are not in any way similar to what happened in Egypt and Tunisia. What happened in those countries was peaceful revolutions demanding freedom and dignity, and all the people agreed on that. As for what is happening in the Kingdom of Bahrain, it is a sectarian strife that aims to eliminate the Sunni presence in it.[83]

Others such as Sheikh Salman Al-Awdah also expressed his regret that protests in Bahrain had slipped into "sectarian tension" and urged an end to the protests but still emphasized the need for dialogue and coexistence.[84] Important too is the role that Bahrain's Muslim Brotherhood has played in supporting the Al-Khalifa regime, despite Saudi Arabia's vehement opposition to the organization in other contexts and its 2014 declaration of the movement as a terrorist organization. The Bahraini branch of the Muslim Brotherhood (*al-Islah* Society) is led by a member of the ruling family, Sheikh Isa bin Muhammad Al-Khalifa, and proclaimed its staunch support for the regime and its efforts to crush the protests. In a statement, the Society expressed its support for the "return of security and stability" in the country, thanks to the Al-Khalifa government and the military effort led by Saudi Arabia, while denouncing the "dangerous scheme that targeted the stability and security of the country driven by foreign agendas and blatant interference by the Iranian regime, and the consequent major rift in the national cohesion among the people of Bahrain, who have known through the covenants only coexistence, affection and compassion."[85] Though Bahrain joined with its allies in designating the Muslim Brotherhood as a terrorist organization in 2017, there appears to remain a tacit understanding between the monarchy and the organization domestically that their shared objective of maintaining the Sunni-dominated status quo necessitates the latter assuming a position of loyalism to the regime.[86] Therefore, the Saudi state has likewise assumed a far less aggressive stance against the Bahraini branch of the Muslim Brotherhood than it has in other contexts.

In Syria, Saudi Arabia assumed a much different position. Long before the Arab uprisings, Saudi Arabia had an interest in "flipping" Syria from Iran's "orbit."[87] Dramatically different from the counterrevolutionary position adopted by the Kingdom in most other contexts post-uprisings, Riyadh was one of the earliest supporters of the political and military opposition against the government of Bashar Al-Assad.[88] As the conflict in Syria began to seriously escalate, sectarian rhetoric and framings of the conflict—by states both in the region and in the West—only deepened communal divisions. Money and weapons were poured by Saudi Arabia into their preferred factions fighting on the ground, often hardline salafi militias. This sectarianization was compounded by Iran, Hezbollah, and various Shi'a militia groups in Iraq pouring resources and fighters into the country to support the Assad regime. Other states supporting the opposition often clashed over their respective support for different factions among the opposition. For Saudi Arabia, Riyadh often came into direct conflict with Qatar during this time due to the latter's support for oppositionists aligned with the Muslim Brotherhood (discussed more in the next chapter). This politicized funding of competing factions within the anti-Assad camp served to fragment much of the opposition while also paving the way for more radical groups to dominate the battlefield.

Calls for *jihad* in Syria were made by several state-backed clerics in Saudi Arabia. Grand Mufti Abdulaziz bin Abdullah Al-Sheikh, Sheikh Salih Al-Fawzan, and Sheikh 'Abd al-Muhsin Al-Abbad all supported what they considered a legitimate *jihad* in Syria but warned specifically against young Saudis going to fight.[89] Sheikh Umar Al-Zayd not only attacked Alawites specifically as "devious" and "treacherous" but also claimed that Bashar Al-Assad and Iran were attempting to expand Shi'a territorial control at the expense of Sunnis.[90] Others such as Sheikh Abdullah Al-Mutlaq stressed the need to support those carrying out the fight and *jihad* in Syria.[91] Over 70 Saudi religious scholars would later issue an appeal for *jihadi* factions in Syria to unite their forces in the fight against Bashar Al-Assad and called upon the broader Muslim community to support their cause.[92] However, despite this recognition by establishment scholars of such a "legitimate *jihad*" against the regime of Bashar Al-Assad, the Kingdom and its personnel stressed that this fight is not for Saudi citizens to partake in.[93] This message grew louder as the war in Syria increasingly gave way to the emergence of extremist groups such as ISIS, who boasted a large number of young Saudi fighters and launched an international campaign of terror, including several attacks within Saudi Arabia.

As the situation in Syria continued to deteriorate and ISIS continued to grow, the attention of Saudi clerics began to shift from supporting the opposition toward denouncing ISIS and distancing Riyadh from the quagmire. This has especially been the case since the rise of Mohammed bin Salman to power in Riyadh and Bashar Al-Assad retaking most of the country with help from Iran and Russia. In 2015, MbS, then Saudi defense minister, reportedly "gave a covert green light for Russia's intervention in Syria."[94] Mohammed bin Salman was especially fearful of a revolution in Syria that would empower political Islamists. According to a lawsuit filed in Washington by former Saudi intelligence operative Saad Al-Jabri, MbS viewed the threat of a "Muslim Brotherhood revolution" in Syria as worse than Assad's survival and gave Russia the go-ahead to "stabilize Syria."[95] Since becoming crown prince and the dominant political actor in Saudi Arabia, MbS has publicly acknowledged that "Bashar is staying," and there has been a significant downturn in both clerical and state attention devoted to Syria.[96]

Similar to how they converged with the state on the domestic Shi'a population and the uprising in Bahrain, Saudi's Sunni Islamists found themselves on the same side as Riyadh when it came to Syria. Saudi religious scholars such as Sheikh Mohamad Al-Arefe—historically connected with the sahwa—called for a jihad to be waged in Syria "in every possible way."[97] Others such as Sheikh Awad Al-Qarni argued that Iran's "Safavid ambitions" were to blame for the violence in Syria, alongside the actions of the regime, Russia, and Israel.[98] Later, following Russia's military intervention to aid Bashar Al-Assad, a consortium of 55 Saudi religious scholars—including several clerics historically associated with the Sahwa—signed a letter denouncing Moscow's involvement and calling on Sunni countries to increase their support for the opposition.[99] The signatories called on *jihadi* factions in Syria to put aside their differences and unite against the regime and its supporters but stopped short of calling for Saudis to join the fight.

The eruption of mass mobilization in Yemen against President Ali Abdullah Saleh in 2011 was likewise a cause for concern in Riyadh, who has long been concerned with maintaining quiet in its backyard.

Indeed, the uprisings "brought millions of people into the streets, protesting against precisely the elite corruption and autocracy that Saudi Arabia (with Western backing) had worked to entrench."[100] After it was clear Saleh could no longer hold on to power, the GCC countries—led by Saudi Arabia—put forward an initiative that stipulated a new power-sharing agreement. Saleh would step down and pass authority to his deputy, Abd Rabu Mansour Hadi, who would then form a unity government that would build a new constitution. This initiative was counterrevolutionary in nature, designed to "preserve Saleh's military and security apparatuses" and reinforce the status quo under the leadership of the current President Hadi.[101]

Despite this initiative, tensions persisted, and in September 2014, armed rebels belonging to Yemen's Houthi movement descended from the north of the country and captured the capital of Sanaa following weeks of anti-government protests. As the Houthis proceeded to push southward in their campaign against the Hadi government, Saudi Arabia and the UAE intervened militarily in support of President Hadi, launching Operation Decisive Storm in 2015. A central objective of this campaign was to maintain the status quo in the country, specifically the protection of an autocrat aligned with their own interests. As Ewan Stein[102] explains, "although backing the 'legitimate' forces of President Abd Rabu Mansour Hadi was portrayed as essential to defeating the Iranian-backed Houthi movement," a significant motivator for Riyadh was to prevent the emergence of a democracy or a hostile authoritarian government in their backyard. The ensuing war in Yemen would quickly devolve into the worst humanitarian crisis in the world since the Second World War.

Both the initial uprising and later war in Yemen were framed by Riyadh as a sectarian struggle against Iranian-backed Houthis, a narrative that was embraced by religious authorities in Saudi Arabia. This is despite the fact that the Houthis are Zaidi Shi'as, which differs considerably from Iranian Twelver Shi'ism and, in matters of jurisprudence, are more similar to Sunni Hanafis. Despite this, Operation Decisive Storm— the largest military expedition undertaken by Saudi Arabia since Desert Storm—relied heavily on sectarian messaging and religious justifications. Immediately following the military intervention, the General Secretariat of the Council of Senior Scholars Sheikh Fahad bin Saad Al-Majid endorsed the move as necessary to defend the people of Yemen and its legitimate government (i.e., the government of Abd Rabu Mansour Hadi):

We pray to Allah Almighty for the safety of all military forces and Yemenis. The Standing Committee of the scholars has already issued a fatwa, number 9,248, giving clear support to the operation.[103]

Denouncing the Houthis as foreign-backed terrorists, Al-Majid called on Muslims across the world to support the military operation in Yemen and save the country from "external forces" (a reference to Iran).[104] Saudi's Grand Mufti called upon businessmen and banks to aid soldiers fighting in the war by paying their bills and absolving their debts back home.[105] The Saudi Ministry of Islamic Affairs organized training courses for Imams close to the Yemeni border on how to counter the dangerous and corrupting nature of "Houthi doctrine" while promoting true "monotheism."[106] Others such as Sheikh Abdulaziz Al-Tarifi[107] and Sheikh Abul Rahman Al-Barrak[108] stressed that *jihad* against the Houthis in Yemen is a duty, with the latter accusing the group of embracing Twelver Shi'ism and being agents of Iran:

> The Houthis are known to have embraced the doctrine of Twelver rejectionism . . . and it is known that they receive support from the rejectionist state of Iran . . . it is the duty of Muslims from Yemen and others to cooperate in supporting their oppressed brothers by defending them, and breaking the thorn of this stray sect of the Houthis, which the state of Iran has used as a bridge to [strengthen] its influence in Yemen.[109]

Again, Saudi Sunni Islamists found themselves in a position of agreement with the state vis-à-vis Yemen. In an interview with Aljazeera, Sheikh Salman Al-Awdah agreed that the military intervention was legitimate and paralleled the regime's narrative that Iran was using the Houthis to advance its own agenda in Yemen.[110] On Twitter, Sheikh Mohamed Al-Arefe accused the Houthis of killing people, destroying mosques and insulting the Quran, and robbing and looting the country, claiming that Operation Decisive Storm was necessary.[111] Sheikh A'id Al-Qarni composed a poem entitled *"labbek ya salman"* (For you, Salman) in support of King Salman launching the operation.[112] Also critical are the extensive relationships Riyadh has maintained with both mainstream and radical Sunni Islamists in Yemen. Indeed, in the effort to defeat the Houthis, Saudi Arabia has provided financial and logistical support to the Yemeni branch of the Muslim Brotherhood—*al-Islah*—despite the group having been designated as a terrorist organization by Riyadh.[113] Additionally, Saudi Arabia and the UAE have both reportedly transferred American-made weaponry to *al-Qaeda* and other hardline salafi militias in Yemen as part of their efforts against the Houthis.[114]

As these examples demonstrate, sectarianism still represents a critical element to Saudi religious soft power, especially as it pertains to competition with Iran and attempts to delegitimize Shi'a calls for change (internally and elsewhere). Critical too is the fact that Sunni Islamists within Saudi Arabia found themselves aligned with the regime within these contexts, and Riyadh maintained a tacit understanding with the Brotherhood in Bahrain and even supported the branch of the organization in Yemen despite labeling the group a terrorist organization and actively working to undermine it elsewhere. Context is paramount: differing strategic environments influence the form these religious soft power strategies take, which identities/ideologies are privileged over others, and how governments conceptualize different threats.

Saudi Identity and Ideology Reformed? MbS, Islam, and the Centralization of Power

The death of King Abdullah bin Abdulaziz Al-Saud in 2015 and the rise of Salman bin Abdulaziz Al-Saud have arguably ushered in one of the most significant shifts in the history of Saudi Arabia. This is primarily a result of the rise to power of King Salman's son, Mohammed bin Salman, popularly referred to as MbS. Initially appointed as deputy crown prince and minister of defense, MbS rose to the position of Crown Prince in 2017 after forcibly sidelining Muhammad bin Nayef, who had held the position since 2015. With the support of his father, he has embarked upon a campaign of power consolidation and centralization, amassing more power than any other individual in the history of the modern Saudi state. In his efforts to establish absolute authority and eliminate alternative power centers capable of challenging his rule, MbS has targeted fellow royals and other elites, journalists, religious clerics, human rights activists, women's rights activists, and many more in an unprecedented wave of repression.

The centralization of power under the sole authority of MbS has resulted in a more personalized form of autocracy within Saudi Arabia. Indeed, MbS has concentrated power in Saudi Arabia to an unprecedented degree, seeking to abrogate and eliminate "the constraints imposed by the collective leadership model that characterized the Saudi regime in the past."[115] In doing so, MbS has "transferred the economic and political responsibilities held by other royals into his own hands, going so far as to subject resistant princes, bureaucrats, and businesspersons to violent repression."[116] Often carried out under the pretense of fighting "corruption," these purges have ultimately been used as a mechanism to solidify MbS' ultimate authority over the state. Critical to these consolidation efforts has been the cult of personality MbS has constructed around himself both at home and abroad. Saudi Arabia and its allies have gone to great lengths presenting MbS as a "reformer" leading the Kingdom into the future, using initiates such as Vision 2030—MbS' grand economic plan to wean Saudi Arabia off oil—as evidence. Other soft power efforts designed to help cultivate this image of "reformer" include hosting prominent sporting events, music festivals, and branches of Western universities.

Religious "Reforms," "Moderate Islam," and a New Nationalism

MbS' efforts to consolidate power and present himself as a "reformer" are most glaring regarding religion. The Crown Prince and his allies—especially in the West—have presented the young leader as a revolutionary reforming Islam in Saudi Arabia. Mohammed bin Salman has vowed to return Saudi Arabia to "moderate Islam," claiming that Riyadh's turn toward and support for more radical interpretations of the religion was a result of the Iranian Revolution of 1979, domestic extremists aligned with the Muslim Brotherhood, and Washington's encouragement of such ideologies during the Cold War to combat socialism and communism. MbS argued in an interview with *TIME* magazine that "Saudi Arabia doesn't spread any extremist ideology" and represents "the biggest victim of extremist ideology" after the state was "hijacked" as a result of the aforementioned forces.[117] This selective reading of history is designed to essentially rewrite Saudi Arabia's past and present the Crown Prince as a renewer of the genuine and moderate Islam that allegedly flourished before 1979. Many in the West have embraced such a narrative, with one *New York Times* columnist describing MbS' reforms as "Saudi Arabia's Arab Spring, at last."[118] Framed in this manner, MbS is depicted as a long-awaited reformer determined to fundamentally restructure the religious basis of Saudi identity and the religio-political vision that has for decades undergirded the Saudi state. But is this really the case?

Under Crown Prince Mohammed bin Salman, Saudi Arabia has indeed witnessed several significant changes, namely, efforts to distance official Saudi history from Wahhabism; allowing women to drive, live alone, and travel without a male guardian; limiting the religious police's powers; permitting public entertainment venues such as cinemas and concerts; and arresting religious clerics and scholars labeled as "extremists" by the regime. However, these developments have occurred alongside MbS' efforts to consolidate his own personal power, which extends into the country's religious sphere. What is occurring in Saudi Arabia is best understood as the restructuring of religion toward this end: religious authority is being centralized under the authority of MbS and brought under the direct control of the monarchy. Moreover, there is an ongoing effort to transition away from religion as the sole central pillar upon which the government seeks to derive its legitimacy (as it has done historically) and move Saudi identity toward a more overt form of nationalism that is being propagated and encouraged by the regime.

Within the religious sphere, MbS is consolidating religious authority and discourse under the sole supervision of the royal palace. As Annelle Sheline and Kristian Ulrichsen[119] argue, "where MbS has truncated the power of the religious establishment, it is to consolidate power into the central state and specifically, to boost his own control." The endeavor to return Saudi Arabia to so-called "moderate Islam" is instead a comprehensive effort by the state to eliminate all independent or dissenting religious voices capable of challenging MbS' desired monopoly on Islam in Saudi Arabia while also projecting an image of "tolerance" and "progress" to the West. It is not an overhaul of the religio-political vision that has historically served as the foundation of the Saudi state, but rather a reorienting of this vision toward MbS' efforts to consolidate ultimate authority. Likewise, the effort to battle "extremist" clerics inside the country represents an offensive against those religious figures who challenge either MbS' absolute authority or his policies, not an assault on this vision, the religious establishment, or Wahhabism itself. Nor is this a matter of extremism: many religious figures who continue to produce more radical content remain in good favor with MbS and still serve in the country's religious establishment. Instead, this is about loyalty and the centralization of religious power.

MbS still sees utility in religion as a political instrument: Islam continues to be used domestically and abroad in the service of political elites. Mohammed bin Salman's alliance with the official religious establishment remains intact, and he has not sought to fundamentally reform Wahhabi doctrine and teachings. Rather, the regime has sought to repurpose these resources to better suit its interests amidst changing domestic, regional, and world contexts.

Islam within Saudi Arabia is still rooted in the same religio-political vision that has been used to legitimize regime policies and authority while discouraging dissent. In 2017 alone, Grand Mufti Abdulaziz Abdullah Al-Sheikh issued eight fatawa warnings against disobeying the "legitimate ruler" (i.e., the monarchy) and stressing allegiance to established authority.[120] MbS himself has been embraced by the religious establishment as a "modernizer" (*muhaddith*) and a "renewer" (*mujaddid*), the latter of which is particularly significant given that it is a term typically used to refer to someone who has rejuvenated the Islamic faith.[121] In 2018, the chief Imam of the Grand Mosque in Mecca, Abdul-Rahman Al-Sudais, praised MbS as a *mujaddid* and openly endorsed his policies in an unprecedented manner:

> The path of reform and moderation in this blessed land . . . through the care and attention from its young, ambitious, divinely inspired reformer crown prince [MbS], continues to blaze forward guided by his vision of innovation and insightful modernism, despite all the failed pressures and threats . . . all threats against his modernizing reforms are bound not only to fail, but will threaten international security, peace, and stability.[122]

The Council of Senior Scholars—still the only religious body in Saudi Arabia permitted to issue fatawa after King Abdullah's decree in 2010—has been critical in endorsing and legitimizing MbS' social policies such as allowing women to drive and his mass "anti-corruption" campaign against fellow royals.[123] Additionally, after the murder of journalist Jamal Khashoggi in the Saudi Consulate in Istanbul in 2018, the Council of Senior Scholars hailed the regime's handling of the matter, stating it "achieve[d] justice and equality in accordance with Islamic law."[124] Following a US intelligence report directly linking MbS to Khashoggi's murder, the Council of Senior Scholars rejected the "negative, false, and unacceptable" assessment, arguing that safeguarding human rights is a "fundamental pillar" of Saudi Arabia.[125]

The religious establishment has also played a central role in denouncing regime critics and legitimizing the regime's repressive measures against them. It has supported MbS in his campaign against mainstream Islamists associated with the sahwa and his broader attempts to target the Muslim Brotherhood. Though the regime often invokes association with the Brotherhood when detaining or silencing critics, the Brotherhood is an "amorphous target" that is "targeted as an intellectual project that blends Islam with politics as much as it is targeted as an actual organization."[126] In other words, any form of Islamism that resides outside of the strict control of the regime is viewed as a threat to the Al-Saud. In short, the official religious establishment remains committed to the religio-political vision that has for decades sought to legitimize and buttress the authority of the Al-Saud while silencing dissent and competing visions.

This new wave of repression has been aided by new anti-terror legislation enacted under MbS, which criminalizes the portraying of the King or Crown Prince, directly or indirectly, "in a manner that brings religion or justice into disrepute."[127] Many high-profile sahwa-related individuals have been arrested in Saudi Arabia under such pretenses and other arbitrary accusations, including Farhan Al-Maliki, Mostafa Hassan, Aid Al-Qarni, Ali Al-Omari, Safar Al-Hawali, Ahmed Al-Amari (died while detained), Ibrahim Nasser, Ibrahim Al-Fares, and Salman Al-Awdah. Crown Prince Mohammed bin Salman has sought to crush all dissenting religio-political visions within the Kingdom. Concerning Al-Awdah, the Saudi state is seeking the death penalty, charging him with being connected to the Muslim Brotherhood and the Qatari government as well as inciting people against the ruler.

MbS has placed the Muslim Brotherhood and the religio-political vision they espouse directly within his crosshairs. During an interview in 2018, MbS claimed that the Muslim Brotherhood was part of a "triangle of evil" that included Iran, *al-Qaeda*, and the Islamic State (ISIS):

> [The] Brotherhood is another extremist organization . . . they want to use the democratic system to rule countries and build shadow caliphates everywhere . . . then they would transform into a real Muslim empire . . . Al-Qaeda leaders, ISIS leaders, they were all Muslim Brotherhood first . . . this is very clear . . . if you see Osama bin Laden, he used to be in the Muslim Brotherhood . . . if you see Baghdadi the leader of ISIS, he used to be from the Muslim Brotherhood . . . actually if you see any terrorist, you will find that he used to be from the Muslim Brotherhood.[128]

The Council of Senior Scholars has also targeted the Muslim Brotherhood under MbS, denouncing the group as an "aberrant and deviating" terrorist organization that does "not represent the method of Islam," but rather "follows its partisan objectives that are running contrary to the guidance of our graceful religion."[129] Pointing to the Saudi educational system, the Crown Prince blamed "elements of the

Muslim Brotherhood organization" for "invading" Saudi schools and spreading extremism, vowing to "eradicate completely" such forces.[130] This "eradication" has resulted in the banning of books written by Brotherhood figures; the dismissal of educators accused of being associated with the group; and the advancement of a wider narrative that Saudi Arabia under MbS is breaking with its extremist past woven by the Brotherhood and its infiltration of Saudi society.[131] MbS has presented his rule as a break from such "extremes," blaming past Saudi behavior that has often encouraged intolerance and violence as a result of these influences.

Under Mohammed bin Salman, Saudi Arabia's historic embrace of intense religiosity is now shifting toward a new form of Saudi nationalism. A new hypernationalism is being actively nurtured by the state as the regime attempts to transition Saudi identity away from a purely Islamic one to a Saudi national identity. In other words, the regime is attempting to substitute a strong Saudi nationalism as the primary legitimizing and unifying force in the country, which has historically been rooted in religion. Though this new nationalism did not appear out of nowhere—its foundation was established during the era of King Abdullah—it has accelerated dramatically under MbS.

This drive toward a new ultranationalism is directed primarily toward Saudi Arabia's young population: it is estimated that over 50 percent of the population is under the age of twenty-five, and this youth bulge is straining the capacity of the traditional Saudi welfare state. Textbooks and state education have been revamped to embrace this new nationalist narrative while distancing the country from pan-Arab or pan-Islamic causes.[132] Also critical is the use of social media for the dissemination of these new narratives: the regime has mobilized an online army of loyalists and automated accounts to promote this new nationalism and the policies pursued by MbS.[133] Vision 2030 is the bedrock of this new nationalist discourse and identity and constitutes the state's promise to its youth of a new economic and social path forward for Saudi Arabia. In such a new nationalistic environment, there has been a considerable increase in the use of the accusations of being a "traitor" and a threat to the nation as a mechanism to target those who challenge either this new state-promoted nationalism, the absolute authority of MbS, or his policies.[134]

However, this reorientation toward overt nationalism does not equate to the decoupling of religion from Saudi identity. Islam continues to be marshaled as a mechanism of state identity both internally and externally. Instead, whereas religion by itself has traditionally served as the basis of Saudi identity, it no longer is the sole source of identification for the Saudi state. A new and intense form of nationalism, encouraged by the regime, is quickly on the rise.

Religion and Saudi Foreign Policy under Mohammed bin Salman

The continued utilization of religion as a source of Saudi identity and the advancement of a religio-political vision that legitimizes the Al-Saud have been apparent in the foreign policy pursued by MbS. Under Crown Prince Mohammed bin Salman, religion remains an important element of Saudi Arabia's foreign policy conduct. Riyadh continues to see political utility in the use of religious soft power abroad. Anti-Shi'ism and the presentation of Saudi Arabia as a "vanguard" of the Sunni community are still regularly deployed by the regime in its conflict with Iran, efforts to crush calls for change among marginalized Shi'a communities, and support its military operation in Yemen or support for armed groups in Syria (addressed above). Anti-Islamism—specifically mainstream Islamism and anti-Muslim Brotherhood rhetoric and policies—and support for counterrevolution throughout the Middle East also remain central to Saudi foreign policy. Riyadh often works in tandem with religious figures and institutions in other countries—such as Egypt and the United Arab Emirates (UAE)—to spread and support a statist religio-political vision of Islam that stresses absolute obedience to established authorities and that delegitimizes opposition. MbS and his regional allies have also pushed hard for the West to adopt a similar stance to mainstream Islamism, thereby embracing the narrative and vision of these political elites, most notably in its efforts to get the United States to designate the Muslim Brotherhood as a terrorist organization.[135] Speaking about the Brotherhood during his interview with *TIME* magazine, the Crown Prince argued that the group's ambitions extend far beyond the Middle East:

> You know what's the biggest danger? They're [the Brotherhood] not in the Middle East because they know that the Middle East is taking good strategy against them in Saudi Arabia, Egypt, UAE, Jordan, and a lot of countries. Their main target is to radicalize Europe. They hope that Europe in 30 years will turn to a Muslim Brotherhood continent, and they want to control the Muslims in Europe by [manipulation] . . . so this will be much more dangerous than the

Cold War, than ISIS, than Al-Qaeda, than whatever we've seen in the last hundred years of history.[136]

This disdain for mainstream Islamism and those who support or tolerate such movements was one of the primary impetuses behind the eruption of the 2017 Gulf Crisis (discussed more in the next chapter). With MbS newly at the helm in Riyadh, a coalition of countries led by Saudi Arabia, the UAE, Egypt, and Bahrain launched an air, land, and naval blockade of Qatar while also severing diplomatic and trade ties with Doha in June 2017. The culmination of tensions resulting from their opposing approaches to the Arab uprisings and political Islamism and the rift between Qatar and the "anti-terror quartet" that launched the blockades even allegedly included initial plans for a military operation against Doha before being dissuaded by the United States.[137] The blockading countries accused Qatar of supporting terrorism while also issuing a list designating numerous individuals and organizations as terrorist entities, including the Doha-based International Union of Muslim Scholars (IUMS) and Yusuf Al-Qaradawi, the main instruments of Qatari religious soft power.[138] Qatar's support for these actors, their initial successes following the overthrow of various longstanding autocrats, and their subsequent promotion of a religio-political vision in direct competition with the one embraced by political elites in Saudi Arabia and elsewhere came to be viewed as an existential threat to their own authority. The Grand Mufti of Saudi Arabia endorsed the blockade, stating that it was done to fight terrorism and ultimately was "in the interests of the future of the people of Qatar."[139] The Council of Senior Scholars denounced the Qatar-based news channel Aljazeera—also critical to Qatari religious soft power efforts—for being the "mouthpiece of terrorist groups."[140] The blockading countries issued a list of demands to Qatar, requiring Doha to sever all ties with the Muslim Brotherhood and other Islamist movements in the region, downgrade its relations with Iran, close Aljazeera, and various other steps if it wanted the blockade to be lifted.

Critical to these efforts aimed at sidelining mainstream Islamism and its supporters has been an extensive, outward-facing campaign designed to present a new "brand" of Saudi Arabia as a beacon of "moderate Islam" throughout the Middle East and the world. This effort to portray Riyadh as a staunch defender of "moderate Islam" is central to MbS' drive to reconstruct perceptions of Saudi Arabia's identity globally as "moderate" and "tolerant" while separating itself from being associated with extremism. Additionally, as stated in Chapter 2, by placing the blame for "radicalism" entirely on alternative readings of Islam, autocrats such as MbS are simultaneously able to deflect attention away from how their own authoritarian policies contribute to extremism while also repressing any they deem as a threat to their own rule under the guise of preventing terrorism. The "moderate Islam" that is embraced by the regime is a statist, apolitical Islam that emphasizes obedience to established authority. Outreach to other religious communities and leaders is paramount to these efforts, for it allows MbS to garner favor with influential actors internationally while also trying to present an image of Riyadh as a rightful authority speaking on behalf of the broader Muslim community, thereby expanding its hegemony over religious discourse and interpretation on a global scale.

Alongside his vows to return Saudi Arabia to its original, "moderate Islam," MbS has begun to designate different preachers to speak publicly about the need to respect other religions.[141] He has established new entities such as the Ideological War Center—a subsidiary of the Ministry of Defense—designed to combat "terrorism and extremism" while raising awareness among Muslims and non-Muslims about "real Islam."[142] Likewise, MbS has established the Global Center to Combat Extremism, also known as "Etidal," which regularly cooperates with international religious leaders in order to advance the "proper reading" of Islamic texts.[143] Central to Riyadh's efforts to take Saudi "moderate Islam" global has been the Muslim World League (MWL) and its secretary-general, Mohammed bin Abdul-Karim Al-Issa. A staunch ally of Crown Prince MbS, Al-Issa and the MWL have been at the center of this campaign. The MWL announced that Saudi Arabia will cease the funding of mosques in foreign countries, which has often been a point of contention with its international partners.[144] In 2019, the MWL launched its global forum for moderate Islam, drawing religious scholars aligned with Saudi Arabia from across the world.[145] The forum and its attendees produced the "Charter of Mecca," which lays forth guidelines for enacting and promoting "moderate Islam."

The MWL and Al-Issa have also spearheaded Saudi Arabia's courting of different religious communities and leaders around the world. In particular, Al-Issa has led Riyadh's outreach to Jewish leaders as part of Saudi Arabia's broader alignment with Israel geopolitically as well as Christian leaders.[146] This has been done to project an image of "tolerance" while also currying favor with influential demographics within Israel and the United States, and stands in stark contrast to how Saudi Arabia has historically sought to present an image of itself as aligned with Palestine.[147] In November 2018, Saudi Arabia hosted a delegation of Christian Evangelical leaders from the United States, who were received by MbS and Al-Issa.[148] A similar delegation visited the Kingdom again in September 2019,[149] and a US Jewish umbrella group—the Conference of Presidents—later led an official visit to the Kingdom, where they were also received by MbS and Al-Issa.[150] In January 2020, Al-Issa led a delegation of Islamic scholars in an unprecedented visit to the site of the Auschwitz concentration camp in Poland, accompanied by representatives of the American Jewish Committee.[151] A year later, Al-Issa was received by Pope Francis at the Vatican.[152] These efforts should be viewed as the strategic use of religious soft power by the Saudi state to portray a global image of itself as "moderate" and "tolerant" while simultaneously cultivating relationships with various influential actors.

Islam has also emerged as a critical tool of soft power in Saudi Arabia's relationships with global powers other than their traditional Western partners. With the return of global multipolarity and great power competition, Saudi Arabia and other Middle East states have increasingly expanded their relationships outside of the West, namely, with Russia and China. Saudi Arabia has sought to project an image of itself to Moscow and Beijing as a lucrative partner in the latter's efforts to control their own sizeable Muslim populations and hedge against religio-political visions that could inspire dissent. Though the role of religion in these relationships is often dwarfed by the dominance of material manifestations—economic, political, or security—it nevertheless plays an important and complementary role, especially under MbS and his efforts to diversify Riyadh's international partnerships. For Riyadh, religious soft power has proved to be a lucrative mechanism in the advancement of mutual interests among the Kingdom, Moscow, and Beijing.

Beginning first with Russia, the individual leading Moscow's religious outreach with Saudi Arabia—and the Middle East more generally—has been Chechnyan president Ramzan Kadyrov. Ratelle[153] explains how he has been described as Russia's "cultural ambassador to the Islamic world," Moscow's "point man in the Middle East," and the Kremlin's "top diplomat" in the region. In many ways, Kadyrov is a natural ally for Saudi Arabia: he is both anti-Iran and anti-Shi'a, sided with Riyadh and its partners in their conflict with Qatar, and has voiced his support for the promotion of so-called "moderate Islam" as understood by the Kingdom and its likeminded acolytes.[154] Like Saudi Arabia, Kadyrov supports a politically quietist and statist conceptualization of Islam that stresses obedience to established authority.

Kadyrov's engagement with Saudi Arabia has increased dramatically in recent years. He attended the visit by Saudi Arabia's King Salman to Moscow in 2017, after which Riyadh agreed to end its religious proselytizing efforts and the funding of mosques in Russia.[155] Kadyrov was also received by Saudi Arabia in 2018 for Eid Al-Adha, where he was presented with "all the diplomatic honors accorded to the representative of a major international partner" and was reportedly granted access to the Prophet Muhammad's room.[156] Later in 2019, the MWL held a conference on religious peace, coexistence, and combating terrorism in Moscow.[157] The MWL stated that Russia was chosen for the location of this conference "due to its distinctive societal harmony and religious and ethnic coexistence patterns." In addition to these diplomatic engagements, a special forces training school was opened in Chechnya in 2019, which has trained security personnel from Saudi Arabia.[158]

Saudi Arabia's religious engagement with China has likewise grown considerably over the past decade. China views its Muslim minority as a serious security threat to its internal cohesion and foreign interests. China has detained over 1 million Muslims and is holding them in internment camps where they face torture, are forced to renounce Islam and pledge loyalty to the Communist Party, and are often executed for their non-compliance.[159] A central objective of Beijing has been to separate its domestic Muslim minority from "global Islam" and keep Muslim states silent regarding the ongoing persecution. Heavily dependent on Chinese trade, investment, and oil markets, Saudi Arabia has not only remained silent but also praised China's efforts to control its domestic Muslim population.

Al-Sudairi[160] explains how "the Saudi government has been keen to reproduce the narratives espoused by Beijing regarding Islam," and Riyadh has gone to great lengths to deploy its religious and spiritual authority to buttress the legitimacy of the Chinese state. In 2013, Saleh Al-Taleb, an Imam of the Grand Mosque in Mecca, "in an extended interview with CCTV, praised the Chinese government's record in dealing with Islam."[161] In 2019, 37 states including Saudi Arabia signed a letter to the president of the United Nations Human Rights Council praising China's "contribution to the international human rights cause" and claiming that China has restored "peace and security" after facing "terrorism, separatism, and extremism in Xinjiang."[162] Likewise, when Saudi Crown Prince Mohammed bin Salman visited China in 2019, he "justified Beijing's actions against Uyghurs and declared that China has the right to take anti-terrorism and de-extremism measures to safeguard national security."[163] The Saudi-based Organization of Islamic

Cooperation has also praised China for "providing care to its Muslim citizens" and stated that it looked "forward to further cooperation between the OIC and the People's Republic of China."[164] Beyond simply praising these efforts, Saudi Arabia has arrested and deported exiled Uyghur Muslims back to China at the request of Beijing.[165]

Riyadh also engages regularly with the Chinese Islamic Association, which is responsible for controlling all Islamic narratives coming into and out of China while driving to "Sinicize Islam." When heads of state or Islamic figures from the Middle East visit China, officials from the Association are always present in the attempt to stress the Islamic legitimacy of the organization. In 2014, Saudi King Salman (then Crown Prince) visited China and was led by the Chinese Islamic Association on tours of different Chinese mosques, and the then-Crown Prince donated $3 million for the construction of Islamic and cultural centers in China.[166] The Association has also established and coordinated Islamic exchange programs with Saudi Arabia, where Chinese Muslims are instructed in the narrative of "moderate Islam," and coordinates the travel of Chinese Muslims to Saudi Arabia for the yearly Hajj.

While still in its early stages, religious cooperation between Saudi Arabia, Russia, and China signifies an emerging trend whereby Riyadh's religious soft power strategies are increasingly accounting for the return of global multipolarity.

Deconstructing Saudi Religious Soft Power

The evolution of Saudi religious soft power following the Arab uprisings—including its internal variations and relation to the other cases discussed in this book—reflects the analytical framework built in Chapter 1 of this book. An amalgamation of the instrumentalist and constructivist paradigms, Saudi religious soft power was influenced by the four underlying causal mechanisms addressed in this framework: (1) foreign threat perceptions; (2) foreign and domestic threat perceptions (i.e., a "two-level game"); (3) identity; and (4) ideology. The ways in which these four causal mechanisms influenced Saudi religious soft power—and the forms these strategies assumed—were shaped by the contexts within which Saudi political elites were operating and the target audiences they sought to influence.

Of these four causal mechanisms, the presence of a domestic threat to the authority and legitimacy of political elites in Riyadh— coupled with and intimately interconnected to the presence of external threats facing Saudi Arabia—had the greatest causal impact on Saudi religious soft power. Deciphering how to respond to the presence of interconnected internal and external threats was the first step of regime calculus within Riyadh, from which Saudi religious soft power would evolve as a coherent strategy to protect the authority and legitimacy of political elites inside Saudi Arabia and their allies abroad. The fact that Saudi elites faced a pressing internal challenge to their own rule resulted in all external stimuli ultimately being filtered through this domestic objective of securing their own authority. Political elites within Saudi Arabia quickly found themselves challenged from all corners, and these challenges are what shaped Riyadh's response to the uprisings and how they ultimately mobilized religion as part of their broader efforts to secure their own interests. As these threats evolved over time and the specific nature of such threats differed between contexts, so too did Saudi foreign policy and religious soft power adapt to address such challenges. The presence of these interconnected threats considerably influenced the identities and ideologies that were constructed by Saudi Arabia to advance the strategic interests of the Al-Saud in the face of such challenges. In other words, the construction and promulgation of particular religious identities and ideologies by Saudi elites—efforts that were central to Riyadh's response to the Arab uprisings—ultimately stemmed from attempts to counter these perceived threats while buttressing their own authority.

The Arab uprisings presented an interconnected combination of domestic and foreign perceived threats to the Al-Saud monarchy. For Saudi Arabia, the presence of a domestic challenge to the legitimacy and authority of the Al-Saud was coupled with a broader existential threat to the prevailing regional authoritarian status quo and balance of power on which they relied and from which they benefited. The challenge posed by "new" or "neo" sahwis struck at the very heart of the religio-political vision that has for decades served as the ideological foundation of the Saudi state. These mainstream Sunni Islamists challenged the state's monopoly on religious practice and interpretation while calling for fundamental reforms and a reconfiguration of the relationship between religion and the state inside Saudi Arabia. This was coupled with mobilization among the Kingdom's marginalized Shi'a minority calling for political reforms, an end to discrimination against the Shi'a in Saudi Arabia, and expressions of solidarity with protesters in Bahrain who were repressed with the help of Saudi military forces. The response by the Al-Saud to the Arab uprisings was filtered through the presence of these domestic threats. Riyadh doubled down on the existing religio-political vision undergirding the Saudi state to legitimize its counterrevolutionary approach—that is, repression—to such challenges. This vision, rooted in a traditionalist ethos that delegitimized protests or challenges to established authority and staunch anti-Shi'ism, would be weaponized both internally and externally to support the interests of Saudi elites.

Externally, the eruption of mass mobilization across the Middle East presented an existential threat to the prevailing regional authoritarian status quo and balance of power that the Al-Saud have relied on and benefited from. The uprisings resulted in intense geopolitical competition between Riyadh and other, more revisionist, competitors vying for strategic influence in the vacuums that emerged following the overthrow of several longstanding autocrats. In particular, the uprisings compounded Saudi Arabia's intense struggle with Iran for regional hegemony, with religious sectarianism being heavily utilized by both sides in this competition. Sectarianism was utilized by the Al-Saud both as a demobilizing mechanism to delegitimize calls for change in places such as Bahrain and Saudi Arabia's Eastern Province and as a mobilizing mechanism to legitimize the uprising and subsequent armed opposition to Bashar Al-Assad in Syria as well as Saudi's military intervention in Yemen in 2015. Additionally, Saudi Arabia was equally threatened by Qatar's support for the ousting of various regional autocrats and Doha's backing of the Muslim Brotherhood, whose early electoral successes in places such as Tunisia, Egypt, and Libya alarmed Saudi leadership. Saudi Arabia would work alongside partners such as Egypt and the UAE to isolate Qatar and undermine their support for such actors. Saudi foreign policy during this period centered around countering these perceived interrelated threats stemming from both domestically and abroad.

The efforts of ruling authorities within Saudi Arabia to construct a particular state identity and project internationally a specific state image—or "brand"—also influenced the religious soft power strategies developed by Riyadh. Such efforts were intimately connected to the types of threats facing the Al-Saud, namely, the presence of both domestic and foreign challenges and the need to balance against both. Saudi political elites had to construct specific internally and externally facing identities for the dual purpose of regime preservation and power projection.

To do so, Saudi Arabia engaged in an identity-balancing act following the Arab uprisings, utilizing different images when operating in different contexts to best advance the strategic imperatives of the

Al-Saud in the face of such threats. The Al-Saud has sought to present itself to the Muslim community as the center of global (Sunni) Islamic authority while also projecting an image of tolerance and moderation to the West. Depicting itself as the ultimate legitimate Islamic authority to both an internal and an external audience, Riyadh strove to assert its "brand" as leader of the Sunni Muslim community following the Arab uprisings, hedging against threats to this identity both internally and externally. This involved the attempted delegitimization of those challenging or rivaling such claims as well as presenting itself as a Sunni "bulwark" against an "expansionist" Shi'a Iran. Saudi Arabia's "branding" efforts were also directed toward the West, championing Riyadh as a leader of "moderate Islam" and a reliable partner in the fight against extremism. Such an image was designed to legitimize Riyadh's intense crackdown domestically and its assertive foreign policy abroad while still maintaining the support of its security partners in the West. Both branding efforts have been remolded following the rise of Crown Prince Mohammed bin Salman to complement his nationalist project and campaign to solidify ultimate authority domestically.

However, this reorientation toward overt nationalism does not equate to the decoupling of religion from Saudi identity. Islam continues to be marshaled as a mechanism of state identity both internally and externally to counter the domestic and foreign threats facing the Al-Saud. Instead, whereas religion by itself has traditionally served as the basis of Saudi identity, it no longer is the sole source of identification for the Saudi state, with elites beginning to turn toward other identity-based formulas to preserve their authority more efficiently moving forward.

Finally, Ideological concerns, specifically pertaining to the supported and constructed religio-political visions embraced by political elites within Saudi Arabia, also had a profound impact on shaping Saudi religious soft power. The specific political threats facing the Al-Saud served to considerably influence the religio-political ethos embraced by Riyadh following the Arab uprisings. Challenged at home and abroad, Saudi Arabia needed the ideological flexibility to legitimize its efforts to preserve power domestically while also projecting power abroad. Saudi political elites continue to depend on a top-down, heavily traditionalist religio-political vision of Islam that equates peaceful protests and calls for change as synonymous with rebellion, which remains strictly prohibited. According to such a statist/quietist vision, all religious practices and interpretations outside of the strict approval of the state constitute illegitimate forms of Islam.

This religio-political vision was marshaled as a legitimizing mechanism buttressing Riyadh's repression at home and aggressive foreign policy abroad as it helped lead the regional counterrevolution. Saudi authorities continue to mobilize Islam as an ideational mechanism to legitimize the rule of the Al-Saud while delegitimizing those proffering alternative conceptualizations of the relationship between religion and politics. Despite the rise of MbS having been portrayed by many as a fundamental break from this vision, the Crown Prince continues to see utility in religion as a political instrument and Islam within Saudi Arabia is still rooted in the same religio-political vision that has been used to legitimize regime policies and authority while discouraging dissent. In other words, religion remains a prominent tool of Saudi statecraft under MbS but has now been largely reoriented to advance his consolidation of personal authority. Additionally, sectarianism, both as an ideological tool of counterrevolution and as a justification for military action, was also critical to Riyadh's efforts in squashing calls for change among various Shi'a communities perceived as threatening as well as supporting armed opposition in Syria and direct military intervention in Yemen. As was demonstrated throughout this chapter, context and target audience often determined which ideological constructs were mobilized according to the interests of political elites in different environments.

Saudi religious soft power embodies how inherently political considerations among ruling elites influence religious outcomes. Instead of religion influencing and constraining policy, what we witnessed in this chapter was the opposite: religion was shaped, molded, and fashioned by the state in accordance with the strategic interests of political elites in Riyadh, specifically their desire to counter perceived domestic and foreign threats to their own authority. The need of political elites to be strategically flexible in order to counter such threats is the reason why these religious soft power strategies often differed dramatically between different contexts. Saudi Arabia marshaled religion as a mechanism to demobilize internally and in places such as Egypt and Bahrain but utilized religion as a mobilizing mechanism in places such as Syria and Yemen in an attempt to push back against Iran. Religious identities and ideologies were central to Saudi religious soft power, yet they were themselves constructed first and foremost by the state to achieve inherently political objectives, namely, regime preservation and power projection. It is the constellation of domestic and foreign threats facing political elites in Riyadh as well as their evolution across time and space that most fundamentally shape the differing ways religion was mobilized as a tool of statecraft by Saudi Arabia following the Arab uprisings.

Conclusion

Religion remains a critical resource used by Riyadh to advance its vast portfolio of interests at home and abroad. Material interests, ideology, and identity are all essential components comprising Saudi Arabia's religious soft power strategies. Saudi religious soft power remains a top-down initiative designed to buttress the authority of the regime while delegitimizing opposition and competing conceptualizations of the relationship between religion and politics. As this chapter has demonstrated, a central objective of the monarchy has been the elimination of alternative religio-political visions and the groups and individuals that proffer them due to the challenge they pose to the authority and legitimacy of the Al-Saud. However, these conflicts with competing groups are not absolute as evidenced by the alignment between the Saudi state and Sunni Islamists vis-à-vis issues such as the uprisings in Bahrain and Yemen, where concerns regarding Iran served to abrogate (to a degree) such divisions. Engaged in a delicate "two-level game" of policy-making, Riyadh molds its religious soft power strategies according to the different contexts it is operating in.

Having been challenged at home and abroad, this drive by Riyadh for hermeneutical hegemony has extended both domestically and internationally following the Arab uprisings. Context and target audience(s) have been critical to these efforts: whether directed toward the Muslim community as a whole, Sunnis or Shi'a, Riyadh's Western partners, or rising powers such as Russia and China, Saudi religious soft power adapts according to the strategic context within which the state is operating. Though the rise to power of Crown Prince Mohammed bin Salman has been depicted as a fundamental "break" from Saudi Arabia's historic relationship with religion, it has instead been shown here that religion is being remolded and recast toward MbS's desire to consolidate absolute power in the Kingdom. In doing so, MbS has sought to eliminate the autonomy of religious actors inside Saudi Arabia while also reworking the identity of the state and its people. This has also included efforts to promote an image of religious "tolerance" and "moderation" abroad while demonizing opposition to MbS or his policies. The new drive toward nationalism by MbS has included the reconstructing of Saudi Arabian history—particularly the historic relationship between Islam and state—to fit this new desired identity and what it ultimately means to be "Saudi." Religious soft power remains central to Riyadh's objectives domestically and internationally.

Chapter 4

QATAR

Qatar's strategy of religious soft power following the Arab uprisings was considerably different from the other two cases addressed in this book. Lacking a formally institutionalized religious establishment, Doha's approach has relied upon individuals, organizations, and networks associated with mainstream political Islamists, primarily the Muslim Brotherhood and its various regional affiliates.

This chapter examines the ways in which inherently political considerations influenced how religion was marshaled as a tool of statecraft by Doha following the Arab uprisings. Facing no considerable political threat at home, the Arab uprisings were viewed by Doha primarily as a strategic opportunity to expand its own influence across the Middle East and must be situated within the context of a broader turn in Qatari foreign policy in the post-1995 period. The absence of this domestic political challenge to the authority of the Al-Thani ruling family allowed Doha to approach the uprisings from a fundamentally different position than either Saudi Arabia or the UAE. Secure in their own authority, the Al-Thani were able to preserve the authoritarian status quo within Qatar while supporting elements of the uprisings abroad to Doha's strategic benefit.

Political elites in Doha mobilized religion via a bottom-up, "republican," and society-oriented approach abroad directed toward the Muslim community in support of the uprisings in Tunisia, Egypt, Libya, and Syria. Qatar's primary instruments of religious soft power—Sheikh Yusuf Al-Qaradawi and the International Union of Muslim Scholars (IUMS)—were instrumental in constructing a new body of Islamic jurisprudence that sought to legitimize peaceful protests against established authority, referred to as *fiqh al-thawra* (the jurisprudence of revolution). However, this enthusiasm was not shared equally across all regional revolutions, with Qatar, Al-Qaradawi, and the IUMS assuming a more nuanced approach vis-à-vis the uprisings in Bahrain and Yemen. The strategic interests of the Al-Thani and the specific context within which they were operating at any given time would ultimately determine how religion was mobilized as a tool of statecraft and what form(s) it assumed.

This chapter begins by first detailing the relationship between Islam and the Qatari state and how Doha has successfully coopted political Islamism since becoming an independent sovereign state in 1971. The next section examines Qatar's response to the Arab uprisings, followed by an overview of Doha's reaction to the growing successes of counterrevolutionary forces in the region. Next, this study investigates how Al-Qaradawi and the IUMS have sought to extend their bottom-up approach by presenting themselves and Qatar as supporters of various "Muslim causes" around the world. Finally, this chapter concludes by connecting the themes and patterns that have comprised Qatari religious soft power post-2010.

Islam in Qatar

Qatar's emergence as a modern state and its relationship with Islam are considerably different from that of Saudi Arabia. Following the Ottoman Empire's decision to renounce their claims to Qatar in 1913, the Anglo-Qatari Treaty of 1916 established British control over the country while also propping up the Al-Thani family as the local authority through whom the UK could exert its influence.[1] The treaty stipulated that the Al-Thani would cede the territory to the British for the latter's protection. It was only when the British announced their decision to withdraw from their occupied territories "east of the Suez" that Qatar gained independence and became its own country in 1971. The emergence of Qatar as its own independent country was not the result of an anti-colonial struggle—as was the case in many of the other countries throughout the Middle East—nor was it the result of a mission to "purify Islam," as happened in neighboring Saudi Arabia. Rather, the Al-Thani ruling family abruptly inherited a sovereign state as a result of British disengagement. In fact, the Al-Thani and other ruling families of the small Gulf states were alarmed at the news of losing British protection. Qatar and several of these other British protectorates entertained the idea of creating a federation in order to combine their strength and hedge against their larger and stronger neighbor, Saudi Arabia, but were unable to agree to common terms. Qatar emerged from its status as a British protectorate as a sovereign traditional monarchy, with power concentrated in the hands of the Al-Thani leadership.

Like Saudi Arabia, Qatar officially adheres to Wahhabism. However, the relationship between state and religion within Qatar is dramatically different from how the two are coupled together in Saudi Arabia. In Qatar, the religious sphere has been defined by a lack of an indigenous clergy and the domination of foreigners. No formal alliance exists between the ulema and the ruling family as it does in Saudi Arabia. Throughout the 1950s to 1980s, Qatar and the Gulf witnessed an influx of Muslim Brotherhood personnel fleeing Arab nationalist governments who were cracking down on the organization and its members in places such as Egypt and Syria. These individuals were critical for the state, which at the time was in the process of building its own educational and judicial systems as well as the government bureaucracy. Additionally, the influx of these Brotherhood personalities was a lucrative mechanism for the Al-Thani and other ruling families in the Gulf to buttress their own "Islamic credentials" while hedging against the rise of Arab nationalist movements throughout the Middle East.

Though the Muslim Brotherhood established an official Qatari branch in 1975, the group voted to dissolve itself in 1999 due primarily to the fact that a formal organizational structure was not needed in an environment where the government and the Brotherhood remained supportive of one another. Moreover, due to the incredibly small native population of Qatar and the ability of the government to co-opt the population and provide its people with necessary social services—the typical means by which the Brotherhood established its influence—a formal organization was largely redundant.[2] Moreover, so long as the Brotherhood remained in the regime's good graces and maintained an outward focus, the Al-Thani had no reason to fear the organization and could capitalize on its popularity throughout the region. Having never assumed a position of opposition against the state, coupled with the regime providing its citizens with access to employment and other social services, the Qatari Brotherhood lacked a domestic mobilizing impetus and instead used their refuge in Doha to focus on external matters. As Freer[3] explains, "the Qatari regime does not place restrictions on the Brotherhood because it does not need to do so," preferring instead to capitalize on the group's networks throughout the Middle East and providing them with a platform through which to disseminate its message, thereby marking its "successful cooptation of political Islam." Contrary to Saudi Arabia, which during this period developed native resources of "sacred capital," Qatar leaned into the networks and personalities of the Muslim Brotherhood.

Religious scholars in Qatar do not have an institutionalized role similar to clerics in Saudi Arabia: there is no official religious office—such as the office of the Grand Mufti in Saudi Arabia—and "the role of ulema within Qatar is relegated to one of personal contacts or informal influence."[4] The Ministry of Islamic Affairs and Endowments was established only in 1993 (twenty-two years after the country's independence) and lacks substantial status or powers. This strategy of informalization was deliberate: as part of its desire to preserve its autonomy from its more powerful Saudi neighbor, Qatar did not desire a strong domestic Wahhabi religious establishment susceptible to Riyadh's influence. As Freer[5] explains, "Qatar's rulers feared that the implementation of religion to legitimize their rule could ultimately confuse their citizens' loyalty, motivating them to follow ulema aligned with the Saudi state rather than becoming devoted to an independent Qatari entity." Therefore, Doha sought to harness the influence of particular personalities connected with the Brotherhood and their networks in order to carve out a distinct religious space for itself not dependent upon the Wahhabi establishment in Saudi Arabia.

No individual represents this approach to political Islam by Qatar better than Sheikh Yusuf Al-Qaradawi. Having left Egypt for Qatar in 1961 and remaining until his death in 2022, Al-Qaradawi was the most prominent cleric for the Muslim Brotherhood and one of the most well-known Islamic figures throughout the world, often being referred to as the Arab world's most popular cleric. Al-Qaradawi established a very close relationship with the Al-Thani ruling family, beginning with Emir Ahmad bin 'Ali Al-Thani, who ruled from 1960 to 1972. The Emir granted the sheikh Qatari citizenship in 1969, and since then, the royal family "became a key supporter of Qaradawi and funded his trips across the world as he visited grassroots Brotherhood-affiliated organizations in Pakistan, Malaysia, Indonesia, Europe, North America, and even as far afield as Japan and South Korea."[6] Later in life, the sheikh would reflect on his close relationship with Qatar, stating, "I am part of Qatar and Qatar is part of me."[7]

Al-Qaradawi helped build Qatar's educational institutions and was the founding dean of the College of Sharia Law at Qatar University in 1977, serving in this position until 1990. Qaradawi was also designated the president of the IUMS upon its creation in 2004. Endorsed by Qatari leadership and based in Doha, the IUMS "emerged out of a concern for the declining independent authority of clerics, and a desire for a universal body that could speak to the contemporary concerns of all Muslims."[8] In particular, the organization sought to present itself as a unique scholarly body not subjugated to state authorities and has adopted an outward-looking, bottom-up approach toward issues facing the global Muslim community.

Sheikh Yusuf Al-Qaradawi and the IUMS represent the foundation of Qatari religious soft power. The official lack of formal institutionalization also provides Qatar, Al-Qaradawi, and the IUMS with a considerable advantage. Being able to distance themselves officially from state authorities, Al-Qaradawi and the IUMS are able to present themselves to the Muslim community as fundamentally different from scholars directly subordinate to the state in places such as Saudi Arabia. This also allows the Al-Thani to either lean into or distance itself from the positions of the IUMS and its officials as it pleases, while also giving the regime the ability to apply pressure if needed without causing intra-governmental tensions.

From 1972 until 1995, Qatar under the rule of Emir Sheikh Khalifa bin Hamad Al-Thani was primarily internally focused as the state was preoccupied with building its domestic institutions and benefited from the US-supported Saudi-led security umbrella in the Gulf. Indeed, for the first roughly two decades following its independence, Qatar was closed off relative to other states in the region, far more interested in internal developments, particularly protecting the newly independent state from its larger neighbor Saudi Arabia.[9] This changed, however, following Qatar's enrichment from oil and natural gas revenues, increased engagement with the United States as part of Washington's assertive foreign policy in the region, and a palace coup that overthrew the Emir and established his son, Sheikh Hamad, as the new ruler. Under Hamad, Qatar sought to assert itself as its own independent regional actor, thereby moving the country out from under the traditional Gulf dominance of Saudi Arabia.

This penchant toward an independent foreign policy by Doha has resulted in the Al-Thani often butting heads with its other Gulf neighbors, particularly Saudi Arabia, which wants Qatar to play a backseat role to Riyadh's dominance in the region. Additionally, Qatar, under the rule of Emir Hamad, greatly strengthened the country's relationship with the United States as a way of hedging against reliance upon its neighbor Saudi Arabia for protection. In 1996, Doha built the Al-Udeid Air Base, which hosts more than 10,000 US servicemen and has proved critical for Washington's power projection and counterterrorism operations in the Middle East as well as the protection of the Al-Thani from foreign threats. Active engagement with the United States is one of the central pillars of contemporary Qatari foreign policy.

A central element to this newfound international engagement and independence was support for mainstream political Islamists associated with the Muslim Brotherhood, with whom the state had cultivated ties for decades. At precisely the same time Qatar sought to "open up" and assert itself abroad, Al-Qaradawi had established himself as one of the most popular Islamic clerics in the world, allowing Doha to tap into his prestige and the networks he maintained. Additionally, the founding of the Doha-based Aljazeera satellite television channel in 1996 helped usher in a new era of Qatari foreign policy and soft power. The channel was revolutionary in the region compared to the dominance of directly state-controlled media. Aljazeera provided a platform to a broad array of different political actors, bolstering Qatar's image as a hub for diplomacy and dialogue while also injecting Doha into the forefront of these debates. Indeed, there is "no better way to subtly tune the ideas that will determine the future of the Arab and Islamic world than to own the stage upon which those ideas are expressed."[10] The growth of Aljazeera coincided with this broader shift in Qatari foreign policy throughout the 2000s, namely, increased emphasis on conflict mediation and diplomacy. Doha has sought to present itself as a regional hub for diplomacy, engaging in mediation efforts from Palestine to Yemen, Lebanon, Sudan, and elsewhere.

The growth of Aljazeera and Doha's efforts at regional conflict mediation have also been particularly useful in providing a platform to mainstream political Islamists and presenting Qatar as a hub for transnational Muslim issues. As Cherribi[11] explains, "in supporting Islamist political movements and the notion of a transnational umma, Aljazeera has succeeded in creating a new model of Islamic society to compete with those underpinning the power structures of traditional regional leaders, Saudi Arabia, Iran, and Egypt." Yusuf Al-Qaradawi's show *Sharia and Life* was the most popular program on the channel for years, accumulating approximately 60 million viewers.[12] Al-Qaradawi benefited from the meteoric growth of Aljazeera, allowing him to spread his teachings and those of his acolytes to the world via live TV. Naturally, the topics covered by Aljazeera and the fact that it has provided a platform to oppositionists have resulted in the channel being viewed by other states in the region as a threat and source of instability.

Qatar's political system has been remarkably stable for an authoritarian country and stands in stark contrast to several of its Gulf neighbors. By the end of the first decade of the twentieth century, Qatar had increasingly capitalized on this domestic stability and sought to project an image of itself to the international community as a hub for conflict mediation and diplomacy in the Middle East. In the Gulf, Qatar maintained cordial relations with its neighbors but continued to compete with some—particularly Saudi Arabia and the UAE—while striving to chart a political path independent of these actors. Qatar's relationships with political Islamists had also developed considerably during this period, which would later become an asset for Doha as it sought to tap into these networks following the Arab uprisings. With no Islamist opposition at home and playing host to figures such as Al-Qaradawi and wide-reaching organizations such as the IUMS, Qatar would be able to capitalize on these cultivated relationships and networks for its own strategic purposes in a way its competitors could not.

Qatar, Islam, and the Arab Uprisings

At the time of the Arab uprisings, Qatar stood out from other countries in the region due to its domestic political stability and lack of significant challenges directed toward the Al-Thani. Indeed, Qatar was "virtually the only state in the broader Middle East in 2011 that had no reason to fear uprisings elsewhere spilling over into its domestic politics."[13] Witnessing almost no public dissent or unrest, the only noteworthy domestic incident that can be attributed to the uprisings was a small meeting convened by a former professor at Qatar University, Ali Al-Kuwari, which was attended only by a total of 73 Qatari citizens and resulted in the publishing of a book, *al-Sha'b yurid al-Islah fi Qatar . . . aidan* (The People Want Reform in Qatar . . . Too), which was immediately banned.[14]

The absence of a significant domestic perceived threat is in stark contrast to the other two cases considered in this book—Saudi Arabia and the UAE—which both faced a significant domestic challenge as a result of the Arab uprisings. This absence is critical: unconstrained by a challenge to their own authority domestically, the Al-Thani were primarily outward facing during this regional wave of mobilization, able to protect the authoritarian status quo that prevailed within Qatar while also seeking to capitalize on these mass movements and the overthrows of longstanding autocrats to alter the regional balance of power in Doha's favor. Building off of its post-1995 shift toward a more independent foreign policy, Doha saw the uprisings as an opportunity to advance its foreign interests and influence while also furthering its independence from its larger, more powerful neighbor, Saudi Arabia.

With the eruption of the Arab uprisings, Qatar was positioned in such a way that it could capitalize on the networks and relationships it had built and "moved away from being a mediator to becoming a more active supporter of change in the Middle East region."[15] It did so by assuming a predominantly bottom-up, "republican," and Muslim-community-oriented approach abroad that allowed the state to differentiate itself from competitors such as Saudi Arabia who relied on top-down repressive measures to maintain its influence. The Al-Thani projected an image of themselves as aligned with the aspirations of the people across the Middle East and provided a platform to religious scholars and institutions that would construct a new religio-political vision attempting to legitimize peaceful popular uprisings. Qatar was able to capitalize on its extensive relationships with political Islamists around the Middle East, primarily the Muslim Brotherhood and its various regional offshoots. Viewing these actors as assets, the Al-Thani were able to build upon their longstanding relations with senior Brotherhood figures based in Doha, allowing Qatar to "reach out directly to the rising groups in Egypt, Libya, and Tunisia that were connected to the Muslim Brotherhood, channeling support, engaging in dialogue, and building connections with those groups which, elected into government in late 2011 and 2012, seemed to be in a position to shape the region's future."[16]

Sheikh Yusuf Al-Qaradawi and the Doha-based IUMS were the principal instruments—that is, "sacred capital"—of Qatari religious soft power during this period as they sought to legitimize the uprisings from a religious perspective. Also critical was Aljazeera, which devoted massive coverage to the uprisings and provided an international platform for Islamist groups and oppositionists. Regularly employing an Islamic lexicon when covering the uprisings, Aljazeera "served as a unifying force for the disparate elements of the unprecedented 'youth bulge,' societal Islamization, and the rise of social media in the Arab world that, once combined, would erupt in the harmonious cries for revolution."[17]

However, despite Qatar's support for revolutionary change in places like Tunisia, Egypt, Libya, and Syria, this enthusiasm disappeared when faced with calls for change in the Gulf region. The Al-Thani, overseeing an authoritarian government themselves, did not embrace the revolutions in Bahrain or Yemen or calls for change in other Gulf countries such as Saudi Arabia or the UAE, desiring instead to maintain the status quo in their immediate neighborhood. These calls for change within the Gulf proved too close to home for the Al-Thani, who viewed such challenges to the status quo within the Gulf as a threat. As will be detailed below, the specific context(s) within which Doha was operating determined the specific messaging and strategies of religious soft power adopted by the state to best advance the interests of the regime.

New Ideological Frontiers and Realpolitik: Qatar in Support of Revolution

As the Arab uprisings unfolded, Qatar's instruments of religious soft power—Al-Qaradawi and the IUMS—responded by putting forward Islamic legal rulings in real time as the protest movements developed, often responding to contrasting edicts issued by regime scholars in places such as Egypt or Saudi Arabia. Amplified by Aljazeera—which focused overwhelmingly on the protests during this period—Al-Qaradawi and the IUMS began constructing what would serve as the foundation for a new body of Islamic religio-political and legal thought, the jurisprudence of revolution (*fiqh al-thawra*). The construction and promulgation of this new body of Islamic jurisprudence by Al-Qaradawi and the IUMS were central to Qatar's response to the Arab uprisings. This new body of scholarship was constructed to legitimize peaceful protests against established authorities from a religious (Islamic) perspective, arguing that such mobilization is fundamentally different from armed rebellion, which has long been denounced in Islamic orthodoxy. Seeking to establish legal guidance on peaceful mobilization, Al-Qaradawi and his allies rooted their arguments concerning confronting tyranny in the Islamic principle of "commanding right and forbidding wrong" (*al-amr bi-l-ma'ruf wa-l-nahy 'an al-munkar*). Diametrically opposed to the legal rulings being issued by regime scholars denouncing the protests and urging obedience to established authority, Al-Qaradawi and the IUMS were the vanguards of a new religio-political framework designed to legitimize the Arab uprisings. Al-Qaradawi's support for the revolutions would result in him being nicknamed "*abu al-thawrat*" ("father of the revolutions").[18]

Addressing the legitimacy of peaceful protests, Al-Qaradawi issued a lengthy *fatwa* arguing:

> Muslims, like all other human beings, have the right to march and hold demonstrations to express their legitimate demands and to communicate their needs to rulers and decision-makers with a voice that cannot be ignored. The voice of the individual may not be heard,

but the voice of the collective is too powerful to ignore, and the more the demonstrators multiply, and the more weighty personalities they have, the more heard and influential their voice is. . . . The evidence of the legitimacy of these marches is that they are matters (customs) of civil life, and [these matters] are permissible. . . . These marches and demonstrations, whether they are taking place to achieve a legitimate purpose, such as calling for Sharia arbitration, the release of detainees without real charge, the suspension of military trials of civilians, or the abolition of the state of emergency that gives rulers absolute powers . . . [the] jurists do not doubt the permissibility [of the protests].

Addressing the question of democracy and its permissibility in Islam, he argued:

Democracy is the best guarantee for the protection of society from oppressive regimes and tyranny . . . we are obliged to adopt the democratic method and mechanisms in order to realize justice and to respect human rights, and to stand against oppressive and tyrannical regimes.[19]

Al-Qaradawi described the protests as fundamentally "Islamic" in nature because they were "demanding freedom, dignity, and social justice, and this is what Islam calls for: people to live in dignity, freedom, and safety."[20] As protests continued to sweep across the region and longstanding autocrats were forced from power, Al-Qaradawi claimed:

If the nineteenth century was the century of capitalism and the twentieth century the century of communism, then the twenty-first century is the century of Islam.[21]

The sheikh projected an image of himself and his allies as fundamentally different from that of the "regime scholars" who sought to prohibit the protests and argued that he and the "ulema who are free"—that is, those who do not serve state institutions—are the ones capable of pronouncing the corruption of rulers.[22] Indeed, the sheikh asserts that "the official religious institutions" of authoritarian regimes pose "one of the greatest dangers" to the Arab Spring because they "disseminate specious arguments" attacking the legitimacy of revolutionary activism."[23] Al-Qaradawi denounced the "reactionary jurisprudence" being issued by regime scholars, imploring them to embrace "revolutionary jurisprudence that works to strengthen the people and purify the government."[24] Addressing such rulings, Al-Qaradawi explains that the Quran is filled with verses prohibiting tyranny and oppression.[25] He describes in-depth his dissatisfaction with regime scholars denouncing the legitimate demands of the protests:

> I do not understand how the verses and hadiths that reject tyranny (zulm) are lost on these [ulema]. Hundreds of verses in the Holy Quran reject tyranny, curse tyrants, express hatred of tyranny and its perpetrators, and that God does not love tyrants . . . Islam teaches us to stand in the face of tyrants, and the Hadiths of the Prophet are many in this regard: "The best jihad is speaking truth before an oppressive authority (sultan ja'ir)" . . . [He also said:] "Whoever among you sees a wrong, let him change it with his hands. If he is unable to do so, let him change it with his tongue. If he is unable to do even this, let him change it with his heart, and that is the weakest level of faith." These [youth protestors] are changing with their tongues. They did not carry swords, nor explode bombs, nor did they aggress against anyone.[26]

It was the revolutions in Tunisia and Egypt, particularly the latter, that laid the foundation for Al-Qaradawi and his allies to construct the foundation of what would become fiqh-al-thawra. The first autocrat to fall would be Zine El-Abidine Ben Ali in Tunisia after roughly 28 days of protests. Throughout this time period, Al-Qaradawi and the IUMS expressed their support for the protesters. When Ben Ali fell in January 2011, Al-Qaradawi argued that the Tunisian people had "shown an example to the Arab and Islamic peoples, and oppressed people in general, that they should not despair nor fear tyrants."[27] The IUMS also congratulated the Tunisian people as well as Ennahda, an Islamist political party inspired by the Muslim Brotherhood, for their electoral victories during the first free election in the country's history. The group hailed the country for being a "pioneer" for the Islamic nation, offering "lessons in peaceful revolutions," as well as "lessons in democracy, pluralism, fair and transparent elections, as witnessed by the whole world," while also calling on Ennahda to "present an honorable model for the Islamic movement in general."[28] In a display of thanks for his support, Rashid Al-Ghannouchi, a co-founder and leader of Ennahda, would describe Al-Qaradawi as the "sheikh of revolutionaries" and one of the biggest supporters of the Arab uprisings.[29]

Though Tunisia was the spark for the region-wide uprisings, it was in Egypt that Al-Qaradawi and the IUMS would exert their most influence, particularly given the sheikh's personal connections to the country. Al-Qaradawi was a staunch supporter of the Egyptian revolution that overthrew Hosni Mubarak, embracing the protesters' demands for dignity and freedom while regularly imploring the scholars of Al-Azhar to stand with demonstrators. On *Sharia and Life*, Al-Qaradawi regularly addressed the Egyptian uprising, lending his emphatic endorsement to the protests:

> I would like to say this to the Egyptian people whom I am greeting now, with their blessed intifada (uprising), revolting against the dire conditions of their lives after being very patient so as to put an end to poverty, hunger, and unemployment: Other are enjoying the wealth of this country, monopolizing our resources and land an [exploiting] all the people and their patience. . . . The people went to the streets in a peaceful manner—in demonstrations, in protest, without sticks, but with prayer beads or Qurans, refusing to leave this life, wanting dignity and freedom and halal [fair] wage. But the security forces countered their protests with live bullets. . . . We saw yesterday dozens of martyrs falling and more than a thousand wounded . . . I ask the people to continue their intifada—continuity is the only way to secure your rights, God willing. . . . To our beloved army, I say that the army's purpose is to protect Egypt in the period to come, a very crucial period. But I ask them not to govern. I don't want to go back in history to another time, to the time of military rule. We want civilians to govern. We want a civilian governance, and if people of the military want to run for office, they should take off their military uniforms and engage in political competition with other civilians according to the rules of the Republic and democracy. . . . What I want to say to the Egyptian regime and especially to Mubarak: I regret to see a regime that is blind and can't see, deaf and can't hear, stupid and can't understand. . . O Mubarak, learn from Ben Ali [of Tunisia], leave on your own feet, before you are forced to leave.[30]

Before Mubarak fell, Al-Qaradawi expressed that Islamists are capable of leading Egypt into the future. The Muslim Brotherhood, he argued, lives for the Egyptian homeland and people as well as the Islamic nation.[31] Following Mubarak's ouster, Al-Qaradawi returned to Egypt's Tahrir Square—the heart of the revolution—to deliver a very symbolic sermon to a massive crowd where he hailed the people of Egypt but warned them to safeguard their revolution: "Don't let anyone steal this revolution from you—those hypocrites who will put on a new face that suits them . . . The revolution isn't over. It has just started to build Egypt . . . guard your revolution."[32] When Egypt's first democratic elections approached, Al-Qaradawi expressed his support for the Muslim Brotherhood. He criticized claims that the group merely sought to seize power for themselves[33] and argued that the interests of Egypt lie with "the arrival of the Muslim Brotherhood and the Islamic movement to power."[34] Following the election of Muslim Brotherhood candidate Mohamed Morsi to the presidency, Al-Qaradawi met with him and congratulated him on his success. Additionally, after having been banned from preaching in Al-Azhar for decades, Al-Qaradawi delivered a sermon at the institution following Morsi's election, where he pronounced its liberation:

> Today we speak from this spot, this Al-Azhar pulpit that has become the pulpit of the entire Sunni world. For years this pulpit was monopolized by whoever monopolized it [i.e., the various Egyptian regimes], but it did not [remain monopolized] forever, for it is the pulpit of Islam, of the Quran and Muhammad, God's prayers and peace be upon him, and therefore it must return to its [real] owners and people.[35]

This outpouring of support from Al-Qaradawi and the IUMS for elements of the uprisings was coupled with various forms of tangible support from the Qatari state, in addition to Doha providing the former with a platform from which to promulgate *fiqh al-thawra* to a global audience. Without a pressing domestic challenge to the authority of the Al-Thani, Doha was able to focus its efforts primarily on restructuring the regional balance of power in its own favor. Doha's Emir, Sheikh Hamad bin Khalifa Al-Thani, sought to project an image of the Al-Thani as defenders of those seeking change and freedoms in the region, explaining that Qatar stood with those in the Middle East "asking for justice and dignity."[36] Emir Hamad also expressed his openness to working and cooperating with moderate Islamist movements—such as the Muslim Brotherhood—stating, "we should not fear them, but let us cooperate with them."[37] Noting Qatar's support for the Egyptian revolution in particular, Al-Qaradawi would hail the Emir as well as Aljazeera, explaining:

> When I learned about the victory of the revolution, I called the Emir of Qatar to congratulate him and thank him. He told me that I played

an essential leadership role. I told him that if Aljazeera had not been there, my voice would not have reached [Tahrir] Square and the people of Egypt.[38]

In Tunisia, following the rise to power of Ennahda, the Qatari National Bank gave Tunis $500 million to support its foreign currency reserves and aid the Ennahda government.[39] Qatar also signed 10 different agreements with the Ennahda government in 2012, including investment and construction deals, humanitarian aid services, and vocational training, and also announced that it would allow the Tunisian armed forces to participate in military drills in Qatar.[40] Additionally, Qatar announced its plans following the revolution to build a $2 billion oil refinery in Tunisia after years of delays.[41] Ennahda leader Rashid Al-Ghannouchi also hailed Qatar for its support, stating Tunisia is happy to "have Qatar as a partner and ally."[42] Similarly, in Egypt, Qatar was quick to embrace and support Mohamed Morsi's government. Qatar immediately provided the new government with over $7.5 billion in emergency loans and direct financial aid.[43] These pledges of financial aid were coupled with numerous promises of Qatari investment within Egypt totaling over $18 billion, both with the ultimate goal of attempting to help stabilize Egypt's turbulent economy and, therefore, the new Muslim Brotherhood government.[44]

Qatar, Al-Qaradawi, and the IUMS were also emphatic supporters of the uprisings in Libya and Syria. However, there is an important difference between these two revolutions and the ones in Tunisia and Egypt, namely, the presence of armed conflict following the virtual disintegration of the Libyan and Syrian states. In Libya, Al-Qaradawi and the IUMS were quick to embrace the protests and benefited from the elaborate contacts and networks established by one of Al-Qaradawi's Libyan students, Ali Al-Sallabi, who served as an intermediary. As the revolution evolved into an armed conflict between Muammar Gaddafi and the Libyan people, Al-Qaradawi issued a fatwa calling for Gaddafi's assassination:

> I urge the commanders, the officers, and the soldiers of the Libyan army not to listen or obey [Gaddafi's orders]. In this case, "hearing and obeying" is haram. The Prophet (peace be upon him) teaches us by saying, "hearing and obeying is an obligation on a person whether one likes the command or not, as long as one is not ordered to disobey God. If he is ordered to disobey God, then there is no such thing as hearing and obeying." Under no circumstance should

a creation disobey the creator. If he [Gaddafi] tells you to attack civilians with fighter jets, I say no! Attack the one who gave you the orders to attack. I give a fatwa to the police and soldiers, who have the capacity to kill Muammar Gaddafi. Whoever can fire a bullet at him and relieve the country and its people from oppression, then they must do so. This man wants to eliminate the people, so I want to protect the people. I give a fatwa to whomever can fire a bullet and rid us of his evil and to rid both Libya and its people from the evil of this man, let them do so. It is not permissible for any officer, whether he is an air force officer or ground officer, it is not permissible for them to obey this man by disobeying God in an injustice.[45]

Following Gaddafi's assassination and the success of the revolution, the IUMS was quick to congratulate the Libyan people for their victory "over the tyrants of darkness."[46] As Libya gradually descended into a state of civil war, Al-Qaradawi and the IUMS continued supporting Islamist actors in the country aligned with the Muslim Brotherhood, who remain opposed to the forces of Khalifa Haftar and the Libyan National Army (LNA), which is backed by Saudi Arabia, the UAE, and Egypt. Doha was also actively involved in the Libyan revolution and its subsequent civil war. Alongside the UAE, Qatar was officially involved in the NATO intervention in Libya in March 2011, contributing fighter jets to the operation and even sending Qatari special forces to fight alongside Libyan revolutionaries.[47] Likewise, as the country slipped into civil war following the overthrow of Gaddafi, Qatar continued to pour money and weapons into Islamist forces connected to the Muslim Brotherhood in their fight against the Saudi–UAE–Egypt-backed LNA, which rapidly evolved into a protracted proxy war that continues to this day.[48]

Al-Qaradawi and the IUMS were also very vocal in their support for the revolutionaries seeking to topple Bashar Al-Assad in Syria. As protests grew across the country, Al-Qaradawi expressed his support for the Syrian people and called for Assad and his allies to leave power, for they "have no place among the honorable."[49] In a joint *fatwa* issued by himself and 100 of his IUMS colleagues, Al-Qaradawi and his colleagues called on the Syrian army to desert their posts and join the opposition, while also calling on Muslim countries everywhere to "support the revolutionaries in Syria with all that they might need, both materially and morally."[50] As the violence in Syria increased and the situation devolved into not only an intense civil war but also a multilayered regional and international proxy war, Al-Qaradawi increasingly called for the arming of the opposition with weapons.[51] In 2013, the sheikh openly called for a *jihad* to be waged in Syria:

> I call on Muslims everywhere to support their [Syrian] brothers . . . everyone who has the ability to fight and use weapons must go to fight. I call on all Muslims to fight with their brothers in Syria.[52]

Al-Qaradawi would continue his calls for Muslims to support Syria: "supporting the Syrians is a duty of every Muslim who believes there is no God but God and that Muhammad is the Messenger of God."[53] He also directly criticized Iran and the Tehran-backed Lebanese group Hezbollah for supporting the Assad regime: "Iran is pushing forward arms and men [to back the Syrian regime], so why do we stand idle? The leader of the party of Satan [referring to Hezbollah] comes to fight the Sunnis . . . now we know what the Iranians want . . . they want continued massacres to kill Sunnis."[54] The IUMS and its officials would also make repeated calls for Turkey and the Gulf states to intervene militarily in Syria[55]

Similar to Libya, Qatar was quick to embrace the revolution in Syria. As early as July 2012, Emir Hamad expressed his support for Arab nations intervening militarily in Syria.[56] As the conflict worsened, Qatar poured money and weapons into their preferred factions among the opposition, namely, Islamist groups aligned with the Muslim Brotherhood.[57] Qatar was engaged in intense competition with Saudi Arabia inside Syria, who feared the rise of the Muslim Brotherhood and instead backed primarily Salafi elements among the opposition. This competition between Doha and Riyadh and the fractionalization of the opposition was one of the primary elements undermining the creation of a unified force against the Assad regime.[58]

Gulf Caveats

The enthusiasm discussed in the previous section by Qatari leadership, Al-Qaradawi, and the IUMS for the revolutions in Tunisia, Egypt, Libya, and Syria disappeared when faced with the prospect of political upheaval in the Gulf region. Qatar remains an autocratic actor with a vested interest in the sustainment of the authoritarian status quo that prevails domestically and within the Gulf. Protest movements that threatened to upend the authoritarian status quo in the Gulf region proved too close to home for Qatari leadership and were viewed as a threat by political elites in Qatar. Therefore, Qatar assumed dramatically different positions vis-à-vis Bahrain, Yemen, and calls for change elsewhere in the Gulf, such as in Saudi Arabia and the UAE. In Bahrain and Yemen in particular, Qatar chose to work underneath the GCC umbrella—led by Saudi Arabia—rather than conducting its foreign policy unilaterally as it had done in other theaters.

In Bahrain, Doha assumed a position concomitant with its other Gulf neighbors that analyzed the uprising through a sectarian framing as a tool of counterrevolution. This was coupled with a near-total absence of coverage of the uprising on Aljazeera, in stark contrast to uprisings elsewhere. *Fiqh al-thawra*, the newly constructed body of Islamic religio-political and legal thought, was not applicable in this case, argued Al-Qaradawi and the IUMS. Al-Qaradawi denounced the uprising in Bahrain as a "sectarian project" inciting "violence, killing, and vandalism."[59] He stated that he is against "fanaticism" and called upon the people of Bahrain to "defend the Arabism and Islamism of Bahrain" by confronting the sectarian project and those who sought to "kidnap" the country (likely a veiled reference to Iran).[60] In a televised sermon, he discussed the protests in Bahrain at length, going to great lengths to distance the events in Bahrain from other instances of revolution in the region:

> There is no people's revolution in Bahrain but a sectarian one . . . what is happening is not like what has happened in Egypt, Tunisia and Libya, but it is the empowerment of some factions via foreign forces on others; thereby it does not include the demands of all of the Bahraini people. The other Arab revolutions, [had] a common denominator of the oppressed against the oppressor, the Bahraini one is a sectarian, with Shiites against Sunnis . . . in Egypt the revolution was inclusive of all Egyptians with all of their different backgrounds, Muslims, Christians, old, young, secular, religious . . . they [the protesters] carried Khamenei's and Nasrallah's pictures as if they belong to Iran and not Bahrain, after all Bahrain belongs to the GCC, and we need them to show real citizenry.[61]

Later, in an interview, Al-Qaradawi referred to the uprising in Bahrain, stating, "this is not a revolution at all and I am in favor of a Saudi—whatever you call it—an expedition into Bahrain, because Bahrain is an Arab country and it should not be Iran's stepping stone."[62] Al-Qaradawi's position was met with criticism by some within the IUMS, including Iraqi Shi'a clerics who were affiliated with the organization, such as

Muhammad 'Ali Al-Taskhiri, who wrote an open letter to the sheikh criticizing him for standing with the regime in Bahrain despite the protests being overwhelmingly peaceful and helping to propagate the false notion that the uprising was purely sectarian in nature.[63] Despite such criticisms, Al-Qaradawi did not change his stance. Nor did the Al-Thani or Aljazeera. In addition to these efforts by Al-Qaradawi to delegitimize the protests in Bahrain, Doha also contributed a small number of troops to the military initiative led by Saudi Arabia and the UAE to crush the uprising.[64]

In Yemen, while Al-Qaradawi did express his support for the protests challenging longstanding autocrat Ali Abdullah Saleh,[65] Qatar took a backseat to Saudi Arabia and supported the GCC initiative led by Riyadh, designed to maintain the status quo by passing power from President Saleh to Vice President Abdrabbuh Mansur Hadi in 2012. Doha continued to play a passive role in supporting the new government up to the Houthi takeover of Sanaa in 2014 and the subsequent military intervention (Operation Decisive Storm) led by Saudi Arabia and the UAE in 2015 in support of Hadi's government. Doha and the International Union of Muslim Scholars provided extensive justification for the military intervention, to which Qatar contributed 1,000 ground troops and various military equipment.[66] The IUMS condemned the "Houthi coup" and the "destruction of Yemen's unity" and called on the Houthis to "uphold Yemeni national interests over any foreign agendas" and engage in dialogue.[67] The Secretary General of the IUMS, Ali Al-Qaradaghi, announced his support for Operation Decisive Storm in order to "liberate" Yemen while also describing the soldiers who died fighting the Houthis as martyrs.[68] However, the IUMS would go silent on Yemen following the eruption of the 2017 Gulf Crisis (discussed below), and Aljazeera's coverage of the war would grow increasingly critical, particularly of the role played by the Saudi-led coalition.[69]

As these two examples demonstrate, Qatar assumed more of a backseat role to developments in Bahrain and Yemen under the broader GCC umbrella in order to help maintain the authoritarian status quo that prevails in the Gulf. Despite Doha's enthusiasm for the revolutions in countries such as Egypt, Libya, or Syria, the prospect of fundamental political change in the Gulf proved too close to home for the Al-Thani. Context proved critical to influencing when and where Qatar, Al-Qaradawi, and the IUMS embraced their newly constructed body of Islamic religio-political and legal thought, *fiqh al-thawra*, versus a strategy designed to sustain the prevailing status quo. Therefore, to best advance the interests of Doha's ruling elite, Qatar's religious soft power strategy inside the Gulf region assumed a considerably different approach than the one projected toward elsewhere in the Middle East.

Doha on the Defensive: Qatar and the Counterrevolution

The immediate enthusiasm spurred by the Arab uprisings and the collapse of various longstanding dictators was short-lived as counterrevolutionary forces quickly consolidated and set out to reverse the gains brought about by the region-wide wave of mass mobilization. This campaign to return the region to the pre-uprisings status quo by states such as Saudi Arabia and the UAE was coupled with the disintegration of Syria and Libya into intense civil and proxy wars, the emergence of ISIS's "caliphate" across parts of Iraq and Syria, and waves of migrants seeking to flee the violence and head to Europe. The counterrevolutionaries portrayed their efforts as needed in order to return "stability" to the Middle East that had been undermined due to the uprisings and set their sights on those who challenged the regional order that had prevailed previously, including Qatar. As a result of this counterrevolutionary offensive, Doha was increasingly forced into a more defensive position.

The 2013 Coup in Egypt

The 2013 military coup in Egypt that overthrew democratically elected President Mohamed Morsi represented the epicenter of the regional counterrevolution. Protests against Morsi emerged alongside efforts by the Egyptian military and its allies—most notably Saudi Arabia and the UAE—to sideline the Muslim Brotherhood and return the country back to the pre-uprisings status quo.[70] During his tenure, Morsi had pursued various unpopular policies leading up to the protests, most notably when he issued a decree granting himself broad powers above the jurisdiction of Egypt's courts, a move that was decried within the country and internationally.[71] The Grand Imam of Egypt's Al-Azhar, Sheikh Ahmed El-Tayeb, sanctioned the protests against Morsi.[72]

Al-Qaradawi and the IUMS were at the forefront of defending Morsi and denouncing the military coup that would soon overthrow him. Regarding the controversial constitutional changes Morsi had made in order to elevate his decrees above the authority of the judiciary, Al-Qaradawi endorsed such amendments, arguing that Morsi was entitled to do so by virtue of "the responsibility placed on his shoulders by Allah" and was doing so in Egypt's best interest.[73] Addressing the protests happening against Morsi and calls for the overthrow of his government, the IUMS stressed that it is obligatory to obey the president because he was democratically elected and called upon the people of Egypt to "stand against preachers of sedition" and mobilize in order to protect the democratic gains of the January 25 revolution.[74] Despite these calls for restraint by Al-Qaradawi and the IUMS, the Egyptian military forcefully overthrew the Morsi government in July 2013, and General Abdel Fattah El-Sisi assumed control of Egypt and embarked on a campaign to crush the Muslim Brotherhood.

Al-Qaradawi and the IUMS emphatically denounced the military coup led by General El-Sisi. The sheikh argued that the coup was led by the "enemies of Islam" and represented a "slander against God" and the Egyptian people, who had triumphed against tyranny during the January 25 revolution.[75] He described the leaders of the coup as "*khawarij*," arguing that Morsi was a legitimate ruler and that overthrowing an elected president—with whom the people willingly entered into a contract based on consensus (*ijma*)—is prohibited in Islam.[76] Al-Qaradawi also criticized the scholars of Al-Azhar who had supported El-Sisi and the coup.[77] In a lengthy *fatwa* published online, Al-Qaradawi expressed his disapproval of the coup and its supporters at length:

> The Egyptians lived thirty years—if not sixty years—deprived of the election of their president . . . until God prepared them, for the first time a president chosen by themselves and of their own free will, which is President Mohamed Morsi . . . the democratically elected President, indisputably and unquestionably, must continue throughout his four-year term, as long as he is able to do his job and is not permanently hindered from working. If he has [made] mistakes, which he himself has admitted, the people and their various political forces must correct [these] mistakes, advise [the government], and be patient with them, but they remain the president of all. As for a group to disobey the president, and give themselves authority over the people, and remove the president and invalidate the constitution, and impose another president and another constitution, it is an act that becomes [entirely] invalid, because they created an authority that was not established by the people, [sic] they violated the covenant of God, and the covenant of the people, and they nullified what was done by a great revolution

carried out by the whole people, and established this democratic system that [the people] dreamed of for eons and sacrificed for it for generations of years and years, until it reached it. . . . As for legitimacy, the Islamic law, which the people of Egypt accepted as their reference in a civil state, not a theocratic religious state, obliges everyone who believes in it and returns to it to obey the legitimately elected president, implement his orders, and respond to his directives in all matters of life, under two conditions: the first condition is that the people should not command a clear disobedience to Allah, which is clear to Muslims. . . . The second condition: not to order the people to do something that [violates] their religion, and enters them into blatant infidelity . . . Those hired by General El-Sisi do not represent the Egyptian people, but a small part of them. The Grand Imam [of Al-Azhar] Dr. Ahmed Al-Tayeb, Chairman of the Council of Senior Scholars—and I am one of them—did not consult us and did not authorize him to speak on our behalf, and he is wrong in his support for the departure from the legitimate president of the country, which is contrary to the consensus of the nation, and did not base his position on the Qur'an or the Sunnah. . . . May Dr. Tayeb deal with Dr. Morsi as he dealt before with Hosni Mubarak! Why is there a double standard? This is a sabotage of the role of Al-Azhar, which always stands with the people, not with the tyrannical ruler. . . . I call from the bottom of my heart to all the Egyptian people, whom I love and redeem . . . I call [on those] in Upper Egypt and Lower Egypt, in cities and villages, in deserts and countryside, I call [on] men and women, young and old, rich and poor, employees and workers, Muslims and Christians, liberals and Islamists, to stand all in one row, to preserve the gains of the revolution: freedom and democracy, and freedom from every dictatorship.[78]

In response to the coup, Al-Qaradawi called upon the Egyptian people to protest El-Sisi while also imploring Arab leaders in the region to stop supporting "the leaders of the coup in Egypt and not to stain their hands with the blood of innocent people."[79] Addressing Saudi Arabia and the UAE specifically, he said that "hundreds are being killed by your billions [of dollars]."[80] He continued to criticize scholars of Al-Azhar, particularly Ali Gomaa and Ahmed Al-Tayeb, for their "toxic *fatawa*" and "politicized rulings," calling on all Arabs and "honest Muslims" to "stand with the oppressed and slandered Egyptian people, until they triumph over their oppressors."[81]

General El-Sisi continued with his coup, granting himself absolute authority while also increasing the levels of repression used against those who stood against him, especially the Muslim Brotherhood and their supporters. On August 14, 2013, at the direction of El-Sisi, Egyptian police and armed forces forcibly dispersed protesters—the majority of whom were Muslim Brotherhood supporters—at two large sit-ins in Cairo, one at al-Nahda Square and a larger one at Rabaa al-Adawiya Square, killing over 1,150 people in what Human Rights Watch described as "one of the world's largest killings of demonstrators in a single day in recent history."[82] The majority of those killed were in the Rabaa Al-Adawiya Square, where, "using armored personnel carriers (APCs), bulldozers, ground forces, and snipers, police and army personnel attacked the makeshift protest encampment, where demonstrators, including women and children, had been camped out for over 45 days, and opened fire on the protesters, killing at least 817 and likely more than 1,000."[83] Referred to popularly as the "Rabaa massacre," the event was met with international condemnation. Al-Qaradawi and the IUMS were also at the forefront of criticizing the El-Sisi regime for the slaughter of unarmed protesters. Al-Qaradawi urged Egyptians to continue demonstrating against El-Sisi while imploring Muslims around the world to stand together against the massacre.[84] He called on "every Egyptian who fears God and fears for his Islam and loves Egypt to come to Rabaa Al-Adawiya and bring his family and children," arguing that it is a religious obligation (*fard al-ayn*) to take to the streets, while also begging Saudi Arabia and the UAE to "return to God" and stop supporting El-Sisi.[85] In a lengthy statement, the IUMS denounced the massacre while calling upon the Egyptian police and military to protect all Egyptians, not just their partisans:

> The Union condemns these heinous massacres that occurred to these peaceful demonstrators defending legitimacy, and holds the leaders of the coup, and those who cooperated with them, and those who supported them, responsible for these massacres before God Almighty and before history and subsequent generations. . . . The Union calls on the leaders of Islamic and Arab countries to assume their responsibilities before God Almighty, and then before history, and generations, to intervene positively and quickly to stop these massacres. . . . The Union calls on the leaders of the free world, loving peace, freedom and democracy, human rights organizations, civil society and the free world, to raise their voices to prevent these massacres, to condemn them, and to do everything in their power

to restore democracy. . . . . Preventing peaceful demonstrations demanding legitimate rights, or dispersing them by force, is contrary to Islamic law, all international laws and human rights. . . . .[The] Union calls on all demonstrators and sit-ins to stand firm.[86]

After the Rabaa massacre, El-Sisi embarked on a campaign to crush the Muslim Brotherhood, officially designating the group a terrorist organization in September 2013 and arresting thousands. Al-Qaradawi denounced the designation, instead describing El-Sisi and the Egyptian military as terrorists.[87] Qatar's Ministry of Foreign Affairs also criticized the move, arguing that the designation was "a prelude to a shoot-to-kill policy."[88] Despite such condemnations and efforts by human rights activists around the world to hold El-Sisi accountable, the new regime's control over the country's political, economic, and social landscapes—coupled with fierce repressive measures and buttressed by allies abroad—has virtually eliminated any space for opposition within Egypt.

The Gulf Crisis

With the counterrevolutionaries increasingly in control across the region, they continued their offensive by going after Qatar, the Muslim Brotherhood, and the IUMS and its officials directly. With tensions running high between Qatar, its Gulf neighbors, and post-2013 Egypt due to Doha's support for elements of the Arab uprisings and popular political Islamist groups, the counterrevolutionaries sought to isolate Doha and crush the Muslim Brotherhood throughout the region. The rise of this increasing external threat for Qatar would force Doha, Al-Qaradawi, and the IUMS deeper into a defensive position.

The first major event came immediately after the rise to power of the new Qatari Emir Sheikh Tamim bin Hamad Al-Thani in June 2013, who instantly came under heavy pressure from states such as Saudi Arabia and the UAE to change key elements of Qatar's foreign policy.[89] According to documents leaked to the press in 2017, Sheikh Tamim signed a series of secret agreements with Doha's Gulf neighbors in 2013 and 2014, which included ending Qatari support for "deviant groups" such as the Muslim Brotherhood, ending support for "antagonistic media" such as Aljazeera, avoiding interference in the internal affairs of Gulf nations, and committing to upholding Egypt's stability post-Morsi.[90] The timing of these events, immediately following the rise of Emir Tamim, was clearly designed to pressure the new ruler into bringing Qatar's foreign policies back in line within the broader GCC fold.

Shortly before these secret agreements were signed and two months after Sheikh Tamim rose to power, Yusuf Al-Qaradawi's flagship program on Aljazeera—*Sharia and Life*—went off air permanently, and the sheikh's weekly Friday sermons were also ended. In an interview years later, Al-Qaradawi would hint at pressures from other Gulf states being the impetus that led to these developments.[91] This is significant, demonstrating that the rise of such external threat perceptions influenced the extent to which Qatar was willing to so publicly and directly provide Al-Qaradawi with a platform. However, Doha's relationships with Al-Qaradawi, the Brotherhood, and Aljazeera would remain intact. Unsatisfied with Qatari progress on the matters addressed in the agreements, Saudi Arabia, Bahrain, and the UAE withdrew their ambassadors from Doha in March 2014, citing the need to protect their "security and stability" and Qatar's continued "interference in their internal affairs."[92] Following this decision, Saudi Arabia, Bahrain, and the UAE would join Egypt in officially designating the Muslim Brotherhood as a terrorist organization.

Tensions between Qatar, Egypt, and its Gulf neighbors continued to escalate, ultimately culminating in what is popularly referred to as the "Gulf crisis." In 2017, Saudi Arabia, the UAE, Bahrain, and Egypt—often referred to as the "anti-terror quartet"—led an air, land, and naval blockade of Qatar while also severing diplomatic and trade ties with Doha. The crisis erupted following the hacking of the Qatar News Agency and the publicizing of alleged statements attributed to the Emir of Qatar, in which he expressed support for Iran, Hamas, Hezbollah, and Israel. Although the Qataris denied the existence of such comments, they were spread widely through different Arab media. US intelligence officials later announced that the UAE was behind the hacking operation.[93] Although the hacks were the alleged "spark" of the 2017 episode, the move was the culmination of tensions that had been brewing since the beginning of the Arab uprisings.

The blockading states accused Qatar of being a supporter and sponsor of terrorism, including groups such as *al-Qaeda*, ISIS, and the Muslim Brotherhood, who were grouped together as synonymous with one another by the "anti-terror" quartet. Sheikh Yusuf Al-Qaradawi and the IUMS were both labeled as terrorist entities, accused of using "Islamic rhetoric as a cover to facilitate terrorist activities."[94] The blockading states issued a list of 13 demands to Qatar, ordering Doha to, among other things, sever ties with "terrorist organizations," specifically the Muslim Brotherhood, ISIS, *al-Qaeda*, and Lebanon's Hezbollah; shut down Aljazeera and its affiliate stations; hand over "terrorist figures" and wanted individuals from Saudi Arabia, the UAE, Egypt, and Bahrain; align itself with other Gulf countries "militarily, politically, socially, and economically"; and agree to all demands within ten days, or the deal would become invalid.[95] Qatar was also ejected from the military operation led by Saudi Arabia and the UAE in Yemen. The blockading states even allegedly included initial plans for a military operation against Doha before being dissuaded by the United States.[96]

The "anti-terror" quartet embarked on a campaign to portray Qatar internationally as a sponsor of terrorism. This was directed especially toward the West, where Saudi Arabia, Egypt, and the UAE, in particular, sought to mobilize their resources as allies within the United States to cast Qatar as the "godfather of terrorist everywhere."[97] They sought to leverage their close relationships with the Donald Trump administration to further isolate Qatar and also pushed Washington to designate the Muslim Brotherhood as a terrorist organization as well.[98] Remaining defiant, Qatar's foreign minister Mohammed bin Abdulrahman Al-Thani stated that Doha is "a platform for peace, not terrorism . . . we are not ready to surrender, and will never be ready to surrender, the independence of our foreign policy."[99]

The IUMS responded strongly to the blockade and accusations leveled against them by the "anti-terror" quartet. They sought to delegitimize the blockades as a source of harm for the Islamic community as a whole, consistent with how their messaging has been rooted in a community-oriented identity. The IUMS immediately denounced the blockades as *haram*.[100] Secretary General of the IUMS, Ali Al-Qaradaghi, blasted the blockade for "tearing the [Islamic] nation" by sowing "division and discord."[101] He argued that Islam forbids "boycott between brothers"[102] and stressed that Qatar is an essential part of "Gulf, Arab, and Islamic cohesion."[103] Regarding the labeling of the IUMS as a terrorist organization, the group denounced the label, stating "these accusations against IUMS are baseless and we consider this attempt to weaken the leadership of an institution that represents 90,000 scholars and hundreds of millions of Muslims for political purposes unacceptable and illogical."[104] Ali Al-Qaradaghi stated that "accusations of terrorism directed at the IUMS by regimes that are hostile to the freedoms of the people and that fund terrorist coups against the will of the peoples are nothing but proof that the IUMS is taking the right path in addressing the problems of the [Islamic] nation."[105] He claimed the expanding popularity of the IUMS "among the people" and its growing strength is why it was classified as a terrorist organization by these countries.[106] Al-Qaradaghi and Raissouni have continued to argue that violence and terrorism are the result of "tyranny, dictatorship, and injustice" and are broader responses to "the counterrevolution that the Arab Spring revolutions were subjected to."[107]

The IUMS also went to great lengths to stress its independence from any political organization or state. Al-Qaradaghi expressed that the IUMS "does not submit to the wishes of a ruler and does not follow the footsteps of a particular country."[108] Raissouni claimed that "there is no country that interferes, asks for something, dictates something or objects to anything in the work of the union,"[109] nor is the organization controlled by the Muslim Brotherhood.[110] The IUMS has continued to present itself as fundamentally different from the "Sultan's scholars" that can be found in places such as Saudi Arabia and Egypt.[111] Again, here we see Al-Qaradawi and the IUMS projecting a community-oriented identity, differentiating themselves from "regime scholars"—that is, scholars directly employed by the state—and therefore a legitimate voice of the Muslim community, not political elites.

Alongside these efforts to isolate Qatar has been a deepening of relations between Doha and Turkey, both of whom sought greater independence in their foreign policies following the uprisings primarily via support for political Islamists. Following the decision of Saudi Arabia, Bahrain, and the UAE to withdraw their ambassadors from Doha in 2014, Turkey established its first overseas military base in the Middle East in Qatar aimed at helping the two countries "confront common enemies" in 2015.[112] Additionally, Qatar demonstrated its support for Turkey following the 2016 coup attempt against President Recep Tayyip Erdogan's government. According to President Erdogan, the Emir of Qatar was the first foreign leader to call him the night of the coup attempt to express Qatar's support and willingness to provide support.[113] The 2017 blockades provided a new impetus to this bilateral relationship. When the blockades against Qatar were launched, part of the terms presented to Doha demanded the closure of the military base that was established in 2015. Turkey's Erdogan strongly denounced the blockades, explaining that Ankara "will not abandon our Qatari brothers."[114] Additionally, immediately following the announcement of the blockades, Turkey's parliament held an emergency session and ratified an agreement allowing additional Turkish troops to be deployed to Qatar.[115] Turkey also air-delivered food supplies to Qatar, and bilateral ties between Doha and Ankara have continued to deepen.

Given the increased importance of the Qatar–Turkey relationship, Al-Qaradawi and the IUMS became much more vocal in their support for Ankara and Erdogan in particular following the increase in tensions within the Gulf, projecting an image of Turkey similar to that of Qatar in relation to supporting efforts for change among the Muslim masses. Secretary General of the IUMS, Ali Al-Qaradaghi, has hailed Turkey for "its great and prominent role in supporting the causes of the Islamic *umma*" following the Arab uprisings.[116] Likewise, Al-Qaradawi has praised the role of Turkey in "uniting Muslims."[117] Following the failed coup attempt against Turkey's president Erdogan in 2016, Al-Qaradawi expressed his support for Ankara, saying that the failure of the coup was a victory of "righteousness over injustice" and was "clear proof" that God stood by his faithful servant, Erdogan.[118] He called upon the governments of Arab and Islamic countries to rally around Turkey in support of Erdogan.[119] The IUMS has continued to deepen its relationship with Turkey following the 2017 Gulf crisis.

Whither the Counterrevolution?

The blockades failed to achieve the objectives stipulated in the list of demands presented to Qatar in 2017. However, the successes of counterrevolutionaries throughout the Middle East have resulted in considerable setbacks for political Islamists. With the Brotherhood and its various affiliates facing persecution and internal schisms over how to best move forward, Qatar's room to maneuver has become more limited. As Diwan[120] explains, "state crackdown on Islamist political movements such as the Muslim Brotherhood—designated as a terrorist organization in the key states of Egypt, Saudi Arabia, and the UAE—narrowed the space for engagement required by Qatar's religious soft power strategy." Doha has survived the blockades launched by the "anti-terror quartet," but with the success of the counterrevolutionaries across the Middle East, the IUMS and its officials have far less tangible influence on regional political developments for now. However, the relationships and networks established by the IUMS and the Al-Thani remain and can be reactivated if the region were to witness another round of mass mobilization. Similarly, having now constructed the foundation of a new body of Islamic religio-political and legal thought designed to legitimize peaceful mass mobilization, Qatar, Al-Qaradawi, and the IUMS can easily remobilize and expand upon this doctrine.

Given that the root causes of the Arab uprisings have only worsened since 2011, this remains a possibility moving forward.

Given the limited room for Qatar's instruments of religious soft power to maneuver in the current Middle East political landscape, there are signs that Doha has been subtly supporting Qatari nationalism, given the broader turn toward such nationalistic sentiments in other Gulf states. Following the 2017 blockades, there has been a considerable increase in state-sponsored nationalism within Qatar as well as state-crafted narratives of Qatari identity.[121] Doha introduced mandatory military conscription for its citizens in 2015 and has been considerably increasing its military capabilities amidst heightened tensions with its Gulf neighbors while also increasingly parading these capabilities during their annual National Day celebrations.[122] Yet, Qatar's instruments of religious soft power have not been mobilized in the service of these efforts as has been done, for example, in Saudi Arabia. The IUMS and its officials remain more pan-Islamic in orientation and have always presented themselves as independent from the Qatari state, which makes such a shift difficult. Focused primarily on issues facing the wider Muslim community and hosting a large number of non-Qatari scholars, it seems unlikely that the IUMS would be used in the service of this new nationalism, lest it sacrifice the image it has sought to procure over the past few decades.

A Community-Oriented Identity Continued: In Pursuit of Other "Muslim Causes"

A central element of Qatar's religious soft power has been an effort to present an image of Doha as a champion of global "Muslim causes." A continuation of its bottom-up society-oriented approach, Qatar has sought to "brand" itself as a leader within the broader global *umma*, using Al-Qaradawi and the IUMS to do so. This often includes using an Islamic lexicon to frame different political issues facing elements of the global Muslim community, which is often amplified using platforms such as Aljazeera. As Freer[123] explains, "Qatar's rulers' endeavor to portray themselves as promoters of the Islamic faith by framing the debate around Islam rather than attempting to diminish its presence or importance."

With the successes of the counterrevolutionaries throughout the Middle East, one area Qatar has been able to carve out a niche for itself is in its support for political prisoners amidst widespread regional crackdowns. The IUMS has praised Doha as the "Kaaba of the oppressed" due to its support for political prisoners and the fact that Qatar has often served as a popular destination for political exiles, especially those associated with the Muslim Brotherhood.[124] In particular, the IUMS has devoted considerable attention to religious scholars, intellectuals, and other prisoners of conscience who have been detained in countries such as Saudi Arabia, Egypt, and the UAE.[125] Following the death of overthrown Egyptian president Mohamed Morsi while imprisoned, Secretary General of the IUMS, Ali Al-Qaradaghi, praised the "steadfastness" of the "martyr Morsi."[126] Likewise, the IUMS has continued to criticize the imprisonment of Sheikh Salman Al-Awdah in Saudi Arabia and the decision of Riyadh to sentence him to death.[127]

However, this activism does not extend to all countries equally: the IUMS has remained almost completely silent on ongoing crackdowns within Bahrain or the increasing number of political detainees in Turkey amidst Ankara's own autocratic turn. Where Qatar has a vested interest in the sustainment of the status quo, the IUMS and other influential scholars within Qatar tend to remain relatively silent regarding those contexts, contradicting the image of independence from the Al-Thani they have sought to project.

Another theater where the IUMS has sought to portray itself as a vanguard of "Muslim causes" is in China, where Beijing is forcefully repressing its Muslim minority to "Sinicize" Islam. Qatar has been able to stand out from many of its neighbors in this regard as the latter increasingly support China's policies vis-à-vis its Muslim Uyghur community and even cooperate with Beijing on the matter. Secretary General Ali Al-Qaradaghi has been very outspoken regarding the arbitrary detention of Muslims in China, imploring Beijing to reverse its policies while also calling on Muslims around the world to speak out against the atrocities taking place.[128] The president of the IUMS, Ahmed Raissouni, argued that "China is working hard to erase the Islam of the Uyghur people by all coercive means, and for years it has been setting up camps where millions of them are mobilized to erase every trace of their culture, faith and Islamic life . . . Beijing is carrying out all forms of oppression and coercion against their people under the pretext of establishing the Chinese identity and fighting extremism."[129] The IUMS issued an official statement on the matter in 2015, stating:

> The International Union of Muslim Scholars followed with great interest the state of religious persecution to which Muslims are

exposed in China in general and in Xinjiang in particular. . . . The 1.6 million square kilometer region, formerly known as East Turkestan, was under Turkish sovereignty for a long time, before the region declared independence as the East Turkestan Republic, which faded under Chinese control under Mao Zedong, dubbed the New Front or Xinjiang. Despite Chinese promises to give the region autonomous status, religiously, culturally, and linguistically, none of this has happened. The Union also recalls that China, which has changed many of its foreign and domestic policies in recent decades and has consequently become one of the world's most influential international powers economically, politically and militarily, but one thing has not changed: that is the internal policy of repression against Muslims! Since the Communists seized power in 1946, Muslims have been forced into mixed marriages, Islamic endowments have been confiscated, preachers and legal teachers have been banned from teaching, most mosques have been demolished, Islamic books have been burned, Islamic schools have been closed, and Muslim leaders have been arrested and imprisoned…The Union calls on international human rights institutions, governments and Islamic organizations to support the people of the Muslim region of Xinjiang, stand with them in the face of the intransigence of their Chinese government, and help the Chinese Muslim people to obtain their innate and legal rights.[130]

The IUMS has also blasted other Middle East countries, such as Egypt, for cooperating with China on the extradition of Uyghur Muslims back to Beijing at the behest of Chinese leadership.[131] Qatar also withdrew from a letter addressed to the United Nations. and signed by 37 countries—including Saudi Arabia and the UAE—that expressed support for China's policies in Xinjiang and toward its Muslim community more generally.[132] However, these actions do not mean that Qatar has abstained from increasing its relationship with a rising China. When withdrawing from the letter, Qatar's permanent representative to the United Nations Ali Al-Mansouri did so cautiously, stating, "we wish to maintain a neutral stance, and we offer our mediation and facilitation services."[133] Moreover, Doha would later vote against a motion in the United Nations. to open a debate about alleged human rights abuses by China against its Uyghur community.[134] Qatar and China have considerably increased their political, economic, and security ties over the past decade.[135] In short, Doha has simultaneously utilized a specific message directed toward the Muslim community through the IUMS while the state has assumed a more nuanced position toward Beijing directly.

Perhaps more than any other theater, Qatar has sought to promote an image/brand of itself as pro-Palestine, particularly as the plight of the Palestinian people has been increasingly cast aside by many Arab states as they grow closer to Israel strategically. Qatar has historically supported Palestinians and has often sought to mediate between Israel and Palestine when tensions have resulted in violence.[136] Doha also provided sanctuary to many Palestinian members of the Muslim Brotherhood during the country's formative years. Yusuf Al-Qaradawi has always presented himself as a staunch upholder of the Palestinian cause, regularly commenting on developments in the occupied territories from his home in Doha.[137] Qatar and Al-Qaradawi have also both maintained public relationships with the organization Hamas, which officially relocated its political headquarters from Syria to Doha following the civil war. Al-Qaradawi and the IUMS remain critical of terrorism accusations against the group, arguing that they are engaged in legitimate resistance against the Israeli occupation. Aljazeera has also proved critical in its extensive coverage of Palestine, particularly developments in Gaza. The news platform regularly addresses "Arab silence" (*assamt al-arabi*) and decries the "passivity of Arab states and governments toward the process of 'de-Arabization' of 'Arab land.'"[138] Palestine was also a routine topic on Al-Qaradawi's show on Aljazeera, *Sharia and Life*.

The IUMS continues to stress the importance of Palestine to its mission and the wider Muslim community.[139] Secretary General Ali Al-Qaradaghi describes Palestine as "the [Islamic] nation's pivotal issue" and argues that "pressure must be exerted on governments and organizations to carry out their responsibilities toward stopping Zionist terrorism in the land of Palestine."[140] The IUMS as a whole has echoed this message, stating:

> The Union urges free peoples in the whole world to support the Palestinian cause, the right of the Palestinian people to defend their land and display it against the usurping foreign occupier, and to support national liberation movements on the land of Palestine instead of harming them or accusing them of falsehood.[141]

The IUMS and its leadership also continue to comment on ongoing developments concerning Israel and Palestine both regionally and globally. For example, Al-Qaradawi and Al-Qaradaghi both decried the decision of the Donald Trump administration to relocate the US embassy to Jerusalem as well as the so-called "deal of the century" marketed by Trump and the Israelis as a genuine solution to the Israel–Palestine conflict.[142] The IUMS, Al-Qaradawi, and other Islamist figures in Qatar also extensively denounced the normalization agreements brokered by the United States between Israel, Bahrain, and the UAE, which were later expanded to also include Sudan and Morocco. Known as the so-called "Abraham Accords," the IUMS denounced the Abraham Accords as "high treason" and stated that the agreement is a "major reward for the crimes of the Zionist occupiers in Al-Quds Al-Sharif, and against the Palestinians, and a tacit recognition of Israel's right to extend its sovereignty over the West Bank."[143] Describing the normalizations as a betrayal of God and the Muslim community, the IUMS argues that the Accords will only further the suffering of the Palestinian people despite being marketed as a peace agreement:

> It is a false and outright lie to invoke these treacherous normalization agreements as bringing benefit to the Palestinian cause, and that what proves the falsehood of this claim is that the Palestinian people, who are directly suffering from the scourge and crimes of this criminal entity, have announced with all its sects and components, its authority and its resistance factions to reject these agreements and consider them a treacherous stab to the Palestinian people in the back.[144]

Al-Qaradaghi described the normalization agreements as "forbidden and void by Sharia, and a major crime, and a betrayal of the rights of God Almighty and His Messenger, the rights of Palestine as a land and people, and the right of our Islamic nation and its martyrs throughout its long history."[145] Referring to the signatories of the Accords, he stated:

> The traitors have muzzled mouths, intimidated peoples and sowed discord in our community, and killed thousands in Egypt, Libya and Yemen, and put [the] scholars and intellectuals in prisons, and beat groups that oppose the Zionist occupation and distorted their reputation [in] the ugliest distortion, and crowned their betrayal with the peace agreement with the Zionist entity.[146]

Yusuf Al-Qaradawi also rejects the normalization agreements, calling for the need to boycott Israel "politically, socially, economically, and culturally."[147] The president of the IUMS, Ahmed Raissouni, argued that normalization threatens to "liquidate the Palestinian cause, and constitutes a new siege against the Palestinian people," who "nevertheless remained firm."[148] He continued, arguing:

> Normalization with the Zionist entity is, first of all, recognition and approval of the usurpation of a Muslim homeland. . . . The danger is that normalization prolongs the life of occupation and aggression, provides it with the reasons for bullying and superiority, and enables it to extend its influence and control in the countries that engaged in normalization with it and open doors to it. Normalization is a partnership with the enemy in its aggression, and it multiplies the burdens, losses and pains on the Palestinian people, who are afflicted by the injustice of their enemies and have now been afflicted by the injustice of their miserable brothers.[149]

Though the IUMS and its officials have assumed a very pro-Palestine stance, Qatar has coupled this messaging with elements of practical engagement with the state of Israel. Despite ruling out the possibility of normalization between the two countries and assuming a much different position than many of its other neighbors, Qatar remains a high-profile intermediary between Hamas and Israel and has been instrumental in providing financial assistance to Gaza.[150] Additionally, a number of Israeli athletes have been allowed to compete in various sporting competitions hosted in Qatar, and the Israeli national anthem was played in Doha following Israeli gymnast Alexander Shatilov winning a gold medal during the 2019 FIG Artistic Gymnastics World Cup series.[151] Later, in 2022, Qatar would allow Israelis to fly directly to Doha for the FIFA World Cup despite no official relations existing between the two states.[152]

Qatar continues to present an image/brand for itself as an upholder of "Muslim causes," building off of its more bottom-up and Muslim-community-oriented strategy of religious soft power. However, this messaging is often coupled with more practical political engagement by the official Qatari state apparatus regarding these issues. Indeed, though Qatar has projected an identity of itself as a champion of grassroots issues facing the Muslim community, this is often coupled with contradicting policies born out of strategic necessity. This approach has provided Doha with flexibility at the political level by allowing the IUMS and its officials to project an image of Qatar to the Muslim community as a vanguard for Muslim issues while simultaneously allowing the state to pursue its interests and craft official policies with more latitude.

Deconstructing Qatari Religious Soft Power

The evolution of Qatari religious soft power following the Arab uprisings—including its internal variations and relation to the other cases discussed in this book—reflects the analytical framework built in Chapter 1 of this book. An amalgamation of the instrumentalist and constructivist paradigms, Qatari religious soft power was influenced by the four underlying causal mechanisms addressed in this framework: (1) foreign threat perceptions; (2) foreign and domestic threat perceptions (i.e., a "two-level game); (3) identity; and (4) ideology. The ways in which these four causal mechanisms influenced Qatari religious soft power—and the particular forms these strategies assumed—were shaped by the contexts within which Qatari political elites were operating and the target audiences they sought to influence.

Of these four causal mechanisms, the absence of a domestic threat to the authority and legitimacy of political elites in Doha had the greatest causal impact on Qatari religious soft power. Qatar encountered the Arab uprisings from a dramatically different perspective than the other two cases discussed in this book. Freed from any considerable domestic challenge to their own authority, the Al-Thani were able to preserve their power domestically and turn outward to advance their strategic interests abroad. The absence of a considerable perceived domestic threat in Qatar allowed Doha the freedom and maneuverability to focus its efforts externally without having to fear or address domestic opposition. This absence had a profound impact on shaping Qatar's response to the uprisings and how they ultimately mobilized religion as part of this response. Qatar benefited from a far wider field of maneuverability than did other states in the region who became consumed in the face of domestic challenges. As a result, they were able to orient their foreign policy—and religious soft power—externally in the efforts to advance their own strategic position abroad.

The uprisings presented Doha with a strategic opportunity to expand its influence, seeking to capitalize on the vacuums emerging from the overthrow of longstanding autocrats, primarily by supporting the Muslim Brotherhood and its various regional offshoots in their own quests for power. With the early successes of political Islamist parties in places such as Tunisia, Egypt, and Libya, such rising forces appeared primed to alter the regional balance and were therefore viewed as appealing partners through which Doha would be able to expand its regional influence. However, this enthusiasm disappeared in the Gulf, where Al-Thani sought to preserve the undemocratic status quo to which they themselves are wedded. In both Bahrain and Yemen, Qatar joined with Saudi Arabia and the UAE to prevent political change and denounce what they framed in sectarian terms as Iranian encroachment. Proving too close to home, Qatar actively worked to preserve the authoritarian status quo in the Gulf, fearful that the emergence of a popular democratic paradigm in the Gulf could jeopardize the foundations of their own rule.

Despite Qatar being able to initially capitalize on the uprisings, Doha's enthusiasm was short-lived as counterrevolutionary forces quickly consolidated and set out to reverse the gains brought about by the region-wide wave of mass mobilization. As the regional counterrevolution, led by Saudi Arabia and the UAE, increasingly assumed a more offensive and dominant position, Qatar found itself forced into a more defensive posture. So too was Qatar's strategy of religious soft power, which became increasingly limited in its maneuverability as political Islamists came under attack by these counterrevolutionary forces. Qatar became particularly isolated following the land, air, and naval blockades launched against it in 2017, led by Saudi Arabia and the UAE. The successes of regional counterrevolutionary forces greatly limited Qatar's freedom of maneuverability that it enjoyed at the apex of the Arab uprisings. Following these efforts to push back directly against Qatar for its policies following the uprisings, Doha has increasingly developed its own military defense capabilities in response.

The absence of a pressing domestic challenge to the authority and legitimacy of the Al-Thani—and the fact that Qatar had successfully coopted mainstream political Islamism—considerably influenced the construction and promulgation of particular religious identities and ideologies by Doha following the Arab uprisings. Qatar sought to project a specific state image—or "brand"—as part of its religious soft power strategy, whereby it embraced a bottom-up, Muslim-community-oriented identity, portraying Doha as a vanguard of "Muslim causes" following the uprisings. By focusing on issues facing Muslims across the world—such as the plight of political prisoners, the deteriorating situation in Palestine, and the oppression of Muslims in China—Doha has sought to depict itself as a champion of such issues. With domestic audiences placated, Doha turned to buttressing its image—and influence—among the broader Muslim community, which in the early phase of the Arab uprisings appeared on the cusp of fundamental political change. The Al-Thani projected an image of themselves as aligned with the aspirations of the people across the Middle East and provided a platform to religious scholars and institutions that would construct a new religio-political vision attempting to legitimize peaceful popular uprisings. Qatar's main instruments of religious soft power—Sheikh Yusuf Al-Qaradawi and the IUMS—have likewise projected a community-oriented identity, regularly seeking to differentiate themselves from "regime scholars"—that is, scholars directly employed by the state—and therefore a legitimate voice of the Muslim community, not political elites.

Though the Al-Thani have increasingly encouraged the development of a more nationalistic "Qatari" identity among its citizenry following the 2017 "Gulf Crisis," it remains to be seen whether the IUMS can—or is willing to—adapt its more pan-Islamic orientation to buttress this new distinctly Qatari nationalism. Additionally, given the successes of counterrevolutionary forces across the region, Qatar has been limited in the extent to which it can project an image of itself as a "vanguard" of change within the region as authoritarian actors have re-entrenched themselves and activists/movements striving for change face increased repression.

Finally, ideological concerns, specifically pertaining to the supported and constructed religio-political visions embraced by political elites within Qatar, also had a profound impact on Qatari religious soft power and were likewise impacted considerably by the lack of a domestic threat to political elites in Doha. The lack of a pressing internal threat to the authority of the Al-Thani considerably influenced the religio-political ethos embraced by Doha following the Arab uprisings, providing Qatar with far more flexibility than other state actors. Doha embraced a bottom-up, "republican," and society-oriented religio-political vision abroad to support the uprisings in places such as Tunisia, Egypt, Libya, and Syria. This approach adopted by Qatar was supported via the construction and promulgation of a new body of Islamic religio-political and legal thought—*fiqh al-thawra* (the jurisprudence of revolution)—designed to legitimize peaceful opposition to established authority from an Islamic perspective within the contemporary nation-state. Al-Qaradawi and the IUMS led this initiative, presenting Islam as a liberating force against injustice and tyranny. Facing no considerable threat at home and portraying itself as a supporter of political reform in the Middle East, the Al-Thani were able to encourage the promotion of this vision without fearing the undermining of their own authority domestically. Doha provided a platform for its architects so long as they remained externally focused.

However, this vision was not applied holistically: in both Bahrain and Yemen, challenges to the prevailing status quo were denounced through sectarian framing as inherently illegitimate. Again, such calls for change within the Gulf were viewed as too close to home for the Al-Thani and potentially jeopardizing for the future stability of their rule if a popular democratic paradigm were to emerge next door. In these contexts, a different religio-political vision was marshaled to protect the interests of Qatari political elites. As was demonstrated throughout this chapter, context and target audience often determined which ideological constructs were mobilized according to the interests of political elites in different environments.

Qatari religious soft power embodies how inherently political considerations among ruling elites influence religious outcomes. Instead of religion influencing and constraining policy, what we witnessed in this chapter was the opposite: religion was shaped, molded, and fashioned by the state in accordance with the strategic interests of political elites in Doha. Facing no considerable domestic threat, the Al-Thani were able to capitalize on the uprisings in a manner distinct from Saudi Arabia or the UAE. The Al-Thani viewed the uprisings primarily as a strategic opportunity and mobilized religion as part of Doha's efforts to capitalize on the wave of mass mobilization that swept throughout the region. Given the absence of internal constraints, they were able to focus their efforts externally without having to fear a domestic challenge to their own authority. Particular religious identities and ideologies were central to Qatari religious soft power, yet they were themselves constructed first and foremost by the state to achieve inherently political objectives. Doha's embrace of a bottom-up, community-oriented, and "republican" conceptualization of Islam abroad designed primarily to legitimize popular mobilization against (certain) established authorities was only possible due to the absence of a pressing domestic challenge to the authority or legitimacy of the Al-Thani.

And yet, in Bahrain and Yemen, Qatar assumed a dramatically different position designed to preserve the illiberal status quo that dominates in the Gulf, proving too close to home for the Al-Thani. Political elites in Doha had to remain strategically flexible in order to best advance their interests, resulting in religion being mobilized in differing ways according to the overall constellation of threats facing the Al-Thani across time and space.

Conclusion

Religious soft power proved to be critical for Qatar as the Arab uprisings swept across the Middle East. Material interests, ideology, and identity are all essential components comprising Doha's religious soft power strategies. In the wake of the uprisings, Qatar assumed a more activist, society-oriented approach in support of the revolutions in Tunisia, Egypt, Libya, and Syria. The absence of a significant domestic political threat was critical for the calculus of the Al-Thani monarchy, allowing them to be almost entirely outward oriented during this period without having to devote considerable resources to preserving their power domestically. However, this calculus did not extend to calls for fundamental change to the status quo within the Gulf region itself. In both Bahrain and Yemen, Qatar—an authoritarian government itself—preferred to operate under the GCC umbrella in order to preserve the status quo in these contexts.

Qatar's strategy of religious soft power—spearheaded by Sheikh Yusuf Al-Qaradawi and the IUMS—was bottom-up in nature and directed internally toward the Muslim community. The formal independence of Al-Qaradawi and the IUMS allowed these actors to present themselves as fundamentally different from "regime scholars" directly affiliated with the state in places such as Saudi Arabia and Egypt. Moreover, Qatar and the IUMS have continued to present themselves as the champions of various "Muslim causes" throughout the world as many other state actors have grown quiet regarding issues facing Muslim compatriots elsewhere. While this strategy was considerably successful during the uprisings and their immediate aftermath, the success of counterrevolutionary actors and the intense crackdown on political Islamist movements have served to limit Qatar's room to maneuver. Indeed, the region's political landscape has shifted markedly toward a deepening of authoritarian rule. Additionally, the international campaign to portray Qatar as a state sponsor of terrorism by the "anti-terror" quartet and their Western allies have also undermined Qatar's image as a regional mediator and peacemaker. Yet, the networks established by Qatar, Al-Qaradawi, and the IUMS remain and can be utilized again if the region were to witness future upheaval. Given that the underlying causes of the Arab uprisings have only worsened, this remains a distinct possibility.

Chapter 5

UNITED ARAB EMIRATES (UAE)

The religious soft power strategy pursued by the United Arab Emirates (UAE) took form during the second, counterrevolutionary phase of the Arab uprisings. This strategy was rooted in ongoing efforts within the Emirates to subordinate Islam to state authority and in longstanding hostility toward Islamism among Abu Dhabi's leadership since the 1990s. Additionally, the increased utilization of religion as a tool of statecraft by the UAE must be situated within the broader context of a turn in Emirati foreign policy toward greater assertiveness abroad. The UAE and its instruments of religious soft power have sought to portray the Emirates as a moderate, tolerant, and progressive country within the Middle East. Abu Dhabi has also sought to champion itself—primarily toward a Western audience—as a source of stability within a region wrecked by revolutionary upheaval, civil wars, and transnational terrorism. In doing so, the UAE has embraced a statist, top-down conceptualization of Islam that renders religion subservient to the state.

This chapter examines the ways in which inherently political considerations influenced how religion was marshaled as a tool of statecraft by Abu Dhabi following the Arab uprisings. To counter what they perceived as an existential threat to their own authority and legitimacy, political elites in the UAE appropriated and constructed religious discourses, doctrines, histories, and symbols in order to most effectively combat the diverse and evolving matrix of threats they encountered following the uprisings. The Emirates embraced a staunchly counterrevolutionary vision that marshaled religion to delegitimize calls for change both internally and throughout the wider region while projecting an image of the UAE to the West rooted in "tolerance" and "moderation" designed to encourage continued support for the Al-Nahyan and their policies.

This chapter begins by first detailing the relationship between religion and the emergence of the UAE as a modern state, namely, how Abu Dhabi grew to fear Islamism—both mainstream and radical—as a threat to its own interests and authority. The next section examines the UAE's response to the Arab uprisings, namely, how the presence of interrelated threats influenced Abu Dhabi's behavior and led to the emergence of the Emirates as a leader of the regional counterrevolution. Next, this study investigates the construction of Emirati religious soft power during the second, counterrevolutionary phase of the Arab uprisings. It details how scholars and institutions aligned with the UAE have sought to affirm the ultimate authority of the state while delegitimizing all forms of Islamism and political activism. This investigation then turns to how the UAE has sought to mobilize "moderate Islam" as a central pillar of their state-branding efforts. Finally, this chapter concludes by connecting the themes and patterns that have comprised Emirati religious soft power post-2010.

Islam in the UAE

The emergence of the UAE as a modern sovereign state shares many parallels with the previously discussed case of Qatar. Known then as the "Trucial States," the seven emirates that now comprise the UAE— Abu Dhabi, Dubai, Sharjah, Ajman, Fujairah, Umm al-Quwain, and Ras al-Khaimah—were under British control until 1971 when the UK followed through on its decision reached in 1968 to withdraw from all of their occupied territories "east of the Suez." Similar to Qatar, the ruling families within the newly independent Emirates were taken by surprise upon Britain's announcement. Their independence was not the result of an anti-colonial struggle nor was British control resented by the ruling families: in fact, following the announcement, the Emir of Abi Dhabi, Sheikh Zayed bin Sultan Al-Nahyan, tried to convince the UK to maintain a military presence in the country after their formal departure.[1]

The abdication of the British led to six of the seven Emirates joining together to form a federation in 1971, with Ras Al-Khaimah joining later in 1972. Abu Dhabi and Dubai, the two largest and wealthiest Emirates, quickly came to dominate the federation. Upon the formation of this federation, "the UAE represented a tribal hierarchy with the political structure subject to the authority of ruling sheikhs," with "very little overt sense of national identity that could transcend these loyalties."[2] Therefore, from its very inception, nation-building within the UAE has focused heavily on the consolidation and legitimization of state authority and the construction of a common sense of shared identity.

Unlike Saudi Arabia and Qatar, the UAE does not adhere to Wahhabism. Abu Dhabi and Dubai adhere to the Maliki school of

Islamic jurisprudence; Sharjah, Umm al-Quwain, Ajman, and Ras al-Khaimah practice the Hanbali school; and the emirate of Fujairah follows the Shafi'i school.[3] Like other states in the Gulf, the seven Emirates that would comprise the UAE witnessed an influx of Muslim Brotherhood personnel throughout the 1950s to 1980s fleeing Arab nationalist governments who were cracking down on the organization and its members across the region. These individuals were critical for the UAE, which at the time was in the process of building its own institutions as well as the government bureaucracy. As Al-Qassemi[4] explains, "the Brothers flourished in the UAE: they were educated, professional, and upwardly mobile individuals who gained employment in various public and private posts, including the judicial and education sector." Additionally, the influx of these Brotherhood personalities was a lucrative mechanism for the ruling families of the Emirates to buttress their own "Islamic credentials" while hedging against the rise of Arab nationalist movements throughout the Middle East.

The influx of individuals associated with the Brotherhood was supported and embraced by ruling families in the Emirates during this time. The UAE branch of the Muslim Brotherhood—*jam'iyyat al-Islah wa-l-Tawjih al-Ijtima'i* (The Society of Reform and Social Counselling), most commonly referred to simply as Islah (reform)—was officially formed in 1974 in Dubai, being approved by the Ministry of Labor and Social Affairs and even receiving financial contributions from the Emir of Dubai, Sheikh Rashid bin Sa'id Al-Maktoum, toward the group's formation.[5] Branches would later be established in Ras Al-Khaimah and Fujairah, and numerous high-profile individuals associated with ruling families throughout the Emirates were affiliated with the organization. Individuals affiliated with Islah came to hold prominent positions throughout Emirati society and were especially present within the newly formed education and judiciary ministries. The group also established informal channels of influence such as social clubs and various charity initiatives.

However, the relationship between Islah and the UAE government would soon change dramatically. Islah gradually developed a more oppositional discourse, seeking to translate its growing influence into tangible change within the Emirates. As Baskan[6] explains, Islah increasingly began "emphasizing the rule of law, demanding respect for human rights, calling for expansion of political participation, and criticizing corruption and other political malpractices." The group also increasingly criticized the UAE's relationship with the United States and began urging an end to foreign military basing in the Gulf (discussed more below).[7] This was coupled with the growing presence of Islah throughout the country, particularly within educational and judicial institutions, as the group rapidly emerged as the most organized and influential non-state actor in the UAE.

The government became concerned about the level of influence held by the group and began considering it as a political threat, especially as Abu Dhabi was attempting to centralize authority within the Emirates under their control. What ensued was a strong crackdown against the organization and the attempted centralization of religion within the UAE and its subjugation to state authority. Dubai's Ministry of Awqaf issued a decree in 1988 stipulating that clerics must "deposit written, advance copies of their Friday sermons with the Ministry and to avoid all areas of controversy and sectarian sensitivity, limiting their remarks to guidance on Islamic practice."[8] Abu Dhabi demanded that the group recede from politics and renounce any external links or affiliations with the Muslim Brotherhood and its general guide in Cairo, but the group refused.[9]

Purges of Islah members and other individuals perceived as sympathetic to the group or its ideology soon took place within the military, education sector, and other government ministries. The government moved to dissolve Islah's board of directors by placing them under the supervision of the Ministry of Social Affairs while also banning Brotherhood officials from holding public office.[10] However, these blows from the UAE government were cushioned by the Emir of Ras Al-Khaimah, Sheikh Saqr bin Muhammad Al-Qasimi, providing the group with refuge and refusing to handover certain leaders of the Brothers to UAE federal authorities.[11]

During the first decades of their independence, the UAE was concerned primarily with domestic consolidation and internal development. Like Qatar, the UAE was a close relative to other states in the region, focused on internal developments and likewise protecting the newly formed federation from its larger neighbors, particularly Saudi Arabia.[12] UAE foreign policy under the Emir of Abu Dhabi Sheikh Zayed bin Sultan Al-Nahyan was quite consistent during this time period, concerned primarily with securing the newly independent state from its larger and more powerful neighbors, Saudi Arabia and Iran. The foreign policy of the UAE during this period was also heavily influenced by a desire to show solidarity with fellow Arabs: "the sense of belonging to a common Arab nation pushed Emirati leaders to pursue a foreign policy of support for the Arab world."[13] Lacking considerable military power as a result of their newfound independence and the dominance of traditional regional powers such as Egypt, Iraq, or Syria, UAE foreign policy during this time revolved around soft power, namely, the provisioning of foreign aid, thanks to rising oil prices: by the late 1970s, the UAE had become the third largest aid donor in the Middle East.[14]

However, the need for enhanced military protection soon became apparent, particularly following Iraq's invasion of Kuwait in 1991. It was at this time that the UAE turned toward the United States as its security guarantor, which was dramatically expanding its military presence in the region. As the United States increasingly rooted its assertive foreign policy in the Middle East within the Gulf, the UAE came to play a central role in Washington's regional presence. Indeed, the 1990s were a turning point for the UAE, which began developing its hard power alongside and often in direct conjunction with the United States. The UAE is unique in that it has actively participated in every US-led military operation in the "broader Middle East" with the exception of the 2003 invasion of Iraq.[15]

Despite the close relationship between the UAE and the United States, the terrorist attacks of September 11, 2001, threatened to jeopardize the relationship. In addition to two of the hijackers being from the Emirates, the FBI would later discover that they and most of the other perpetrators had flown directly to the United States from the UAE. Moreover, the 9/11 commission and other investigations would soon shed light on the massive amounts of terrorism financing that had been funneled through the Emirates. The UAE responded by doubling down on their relationship with the United States, serving as a key partner in the broader "war on terror" and hosting a large number of US military and intelligence personnel.

It is in the post-9/11 period that the most profound reshaping of Emirati politics would take place, driven by the rise of Mohammed bin Zayed Al-Nahyan (MbZ). The third son of Sheikh Zayed, MbZ, became chief of staff of the military in 1992 and, upon the death of his father in 2004, was already the de facto decision-maker in the armed forces and much of the country, with leaked US cables from 2009 describing the young leader as "the man who runs the United Arab Emirates."[16] Though the half-brother of MbZ, Sheikh Khalifa bin Zayed Al-Nahyan, assumed the rulership of Abu Dhabi and the presidency of the UAE following Sheikh Zayed's death, MbZ quickly became "the de facto center of influence and authority," first within Abu Dhabi and then throughout the UAE as a whole."[17] The growth of Mohammed bin Zayed's power also coincided with the rise of Abu Dhabi over Dubai as the political powerhouse of the Emirates, with the latter focused primarily on "economic prowess rather than political dominance" and suffering because of the 2008 global financial crisis.[18]

Mohammed bin Zayed is responsible for directing UAE policy in the post-9/11 era. He continued to place great emphasis on the Emirates' relationship with the United States and assumed a more assertive approach abroad compared to Sheikh Zayed. Additionally, MbZ was particularly fixated on the perceived threat posed by Islamists to the UAE. A series of leaked US diplomatic cables have quoted MbZ describing the Muslim Brotherhood as the UAE's "mortal enemy" and asserting that Islah members are "standard bearers for an essentially foreign ideology."[19] Others report MbZ as arguing that the UAE is engaged in a "culture war" with the Brotherhood,[20] while one in particular quoted the young ruler as disagreeing with US democracy promotion in the region, arguing: "the Middle East . . . is not California . . . while members of the U.S. Congress and Senate are loyal to their states and their constituencies, the masses in the Middle East would tend to go with their hearts and vote overwhelmingly for the Muslim Brotherhood and the jihadists represented by Hamas and Hezbollah."[21]

Given this antipathy toward political Islamism, MbZ continued the campaign against Islah in the post-9/11 period, seeking to crush the group under the umbrella of the "war on terror" and bring all forms of Islam under the direct control of the state. Hundreds were arrested and stripped of their position within the government under the pretext of fighting "terrorism." Efforts to convince Islah to disband itself ultimately failed, with the group refusing to dissolve and still benefiting from the refuge provided by the Emir of Ras Al-Khaimah, Sheikh Saqr bin Muhammad Al-Qasimi. UAE authorities also increased their supervision of mosques, preachers, and sermons delivered within the country.

MbZ has spearheaded the efforts of the UAE to comprehensively "rebrand" itself post-9/11. The Emirates has sought to project an image of itself internationally as "moderate" and "tolerant," while simultaneously ingraining itself deeply within the global economy and rapidly emerging as an economic powerhouse in the Middle East. This has included extensive security cooperation with the United States. Additionally, there have been increased efforts at home toward constructing a more common, unified Emirati identity and a sense of loyalty among the citizenry vis-à-vis the state.[22] The UAE has used its massive wealth to promote a centralized and top-down narrative regarding national heritage and culture.[23] Critical to these efforts have been extensive education reforms, designed to promote a stronger sense of national identity while establishing the state as the sole legitimate interpreter of Islam.[24]

By the end of the first decade of the twenty-first century, the UAE had evolved considerably. MbZ accelerated the project of power consolidation and centralization, turning himself and Abu Dhabi into the primary power brokers across the country. Viewing political Islamists as anathema to the interests of the ruling elite, the UAE federal government adopted a number of measures designed to undermine Islah while simultaneously bringing Islam under the sole authority of the state. Abu Dhabi has embraced and expanded upon a religio-political vision rooted in the subordination of religion to state authorities. Indeed, MbZ continues to embrace a religio-political vision that renders religion subservient to the state, the latter of which is the only legitimate body permitted to regulate Islamic practice and interpretation. This has also resulted in a broader securitization of Emirati society and a strengthening of authoritarianism. Indeed, according to the U.S. Department of State, the UAE government "controls virtually all Sunni mosques, prohibits proselytizing, and restricts the freedom of assembly and association."[25] Abu Dhabi "funds or subsidizes almost 95 percent of Sunni mosques and employs all Sunni imams."[26]

During this period, the UAE also emerged as a regional economic powerhouse immersed within the broader global capitalist economy. However, this newfound economic prowess was not felt equally throughout the Emirates, with wealth being disproportionately concentrated in Abu Dhabi and Dubai. Additionally, the UAE's relationship with its primary security guarantor, the United States, continued to remain paramount to Emirati leadership. Abu Dhabi was able to greatly expand its military capabilities with direct American help and has engaged in numerous US-led military endeavors throughout the broader Middle East. The UAE during this period placed great emphasis on projecting a "modern," "progressive," and "tolerant" image of itself internationally, seeking to present the Emirates as fundamentally different from the rest of the region. As will be demonstrated below, the eruption of the Arab uprisings would drive both initiatives into overdrive as MbZ sought to help curtail the tide of regional mass mobilization.

The UAE, Islam, and the Arab Uprisings

Emirati leadership interpreted the eruption of the Arab uprisings as an existential threat to their own authority as well as the broader authoritarian status quo and prevailing regional balance of power from which they have traditionally benefited. The presence of both internal and external perceived threats compounded concerns among Emirati leadership. Domestically, the regime was challenged to a far lesser extent than other states in the region. Nevertheless, the response of Emirati authorities was swift and expansive, viewing such opposition as intimately connected to broader calls for change throughout the Middle East. Indeed, though the UAE witnessed domestic forms of protest and opposition that were unlikely to considerably challenge the existence of the regime, the response by Abu Dhabi was unwavering. The fact that Islah, in conjunction with some elements of secular opposition within the UAE, was at the forefront of calls for change within the Emirates only fueled Mohammed bin Zayed's personal disdain for political Islamism.

With the death of the Emir of Ras Al-Khaimah, Sheikh Saqr bin Muhammad Al-Qasimi, in 2010, happening the year prior, Islah had lost its layer of protection historically provided by the ruler, making the group far more vulnerable to state repression. The rise of political Islamist parties across the region greatly exacerbated these concerns, ultimately leading to the intense securitization of UAE policies both at home and abroad. Externally, the UAE viewed the uprisings as a threat to the regional authoritarian status quo and balance of power, both of which Emirati political elites depend on for the sustainment of their own interests. To counter these perceived domestic and foreign threats, the UAE would become a leading counterrevolutionary force in the Middle East. However, the uprisings also presented the Emirates with a strategic opportunity, namely, the ability to wield the economic and military power it had amassed—the latter with the help of the United States—over the previous decade. UAE foreign policy following the uprisings was designed not just to counter perceived threats but also to assert the Emirates as a major regional power broker.

The Arab uprisings dramatically accelerated several trends that were already underway within the Emirates, such as the consolidation of power at the federal level around Abu Dhabi, the centralization of authority around MbZ in particular, the intense crackdown on all forms of Islam outside of direct state control, and a shift in Emirati foreign policy toward greater assertiveness abroad. Indeed, in the post-uprisings period, MbZ has served as the architect of UAE policy, driving the Emirates in a more autocratic direction while also pushing the country to become one of the most geopolitically active states in the region. Alongside Saudi Arabia, the UAE has helped lead the regional counterrevolution, using the considerable economic and military power it had been developing over the past two decades.

Though the UAE was staunchly against the rise of the Muslim Brotherhood across the region, Abu Dhabi did not immediately lean into religion following the Arab uprisings as happened in Saudi Arabia or Qatar. This is because in 2011/2012, the UAE largely lacked the resources (i.e., "sacred capital") for an effective religious soft power strategy. Indeed, the Emirates lacked strong domestic religious institutions or influential *ulema* capable of reaching a wide audience, which were possessed by both Riyadh and Doha. Abu Dhabi would have to first acquire such sacred capital before it could formulate an effective religious soft power strategy. The tools of UAE religious soft power would be developed during the second, counterrevolutionary, phase of the Arab uprisings.

Interrelated Threats and ... Opportunities?

Relative to other states in the region, including Saudi Arabia, the UAE witnessed considerably lower levels of domestic opposition as a result of the Arab uprisings. Despite this, the limited displays of activism inspired by the uprisings—coupled with the successes of revolutions elsewhere in the region—sent shockwaves throughout Emirati leadership and greatly influenced Abu Dhabi's reaction. The presence of a perceived domestic threat was critical to the hardline approach the UAE would assume toward the Arab uprisings as a whole. These domestic concerns were intimately connected with externally perceived threats as a result of the uprisings. Abu Dhabi feared that the successful emergence of a popular democratic paradigm within the Middle East would undermine their own legitimacy and inspire opposition against the monarchy. Additionally, the existing regional balance of power—from which Abu Dhabi has historically benefited—was jeopardized by more revisionist actors seeking to advance their own strategic imperatives. The answer to such threats was an unwavering strategy of counterrevolution at home and abroad.

Expression of opposition within the UAE was done primarily through online discussion forums and petitions calling for political reform. One online discussion forum in particular, UAEHewar.net (no longer accessible), was established in 2009 and "quickly gained a reputation as the place to put forth grievances, challenge the authorities, and discuss the country's future."[27] Given the very authoritarian and securitized nature of the UAE, the website provided an outlet for the expression of dissent and for Emiratis to engage with others on political, economic, and social issues. Discussions on the site addressed human, civil, and political rights within the Emirates.[28] Upon the eruption of the Arab uprisings, discussions pertaining to the revolutions taking place across the region and the shortcomings of authorities within the UAE began to emerge, as did petitions calling for political change.[29] The site has since been taken down.

One petition, in particular, emerged as the most popular in terms of the number of signatories and was delivered to the ruler of Abu Dhabi, calling for an elected parliament, the need to push the country toward a constitutional monarchy, and so on. Addressed to Sheikh Khalifa, the petition was signed by over 130 Emirati intellectuals, many of whom were affiliated with Islah, but also included endorsements from a number of pro-democracy activists and other nominally secular institutions. The petition stated:

> We, the undersigned, a group of citizens of the United Arab Emirates, have the honor to extend to your Highness [Sheikh Khalifa] and to Their Highnesses of the members of the Supreme Council of the Union the utmost appreciation and respect. We salute Your Highness for your blessed efforts to achieve pride and dignity for your sons and the people of the United Arab Emirates. The United Arab Emirates has, throughout its bright history, and continues to be, in complete harmony between the leadership and the people, and considers participation in decision-making as part of the traditions and customs of this nation since before the establishment of the state and beyond, and we are determined to continue this idea of participation in the making of decisions, and this we consider a source of pride and glory, as a result of the insightful vision of the late Sheikh Zayed bin Sultan Al-Nahyan, founder of the state, and his brothers, members of the Supreme Council and Rulers of the Emirates, when they put national participation as one of the foundations of the constitution that, in its introduction, reads: " . . . and to move it towards a representative democratic system with integrated pillars in a society free from fear . . ." The FNC [Federal National Council] was only the nucleus of this participation. However, efforts to grow national participation in political decisions in the country for 39 years have not changed as stipulated in the constitution. We are fully convinced that Your Highness is aware that the rapid regional and international developments require the development of the

process of national participation. Based on our deep belief in Your Highness's keenness on the interest of this country and its children, who are your children, and our belief in Your Highness's keenness to communicate permanently with citizens, we submit to Your Highness and to Their Highnesses the Members of the Supreme Council of the Union a request to reconsider Supreme Council Resolution No. 4 of 2006, Federal Resolution No. 2 of 2011 and Resolution No. 3 of 2006 on determining the method of selecting the representatives of the Emirates in the Federal National Council in a manner that achieves the following aspirations: 1- The election of all members of the Federal National Council by all citizens as applied in democratic countries around the world. 2- Amending the constitutional articles related to the Federal National Council to ensure that it has full legislative and supervisory powers. May God grant you success for the good of this country and the future of its generations, and help you shoulder your responsibilities in serving your country and your people.[30]

The petition was also endorsed by four different civil society organizations within the UAE—the Lawyer's Association, the Teacher's Association, the Al-Shuhuh National Heritage Association, and the United Arab Emirates University Faculty Association—which would later issue their own joint letter stating that "civil society in UAE considers that the time has come to ensure the right of political participation of every citizen, with direct elections for a council with full federal oversight and legislative powers."[31] In addition to these petitions, elements of dissent were also expressed on social media. One individual in particular, Mohammad Abdul Razzaq Al-Siddiq, was very active online during the early stages of the regional uprisings, calling for change within the UAE while criticizing Emirati leadership. A leader of Islah, Al-Siddiq argued that the UAE has "lost the legacy of love that Zayed built for the Emirates in the hearts of the Arab peoples,"[32] while praising Qatar for coming to the aid of the oppressed.[33] He lambasted the "criminals from the security apparatus" for "corrupting the Friday sermon" and humiliating preachers and Imams.[34] The UAE security apparatus, he argued, wants to "kill our mosques, our sermons, our religion, and spoil our youth with parties of debauchery"[35] and claimed it is not permissible to turn the mosque into a tool of propaganda for leaders.[36] Despite Al-Siddiq's efforts, these posts did not gain much traction or popularity online, many receiving only a few "likes" and "retweets" on Twitter.

It is important to note the considerable difference in tone and demands articulated within the above petition compared to calls for change happening elsewhere in the region at the time. The petition did not call for regime overthrow, nor did it lead to street protests, sit-ins, or other forms of public dissent. While some such as Al-Siddiq engaged in more direct criticisms, these posts did not garner the type of attention that was gained by Islamists elsewhere in the region such as Salman Al-Awdah or Yusuf Al-Qaradawi. Yet, the petition transcribed above was rather significant in that it "marked the first time that the secular and Islamist opposition came together in such a public political undertaking."[37] More broadly, "Islah's commitment to keep pushing for evolution towards democracy—in line with a clause in the UAE constitution of 1971—has effectively placed it into direct confrontation with the country's now committedly apolitical ruling families."[38] Such demands were antithetical not only to the UAE's highly authoritarian and securitized political landscape but also to Abu Dhabi's efforts to consolidate and centralize its own authority over the seven Emirates that comprise the UAE. Despite the lack of traction garnered by these acts, a nerve was struck among Emirati leadership, who viewed these developments as a pressing domestic threat inexorably linked to a region in upheaval.

These domestic developments within the Emirates were compounded by the rise of mass mobilization throughout the wider Middle East as a result of the Arab uprisings. Like Saudi Arabia, the UAE was alarmed by the eruption of the uprisings across the region. Not only the emergence of a popular democratic paradigm within the region would challenge the authoritarian form of governance that dominates in the Emirates, but also a fundamental reworking of state-society relations and regional economies could seriously undermine the crony capitalist system that has flourished within the UAE, leading to the enrichment of the ruling families and the emergence of Abu Dhabi and Dubai as financial powerhouses. Moreover, the early successes of mainstream Islamist groups—specifically the Muslim Brotherhood and various regional affiliates—in many of the vacuums that emerged following the overthrow of different rulers were of grave concern to Abu Dhabi, which feared that such successes would inspire Islamists within the UAE and possibly alter the regional balance of power in favor of states that supported the Brotherhood, such as Qatar and Turkey.

However, though the UAE faced a wide spectrum of threats following the Arab uprisings, this period would also present the Emirates with a grand opportunity. Indeed, the UAE quickly emerged determined to use its newfound economic and military resources to crush all forms of domestic opposition and assert itself abroad as a leading counterrevolutionary actor in the new Middle East.

The Regime Responds: Abu Dhabi and the Counterrevolution

The immediate response of the UAE to the Arab uprisings did not involve the mobilization of religion. Instead, the Emirates rooted their reaction in various economic, diplomatic, and military initiatives, ultimately seeking to crush mainstream political Islamism at home and abroad while also asserting the UAE as a major regional power broker. Both domestically and abroad, political elites within the Emirates embraced an unrelenting strategy of counterrevolution as the solution to the Arab uprisings.

At home, the regime was unrelenting: it sought to make an example out of those who had voiced opposition and moved to crush Islah as an organization. The crackdown was immediate, with the state arresting dozens of signatories while stripping others of their citizenship, accusing them of publicly insulting Emirati leadership while harming state security and having connections with "foreign organizations and outside agendas."[39] Emirati authorities accused Islah of possessing an armed wing that aimed to establish an "Islamic state" in the Gulf, which has continued to be denied by family members of the detained.[40] The most dramatic move by UAE authorities came in 2013 when 94 individuals—the majority of whom were associated with Islah—were sentenced under the pretext of compromising state security. Prosecutors claimed the individuals were guilty of the following:

> They launched, established and ran an organization seeking to oppose the basic principles of the UAE system of governance and to seize power. . . . The organization announced its declared principles as being the teaching and virtues of Islam, but their undeclared aims were, in fact, to seek to seize power and the state's system of governance and to oppose the basic principles of this system. . . . They also communicated with the international Muslim Brotherhood organization and other similar organizations based outside the state, and asked them for help, expertise and financial support to serve their undeclared goal of seizing power.[41]

Those arrested included academics, economists, lawyers, medical professionals, and even a member of Ras Al-Khaimah's ruling family,

Sheikh Sultan al-Qassimi. Mohammad Abdul Razzaq Al-Siddiq was also detained for his outspoken criticism, and his family would later be stripped of their citizenship.[42] Abu Dhabi dissolved the boards of the Teachers' Association and the Lawyers' Association, both of which had endorsed the petition sent to Sheikh Khalifa.[43] Additionally, in 2013, UAE authorities arrested 11 Egyptian citizens, alleging they were members of the Muslim Brotherhood in Cairo aiding Islah in their efforts to overthrow the Emirates.[44] The following year, 20 more Egyptian citizens were arrested on similar charges.[45] As a result of the government crackdown, Islah as an organization was crippled and forced underground, with much of its leadership in jail or having fled abroad.

State repression during this period was also coupled with forms of co-optation. Many who voiced opposition during this period were located in the northern, poorer Emirates of the UAE, such as Ras Al-Khaimah, Fujairah, and Ajman. In order to stymie opposition against the richer Emirates of Abu Dhabi and Dubai, the regime responded with a series of aid packages, investments, and wage hikes designed to quell such frustrations. Right before the above petition was submitted to Sheikh Khalifa, Abu Dhabi announced that $1.5 billion would be invested in various utility services in the northern Emirates.[46] This was coupled with a 70 percent pension increase for military personnel and their families within the Emirates;[47] a 100 percent salary increase for judicial authorities, Ministry of Health employees, and government teachers;[48] and the announcement of a monetary fund worth almost $3 billion to help citizens with limited income pay their personal loans.[49]

A central pillar of the UAE's response to the Arab uprisings has been the desire of Abu Dhabi to isolate and weaken the Muslim Brotherhood both within the UAE and across the Middle East. The Brotherhood and its affiliates, including Islah, are viewed as a serious threat to political elites in the UAE because the group embraces a competing religio-political vision that challenges state monopoly on religion and the highly authoritarian system operated by Abu Dhabi. In the immediate aftermath of the uprisings, the UAE's foreign minister, Sheikh Abdullah Bin Zayed Al-Nahyan, denounced the Brotherhood as "an organization which encroaches upon the sovereignty and integrity of nations" and called for other Gulf nations to cooperate against the group.[50] On August 20, 2014, Abu Dhabi issued new terrorism legislation—Terrorism Law No. 7 of 2014—which grants the government sweeping new powers designed to criminalize all forms of dissent, including peaceful opposition to the government, as acts of "terrorism."[51] That same year, the UAE officially labeled eighty-three organizations—including Islah and the Muslim Brotherhood—as terrorist organizations, along with a number of Western-based Muslim organizations such as the Council on American-Islamic Relations (CAIR), the Muslim Association of Britain, Islamic Council Norway, and many more.[52] Commenting on the designations, Emirati minister of foreign affairs at the time, Sheikh Abdullah bin Zayed, sought to justify their position:

> Our threshold is quite low when you talk about extremism. We cannot accept incitement or funding when we look at some of these organizations. . . . For many countries the definition of terror is that you have to carry a weapon and terrorize people. For us it's far beyond that. We cannot tolerate even the smallest and tiniest amount of terrorism. . . . They are trying to hijack our religion. It's not about them not liking other religions. No, they don't like our religion. They don't like the way we practice our Islam.[53]

The following year, the UAE would arrest forty-one individuals, accusing them of trying to "seize power and establish a caliphate" in the Gulf.[54] Emirati leadership continues to equate the Brotherhood with terrorist organizations such as ISIS and *al-Qaeda*, with senior officials describing the group as "the gateway drug to *jihadism* of all kinds."[55] Such depictions are deliberate: by equating the Brotherhood with known and acknowledged global terrorist organizations, Emirati authorities present their repressive policies toward the group and its affiliates as legitimate counterterrorism efforts.

In addition to these terrorism designations, the UAE assumed a much more assertive diplomatic, economic, and military stance abroad following the uprisings. Indeed, though the uprisings represented a threat to the status quo favored by Abu Dhabi, they also presented the UAE with an opportunity to assert itself geopolitically. This sentiment was summarized well by Emirati Anwar Gargash, the former minister of state for foreign affairs, who stated:

> There is a very rapidly changing status quo in the region characterized by political instability and violent extremism, and we have seen it since the Arab Spring started in 2011. . . . This added more risks in an already risky environment. . . . There are many regional challenges so we should have the potential to face these threats. As [much as] the UAE and other countries need regional allies, we have to start with our own self-power and potential.[56]

The forceful deployment of UAE "self-power and potential" has dominated Emirati foreign policy following the Arab uprisings. The UAE has sought to help lead the regional counterrevolution while establishing the Emirates as a major regional power broker. Throughout the Middle East, the Emirates has increasingly used its growing economic, diplomatic, and military prowess to crush political Islamism and advance Emirati influence abroad. Indeed, following the Arab uprisings, the UAE has quickly become one of the most geopolitically active and interventionist states in the Middle East.[57]

When the Arab uprisings (2010–11) were sparked by the revolution in Tunisia, the UAE was largely absent from trying to influence events in Tunis due to the peripheral nature of the country to Emirati strategic interests. Nonetheless, following the successful election of the Muslim Brotherhood offshoot Ennahda to power and the pouring of Qatari support into the country for the new government, the UAE halted its investments in the country and withdrew its ambassador in 2013, claiming that Tunisia's future was too "uncertain."[58] During this time, the UAE gradually began building relations with Ennahda's primary opposition, Nidaa Tounes, which has best been described as an "alliance of secularists and old regime figures."[59] Following the successful election of Nidaa Tounes in 2014, relations between Tunisia and the UAE gradually increased. In early 2015, UAE Minister for Foreign Affairs Abdullah bin Zayed Al-Nahyan traveled to Tunisia to meet with President Beji Caid Essebsi, the founder of Nidaa Tounes.[60] Later, following the death of President Essebsi and the election of Kais Saied, the UAE would emerge as a strong supporter of the coup led by President Saied in 2021, ultimately returning the country to authoritarian rule.[61]

The revolution in Egypt was far more consequential for the UAE, due to the central position Cairo has historically held in the Arab world. After protests had swept across Egypt, the UAE Minister for Foreign Affairs Abdullah bin Zayed Al-Nahyan was the only Arab leader to meet with embattled Egyptian president Hosni Mubarak, following a statement issued by the Emirates denouncing all "foreign attempts to interfere in the internal affairs of Egypt."[62] After the overthrow of Mubarak, the UAE maintained its support for the Supreme Council of the Armed Forces (SCAF) during the transitional period immediately following the revolution. Upon Egypt's presidential elections, the UAE supported candidate Ahmad Shafik (the prime minister under Mubarak), who would flee to the Emirates following his defeat and the election of Mohamed Morsi. The Emirates would play a central role in encouraging the military coup that overthrew Morsi in 2013, namely, by helping to finance the Tamarod movement that took to the streets against the president.[63] After General Abdel Fattah El-Sisi assumed the presidency, he was immediately embraced by the UAE, which moved quickly to support the new regime with a $4.9 billion aid package and over $14 billion in investments in the first two years of El-Sisi's rule.[64]

In Bahrain, Libya, and Yemen, the UAE was directly involved militarily. Facing an uprising against the Al-Khalifa ruling family, Bahrain witnessed a military intervention led by Saudi Arabia and the UAE to squash the protests and maintain the status quo. Approximately 500 UAE police officers accompanied 1,000 Saudi troops into Bahrain to forcibly suppress demonstrations against the Al-Khalifa monarchy.[65] Like Riyadh, Abu Dhabi maintains a tacit understanding with the Muslim Brotherhood in Bahrain due to the latter's role in helping buttress regime authority. In Libya, the UAE participated in the NATO intervention against Gaddafi by contributing 12 warplanes to help enforce the no-fly zone over the country.[66] After the disintegration of the Libyan state and its slide into civil war, the Emirates has been very active in the ongoing proxy war taking place within the country, seeking to crush Brotherhood influence. The UAE has emerged as one of the strongest supporters of the anti-Brotherhood Libyan National Army (LNA) led by General Khalifa Haftar—which is opposed to the internationally recognized Government of National Accord—providing the LNA with large quantities of weaponry, directly carrying out air strikes and drone strikes to support Haftar's forces, and reportedly funding Russian mercenaries fighting on behalf of the LNA.[67] The UAE has also reportedly supported monetarily Salafi militants fighting alongside Haftar.[68]

Finally, in Yemen, the UAE endorsed the Saudi-led GCC initiative in 2011 that witnessed the transfer of power from President Ali Abdullah Saleh to his vice president, Abdrabbuh Mansour Hadi. In 2015, the Emirates joined with Saudi Arabia to launch a military intervention in Yemen to support the Hadi government following the fall of Sanaa to the Houthi movement. However, in the fight against the Houthis, tensions have ballooned between Abu Dhabi and Riyadh due to the latter's cooperation with Yemen's Muslim Brotherhood affiliate— also called Islah—much to the dismay of the UAE. Abu Dhabi has remained concerned that the rising influence of the Yemeni branch of the Muslim Brotherhood would empower the UAE branch. Therefore, the Emiratis have backed the Southern Separatist Movement (*hirak al-janubi*), which seeks independence for southern Yemen, and certain Salafi groups in Aden and Taiz as a counterbalance to the Muslim

Brotherhood.[69] In doing so, US weapons possessed by the UAE have also reportedly been transferred to *al-Qaeda*-linked fighters and other hardline Salafi militias in the attempt to counterbalance Islah and aid the fight against the Houthis, and Abu Dhabi has reportedly directed assassination campaigns using ex-US soldiers as mercenaries to target Islah's leadership.[70]

The approach by the UAE to the uprising and subsequent civil war in Syria has been markedly different than the other two cases discussed in this book. The Emirates has not embraced anti-Assad revolutionaries due to the strong presence of Islamists among the opposition, specifically groups affiliated with the Muslim Brotherhood. Mohamed bin Zayed has warned that the alternative to Assad is worse than the status quo.[71] However, the UAE did participate in the international coalition against ISIS across Syria and Iraq. The Emirates has demonstrated its backing of Syrian President Bashar Al-Assad by expressing support for Russia's military intervention in 2015, participating with Moscow in "counterterrorism operations," reopening its embassy in Damascus in 2018, and urging the Arab League and the broader international community to take Assad back, whom Abu Dhabi praised for his "wise leadership."[72] Later, in 2022, Bashar Al-Assad was embraced by MbZ in Abu Dhabi in his first trip to an Arab state since the 2011 uprising.[73]

Given the UAE's antipathy for political Islamists and its desire to lead the regional counterrevolution, it is clear why it—along with Saudi Arabia—spearheaded the 2017 air, land, and naval blockades of Qatar. As explained in the two previous chapters, the blockades were designed to pressure Qatar into changing its more activist foreign policy, particularly its support for the Muslim Brotherhood. Political elites in the UAE viewed Qatar's support for such forces as a direct threat to their own interests. The UAE played a central role in attempting to portray Doha to Western audiences as a state sponsor of terrorism. Abu Dhabi devoted considerable financial resources toward lobbying within Western countries, particularly the United States, attempting to project an image of Qatar as a supporter of terrorist movements.[74] Mohammed bin Zayed also sought to leverage his close personal ties with members of the Donald Trump administration in the hopes of getting Washington on board, albeit to little avail.

Complementing these assertive foreign policy efforts abroad was the strategic use of social media and various different mechanisms of surveillance by authorities within the UAE. Troll armies of fake accounts numbering in the thousands have been removed from platforms such as Facebook, Twitter, and Instagram after being linked to the UAE government. The content produced and promoted by these accounts overwhelmingly targeted Qatar, the Muslim Brotherhood, and other perceived enemies of the Emirates while supporting UAE policies throughout the region.[75] Emirati surveillance efforts have also increased dramatically following the uprisings. A comprehensive investigation published by Reuters in December 2019 documents how former Western security officials and various intelligence contractors established a surveillance powerhouse in the UAE, now controlled and directed by the Emirati firm DarkMatter.[76] Originally led by former US counterterrorism czar Richard Clark in 2008, when he was serving as a consultant for the UAE, the secret unit was initially designed to assist the Emiratis in fighting terrorism. However, as revealed by the *Reuters* investigation, those targeted by the unit expanded to all those deemed as foes by the UAE government, particularly following the Arab uprisings. New targets grew to include women's rights activists in Saudi Arabia, diplomats at the United Nations, personnel at FIFA, human rights activists, journalists, political dissidents, Qatari government officials, and US citizens.[77]

MbZ Solidifies Control

The period following the Arab uprisings presented an opportunity for Mohammed bin Zayed to further consolidate his own power. At the time of the uprisings, MbZ had already established himself as the de facto authority within the Emirates. However, the post-uprisings period would witness the consolidation of centralized power within Abu Dhabi and, more specifically, in the hands of MbZ. As the architect of the UAE's response to the uprisings, MbZ's authority was further entrenched following Sheikh Khalifa suffering a stroke in 2014 and largely withdrawing from the public sphere.[78] Similar to Mohammed bin Salman (MbS) in Saudi Arabia, MbZ has embarked upon a campaign of power consolidation and centralization, eliminating institutional constraints while amassing more power than any other individual in the history of the UAE. This includes, among other developments, bringing religion within the Emirates under his direct control. Later, in 2022, MbZ would assume the presidency following the death of Sheikh Khalifa, cementing his absolute control over the Emirates.

The continued rise of MbZ has corresponded with the increased securitization of the Emirates and the emergence of what has been referred to as a "militarized hypernationalism."[79] In addition to reinstituting the military draft in 2014, MbZ has overseen a dramatic increase in the acquisition of military hardware and technology by the Emirates, primarily from the United States but also Russia and China.[80] Indeed, US weapons exports to the UAE have increased considerably, as has military spending within the Emirates.[81] Since 2015, the UAE has introduced a new holiday, "Commemoration Day" (or "Martyr's Day"), to honor the Emirati military and fallen soldiers.[82] Mohammed bin Zayed has also focused heavily on efforts to construct a cohesive national identity within the Emirates.[83] Initiatives designed to foster such a shared sense of identity include the "Year of National Identity" and "Year of Zayed" recently hosted in the UAE, the introduction of various national museums and libraries, and expanded emphasis on the annual "national day" celebrations.[84] Education within the Emirates has also continued to be heavily reformed, with MbZ directing curricula to focus heavily on Emirati national identity and the creation of "entrepreneurial, self-reliant, and achievement-oriented Emirati citizens."[85]

Islam within the Emirates has been oriented toward the objectives of securing MbZ's ultimate authority and shifting popular identity across the Emirates toward a more unified, Emirati identity. Absolute obedience to Emirati authorities and this shift toward overt nationalism have both been coupled with forms of religious legitimization, particularly in the education sector. Islamic education in the UAE—mandatory in public and private schooling, grades 1 through 12—has been reformed to encourage loyalism to established authority as a religious obligation, promote a unified Emirati identity and the notion of an economically "productive citizen," and advance the religious legitimization of modern capitalist thinking.[86]

The UAE Accumulates "Sacred Capital"

The building of Emirati soft power is considerably different from the other two cases discussed in this book. Historically, similar to Qatar but unlike Saudi Arabia, there has never been a strong domestic religious establishment within the UAE. However, unlike Qatar—which was able to capitalize on the presence of heavyweight scholars such as Sheikh Yusuf Al-Qaradawi and good relations with non-state movements such as the Muslim Brotherhood—the UAE did not possess influential religious scholars, and the local branch of the Brotherhood, Islah, had assumed an oppositional stance toward the state.

At the time of the Arab uprisings, the Emirates lacked the resources—influential institutions or scholars, that is, "sacred capital"—to manufacture a strong religious soft power strategy, aside from depicting themselves as opposed to more "extreme" interpretations of Islam, which they had already been engaged in post-9/11. Indeed, the emergence of Emirati religious soft power as a cohesive strategy—equipped with capable sacred capital—is a relatively new enterprise. The construction of such a strategy occurred during the second, counterrevolutionary, phase of the Arab uprisings. The increased utilization of Islam as a form of soft power by the UAE must be viewed through the lens of a broader shift in Emirati foreign policy toward a more assertive posture and the increased mobilization of hard power by Abu Dhabi abroad.

Emirati religious soft power emerged out of ongoing efforts within the UAE to construct a religio-political vision of Islam as subordinated to the state, thereby establishing a strict state monopoly on religious practice and interpretation. The UAE has sought to construct an Islam that is subservient to the state, incapable of challenging the authority or policies pursued by the regime. This top-down, state-controlled Islam is designed to complement the UAE's counterrevolutionary ethos, the state's increasing nationalist orientation, MbZ's personal consolidation of power, and broader state-branding initiatives directed primarily toward the West.

Therefore, UAE religious soft power has focused primarily on promoting a religio-political vision emphasizing political quietism and absolute obedience to established authority, as well as emphasizing the notions of "moderation" and "tolerance" to project an image of the Emirates as a modern, stable, and progressive presence in the Middle East.

The UAE's Rising Stars

In the post-uprisings period, UAE authorities have sought to build their own instruments of religious soft power to advance their objectives domestically and internationally. Two individuals in particular—Sheikh Abdullah bin Bayyah and Hamza Yusuf—have emerged as the vanguard figures of Emirati religious soft power and the foundation of the UAE's sacred capital. When the Arab uprisings erupted across the Middle East, neither bin Bayyah nor Yusuf was formally affiliated with the UAE. Sheikh Abdullah bin Bayyah (born 1935) is an internationally renowned Islamic scholar from Mauritania and is currently a professor of Islamic studies at King Abdulaziz University in Jeddah, Saudi Arabia. A prominent Sufi scholar, bin Bayyah has emerged as one of the foremost critics of Islamic extremism and has worked in conjunction with different Arab and Western governments on various religious initiatives for decades. Bin Bayyah served as Sheikh Yusuf Al-Qaradawi's deputy at the European Council for Fatwa and Research as well as the International Union of Muslim Scholars (IUMS) until his resignation in 2013 (addressed below). Throughout his career, bin Bayyah has maintained a close relationship with the ruling Al-Nahyan family in Abu Dhabi, regularly participating in various lectures and other events within the UAE as an honored guest throughout the 2000s.[87]

Hamza Yusuf is an American convert to Islam and a co-founder of Zaytuna College, established in 2008 as the first accredited Muslim undergraduate college in the United States. A close student and colleague of bin Bayyah's, Yusuf has been recognized as one of the most influential Islamic scholars within the West.[88] Yusuf has developed a close relationship with Washington, having advised both Democratic and Republican presidents. Bin Bayyah and Yusuf continue to work closely together, with the latter serving regularly as the Sheikh's translator.

Sheikh Abdullah bin Bayyah and Hamza Yusuf approached the beginning of the Arab uprisings with caution. Not yet formally affiliated with any government, both bin Bayyah and Yusuf assumed what can be considered a more ambiguous stance at the outset of the region-wide mobilizations. Sheikh bin Bayyah expressed throughout 2011 that he was not a supporter of revolution, but since the region had already witnessed such phenomenon, it is now necessary to deal with such realities.[89] Sheikh bin Bayyah stood out in stark contrast to many of his IUMS colleagues who had embraced the revolutions and began constructing religious arguments in support of these protests. During an interview in October 2011, when asked about the protests across the region, bin Bayyah argued that the issue was "complex" without outright rejecting or supporting the regional uprisings.[90] He expressed his fear regarding what would ultimately arise following these regional revolutions, arguing that they might "fail to achieve their desired hopes due to conflict, fragmentation, and concerns for personal and factional interests."[91] He discussed these fears at length:

> We fear, in reality, that the consequence of these revolutions will be disagreements, discord, and civil war. We do not belittle the significance of these revolutions. We do not belittle the significance

of these youths standing up without protection for the sake of the interests of the country and for the sake of putting an end to this overwhelming danger and this nightmare that has weighed heavily upon the umma's chest for a long time. It did not permit it to express its freedom and creativity. This is a situation that is unacceptable. Yet, despite this, and alongside this, there is a fear that these revolutions will not reach the desired outcome. There is a wise person who says, "revolution is a bulldozer," it bulldozes everything before it. But it needs a construction engineer to undertake building thereafter. The revolutions are bulldozing, but where are these sensible people, these engineers who can build a new edifice which we hope will be an expansive edifice that will accommodate all the sons of the nation, in which there is no ostracizing of one group by another, in which there is no fighting about [one's] existence. Let me say that existential fights result in annihilation. Thus, we propose to people that they work toward coexistence, work toward building.[92]

The tensions between bin Bayyah's more tepid approach to the uprisings and the strong support for the revolutions displayed by many of his colleagues at the IUMS—particularly Sheikh Yusuf Al-Qaradawi—eventually led to his resignation from the organization. In his resignation letter, bin Bayyah expressed that the "modest role" he was attempting to play in the "cause of reform and reconciliation" required an approach that "does not fit" with his position at the IUMS.[93] Sheikh bin Bayyah would soon find a new institutional home in the Emirates.

During the early days of the Arab uprisings, Hamza Yusuf expressed support for regional protests via a series of blog posts. Discussing the revolution in Tunisia, he explains that "Tunisia is a stunningly beautiful country with a great history and a bright and talented people, but corruption, cruelty, and the ineptitude of leaders unable to gauge the frustration of their people has led to the current crisis."[94] He described the revolution that brought down President Ben Ali as "a genuine uprising of people who are sick and tired of the corruption and cruelty of a state apparatus."[95] Addressing the revolution in Egypt, Yusuf applauded the people for seeking a new "social contract" in the "land of the Pharaohs."[96] He described the revolution as "a historic turn in the largest Arab nation, a widespread non-ideological movement, fueled by the long-repressed aspirations of the majority of Egyptians."[97] The Egyptian people, he argues, are "challenging their government, courageously defying the fear factor so ruthlessly cultivated in the belly of the bestial state security apparatus."[98] Yusuf even implored the United States to involve itself by supporting the revolution:

> America, where are you? The people of Egypt are clamoring for the very right of dissolving the social contract with their current government due to its long string of abuses, a right enshrined in our nation's foundational document. It behooves America to lend a helping hand to Egypt's people at this crucial moment.[99]

Yusuf adopted similar language when addressing the revolution in Libya. Gaddafi, Yusuf stated, reminded him of Shakespeare's tyrant, Richard III, in that he was "conniving, mutant, dark, and absolutely cruel, with no concern for his family, friends, or companions, let alone the people he rules over."[100] Yusuf emphasized his "hope that Gaddafi's reign comes to an end soon for the sake of Libya's beautiful people."[101] However, this enthusiasm for the regional protest movements calling for change would not last. Yusuf's rhetoric soon shifted toward the need to uphold stability and order within the region. In particular, he began expressing high praise for monarchial forms of government. In a televised interview, Yusuf explained: "Firstly, kings are incorruptible unlike those who do not possess great wealth. . . . As for a king, he is satiated. He has everything. He does not need anything."[102] As will be explained at length below, the pro-monarchy framework would later be used in service of the Al-Nahyan in the UAE.

Institutionalization

As counterrevolutionary forces began gaining the upper hand throughout the region and several states devolved into protracted civil and proxy wars, the UAE came to see natural allies in the personalities of Sheikh bin Bayyah and Hamza Yusuf. The notion that the Islamic community and the Middle East must return to a state of "stability," "moderation," and "tolerance" has assumed a central position in Emirati religious soft power and is often presented as a legitimizing mechanism for the UAE's counterrevolutionary policies. As they assumed the mantle of the regional counterrevolution alongside Saudi Arabia, the UAE partnered with bin Bayyah and Yusuf in their efforts to bring Islam under the exclusive authority of the state and export its counterrevolutionary vision. These two scholars have become central to Abu Dhabi's religious soft power strategy designed to counter perceived domestic and foreign threats, balance against competing ideologies while promulgating a religio-political vision rooted in a statist conceptualization of Islam, and project a specific image of the Emirates as part of its broader state-branding efforts.

The Emirates has sought to harness the influence and prestige of bin Bayyah, Yusuf, and several other scholars via a process of institutionalization. The creation of formal institutions within the Emirates during the second, counterrevolutionary, phase of the Arab uprisings has allowed Abu Dhabi to cement its religio-political vision domestically and promote it abroad via its new sources of sacred capital. As Amasha[103] explains, "after the July 2013 coup in Egypt, the UAE established institutions that were envisioned to ideologically legitimize the counterrevolutionary camp and delegitimize its dissidents (especially the Ikhwani [Muslim Brotherhood] and *jihadist* discourse)."

In 2014, the UAE announced the formation of two institutions designed to serve these ends: the Muslim Council of Elders (MCE) and the Forum for Promoting Peace in Muslim Societies (FPPMS). The MCE is headed by Sheikh bin Bayyah and Ahmed El-Tayeb, the current Grand Imam of Al-Azhar in Egypt. The stated mission of the MCE is to "restore the role of scholars, to use their expertise to improve Muslim societies and to help eliminate causes of fragmentation and to promote reconciliation."[104] It describes itself as "the first institutional body that aims to bring the Islamic nation together by extinguishing the fire that threatens Islam's humanitarian values and principles of tolerance, and putting an end to the sectarianism and violence that have plagued the Muslim world for decades." The FPPMS was created alongside the MCE and is headed by Sheikh bin Bayyah as its president and Hamza Yusuf as its vice president. The forum is focused primarily on interfaith relations—particularly among the three Abrahamic faiths—and "clarifying" the teachings of Islam. It seeks to emphasize the "priority of peace," which it claims is the ultimate objective and foundation for rights and justice.[105] The FPPMS is officially sponsored by UAE Minister of Foreign Affairs Abdullah bin Zayed, who claimed the organization is a necessary response to the "strife" (*fitna*) and "grave mistakes" currently plaguing the Muslim community, which can only be solved by state leaders and religious scholars working together to "remedy the crisis the [Islamic] nation is going through."[106] Presented as a way to "return" to genuine Islamic values that have been cast aside in recent decades, Mohamed bin Zayed claims the FPPMS presents a platform for scholars to confront those who promote "sedition and chaos."[107] The

UAE, and its newly founded institutions, is presented as a haven for solutions to such issues.

This narrative of the need to end the current state of *fitna* and return to "peace," "moderation," and "stability"—and the critical role of the Emirates and its leadership in doing so—will assume a central role in the messaging advanced by the UAE and its new institutions, as will be discussed at length below. The statist religio-political vision proffered by the UAE is presented as a solution to the destabilizing forces plaguing the Middle East. To achieve this objective, the UAE has built a number of additional institutions alongside the MCE and the FPPMS. In 2018, the Emirates announced the formation of an institution that now resides at the heart of such efforts: the UAE Fatwa Council, headed by Sheikh Abdullah bin Bayyah. The sole body responsible for issuing Islamic rulings within the UAE, the Fatwa Council was formed in order to centralize religious authority within the Emirates.

The Council embodies the religio-political vision embraced by Emirati authorities. It has the exclusive authority to "grant licenses to issue *fatawa*, train muftis and develop their skills, as well as to conduct related studies in co-ordination with the country's General Authority of Islamic Affairs and Endowments."[108] Upon his appointment as chairman of the Council, Sheikh bin Bayyah formally became an employee of the state and is effectively the highest ranking Islamic official within the UAE. He argues that the purpose of the formation of the Council was to achieve the goal of "controlling, institutionalizing and unifying" the issuing of *fatawa* to protect the community from "rogue" rulings that threaten peace and stability.[109] Hamza Yusuf is also a member of the Council. Under the direct supervision of the state, the Fatwa Council is the epicenter of Abu Dhabi's institutionalized sacred capital.

A number of other institutions have also been created by Abu Dhabi with a specific focus on international "branding" initiatives for the UAE, namely, the promotion of "moderate Islam" and tolerance. These initiatives are primarily directed toward the West in an effort to promote a specific international image of the UAE (discussed more below). For example, in 2016, the UAE announced the National Program for Tolerance and the establishment of an official minister of tolerance, currently held by Sheikh Nahyan Mabarak Al-Nahyan. The Ministry explains that "tolerance is one of the deep-rooted values in the genuine community of UAE, which are derived from the moderation of the true Islam, the noble Arab customs and traditions, and from the wisdom and legacy of [Sheikh] Zayed."[110] The Ministry also has a strong international focus, describing itself and the UAE as "a global capital, where civilizations of East and West converge to enhance peace and rapprochement among all peoples."[111] Other institutions such as the Tabah Foundation and the al-Muwatta Center, both headed by bin Bayyah, were likewise created to promote a return to "moderation" and "tolerance" as the core foundations of Islam.

In addition to these domestic initiatives, the UAE has increasingly worked with Egypt's Al-Azhar to capitalize on the historic institution's prestige and reach to promote a shared counterrevolutionary vision, expanding Abu Dhabi's pool of sacred capital. As has been mentioned, leading Egyptian Islamic figures such as Ahmed El-Tayeb, the Grand Imam of Al-Azhar, hold leadership positions within these newly formed institutions based in the UAE. El-Tayeb and other Egyptian Islamic figures often participate in international conferences and other initiatives hosted by institutions based in the Emirates. In addition to participating in such events, El-Tayeb has been recognized by the Emirates through a series of awards, most notably the Sheikh Zayed Book Award's "Cultural Personality of the Year" prize in April 2013 and, shortly following the 2013 military coup in Egypt, which El-Tayeb endorsed, the Dubai International Holy Quran Award's "Islamic Personality of the Year."[112] Upon a visit to Egypt's Al-Azhar in 2014, Mohammed bin Zayed praised the university and expressed his "profound appreciation and respect for the message of this grand institution in promoting the tolerant image and teachings of Islam and its role in preserving Egypt's national fabric as a united and coherent entity as well as its honorable role and stand against deviated ideas, extremists and fanatic trends."[113] The UAE has donated large sums of money to Al-Azhar following the Arab uprisings, and the university is reportedly working with Abu Dhabi to open an affiliated college in the Emirates.[114]

Islam and Political Authority: Abu Dhabi's Statist Vision

Central to the UAE's formulation of its religious soft power strategy following the Arab uprisings has been the construction of a religio-political vision that combines strict Islamic traditionalism with the concept of the modern nation-state and the legitimization of authoritarian rule. Emirati religious soft power has sought to affirm the ultimate, unquestionable authority of the state while projecting an image of the Emirates as a force for peace, stability, and tolerance in the Middle East. Sheikh Abdullah bin Bayyah, Hamza Yusuf, and the myriad institutions built by the UAE following the Arab uprisings are critical to these efforts and represent the instruments of Emirati religious soft power. Collectively, these actors present themselves—and their sponsor, the UAE—as the forces capable of returning the Muslim community and the Middle East to a state of perceived stability. In doing so, they have focused heavily on constructing what Quisay and Parker[115] refer to as a "theology of obedience." This religio-political doctrine has its roots in traditionalist conceptualizations regarding the relationship between Islam and political authority discussed in Chapter 2 but has been adapted for the modern nation-state and the legitimization of modern authoritarian rule. Indeed, Sheikh bin Bayyah, Hamza Yusuf, and the various newly created institutions within the Emirates have worked to construct Islamic justifications for a form of what has been referred to as "modernist authoritarianism."[116]

Sheikh bin Bayyah, Hamza Yusuf, and the newly formed institutions within the UAE present themselves as the actors capable of rolling back the current state of "war" and "chaos" currently plaguing the Muslim community and the broader Middle East. In doing so, they have constructed what Warren[117] refers to as the "jurisprudence of peace." They argue that the way to return to a state of "peace," "moderation," and "stability" is through a formal alliance between the *ulema* and the state. According to bin Bayyah, such an alliance is necessary in order to counter "abnormal and deviant" *fatawa* and the proliferation of individuals, groups, and organizations issuing Islamic legal rulings, resulting in what he refers to as the "chaos of the *fatwa*."[118] Warren[119] details how this idea has long been a focus of bin Bayyah, but that this issue has become an increasingly prominent aspect of the sheikh's discourse following the Arab uprisings. For bin Bayyah, the solution to this problem is a formal alliance between select *ulema* and the nation-state via initiatives such as the UAE Fatwa Council. Indeed, bin Bayyah explains that the Council's purpose is the "controlling, institutionalizing, and unifying" of Islamic rulings in order to protect against "rogue *fatawa* and destructive currents" that threaten "spiritual security" as well as "civil, social, regional, and even international peace."[120] In short, his solution is subordinating religion underneath the direct control of the state.

It is in this context that Sheikh bin Bayyah has expressed skepticism regarding the introduction of democracy to the Middle East, which itself represents an existential threat to political elites in the UAE. Indeed, the Sheikh does not view democracy as the solution to current problems plaguing the Middle East. In his Framework Speech for the Forum for Promoting Peace in Muslim Societies, he states:

> As some Westerners have observed, democracy is the best of the worst. Our purpose here today is not to discuss its benefits and disadvantages, but to consider if Western democracy is capable of resolving fundamental differences and the absence of common ground in our communities. After our experiences with wars that have taken the lives of millions, should we explore different solutions for Muslim societies? Scholars everywhere must condemn fighting and exclusion and commit themselves to peace. Without abolishing the Western concept of democracy, which gives a voice to every individual in societies that are prepared for it, we must establish a series of guarantees so that it promotes peace rather than wars and conflict. We must also be seriously committed to seeking peaceful coexistence and shared benefits. . . . The German philosopher Leo Strauss said, "the pervading evil of democracy is the tyranny of the majority, where the majority, even if by a small percentage, consolidates wealth and power, while the minority is left poor and oppressed. This could last a very long time since the ruling party will resort to any means to remain in power."
>
> Is it not our right and obligation to find a better political solution than democracy and to establish a system based on the principles of consultation (shurah) and higher justice? When we speak of democracy and shurah, we are referring to the true forms of these systems rather than the hypocritical ones we have seen with the corrupt elections in some Arab states. Our approach must employ transparency and goodwill. No party should use victory to inflict financial, moral, religious, or worldly damage on another party. There should be no monopolization, and guarantees must be provided for coexistence, compromise, and mutual concessions. Vengeance, claims of absolute truth, and distorted historical and religious interpretations must be avoided to ensure harmony and accord.
>
> In societies that are not yet ready, the call for democracy is essentially a call for war. Since the human and financial costs of establishing democracy may be very high in societies without common ground, justice in its Islamic sense must be established as a foundation for peace and security . . . democracy should be approached with reservations and must never become a religion. The concept of modernity must also be reconsidered, for modernity does not mean Westernization and moral decline, but, rather, that

we should hold onto our origins while engaging the present era with unity and solidarity rather than with rivalry and confrontation.[121]

Bin Bayyah's discussion of democracy is filled with warnings regarding how the implementation of such a system in societies that are "not ready" for it can result in instability and war. He argues that calling for democracy in such contexts is, essentially, "a call for war." Bin Bayyah also urges the rethinking of what constitutes "modernity" and suggests that the governing systems in the Middle East should not have to mirror Western conceptualizations of what constitutes a legitimate political order. This argument fits well with the narratives espoused by Emirati leadership. Indeed, in an interview with CNN following the outbreak of the Arab uprisings, the ruler of Dubai, Sheikh Mohammed bin Rashid Al-Maktoum, stated, "we have our own democracy. You cannot transport your democracy to us."[122] Nowhere in the rhetoric of bin Bayyah or UAE officials is there a consideration of how the authoritarian status quo that dominates the Middle East could be the source of the instability the region is currently witnessing. Bin Bayyah and Emirati leadership are engaging in what can be considered almost a reverse orientalism: by portraying Muslims and Arabs as "not ready" for democracy and in need of their own unique system of governance, they seek to present themselves as the only viable option for maintaining peace and stability to their Western supporters.

The Arab uprisings, bin Bayyah argues, "deviated from reason, human dignity, morality, and societal benefit."[123] Instead of striving toward the establishment of justice or certain political or human rights, bin Bayyah places a premium on the establishment of "peace." During a panel at the Council on Foreign Relations in Washington, D.C., bin Bayyah explained:

> We believe peace is actually the first right, the first human right. If we want to go to war until all the rights are established and all the wrongs are redressed, then as far as I can tell we'll just annihilate ourselves. The last rights up to the last man, this is a dilemma, it's a dilemma. We believe that we have to change this discourse and recognize that peace is what will pave the road to achieving those rights and life itself. We're not denying grievances, we're not denying the rights of people. Citizens have rights, citizens have rights to have their wrongs redressed. These are sound rights, we all believe in them. But we don't think the road to war or the road of war is the sound road to achieving those rights.[124]

Again, bin Bayyah here stresses the imperative of "peace" over all else, at times insinuating that the drive toward rights or justice is akin to "the road of war." Peaceful protests and calls for change are not differentiated from armed rebellion or acts of terrorism, with all of these phenomena falling under the broad category of "*fitna*" or "war" in bin Bayyah's discourse. Such a discourse narrative is designed to delegitimize all calls for political change by making them synonymous with calls to war, instability, and so on. Instead, bin Bayyah emphasizes the need for obedience. According to bin Bayyah, the *ulema* is not endowed with the right to challenge the ruler, for only the latter is knowledgeable of the nuances necessary for conducting statecraft. He argues that the *ulema* does "not know the facts of the matter or the consequences of particular courses of action" and may not be cognizant of "internal tensions, or external concerns that may lead to civil war, which need to be taken into account in matters of [the] state."[125] Only the ruler, he argues, has the legitimate right to make decisions:

> The religious leaders are not political leaders, which means they should not wear political clothes. This is why we said that only the political leadership has the absolute and exclusive authority to make decisions.[126]

For Sheikh bin Bayyah, obedience to established (state) authority is the only legitimate mechanism through which to achieve his understanding of "peace." The Sheikh argues that obedience is obligatory even if that means waiving one's rights for the collective interest of society:

> Scholars understand obedience based on sound hadiths, established texts, and agreed upon goals and principles, the most important of which are preventing harm, avoiding bloodshed, ensuring peace and stability, promoting good, and repelling evil. Obedience may be expressed by carrying out the law, and this cannot be denied. However, obedience may also be expressed by waiving one's rights, as the Quran says, "Repel evil with that which is best." This second option, waiving one's rights, is a strong moral position and must not be confused with defeat. It earns the admiration of others and forces them to reconsider their positions. As the prophets and saints demonstrate, it is a sublime and honorable position to take. It must not be misunderstood as surrendering to injustice for the sake of peace, for one who makes this choice seeks peace by more just and merciful means, and seeks also to reform the oppressor who is

regarded with pity as a victim of his desires. By waiving one's rights, one chooses reform over discipline. Whoever dismissed this second type of obedience fails to take five issues into consideration:

[1] Evidence from various hadiths, primarily from Sahih Muslim, which was consented upon as narrated by al-Hafiz ibn Hajar and others. [2] The importance placed on avoiding bloodshed in Islam. [3] The preservation of the collective interest of society, which takes precedence over avoiding evil, as can be seen when Harun, Allah's peace and blessings be upon him, said to his brother Musa, Allah's peace and blessings be upon him, "I was afraid that you might say, 'you have divided the Children of Israel and disobeyed my orders.'" [4] The unknown consequences of inciting tribulations (fitan). [5] The understanding that peace offers more opportunities to address issues of concern than do war and conflict.[127]

Hamza Yusuf has expressed similar concerns. He argues that "We do not accept any rebellion (*khurūj*) against our leaders or our public affairs even if they are oppressive."[128] Discussing the Syrian revolution and the collapse of the country into civil war, Yusuf states, "Allah can humiliate whoever he pleases. If you humiliate a ruler, God will humiliate you."[129] His rhetoric mirrors that of bin Bayyah's, arguing that "peace" is the ultimate objective, which is being realized by figures such as bin Bayyah and the Al-Nahyan in the UAE:

The pursuit of peace is a most noble human endeavor. The Qur'an states, "Now if they incline towards peace, then incline to it, and place your trust in God, for God is the all-hearing, the all-knowing. And if they mean to deceive you, surely you can count on God" (8:61–62). This verse indicates that one should not avoid reconciliation out of fear that it may only be an enemy's subterfuge. That is not our teaching. We are asked to seek peace and place our trust in God. Such is the preciousness of peace that its mere possibility, however remote, demands our most sincere and faithful efforts. The New Testament also reminds us, in words attributed to Jesus, peace be upon him, "Blessed are the peacemakers, for they shall be called the dependents of God."

Shaykh Abdullah bin Bayyah is a peacemaker and has placed his trust in God. He believes that peace is not simply the starting point but the only point. War, should it arise, is a disruptive suspension of peace, one that all men of intelligence should seek to end by any means necessary. Shaykh Abdullah once said that the only blessing in war is that when it befalls men, they fervently hope for peace. As for those who claim that calling to peace is canceling out jihad, the converse is true, as Shaykh Abdullah cogently argues: Jihad is not war, and while it does have military applications, Muslims waging war on other Muslims is not one of them. That is called fitnah, something our Prophet, God's peace and blessings upon him, shunned so much that he sought refuge from it.

Shaykh Abdullah, a master of usul—the tools of ijtihad—and a man who profoundly understands the time we live in, is uniquely qualified to determine when the military application of jihad is valid and when it is not. Hence, his call for peace, far from cancelling out jihad, is itself an act of jihad. The pre-Islamic Jahili Arabs knew war all too well, as they lived in societies rife with strife: blood vengeance was their way, and the cycles of violence, like a millstone grinding its grain, constantly ground the bones of their bodies. When Islam appeared as an oasis in the desolate desert where wars were far too common, and the Prophet Muhammad, God's peace and blessings upon him, offered another path, the path of peace through submission, the Arabs saw a way out of their wanton violence that invariably left children without fathers and women without husbands.

A new world order was born, and though not immune at times to violence, it was one in which learning, science, and commerce prevailed, not war, violence, and vengeance. These became the pursuits of men who went forth to form societies that became some of the most tolerant and peaceful in human history. But that was then: this is now a turbulent time for Muslims. Failed states, senseless violence, and teeming refugees now characterize large parts of the Muslim world.

Despite these troubles, some Muslims are still calling, like premodern physicians, for a bloodletting to cure the social body. But blood leads only to more blood, and the body, far from being healed, is further sapped and drained of its strength. Much like the premodern patient whose bloodletting often led to his demise, today's victims of this militant bleeding are drowned in rubble, dazed and confused, wondering when it will all end. Shaykh Abdullah is calling Muslims to end the madness and restore the way of the Prophet Muhammad, God's peace and blessings upon him, the way of peace and prosperity. He is reminding us by using our own sources—the Qur'an, the Sunnah, and the prescriptions of our pious predecessors—that peace, not war, is the only way out. For those who would believe otherwise, let them contemplate the words our

Prophet, God's peace and blessings upon him, repeated throughout his life after each daily prayer: "O Allah, You are Peace, and from You is Peace, and to You returns Peace, so let us live, O our Lord, in Peace."

Shaykh Zayed Al-Nahyan, the Father of the United Arab Emirates, was committed to peace and unity, and it is no surprise that his honorable sons, following in his illustrious footsteps, would be the ones to host and support this powerful initiative from Islam's teaching by the great Mauritanian scholar, Shaykh Abdallah b. Bayyah. With war being waged on peace all around us, Shaykh Abdallah's message is a simple cure: Wage war on war in order to have peace upon peace. For war is not the way: peace is the path. The path is peace.[130]

This "theology of obedience" and "jurisprudence of peace" constructed by Sheikh bin Bayyah and Hamza Yusuf have laid the groundwork for a modernist authoritarianism buttressed by Islamic justifications. By affirming the ultimate authority of the state, these two scholars have built a religio-political vision that delegitimizes all calls for change—whether peaceful or violent—by labeling them as sources of inherent instability. By maintaining a strict emphasis on religious misinterpretations as the source for this "chaos" and instability, they divert attention away from any discussion of how the policies pursued by states throughout the Middle East have fueled the underlying sources of instability in the region.

It is critical to mention the myriad issues that are absent from the discourse of bin Bayyah and Yusuf. As the counterrevolution successfully swept throughout the region, both scholars have remained silent regarding political prisoners, the intensification of authoritarian rule, and human rights abuses across the Middle East, the UAE's various military interventions and initiatives, and so on. Nor have they chosen to engage directly with the body of jurisprudence—the jurisprudence of revolution (*fiqh al-thawra*)—produced during the early stages of the uprisings that seeks to justify peaceful opposition to established authority by distinguishing such actions from armed rebellion. As will be discussed below, these discourses and the religio-political vision constructed by bin Bayyah and Yusuf have been externalized as part of the UAE's branding efforts designed to present Abu Dhabi to its Western partners as a source of stability and peace in a troubled region.

A Western-Oriented Identity: The UAE and "Moderate Islam" Abroad

Central to the UAE's religious soft power strategy is the projection of an image of the Emirates as a source of peace, stability, and progress in a turbulent Middle East region. This carefully constructed "global brand"—directed toward the West, particularly the United States, which remains Abu Dhabi's security guarantor—utilizes "tolerance" and "moderation" as geopolitical instruments. In doing so, the Emirates seeks to bolster its "credibility as a moderate, capable, proactive Arab partner to the United States that is willing to shoulder some of the burden in maintaining Gulf security—unusual in a region where Washington has been repeatedly called on to act as a policeman."[131] As the UAE increasingly wields its accumulated hard power abroad, this image—directed primarily to Western audiences, particularly the United States—is designed to complement these efforts and construct an identity of the Emirates as a "progressive" actor pushing the region back toward "stability."

The promotion of so-called "moderate Islam" as intrinsic to Emirati national identity and politics remains critical to these efforts. As was discussed in Chapter 2, by equating all forms of Islamism (both mainstream and radical) as synonymous with one another, this constructed dichotomy serves to divide Muslims into arbitrary categories of "good" or "bad."[132] The Islam practiced and promoted by the regimes in the Middle East is presented to the West as "good" and "moderate" and is designed to depict these governments as the best—perhaps only—partners capable of working with the West to combat "bad" and "extreme" Islam.

By placing the blame for such "radicalism" entirely on alternative readings of Islam—and framing the solution to such phenomena as the need to reform Islam internally—these governments are simultaneously able to deflect attention away from how their authoritarian policies contribute to extremism while also repressing any they deem as a threat to their own rule under the guise of preventing terrorism and returning the religion to a state of "moderation" and "peace." This framing allows countries such as the UAE to control discussions surrounding Islam, reform, and politics, asserting itself to the forefront of such conversations while presenting themselves as "a center of Islamic reform in American eyes, which in turn helps maintain U.S. interest in the Al-Nahyan's security in the face of both external and internal challenges."[133]

The UAE presents itself to Western audiences as a haven for "moderation" and "tolerance" in the Middle East, constructing an identity that appeals to its international supporters. Abu Dhabi stresses that "values of inclusion, mutual respect and religious freedom have been ingrained in the UAE's DNA since before the country's founding in 1971."[134] According to the UAE embassy in the United States, the Emirates "has a forward-looking vision for the Middle East region—a path that promotes moderate Islam, empowers women, teaches inclusion, encourages innovation and welcomes global engagement."[135] The year 2019 was proclaimed the "Year of Tolerance" within the Emirates, further advancing this image of the UAE as a source of "stability and prosperity" in the Middle East.[136] A leading element of this state-branding campaign is the equating of all forms of Islamism—mainstream and radical—as synonymous with extremism, and all forms of activism or dissent as catalysts for instability. By delegitimizing these actors, only the state and aligned *ulema* are presented as the "legitimate" representatives of Islam, thereby establishing state hegemony over Islamic practice and interpretation.

The attempted delegitimization of mainstream Islamism, particularly the Muslim Brotherhood and its various regional offshoots and affiliates, is thus a primary objective of UAE religious soft power. The Brotherhood has been denounced by the UAE Fatwa Council as a terrorist organization that seeks to "instigate divisions, trigger conflicts and shed blood" and has urged Muslims to avoid the organization "due to its support for violent extremist groups, disputes with leaderships, and disobedience."[137] Both the MCE and the FPPMS have targeted Qatar due to Doha's support for the group, calling upon the Al-Thani to "ensure Arab unity, review its stances, commit to its pledges to end its support for terrorism and stop providing refuge for extremist groups, to not interfere in the affairs of other countries and affect their stability, as well as to commit to good neighborliness and respect the sovereignty of other countries and their independence."[138] Following the blockades launched against Qatar in 2017, the FPPMS issued the following statement in support of the move:

> The Forum Promoting Peace in Muslim Societies, which brings together dozens of ulema, was established in Abu Dhabi, the capital of the UAE—a country of tolerance and peace-making—to call for peace, love, and harmony between the sons and daughters of the Arab and Islamic umma and humanity as a whole; and in order to combat radicalism, extremism, and terrorism. In its annual gatherings and

its various initiatives, the Forum has ceaselessly been calling for solidarity and cooperation between all actors: governments, ulama, and the educated classes, being convinced that terrorism will not be defeated, nor the disease eradicated, except through such solidarity; and due to [the Forum's] intense desire for the spirit of solidarity and its confidence that the logic of cooperation will prevail, because this is the only way for the umma to reach safety.

The Forum has followed with extreme unease the activities of the Qatari government in ripping apart Arab ranks, rebelling against the Gulf family, and insulting the generous faith of Islam by supporting terrorist groups, inciting political instability in safe countries, and inflaming sectarian conflict. [This] has led to remedial efforts by the countries of the Gulf Cooperation Council and several Arab and Islamic countries to limit the evil that stems from the actions of the Qatari government that aim at demolishing the foundations of stability and security in the region. The Presidency of the Forum Promoting Peace, and the Secretariat-General call to the brotherly state of Qatar to reconsider its position, return to the embrace of the Gulf family, relinquish its errors, return to Arab and Islamic ranks in fighting terrorism, and promote unity and stability. Wisdom requires that it rectify its errors and reconsider its stances. As is mentioned in the epistle of [the second Caliph] Umar ibn al-Khattab, may God be pleased with him, "Returning to the truth is better than persisting in falsehood."[139]

In the attempt to delegitimize alternative sources of Islamic authority and competing religio-political visions, the UAE has spearheaded a number of initiatives to define what constitutes "legitimate" Islam. Still directed primarily toward an international—particularly, Western— audience, such initiatives gather together Islamic scholars from across the world to establish a global hegemony on Islamic discourse, practice, and interpretation. Simultaneously, such initiatives are designed to buttress the image of the Emirates abroad as a proper Islamic authority, returning the religion and the Middle East to a state of "stability."

One such initiative was the 2016 International Conference on Sunni Islam co-organized by religious leaders from the UAE, Egypt, and Russia to discuss the question, "who is a Sunni?" Hosted in the Chechen Republic capital of Grozny, the conference was attended by roughly 200 Sunni scholars from around the world and was designed to "establish a moderate approach to political Islamism" and restore vitality to Egypt's Al-Azhar.[140] Those present at the conference included, among others,

Ahmed El-Tayeb, the Grand Imam of Egypt's Al-Azhar and Chairman of the UAE-based MCE; Shawki Allam, the Grand Mufti of Egypt; Ali Gomaa, the former Grand Mufti of Egypt; Abdul Fattah Al-Bizm, the Mufti of Damascus, Syria; and Habib Ali Jifri, head of the UAE-based Tabah Foundation.[141] The conference "identified Wahhabism, Salafism, and the Muslim Brotherhood as 'misguided' interpretations of Islam, much like the Islamic State," and those present "concurred that Russia should establish a satellite channel to convey 'a truthful message of Islam' to counter Aljazeera's support for the Muslim Brotherhood."[142]

Another such initiative was an international conference held in Morocco in 2016, co-organized by the UAE-based FPPMS, and ending with the signing of the "Marrakesh Declaration." Endorsed by dozens of Islamic scholars and representatives from the United Nations and various different governments, the Marrakesh Declaration mirrors the religious rhetoric promoted by the Emirates and was focused primarily on the rights of religious minorities within Muslim-majority countries. In the Foreword, Hamza Yusuf explains the origins of the document, arguing that it emerged in the context of the Arab uprisings:

> The provenance of the Marrakesh Declaration can be traced back to the turmoil and tragedies unleashed by the protests and revolutionary fervor that spread across Arab lands in the past decade. The incendiary ethos of the movements represented a loss of reason, morality, and human dignity, and led to widespread chaos, confusion, and civil wars. And amidst all the death and devastation arose ideologies inimical to Islam and its teachings and values, especially in their persecution of religious minorities in predominantly Muslim countries.[143]

Sheikh bin Bayyah expresses similar arguments within his essay of the Marrakesh Declaration, highlighting the surge of "globally cascading violence," "chaos and conflagration," and the "current state of civil strife" afflicting the Muslim community.[144] Focusing specifically on religious minorities within Muslim-majority countries, he argues, "perhaps one of the most compelling challenges today concerns that of faith-based minorities in Muslim-majority lands. Taking on this challenge is one of the duties of our time, given that today's Muslim communities need a new reading of their social formations and the nature of their national fabric in the contemporary context and the sacred law of Islam, so it can be reconciled with international standards."[145] The "journey" to address this issue, bin Bayyah explains, "began when protests in the

Arab world deviated from reason, human dignity, morality, and societal benefit."[146] Despite the "chaos" and "conflagration" that has ensued following the Arab uprisings, Sheikh bin Bayyah, Hamza Yusuf, and the other scholars present at the signing of the Marrakesh Declaration presented themselves to an international audience as the ones capable of charting a new path for "peace" and "stability."

Interfaith initiatives have likewise assumed a central position in the religious soft power efforts of the UAE. Engagement with other faith communities and leaders abroad not only further advances an image of the Emirates as a tolerant and progressive actor but also presents an opportunity for Abu Dhabi and its aligned scholars and institutions to project themselves internationally as the "legitimate" representatives of the global Muslim community. The closeness of Sheikh bin Bayyah and Hamza Yusuf to various Western governments, particularly Washington, is very helpful in this regard. Both bin Bayyah and Yusuf regularly present the UAE as a vanguard of tolerance, peace, and stability in the Middle East.[147] Similarly, Sheikh bin Bayyah has been praised by the US government as a global voice for moderation and tolerance, while Yusuf continues to be considered one of the most influential Muslim scholars in the West, having worked with numerous administrations in Washington and even serving as a formal advisor to the Trump administration via the "Commission on Unalienable Rights."[148] Sheikh bin Bayyah hailed Yusuf's appointment, stating that his fellow Fatwa Council members "serve as global ambassadors who portray a bright image of the UAE, which has become a model for tolerance and a generous aid donor thanks to the directives of President His Highness Sheikh Khalifa bin Zayed Al-Nahyan for promoting and upholding human rights and fostering inter-cultural dialogue."[149]

The number of interfaith initiatives spearheaded by the UAE or involving institutions based in the Emirates is substantial. In particular, the Emirates has gone to extensive lengths to present itself as a central hub for coexistence and tolerance between the three Abrahamic faiths of Islam, Christianity, and Judaism. Programs such as the UAE's Alliance of Virtue seek to "bring together religious leaders of good-will for the benefit of humanity," and its committee comprises leading Muslim, Christian, and Jewish individuals from around the world.[150] The newly formed Jewish Council of the Emirates serves as the representative body of Jews within the UAE, and in 2019, NYU Chaplain Rabbi Yehuda Sarna was named as the country's first chief rabbi.[151] Also in 2019, Pope Francis traveled to the UAE, where he delivered a Catholic mass and, in conjunction with the Grand Imam of Egypt Ahmed

El-Tayeb, signed the document on "Human Fraternity for World Peace and Living Together."[152] Following the Pope's visit, the UAE announced it was creating the "Abrahamic Family House" complex, which will include a church, mosque, and synagogue.[153] The UAE also hosts a number of worship centers domestically that cater to other religious faiths outside of the Abrahamic tradition, including Hindu, Sikh, and Buddhist temples.[154]

More than any of the other efforts pursued by the UAE, the crowning jewel of the Emirates' interfaith initiatives remains the so-called "Abraham Accords." Ratified under the administration of President Donald Trump in 2020, the Abraham Accords involved the formal normalization of relations between Israel, the UAE, and Bahrain and were later expanded to include Morocco and Sudan as well. These four states joined Egypt and Jordan in formally establishing relations with the state of Israel. The Accords were marketed as a way forward for the Israel–Palestine conflict and a broader framework for "Middle East peace." When the Abraham Accords were announced, signatories emphasized how this historic declaration would be a tool for "maintaining and strengthening peace in the Middle East and around the world based on mutual understanding and coexistence."[155] The UAE described the Accords as a "catalyst for wider change in the Middle East" and a mechanism to "promote regional security, prosperity, and peace for years to come."[156] Former president Donald Trump's son-in-law Jared Kushner, one of the architects of the Accords, claimed that the agreements established "a new paradigm" in the Middle East and have "captured the imaginations of the whole region."[157] However, critics argue that the Abraham Accords are fundamentally oriented toward the advancing of shared political objectives.[158]

The Abraham Accords have been embraced by the UAE's religious soft power network as evidence of Abu Dhabi's "progressive" vision and identity. In a video interview following the signing of the Accords, Sheikh bin Bayyah hailed Emirati leadership for the initiative:

> The initiative that we launched is a futuristic initiative as it represents the vision of the state of the UAE. The great state of the UAE, as embodied by the founder Sheikh Zayed. It was a futuristic vision. This is why the religious leaders of the three Abrahamic religions have called for making peace which is a central value for the three religions. . . . [National] Interests which are beneficial are only decided by the political leadership. They know very well the real benefits and act according to these benefits . . . We have complete

trust in his highness Sheikh Mohammed bin Zayed, may God protect him. This is what the Emirates Fatwa council has agreed upon, that the religious leaders work with us hand in hand to make peace, to look for coexistence and to look for ways to reinforce peace and these values in other leaders and Muslim and non-Muslim peoples.[159]

The UAE Fatwa Council issued the following statement supporting the Accords: "Given that the supreme interest is the de jure determinant of the acts undertaken by the Sovereign Ruler who is the only one that can determine the nation's supreme interests and responsibilities in relation to war and peace, and the relations between nations, the Emirates Fatwa Council blesses the wise leadership's acts for the supreme good for the nation and its people."[160] Likewise, the FPPMS expressed their support for the Accords and the UAE's broader efforts to establish "peace and stability" in the world.[161] Following the signing of the Abraham Accords, the UAE has continued to work closely with Jewish and Christian communities within the West in their shared efforts to promote an image of the Emirates as a force for moderation, peace, and stability in the Middle East. Such initiatives remain critical to the construction of Emirati identity as an actor striving for interfaith "peace" and overall "stability" in the Middle East.

Deconstructing Emirati Religious Soft Power

The evolution of Emirati religious soft power following the Arab uprisings—including its internal variations and relation to the other cases discussed in this book—reflects the analytical framework built in Chapter 1 of this study. An amalgamation of the instrumentalist and constructivist paradigms, Emirati religious soft power was influenced by the four underlying causal mechanisms addressed in this framework: (1) foreign threat perceptions; (2) foreign and domestic threat perceptions (i.e., a "two-level game"); (3) identity; and (4) ideology. The ways in which these four causal mechanisms influenced Emirati religious soft power—and the particular forms these strategies assumed—were shaped by the contexts within which Emirati political elites were operating and the target audiences they sought to influence.

Of these four causal mechanisms, the presence of a domestic threat to the authority and legitimacy of political elites in Abu Dhabi—coupled with and intimately interconnected to the presence of external threats facing the UAE—had the greatest causal impact on Emirati religious soft power. As was discussed, the UAE did not immediately mobilize religion in the efforts to counter such threats to the extent that Saudi Arabia and Qatar did following the uprisings. Instead, Abu Dhabi turned primarily to its newly accumulated wealth and military prowess. Emirati leadership interpreted the eruption of the Arab uprisings as an existential threat to their own authority as well as the broader authoritarian status quo and prevailing regional balance of power from which they have traditionally benefited.

Despite the domestic threat faced by the Al-Nahyan not equaling the levels of opposition witnessed in other countries during the uprisings, Abu Dhabi nonetheless perceived these domestic challenges through an existential lens. The fact that the UAE branch of the Muslim Brotherhood, Islah, along with some elements of secular opposition within the Emirates, was at the forefront of calls for change fueled Abu Dhabi's disdain for political Islamism and raised the perceived threat levels among Emirati political elites. The rise of political Islamist parties across the region greatly exacerbated these concerns. External stimuli came to be filtered through the domestic objective among Emirati political elites to preserve their own authority. Though Abu Dhabi was challenged domestically to a far lesser extent than other states in the region, the response of Emirati authorities was swift and expansive, viewing such opposition as intimately connected to broader calls for change throughout the Middle East. As these threats evolved over time and the specific nature of such threats differed between contexts, so too did Emirati foreign policy and religious soft power adapt to address such challenges. This ultimately led to the further consolidation of religious oversight in the hands of Emirati political elites and a wider securitization of UAE policies at home.

Externally, the UAE viewed the uprisings as a threat to the regional authoritarian status quo and balance of power, both of which Emirati political elites depend on for the sustainment of their own interests. To counter these threats to the status quo, the UAE would become a leading counterrevolutionary force in the Middle East, mobilizing the economic and military power it had amassed—the latter with the help of the United States—over the previous decade. Indeed, though the uprisings represented a threat to Emirati political elites, they also presented the Emirates with a strategic opportunity, namely, by asserting itself as a major regional powerbroker. Central to this new assertiveness abroad was the targeting of not just political Islamist groups but also their state supporters, namely, Qatar. The UAE, alongside Saudi Arabia, led the efforts to isolate Qatar and undermine their support for such actors.

UAE foreign policy during this period centered around countering these perceived interrelated threats stemming from both domestically and abroad.

The efforts of ruling authorities within the UAE to construct a particular state identity and project a specific state image—or "brand"— also heavily influenced the religious soft power strategies developed by Abu Dhabi. Such efforts were intimately connected to the types of threats facing the Al-Nahyan, namely, the presence of both domestic and foreign challenges and the need to balance against both. The specific political threats facing the Al-Nahyan served to considerably influence the religio-political ethos embraced by Abu Dhabi following the Arab uprisings. Emirati political elites had to construct specific internally and externally facing identities for the dual purpose of regime preservation and power projection.

The UAE has sought to project an image of itself as a beacon of religious "moderation," "tolerance," and overall "stability" within the Middle East to a primarily Western audience to best advance the strategic imperatives of Abu Dhabi in the face of such threats. This endeavor by Abu Dhabi to brand itself as a vanguard of "moderate Islam" within a turbulent Middle East was designed primarily to garner external (Western) support for its domestic and regional policies by portraying its rivals—be they state actors or non-state actors—as sources of intolerance and instability. Several institutions were created during the second, counterrevolutionary phase of the Arab uprisings to help project such an image to international audiences. Such an image was designed to legitimize Abu Dhabi's intense crackdown domestically and its assertive foreign policy abroad while still maintaining the support of its security partners in the West. As the UAE increasingly wields its accumulated hard power abroad, this image—directed primarily to Western audiences, particularly the United States—is designed to complement these efforts and construct an identity of the Emirates as a "progressive" actor pushing the region back toward "stability."

Finally, ideological concerns, specifically pertaining to the supported and constructed religio-political visions embraced by political elites within the UAE, also had a profound impact on Emirati religious soft power. Challenged at home and abroad, the UAE needed the ideological flexibility to legitimize its efforts to preserve power domestically while also projecting power abroad. It sought to delegitimize domestic and regional calls for reform by criminalizing all forms of religio-political expression outside of the direct control of the state. The UAE embraced a top-down, statist religio-political vision that renders religion subservient to the state. This vision emphasizes political quietism and absolute obedience to established authority, thereby establishing a strict state monopoly on religious practice and interpretation. The statist religio-political vision proffered by the UAE is presented as a solution to the destabilizing forces plaguing the Middle East. This religio-political vision was marshaled as a legitimizing mechanism buttressing Abu Dhabi's repression at home and aggressive foreign policy abroad as it helped lead the regional counterrevolution.

Central to this ideological vision are the notions of "tolerance," "moderation," and "stability" and how religio-political forces that reside outside of state control are a threat to each. Islamic interpretations or practices outside of strict state control are delegitimized as sources of chaos, intolerance, and *fitna*. So too are calls for change that challenge the ultimate authority of the state. The promulgation of this vision would not materialize into a cohesive strategy until the second, counterrevolutionary phase of the Arab uprisings, when the Emirates embarked on a new campaign of institutionalization to cement this vision in the UAE and project it abroad.

Emirati religious soft power embodies how inherently political considerations among ruling elites influences religious outcomes. Instead of religion influencing and constraining policy, what we witnessed in this chapter was the opposite: religion was shaped, molded, and fashioned by the state in accordance with the strategic interests of political elites in Abu Dhabi, specifically their desire to counter perceived domestic and foreign threats to their own authority. The UAE's embrace of a counterrevolutionary, heavily authoritarian conceptualization of Islam was designed to delegitimize and eliminate all challenges to political elites within the Emirates as well as calls for change elsewhere in the region. Complementing this heavily authoritarian vision was a deliberate effort to project an image of religious "tolerance" and "moderation" to the UAE's Western supporters designed to present the Emirates as a force for positive change in the region and maintain security support for Abu Dhabi. Particular religious identities and ideologies were central to Emirati religious soft power, yet they were themselves constructed first and foremost by the state to achieve inherently political objectives, namely, regime preservation and power projection. It is the constellation of domestic and foreign threats facing political elites in Abu Dhabi as well as their evolution across time and space that most fundamentally shapes the differing ways religion was mobilized as a tool of statecraft by the UAE following the Arab uprisings.

Conclusion

Compared to the other two case studies discussed in this book, Emirati religious soft power as a comprehensive and formal strategy is a relatively new enterprise. At the time of the Arab uprisings, the UAE lacked the necessary resources—influential scholars or institutions—to project religious influence abroad. Therefore, during the counterrevolutionary phase, Abu Dhabi underwent an extensive campaign of institutionalization to manufacture such resources. The UAE was able to construct a religious soft power strategy in such a way that it fit with Abu Dhabi's statist, counterrevolutionary, and ultra-authoritarian vision. Unlike Saudi Arabia, the UAE never possessed strong domestic Islamic institutions. Unlike Qatar, the UAE did not co-opt political Islamist and viewed them as a threat, therefore choosing instead to repress them. When the Emirates moved to construct their strategy of religious soft power, they were able to begin from a relatively clean slate, constructing it in such a way that aligned perfectly with regime interests. MbZ, the architect of this strategy, has molded religion within the Emirates in such a way that buttresses his own authority and places his policies above questioning. With the death of Sheikh Khalifa in 2022 and the rise of MbZ to the presidency within the UAE, this strategy can be expected to continue and intensify.

The UAE's strategy of religious soft power—coupled with the increase in the wielding of economic and military power by the Emirates—has reaped considerable rewards for Abu Dhabi. The regional crackdown on political Islamist movements has served to eliminate the primary perceived threat by UAE leadership. Within the Emirates, Islah has been driven underground, with much of its senior leadership either imprisoned or fleeing abroad. Regionally, the Muslim Brotherhood has faced a wave of repression that has similarly weakened the group's ability to organize or mobilize in the near future. Given these setbacks, Qatar—a primary competitor of Abu Dhabi—has seen its strategy of religious soft power undermined for the time being. The Emirates, on the other hand, has been very successful in capitalizing on the post-uprisings period to assert itself as a major powerbroker in the Middle East and leader of the regional counterrevolution.

Moreover, the UAE's strategy of portraying itself to a Western audience as a source of tolerance, moderation, and stability within the region has reaped considerable benefits. By painting instability in the Middle East as a religious issue, Abu Dhabi has molded discourse surrounding solutions to such problems in a way that neglects the role of authoritarian actors or their policies in fueling widespread grievances. Akin to a form of reverse orientalism, Sheikh bin Bayyah, Hamza Yusuf, and Emirati leadership have portrayed the region as "not ready" for democracy, arguing that Islam—not political systems—needs a fundamental reform. By framing regional instability in this way, the Emirates is able to bypass discussions pertaining to political, economic, or social grievances that resulted in widespread mobilization across the region, instead focusing on the promotion of a vague and abstract "peace."

CONCLUSION

The purpose of this research was to construct a theoretical framework capable of analyzing the differing and often contradictory ways religion is utilized by state actors as a tool of statecraft, particularly within the contemporary Middle East. This study sought to flip the causal script by examining the ways in which political considerations impact how religion is marshaled as a tool of foreign policy. Instead of religion influencing political outcomes, this analysis examined how politics influences religious outcomes. Demonstrated herein is how states appropriate and construct religious discourses, doctrines, histories, and symbols according primarily to the particular threats facing political elites at a given time within specific contexts. The specific threats facing political elites in different contexts, the target audience(s) they sought to influence, and the religious resources available to political elites served to influence and constrain how religion was coupled with a state's broader foreign policy conduct.

The framework of religious soft power created in this book was applied to the cases of Saudi Arabia, Qatar, and the UAE following the Arab uprisings. The religious soft power strategies of these states are a complex amalgamation of material, identity-based, and ideational variables. Yet, all these strategies centered on how best to advance the interests of political elites. These strategies involved the construction of specific identities and ideologies for the advancement of what are inherently political objectives, namely, the imperatives of regime preservation and power projection. The variation observed both between and within the religious soft power strategies of Saudi Arabia, Qatar, and the UAE was primarily the result of how political elites within these three countries maneuvered in the face of a diverse and evolving matrix of perceived threats following the Arab uprisings.

Comparing the Religious Soft Power Strategies of Saudi Arabia, Qatar, and the UAE

After establishing the theoretical framework of religious soft power, this study conducted three in-depth case studies first utilizing process-tracing to detail the causal sequence as it developed and evolved within Saudi Arabia, Qatar, and the UAE, then employing a cross-case comparison in order to juxtapose these sequences and what drove the variation between them. These three cases were chosen not only because they represent the full variation of the dependent variable in question but also due to the broader shift of power within the Middle East toward the Gulf. Awash with oil (and in the case of Qatar, natural gas) revenues; relatively stable compared to "traditional" powers in the region such as Egypt, Syria, and Iraq who are consumed with internal developments; and the lynchpin of American hegemony in the Middle East, the Gulf states are among the primary drivers of political, economic, and military developments in the region.

The variation observed across the three cases examined in this book was determined primarily by the four interconnected causal mechanisms addressed in this analysis: (1) foreign threat perceptions; (2) foreign and domestic threat perceptions (i.e., a "two-level game"); (3) identity; and (4) ideology. These four interconnected mechanisms drove regime policy following the Arab uprisings and helped determine the nature and objectives of the religious soft power strategies constructed by Saudi Arabia, Qatar, and the UAE.

Of these four causal mechanisms, the presence or absence of a perceived domestic threat to regime authority—coupled with and intimately interconnected to the presence of external threats—had the greatest causal impact on the religious soft power strategies adopted by Saudi Arabia, Qatar, and the UAE. Deciphering how to respond to specific threats facing political elites within these three countries was the first step of regime calculus when Riyadh, Doha, and Abu Dhabi encountered the Arab uprisings. It represented the starting point from which Saudi, Qatari, and Emirati religious soft power would emerge as a coherent strategy to protect the authority and legitimacy of political elites within these three cases and project their influence abroad.

Both facing domestic threats viewed by political elites as existential, Saudi Arabia and the UAE approached the Arab uprisings from a fundamentally different position than Qatar. The presence and nature of these threats molded the identities and ideologies that were constructed and embraced by political elites in the efforts of regime preservation and power projection. As these threats evolved over time, so too did their religious soft power strategies in order to preserve and protect the interests of political elites. Instead of religion driving political outcomes—as is commonly assumed in academic and policy analyses focusing on the Middle East—what we witnessed in this research was the opposite: how primarily political considerations drove religious outcomes.

The absence of a considerable perceived domestic threat in Qatar allowed Doha the freedom and maneuverability to focus its efforts externally without having to fear or address domestic opposition. Secured domestically, the Al-Thani benefited from a far wider field of maneuverability than did other states in the region, who became consumed in the face of domestic challenges. This is considerably different from Saudi Arabia and the UAE, both of whom had to deal with the presence of domestic opposition while also attempting to influence events abroad in the wake of the Arab uprisings. Both Saudi Arabia and the UAE interpreted the uprisings through an existential lens primarily because of this domestic opposition. Important too is the intensity of the perceived domestic threat faced by leadership within Saudi Arabia and the UAE. The threat faced by the Al-Saud in Riyadh was arguably more considerable than the threat faced by the Al-Nahyan in Abu Dhabi. Riyadh found itself facing considerable internal opposition from mainstream Sunni Islamists and its marginalized Shi'a population, the latter of which was compounded by widespread Shi'a mobilization across the King Fahd Causeway in Bahrain. On the other hand, Abu Dhabi faced a considerably less-threatening domestic threat. The fact that the UAE branch of the Muslim Brotherhood, Islah, along with some elements of secular opposition within the Emirates, was at the forefront of calls for change fueled Abu Dhabi's disdain for political Islamism and raised the perceived threat levels among Emirati political elites, as did the success of political Islamist movements elsewhere in the region. The response of regime leadership was uncompromising due to the existential lens through which this threat was interpreted.

The presence or absence of a perceived domestic threat was coupled with how regime leadership in Saudi Arabia, Qatar, and the UAE discerned foreign threats that either emerged or were compounded by the events of the Arab uprisings. None of the three states addressed in this book witnessed regime collapse or devolved into civil war as happened to other states in the region. For Qatar, this, combined with the lack of a significant domestic threat, allowed Doha to be primarily externally facing during the Arab uprisings. The uprisings presented Doha with an opportunity to expand its influence, seeking to capitalize on the vacuums emerging from the overthrow of longstanding autocrats, primarily by supporting the Muslim Brotherhood and its various regional offshoots in their own quests for power. With the early successes of political Islamist parties in places such as Tunisia, Egypt, and Libya, such rising forces appeared primed to alter the regional balance and were therefore viewed as appealing partners through which Doha would be able to expand its regional influence.

Yet, this enthusiasm disappeared in the Gulf, where Al-Thani sought to preserve the undemocratic status quo to which they themselves are wedded and feared a future challenge to their own authority could emerge from the presence of a popular democratic paradigm that close to home. In both Bahrain and Yemen, Qatar joined with Saudi Arabia and the UAE to prevent political change and denounce what they framed in sectarian terms as Iranian encroachment. Additionally, the Al-Thani would assume a more defensive posture following the land, air, and naval blockades launched against Qatar in 2017, led by Saudi Arabia and the UAE. Qatar's strategy of religious soft power became increasingly limited in its maneuverability as counterrevolutionary forces across the region gained the upper hand and political Islamists came under intense attack.

For Saudi Arabia and the UAE, the presence of domestic opposition was coupled with an existential threat to the prevailing regional authoritarian status quo and balance of power on which they relied and benefited from. This threat was intimately connected to domestic opposition that emerged in both Saudi Arabia and the UAE. Saudi and Emirati foreign policy during this period centered around countering these perceived interrelated threats stemming from both domestically and abroad. The uprisings compounded Saudi Arabia's intense struggle with Iran for regional hegemony, with religious sectarianism being heavily utilized by both sides in this competition. Additionally, Riyadh was equally threatened by Qatar's support for the ousting of various regional autocrats and Doha's backing of the Muslim Brotherhood, whose early electoral successes in places such as Tunisia, Egypt, and Libya alarmed Saudi leadership. In Syria, Riyadh saw an opportunity to push back against Iran by supporting and arming the opposition to President Bashar Al-Assad, hoping to weaken Tehran's regional alliances. Like Saudi Arabia, the UAE feared the empowerment of political Islamists—particularly the Muslim Brotherhood—throughout the region and Qatar's active support for such movements, as well as Iran's efforts to alter the regional balance of power in their own favor. The uprisings presented Abu Dhabi with an element of opportunity, namely, the ability to wield the considerable hard power they accumulated over the previous two decades to assert themselves as a major regional powerbroker. The UAE would emerge as a leader of the regional counterrevolution, seeking to expand its influence across the Middle East in the process.

The combination—or absence—of these interrelated threats considerably influenced the identities that were constructed and/or appropriated by Riyadh, Doha, and Abu Dhabi following the Arab uprisings. Such threats established the parameters within which ruling elites in these three countries molded and wielded deliberately constructed identities according to the specific contexts within which they were operating. Efforts to construct particular state identities and project internationally a specific state image, or "brand," considerably influenced the religious soft power strategies adopted by the three cases in this book and were intimately connected to the specific threats facing political elites.

Beginning first with Qatar, the absence of a pressing domestic challenge to the authority and legitimacy of the Al-Thani—and the fact that Doha had successfully co-opted mainstream political Islamism—resulted in Doha turning to buttress its image—and influence—among the broader Muslim community, which in the early phase of the Arab uprisings appeared on the cusp of fundamental political change. Qatar sought to project an image of itself as a vanguard of "Muslim causes" following the uprisings, specifically projecting this image to primarily Muslim audiences. By focusing on issues facing Muslims across the world—such as the plight of political prisoners, the deteriorating situation in Palestine, and the oppression of Muslims in China—Doha sought to depict itself as a champion of such issues. This approach was also intimately connected with how Qatar has historically sought to construct its identity internally, encouraging citizens to view themselves as part of the broader global Muslim community. However, following efforts by different actors to push back against Doha for its regional policies—particularly the blockades constituting the 2017 "Gulf Crisis"—the Al-Thani have increasingly encouraged the development of a more nationalistic "Qatari" identity among its citizenry. Additionally, given the successes of counterrevolutionary forces across the region, Qatar has been limited in the extent to which it can project an image of itself as a "vanguard" of change within the region as authoritarian actors have re-entrenched themselves and activists/movements striving for change face increased repression.

Unlike Qatar, the UAE sought to project an image of itself as a beacon of religious "moderation," "tolerance," and overall "stability" within the Middle East to a primarily Western audience to best advance the strategic imperatives of Abu Dhabi in the face of the interrelated threats it faced. This endeavor by Abu Dhabi to brand itself as a vanguard of "moderate Islam" within a turbulent Middle East was designed primarily to garner external (Western) support for its domestic and regional policies by portraying its rivals—be they state actors or non-state actors—as sources of intolerance and instability. Such an image was designed to legitimize Abu Dhabi's intense crackdown domestically and its assertive foreign policy abroad while still maintaining the support of its security partners in the West. Domestically, Abu Dhabi projected an image of itself as a legitimate Islamic authority against which protests were strictly prohibited to delegitimize those calling for reforms. Religion inside the UAE was one of the many mechanisms used to promote and legitimize a cohesive "Emirati" identity as Abu Dhabi increasingly encourages the growth of nationalism internally.

Finally, in many ways, Saudi Arabia engaged in an identity-balancing act following the Arab uprisings, utilizing different images when operating in different contexts in order to best advance the strategic imperatives of the Al-Saud in the face of such threats. The Al-Saud has sought to present itself to the Muslim community as the center of global (Sunni) Islamic authority while also projecting an image of tolerance and moderation to the West. Depicting itself as the ultimate legitimate Islamic authority to both an internal and an external audience, Riyadh strove to assert its "brand" as a leader of the Sunni Muslim community following the Arab uprisings, hedging against threats to this identity both internally and externally. This involved the attempted delegitimization of those challenging or rivaling such claims as well as presenting itself as a Sunni "bulwark" against an "expansionist" Shi'a Iran. Saudi Arabia's "branding" efforts were also directed toward the West, championing Riyadh as a leader of "moderate Islam" and a reliable partner in the fight against extremism. Such an image was designed to legitimize Riyadh's intense crackdown domestically and its assertive foreign policy abroad while still maintaining the support of its security partners in the West. Both branding efforts have been remolded following the rise of Crown Prince Mohammed bin Salman to complement his nationalist project and campaign to solidify ultimate authority domestically.

Ideological concerns, specifically pertaining to the supported and constructed religio-political visions embraced by leadership in the three countries under examination, also influenced the religious soft power strategies of the three cases addressed in this book and were likewise intimately connected to the specific threats facing political elites. The specific threats facing political elites in Saudi Arabia, Qatar, and the UAE considerably influenced the religio-political ethos they embraced as they maneuvered ideologically to counter such challenges and promote their own interests.

Beginning first with Qatar, Doha embraced a bottom-up, "republican," society-oriented religio-political vision abroad to support the uprisings in places such as Tunisia, Egypt, Libya, and Syria. This approach adopted by Qatar was supported via the construction of a new body of Islamic jurisprudence—*fiqh al-thawra* (the jurisprudence of revolution)—designed to legitimize peaceful opposition to established authority within the contemporary nation-state. Facing no considerable threat at home and portraying itself as a supporter of political reform in the Middle East, the Al-Thani were able to encourage the promotion of this vision without fearing the undermining of their own authority domestically. Doha provided a platform for its architects so long as they remained externally focused. However, this vision was not applied holistically: in both Bahrain and Yemen, challenges to the prevailing status quo were denounced through sectarian framing as inherently illegitimate. Again, such calls for change within the Gulf were viewed as too close to home for the Al-Thani and potentially jeopardizing the future stability of their rule if a popular democratic paradigm were to emerge next door.

On the other hand, the UAE embraced a religio-political vision diametrically opposed to fiqh al-thawra. Indeed, Abu Dhabi constructed a top-down, statist conceptualization of Islam that renders religion subservient to the state, which maintains ultimate authority. Central to this ideological vision are the notions of "tolerance," "moderation," and "stability" and how religio-political forces that reside outside of state control are a threat to each. This vision emphasizes political quietism and absolute obedience to established authority, thereby establishing a strict state monopoly on religious practice and interpretation. The statist religio-political vision proffered by the UAE is presented as a solution to the destabilizing forces plaguing the Middle East. Islamic interpretations or practices outside of strict state control are delegitimized as sources of chaos, intolerance, and fitna. So too are calls for change that challenge the ultimate authority of the state. This religio-political vision was marshaled as a legitimizing mechanism buttressing Abu Dhabi's repression at home and aggressive foreign policy abroad as it helped lead the regional counterrevolution. The Emirates embarked on a new campaign of institutionalization following the uprisings to cement this vision in the UAE and project it abroad.

Finally, Saudi Arabia embraced a top-down, heavily traditionalist religio-political vision of Islam that equates peaceful protests and calls for change as synonymous with rebellion, which remains strictly prohibited. Like in the UAE, this quietist vision seeks to delegitimize all religious practice and interpretation outside of the strict approval of the state. This religio-political vision was marshaled as a legitimizing mechanism buttressing Riyadh's domestic policies—namely, repression at home—and aggressive foreign policy abroad as it helped lead the regional counterrevolution. Sectarianism, both as an ideological tool of counterrevolution and as a justification for military action, was also critical to Riyadh's efforts in quashing calls for change perceived as threatening and supporting armed opposition in Syria and direct military intervention in Yemen. Saudi authorities continue to mobilize Islam as an ideational mechanism to legitimize the rule of the Al-Saud while delegitimizing those proffering alternative conceptualizations of the relationship between religion and politics.

The variation observed between these three cases and the myriad different, and often competing, ways religion was marshaled by these actors as a tool of statecraft was primarily the result of inherently political phenomena. In flipping the causal arrow, this research challenged conventional assumptions regarding the relationship between religion and politics, demonstrating how political considerations impact religious outcomes. The framework of religious soft power developed herein provides a powerful new analytical lens through which to reassess the relationship between religion and international politics.

Scholarly and Policy Implications

The research conducted in this book yields considerable scholarly and policy-oriented implications.

Beginning first with the broadest level of scholarly and theoretical debates, this research contributes considerably to the academic community's understanding of the role of religion as it relates to foreign policy within an increasingly post-liberal world order. As the United States' moment of unipolarity increasingly comes to an end and other actors with alternative histories, threat perceptions, identities, ideologies, and so on, begin to assert themselves more forcefully—whether at a regional or global level—understanding the motivations of such actors and the causal agents driving their actions will be imperative. By bridging the instrumentalist and constructivist paradigms—and the underlying causal mechanisms within them—the framework of religious soft power provides a powerful new analytical lens through which to examine such relationships. In particular, the novel contribution of this research is how it challenges conventional understandings of the relationship between religion and foreign policy, flipping the causal arrow and creating a new analytical lens through which to examine how political considerations impact religious outcomes.

It is the intersection of inherently political phenomena—the need to counter perceived threats at both the domestic and international levels—that has the most causal impact on the variation between how different states harness religion as a tool of statecraft. Indeed, this constellation—or matrix—of threats is the originating point from which political elites mobilize religious narratives, doctrines, jurisprudence, identities, and so on to preserve their own authority. When a domestic threat to regime elites is present, the state must devote resources to combating this internal challenge and preserving the legitimacy of the status quo. If this internal threat is compounded by an interconnected external threat—and if this interrelated threat is perceived by regime leadership as existential in nature—the foreign policy conduct of the state will be centered around combating these intimately tethered threats to political elites. When a domestic threat is absent or at a level perceived as insignificant enough to considerably challenge the authority of regime elites, the state will benefit from a far wider field of maneuverability given that political elites will have more flexibility to divert their resources to advancing their interests externally without the fear of being challenged internally. Regime preservation will be far easier to maintain, allowing political elites to shift their focus more toward power projection. The form(s) religion assumes will be influenced by these threat perceptions, meaning political elites will pick and choose—or, where absent, construct their own—religious narratives, doctrines, jurisprudence, and identities through which to best preserve and advance their own strategic interests.

Second, this research contributes to debates surrounding Islam and its relationship with politics. Within numerous academic and policy circles, there has been a tendency to assume that ideology and/or identity are the primary drivers of how Muslim states utilize Islam as part of their domestic and foreign policies. The idea that Islam—due to being "unique" or "exceptional"[1]—somehow abrogates traditional political science categories and that the behavior of Muslim heads of state is the result of some immutable Islamic influence does not hold up to scrutiny here. Instead, this research explains how political considerations and elite interests—namely, desires to counter threats to preserve regime authority and project power abroad—drive how Islam is marshaled as a tool of statecraft. Instead of Islam being "exceptional" and requiring unique tools of analysis, conventional political science categories remain capable of explaining most of the variation between and within these cases.

This research also contributes considerably to the scholarly debates surrounding the emergence of a new regional order in the Middle East following the 2011 Arab uprisings and the role of religion within this order. Geopolitical power in the Middle East has continued to shift toward the Gulf, allowing states such as Saudi Arabia, Qatar, and the UAE to amass unprecedented levels of regional and global influence. Regional geopolitical competitions now largely revolve around Gulf actors, who have expanded their foreign policy activities to almost every corner of the broader Middle East. The mobilization of religion in pursuit of these foreign policy objectives is commonplace. Following the uprisings, much has been written concerning the regional rivalry between Saudi Arabia and Iran, particularly how each has mobilized Sunni and Shi'a Islam (respectively) to advance their own interests. However, this research focuses on the often-overlooked dimension of intra-Sunni competition. Indeed, one of the most defining features of the post-2011 uprisings period has been the vociferous struggle over religious authority within Sunnism between what can be called the "post-Islamists" (Muslim Brotherhood and aligned groups), radical Salafi-jihadist groups (such as Daesh and *al-Qaeda*), and established state religious institutions.

This research explores in depth this intra-Sunni struggle for religio-political authority and how this competition influenced foreign policy decision-making. It demonstrates how different actors adopt and construct different—at times, contradicting—Islamic narratives, symbols, histories, and jurisprudence to advance their own interests and balance against competing conceptualizations regarding the relationship between Islam and politics. Furthermore, this book explores how religion has been repurposed in certain ways to buttress the increasingly top-down nationalist reorientations currently underway throughout many of the Gulf monarchies. As the matrix of threats facing political elites in these countries has evolved, so too have their strategies of religious soft power to counter them, with religion now increasingly used to supplement the government-sponsored ultranationalism being promoted across the Gulf.

The findings produced by this book also contain considerable policy implications, particularly for the United States, which remains the unparalleled military power within the region and the upholder of the political and security status quo. American foreign policy in the Middle East—particularly as it relates to Islam—has been littered with orientalist preconceptions and fundamental misunderstandings of the region's political, social, and religious landscapes. First, a serious disconnect remains between how US policymakers conceptualize Islam—and the supposed "Islamic motivations" of different actors in the region—and how religion is instrumentalized by different actors to advance their own strategic interests. The cases discussed in this book spotlight the politics that often surround the utilization of religion as a tool of statecraft, whether it be to counter perceived domestic or foreign threats, project a particular "brand" to an international audience, or promote a particular ideological vision regarding the relationship between Islam and political authority.

Of particular interest for the West is the examination herein detailing the inherently political context within which the international promotion of religious tolerance and "moderate Islam" is currently taking form. Indeed, the new international enterprise of "moderate Islam" pursued by various states within the Middle East has been used as a mechanism by these actors to present themselves as champions of tolerance, moderation, and stability while delegitimizing alternative centers of religious authority or calls for change as inherently "extreme" and destabilizing. Such discourse resonates in many circles within the West due to the continued prevalence of orientalist and Islamophobic influences. Though such efforts remain directed primarily toward the West, they have also evolved to include other global powers, particularly Russia and China, as they expand their presence in the Middle East. While the overwhelming majority of analyses examining the increasing role of Moscow and Beijing in the Middle East tend to focus on their expanding political, economic, and military footprints, this research has highlighted how religious soft power also plays an important role in these relationships.

Lastly, an area of both scholarly and policy importance addressed in this book concerns the relationship between Islam, democracy, and authoritarianism. Debates regarding the compatibility of Islam and democracy have traditionally focused exclusively on whether Islam as a faith tradition can reconcile itself with the primary tenets of a pluralistic and democratic political system.[2] Regularly absent from such discussions is how state authorities within Muslim-majority countries often have a vested interest in swaying such debates to advance their own objectives. This is particularly the case within the Middle East, where state actors seek to preserve the regional authoritarian status quo. In many ways, by capitalizing on ignorance concerning Islam in the West and often widespread feelings of Islamophobia, such actors are able to present themselves as the only ones capable of ensuring "stability" and "order" in a region where the inhabitants are "not ready" for democracy.

In addition to these considerable scholarly and policy-oriented implications of the research herein, this book spotlights a lucrative area of future research: analyzing these religious soft power strategies from the perspective of the religious "consumer." As explained in the introduction, the analysis herein has examined religious soft power strategies as advanced by state actors—the "producers" of such strategies—but it remains to be seen how those on the receiving end of these strategies interpreted and internalized these efforts. In other words, how effective are these religious soft power strategies among target audiences? Are the instruments of these religious soft power strategies—the specific scholars and institutions—viewed widely as authoritative and legitimate by the Muslim community? Are some viewed as more legitimate than others? Are they viewed as legitimate representatives of Islam by those in the West? Such questions remain to be answered. It is my hope that the framework and empirical evidence detailed in this book will serve as a foundation for future research on religious soft power as a tool of statecraft and the ever-evolving relationship between Islam and politics in the Middle East.

The Future of Religious Soft Power in the Middle East

Religious soft power in the Middle East will continue to be influenced by internal circumstances within specific countries as well as wider regional and international developments. Though these contexts are rapidly evolving, the four causal mechanisms addressed within this book will continue to guide how states ultimately interpret and respond to such phenomena. Religion as a tool of statecraft will be constructed and instrumentalized according to the specific context within which these states are operating at any given time. Still, religion as a mechanism of soft power is but one "tool" at the disposal of the state and is complemented by other soft power initiatives as well as the use of hard power.

For now, it appears counterrevolutionary forces have emerged victorious in the period following the Arab uprisings. Civil society in the Middle East—both secular and religious—has largely been driven underground. Authoritarian rule across the Middle East has become more intensified and personalized, with "strongman" personalities such as Saudi Crown Prince Mohammed bin Salman, UAE president Mohammed bin Zayed, Tunisian president Kais Saied, and Egyptian president Abdel Fattah El-Sisi amassing unprecedented levels of executive power in their countries. This has gone hand in hand with the intensification of repression throughout the region. Economically, the IMF continues to issue warnings over the horrendous devolution of economies across the Middle East and North Africa due to chronic mismanagement and corruption as well as external shocks such as the war in Ukraine.

However, the notion that such trends are sustainable over the long term neglects the growing animosity throughout the Middle East toward state authorities. Notably, the war in Gaza has shattered the façade of stability presented by regional counterrevolutionary forces. Hamas's attack against Israel on October 7, 2023, and Israel's subsequent military campaign in Gaza have resulted in the annihilation of life and infrastructure in the enclave while dragging the region to the brink of full-scale war. In the wake of the war in Gaza, the three countries addressed in this book have largely continued their existing religious soft power strategies.

Qatar has continued its community-oriented, bottom-up approach, using its relationship with Hamas to position itself diplomatically as a mediator—namely, the effort to broker an enduring ceasefire in Gaza. The IUMS has repeatedly condemned Israel's actions in Gaza, denouncing Israel's actions as "genocide" and arguing it is an "Islamic duty" for Arab and Islamic governments to intervene in order to prevent "mass destruction."[3] Saudi Arabia has been engaged in a delicate balancing act. This has included criticizing Israel's actions rhetorically—and hosting a summit of Islamic nations to condemn Israel's actions—while still maintaining its unofficial strategic ties with Israel, in particular, its attempt to proceed with a US-led "megadeal" that would entail Israel–Saudi normalization and unprecedented concessions granted to the Kingdom from the United States in return.[4] Sheikh Abdulrahman Al-Sudais, Imam of the Grand Mosque in Mecca, prayed for God to grant the Palestinians victory but coupled this with saying the mosque is a place for worship, not the airing of political slogans.[5] The UAE, also rhetorically critical of Israel's actions, has not disrupted its relationship with Israel in any meaningful way, nor is it likely to do so. Abdullah Bin Bayyah and the UAE Fatwa Council have been silent on Gaza, with the Council keeping its focus limited to humanitarian efforts directed by Abu Dhabi.[6] Keen to maintain its strategic relationship with Israel, the UAE remains a party to the Abraham Accords.

Even when the war in Gaza ends, the underlying sources of future instability and conflict across the Middle East will remain. As the grievances that were at the heart of the Arab uprisings grow considerably worse and new fault lines emerge, so too will popular discontent and the likelihood of unrest increase considerably. It can be expected that the strategic wielding of religion will continue to play a role in these struggles.

NOTES

Introduction

1. Bettiza, Gregorio. "States, Religions, and Power: Highlighting the Role of Sacred Capital in World Politics." *Berkley Center for Religion, Peace, and World Affairs*, March 30, 2020, https://berkleycenter.georgetown.edu/publications/states-religions-and-power-highlighting-the-role-of-sacred-capital-in-world-politics.
2. Ayoob, Mohammed. "Political Islam: Image and Reality." *World Policy Journal*, Vol. 21, No. 3, 2004, pp. 1–14.
3. Darwich, May. "The Challenge of Bridging IR and Area Studies in Middle East International Relations Teaching." *LSE Middle East Center Blog*, August 15, 2018, https://blogs.lse.ac.uk/mec/2015/08/18/the-challenge-of-bridging-ir-and-area-studies-in-middle-east-international-relations-teaching/.
4. Lewis, Bernard. "The Roots of Muslim Rage." *The Atlantic*, September 1990, https://www.theatlantic.com/magazine/archive/1990/09/the-roots-of-muslim-rage/304643/.
5. Huntington, Samuel. *The Clash of Civilizations and the Remaking of World Order*. Simon and Schuster, 1996.
6. Bolling, Landrum. "Religion and Politics in the Middle East Conflicts." *Middle East Journal*, Vol. 45, No. 1, 1991, pp. 125–30.
7. Hamid, Shadi. *Islamic Exceptionalism: How the Struggle Over Islam is Reshaping the World*. St. Martin's Press, 2016.
8. Gerring, John. "What is a Case Study and What is it Good for?" *The American Political Science Review*, Vol. 98, No. 2, 2004, pp. 341–54.
9. Beach, Derek. "Process-Tracing Methods in Social Science." *Oxford Research Encyclopedias*, 2017.
10. Collier, David. "Understanding Process Tracing." *Political Science and Politics*, Vol. 44, No. 4, 2011, pp. 823–30.
11. Goldstone, Jack. "Comparative Historical Analysis and Knowledge Accumulation in the Study of Revolutions." in *Comparative Historical Analysis in the Social Sciences*, ed. James Mahoney and Dietrich Rueschemeyer. Cambridge University Press, 2003, pp. 41–90.
12. George, Alexander and Bennett, Andrew. *Case Studies and Theory Development in the Social Sciences*. MIT Press, 2005.
13. Ibid.
14. Przeworski, Adam and Teune, Henry. *The Logic of Comparative Social Inquiry*. John Wiley and Sons, 1970.

15 Lynch, Mark. *The New Arab Wars: Uprisings and Anarchy in the Middle East*. Public Affairs, 2017.
16 Freer, Courtney. *Rentier Islamism: The Influence of the Muslim Brotherhood in Gulf Monarchies*. Oxford University Press, 2018.

Chapter 1

1 Fischer, Markus. "Culture and Foreign Politics." In *The Limits of Culture: Islam and Foreign Policy*, ed. Brenda Shaffer. MIT Press, 2006, pp. 27–64.
2 Ibid.
3 Houghton, David. "Reinvigorating the Study of Foreign Policy Decision Making: Toward a Constructivist Approach." *Foreign Policy Analysis*, Vol. 3, No. 1, 2007, pp. 24–45.
4 Ruggie, John. *Constructing the World Polity: Essays on International Institutionalization*. Routledge, 1998.
5 Wendt, Alexander. *Social Theory of International Politics*. Cambridge University Press, 1999.
6 Haynes, Jeffrey. ""Religion and International Relations: What Do We Know and How Do We Know It?"" *Religions*, Vol. 12, No. 5, 2021, pp. 1–14.
7 Adiong, Nassef Manabilang, et al. *Islam in International Relations: Politics and Paradigms*. Routledge, 2018; Berger, Maurits. *Religion and Islam in Contemporary International Relations*. Netherlands Institute of International Relations, 2010; Fox, Jonathan and Sandler, Shmuel. *Brining Religion into International Relations*. Palgrave Macmillan, 2004; Fox, Jonathan and Sandal, Nukhet. "Toward Integrating Religion into International Relations Theory." *Zeitschrift für internationale Beziehungen*, Vol. 17, No. 1, 2010, pp. 149–59; Fox, Jonathan and Sandal, Nukhet. "Integrating Religion into International Affairs." In *Routledge Handbook of Religion and Politics*, ed. Jeffrey Haynes. Routledge, 2016, pp. 270–83; Sandal, Nukhet. *Religion in International Relations: Interactions and Possibilities*. Routledge, 2015; Sandal, Nukhet and James, Patrick. "Religion and International Relations Theory: Towards a Mutual Understanding." *European Journal of International Relations*, Vol. 17, No. 1, 2010, pp. 3–25; Sheikh, Mona Kanwal. "How Does Religion Matter? Pathways to Religion in International Relations." *Review of International Studies*, Vol. 38, No. 1, 2012, pp. 365–92; Snyder, Jack. *Religion and International Relations*. Columbia University Press, 2011.
8 Mandaville, Peter and Hamid, Shadi. "Islam as Statecraft: How Governments Use Religion in Foreign Policy." *Brooking Institution*, 2018.
9 Acharya, Amitav. *The End of American World Order*. Polity, 2018.
10 Fox and Sandler. *Brining Religion into International Relations*.

11 Haynes, Jeffrey. "Religion in Foreign Policy." In *The Oxford Encyclopedia of Foreign Policy Analysis*, ed. Cameron G. Thies. Oxford University Press, 2017.
12 Hill, Christopher. *The Changing Politics of Foreign Policy*. Palgrave, 2003.
13 Putnam, Robert. "Diplomacy and Domestic Politics: The Logic of Two-Level Games." *International Organization*, Vol. 42, No. 3, 1998, pp. 427–69.
14 Neack, Laura. *The New Foreign Policy: Complex Interactions, Competing Interests*. Rowman and Littlefield, 2014.
15 Maoz, Zeev and Henderson, Errol. *Scriptures, Shrines, Scapegoats, and World Politics*. University of Michigan Press, 2020.
16 Tabaar, Mohammad Ayatollahi. *Religious Statecraft: The Politics of Islam in Iran*. Columbia University Press, 2018.
17 Maoz and Henderson. *Scriptures, Shrines, Scapegoats, and World Politics*.
18 Tabaar. *Religious Statecraft*.
19 Maoz and Henderson. *Scriptures, Shrines, Scapegoats, and World Politics*.
20 Ibid.
21 Huang, Reyko. "Religious Instrumentalism in Violent Conflict." *Ethnopolitics*, Vol. 19, No. 2, 2020, pp. 150–61.
22 See Walzer, Michael. "The New Tribalism." *Dissent Magazine*, Spring 1992, https://www.dissentmagazine.org/article/the-new-tribalism; Kaplan, Robert. *The Coming Anarchy: Shattering the Dreams of the Post-Cold War*. Vintage, 2001; Lewis, Bernard. "The Roots of Muslim Rage." *The Atlantic*, September 1990, https://www.theatlantic.com/magazine/archive/1990/09/the-roots-of-muslim-rage/304643/; Cook, Michael. *Ancient Religion, Modern Politics: The Islamic Case in Comparative Perspective*. Princeton University Press, 2016; Isaacs, Harold. *Idols of the Tribe: Group Identity and Political Change*. Harvard University Press, 1989; Conner, Walker. *Ethnonationalism*. Princeton University Press, 1993, and so on. However, no work better encapsulates the primordialist camp than Huntington, Samuel. *The Clash of Civilizations and the Remaking of World Order*. Simon and Schuster, 1996.
23 Huntington, Samuel. *The Clash of Civilizations and the Remaking of World Order*. Simon and Schuster, 1996.
24 Fox and Sandal. "Toward Integrating Religion into International Relations Theory."
25 Fox and Sandler. *Brining Religion into International Relations*.
26 Geertz, Clifford. *Islam Observed: Religious Development in Morocco and Indonesia*. University of Chicago Press, 1971; Hodgson, Marshall. *The Venture of Islam*. University of Chicago Press, 1974; Asad, Talal. *The Idea of an Anthropology of Islam*. Georgetown University Press, 1986; Ahmed, Shahab. *What is Islam? The Importance of Being Islamic*. Princeton University Press, 2016.

27 Aydin, Cemil. *The Idea of the Muslim World: A Global Intellectual History*. Harvard University Press, 2019.
28 Stein, Sabina. "Competing Political Science Perspectives on the Role of Religion in Conflict." Center for Security Studies, ZTH Zurich, 2011, https://css.ethz.ch/content/dam/ethz/special-interest/gess/cis/center-for-securities-studies/pdfs/Politorbis-52-21-26.pdf.
29 Sheikh. "How Does Religion Matter?"
30 Huang. "Religious Instrumentalism in Violent Conflict."
31 Maoz and Henderson. *Scriptures, Shrines, Scapegoats, and World Politics*.
32 Fischer. "Culture and Foreign Politics."
33 Ibid.
34 Tambiah, S. J. *Buddhism Betrayed? Religion, Politics, and Violence in Sri Lanka*. University of Chicago Press, 1992.
35 Wilhelmsen, J. "Between a Rock and a Hard Place: The Islamization of the Chechen Separatist Movement." *Europe-Asia Studies*, Vol. 57, No. 1, 2005, pp. 35–59.
36 Tabaar. *Religious Statecraft*.
37 Kaufman, Stuart. *Modern Hatreds: The Symbolic Politics of Ethnic War*. Cornell University Press, 2001.
38 Phillips, Christopher. *The Battle for Syria: International Rivalry in the New Middle East*. Yale University Press, 2016.
39 Maoz and Henderson. *Scriptures, Shrines, Scapegoats, and World Politics*.
40 Wehrey, Frederic. *Beyond Sunni and Shia: The Roots of Sectarianism in a Changing Middle East*. Oxford University Press, 2018; Hashemi, Nader and Postel, Danny. *Sectarianization: Mapping the New Politics of the Middle East*. Oxford University Press, 2017; Abdo, Geneive. *The New Sectarianism: The Arab Uprisings and the Rebirth of the Sunni-Shia Divide*. Oxford University Press, 2016; Cammett, Melani, et al. *A Political Economy of the Middle East*. Routledge, 2013; Gengler, Justin. *Group Conflict and Political Mobilization in Bahrain and the Arab Gulf: Rethinking the Rentier State*. Indiana University Press, 2015.
41 Nasr, Vali. "The Rise of Muslim Democracy." *Journal of Democracy*, Vol. 16, No. 2, 2005, pp. 13–27; Schwedler, Jillian. *Faith in Moderation: Islamist Parties in Jordan and Yemen*. Cambridge University Press, 2007; Yadav, Stacey. "Understanding What Islamists Want: Public Debate and Contestation in Lebanon and Yemen." *Middle East Journal*, Vol. 64, No. 2, 2010, pp. 199–213; Masoud, Tarek. *Counting Islam: Religion, Class, and Elections in Egypt*. Cambridge University Press, 2014; Warner, Carolyn. "Christian Democracy in Italy: An Alternative Path to Religious Party Moderation." *Party Politics*, Vol. 19, No. 2, 2013, pp. 256–76; Pahwa, Sumita. "Pathways of Islamist Adaptation: The Egyptian Muslim Brothers' Lessons for Inclusion Moderation Theory." *Democratization*, Vol. 24, No. 6, 2017, pp. 1066–84.

42 Stein. "Competing Political Science Perspectives on the Role of Religion in Conflict."
43 Fischer. "Culture and Foreign Politics."
44 Tabaar. *Religious Statecraft.*
45 Ibid.
46 Fischer. "Culture and Foreign Politics."
47 Flockhart, Trine. "Constructivism and Foreign Policy." In *Foreign Policy: Theories, Actors, Cases*, ed. Steve Smith et al. Oxford University Press, 2016, pp. 79–94.
48 Fox and Sandal. "Toward Integrating Religion into International Relations Theory."
49 Fischer. "Culture and Foreign Politics."
50 Houghton. "Reinvigorating the Study of Foreign Policy Decision Making."
51 Ruggie. *Constructing the World Polity.*
52 Wendt. *Social Theory of International Politics.*
53 Maoz and Henderson. *Scriptures, Shrines, Scapegoats, and World Politics.*
54 Ibid.
55 Hopf, Ted. "The Promise of Constructivism in International Relations Theory." *International Security*, Vol. 23, No. 1, 1998, pp. 171–200.
56 Wendt, Alexander. "Anarchy is What States Make of It." *International Organization*, Vol. 46, No. 3, 1992, pp. 391–425.
57 Warner, Carolyn and Walker, Stephen. "Thinking About the Role of Religion in Foreign Policy: A Framework for Analysis." *Foreign Policy Analysis*, Vol. 7, No. 1, 2011, pp. 113–35.
58 Fox and Sandal. "Toward Integrating Religion into International Relations Theory."
59 Hurd, Ian. "Legitimacy and Authority in International Politics." *International Organization*, Vol. 53, No. 2, 1999, pp. 379–408.
60 Fox and Sandal. "Integrating Religion into International Affairs."
61 Barnett, Michael and Telhami, Shibley. *Identity and Foreign Policy in the Middle East.* Cornell University Press, 2002.
62 Hene, Peter. *Religious Appeals in Power Politics.* Cornell University Press, 2023.
63 Salloukh, B. "Overlapping Contests and Middle East International Relations: The Return of the Weak Arab State." *American Political Science Association*, Vol. 50, No. 3, 2017, pp. 660–3.
64 Haas, Mark. "Ideological Polarity and Balancing in Great Power Politics." *Security Studies*, Vol. 23, No. 4, 2014, pp. 715–53.
65 Freer, Courtney. *Rentier Islamism: The Influence of the Muslim Brotherhood in Gulf Monarchies.* Oxford University Press, 2018.
66 Nexon, Daniel. "Religion and International Relations: No Leap of Faith Required." In *Religion and International Relations Theory*, ed. Jack Snyder. Columbia University Press, 2011, pp. 141–67.

67 Ibid.
68 Fox and Sandal. "Toward Integrating Religion into International Relations Theory."
69 Tabaar. *Religious Statecraft.*
70 Ibid.
71 Fearon, James. "Domestic Politics, Foreign Policy, and Theories of International Relations." *Annual Review of Political Science*, Vol. 1, No. 1, 1998, pp. 289–313.
72 Tayfur, Fatih M. "Systemic-Structural Approaches, World-System Analysis, and the Study of Foreign Policy." *METU Studies in Development*, Vol. 27, No. 3–4, 2000, pp. 265–99.
73 Waltz, Kenneth. *Theory of International Politics*. Addison-Wesley Publishing Co., 1979.
74 Ibid.
75 Hinnebusch, Raymond. *The International Politics of the Middle East*. Manchester University Press, 2015.
76 Walt, Stephen. *The Origins of Alliances*. Cornell University Press, 1987.
77 Davis, James. *Threats and Promises: The Pursuit of International Influence*. Johns Hopkins University Press, 2000.
78 Walt. *The Origins of Alliances.*
79 Putnam. "Diplomacy and Domestic Politics."
80 Neack. *The New Foreign Policy.*
81 Hagan, Joe. "Domestic Political Explanations in the Analysis of Foreign Policy." In *Foreign Policy Analysis: Continuity and Change in its Second Generation*, ed. Laura Neack, et al. Pearson, 1995, pp. 117–44.
82 Moravcsik, Andrew. "Taking Preferences Seriously: A Liberal Theory of International Relations." *International Organization*, Vol. 51, No. 4, 1997, pp. 513–53.
83 Snyder, Jack. *Myths of Empire: Domestic Politics and International Ambition*. Cornell University Press, 1991.
84 Hagan. "Domestic Political Explanations in the Analysis of Foreign Policy."
85 Tayfur. "Systemic-Structural Approaches, World-System Analysis, and the Study of Foreign Policy."
86 Russett, Bruce, et al. "The Democratic Peace." *International Security*, Vol. 19, No. 4, 1995, pp. 164–84.
87 Levy, Jack. "Domestic Politics and War." *The Journal of Interdisciplinary History*, Vol. 18, No. 4, 1988, pp. 653–73; Tir, J. and Jasinski, M. "Domestic-Level Diversionary Theory of War: Targeting Ethnic Minorities." *Journal of Conflict Resolution*, Vol. 52, No. 5, 2008, pp. 641–64; Tabaar. *Religious Statecraft.*
88 Risse-Kappen, Thomas. "Public Opinion, Domestic Structure, and Foreign Policy in Liberal Democracies." *World Politics*, Vol. 43, No. 1, 1991, pp. 479–512.

89 Dahl, Robert. *Who Governs?* Yale University Press, 1963.
90 Hagan. "Domestic Political Explanations in the Analysis of Foreign Policy."
91 David, Steven. "Explaining Third World Alignment." *World Politics*, Vol. 43, No. 1, 1991, pp. 233–56.
92 Ibid.
93 Ibid.
94 Harknett, Richard and Vandenberg, Jeffrey. "Alignment Theory and Interrelated Threats: Jordan and the Persian Gulf Crisis." *Security Studies*, Vol. 6, No. 3, 1997, pp. 112–53.
95 Ibid.
96 Chafetz, Glenn, et. al. "Introduction: Tracing the Influence of Identity on Foreign Policy." *Security Studies*, Vol. 8, No. 2–3, 1998, pp. 7–22.
97 Ibid.
98 Finnemore, Martha. *Defining State Interests: National Interests in International Society*. Cornell University Press, 1996.
99 Wendt. *Social Theory of International Politics*.
100 Hopf. "The Promise of Constructivism in International Relations Theory."
101 Jervis, Robert. *Perception and Misperception in International Politics*. Princeton University Press, 1976.
102 Chafetz et al. "Introduction."
103 Barnett and Telhami. *Identity and Foreign Policy in the Middle East*.
104 Kahl, Colin. "Constructing a Separate Peace: Constructivism, Collective Liberal Identity, and Democratic Peace." *Security Studies*, Vol. 8, No. 2–3, 1998, pp. 94–144.
105 Huntington. *The Clash of Civilizations and the Remaking of World Order*.
106 Al-Nakib, Farah. "Modernity and the Arab Gulf States: The Politics of Heritage, Memory, and Forgetting." In *Routledge Handbook of Persian Gulf Politics*, ed. Mehran Kamrava. Routledge, 2020, pp. 57–82.
107 Holtsi, Kal. "National Role Conceptions in the Study of Foreign Policy." *International Studies Quarterly*, Vol. 14, No. 1, 1970, pp. 233–309.
108 Walker, Stephen. "Symbolic Interactionism and International Politics: Role Theory's Contribution to International Organization." In *Contending Dramas: A Cognitive Approach to International Organizations*, ed. Martha Cottam and Zhiyu Shi. Praeger, 1992.
109 Chafetz, et al. "Introduction."
110 Hinnebusch, Raymond and Ehteshami, Anoushiravan. "Foreign Policymaking in the Middle East: Complex Realism." In *International Relations of the Middle East*, ed. Louise Fawcett. Oxford University Press, 2019, pp. 249–70.
111 Rousseau, David and Garcia-Retamero, Rocio. "Identity, Power, and Threat Perception." *Journal of Conflict Resolution*, Vol. 51, No. 5, 2007, pp. 744–71.

112 Henne, Peter. *Religious Appeals in Power Politics*. Cornell University Press, 2023.
113 Van Ham, Peter. "The Rise of the Brand State: The Postmodern Politics of Image and Reputation." *Foreign Affairs*, Vol. 80, No. 5, 2001, pp. 2–6.
114 Fan, Ying. "Branding the Nation: Towards a Better Understanding." *Place Branding and Diplomacy*, Vol. 6, No. 1, 2010, pp. 97–103.
115 Risen, Clay. ""Branding Nations." *New York Times*, December 11, 2005, https://www.nytimes.com/2005/12/11/magazine/branding-nations.html.
116 Gries, Peter and Chun Yam, Paton Pak. "Ideology and International Relations." *Current Opinion in Behavioral Sciences*, Vol. 34, No. 1, 2020, pp. 135–41.
117 Gould-Davies, Nigel. "Rethinking the Role of Ideology in International Politics During the Cold War." *Journal of Cold War Studies*, Vol. 1, No. 1, 1999, pp. 90–109.
118 Keohane, Robert and Goldstein, Judith. *Ideas and Foreign Policy: Beliefs, Institutions, and Political Change*. Cornell University Press, 1993.
119 Gries and Chun Yam. "Ideology and International Relations."
120 Ibid.
121 Hunt, Michael. *Ideology and U.S. Foreign Policy*. Yale University Press, 1987.
122 Chen, Jian. *Mao's China and the Cold War*. The University of North Carolina Press, 2001.
123 Brands, Hal. "Democracy vs. Authoritarianism: How Ideology Shapes Great-Power Conflict." *Survival*, Vol. 60, No. 1, 2018, pp. 61–114.
124 Kroenig, Matthew. *The Return of Great Power Rivalry: Democracy versus Autocracy from the Ancient World to the U.S. and China*. Oxford University Press, 2020.
125 Rubin, Lawrence. *Islam in the Balance: Ideational Threats in Arab Politics*. Stanford University Press, 2014.
126 Gould-Davies. "Rethinking the Role of Ideology in International Politics During the Cold War."
127 Ibid.
128 Ibid.
129 Ibid.
130 Haas, Mark. *The Ideological Origins of Great Power Politics, 1789-1989*. Cornell University Press, 2005.
131 Meibauer, Gustav. ""Interests, Ideas, and the Study of State Behaviour in Neoclassical Realism."' *Review of International Studies*, Vol. 46, No. 1, 2019, 20--36.
132 Levi, Werner. "Ideology, Interests, and Foreign Policy." *International Studies Quarterly*, Vol. 14, No. 1, 1970, pp. 1–31.
133 Ibid.
134 Freeden, Michael. *Ideologies and Political Theory: A Conceptual Approach*. Oxford University Press, 1996.

135 Ugarriza, Juan and Craig, Matthew. "The Relevance of Ideology to Contemporary Armed Conflicts: A Quantitative Analysis of Former Combatants in Columbia." *Journal of Conflict Resolution*, Vol. 57, No. 3, 2013, pp. 445–77.
136 Nye, Joseph. *Soft Power: The Means to Success in World Politics*. Public Affairs, 2004.
137 Ibid.
138 Nye, Joseph. "Soft Power." *Foreign Policy*, 1990.
139 Nye. *Soft Power*.
140 Haynes, Jeffrey. *Religious Transnational Actors and Soft Power*. Routledge, 2012.
141 Haynes, Jeffrey. "Religion and Foreign Policy Making in the USA, India, and Iran: Towards a Research Agenda." *Third World Quarterly*, Vol. 29, No. 1, 2008, pp. 143–65.
142 Ibid.
143 Diwan, Kristin. "Clerical Associations in Qatar and the United Arab Emirates: Soft Power Competition in Islamic Politics." *International Affairs*, Vol. 97, No. 4, 2021, pp. 945–63.
144 Mandaville and Hamid. "Islam as Statecraft."
145 Mandaville, Peter. *The Geopolitics of Religious Soft Power: How States Use Religion in Foreign Policy*. Oxford University Press, 2023.
146 Bettiza, Gregorio. "States, Religions, and Power: Highlighting the Role of Sacred Capital in World Politics." *Berkley Center for Religion, Peace, and World Affairs*, March 30, 2020, https://berkleycenter.georgetown.edu/publications/states-religions-and-power-highlighting-the-role-of-sacred-capital-in-world-politics.
147 Ibid.
148 Nye. "Soft Power."

Chapter 2

1 Darwich, May. "The Challenge of Bridging IR and Area Studies in Middle East International Relations Teaching." *LSE Middle East Center Blog*, August 15, 2018, https://blogs.lse.ac.uk/mec/2015/08/18/the-challenge-of-bridging-ir-and-area-studies-in-middle-east-international-relations-teaching/.
2 Said, Edward. *Orientalism*. Pantheon Books, 1978.
3 Lewis, Bernard. "The Roots of Muslim Rage." *The Atlantic*, September 1990, https://www.theatlantic.com/magazine/archive/1990/09/the-roots-of-muslim-rage/304643/.
4 Huntington, Samuel. *The Clash of Civilizations and the Remaking of World Order*. Simon and Schuster, 1996.
5 Ibid.

6. Aydin, Cemil. *The Idea of the Muslim World: A Global Intellectual History*. Harvard University Press, 2019.
7. Geertz, Clifford. *Islam Observed: Religious Development in Morocco and Indonesia*. University of Chicago Press, 1971; Hodgson, Marshall. *The Venture of Islam*. University of Chicago Press, 1974; Asad, Talal. *The Idea of an Anthropology of Islam*. Georgetown University Press, 1986; Ahmed, Shahab. *What is Islam? The Importance of Being Islamic*. Princeton University Press, 2016.
8. Piscatori, James. *Islam in the Political Process*. Cambridge University Press, 1993.
9. Esposito, John. *The Future of Islam*. Oxford University Press, 2010.
10. Mayer, Ann Elizabeth. *Islam and Human Rights: Tradition and Politics*. Westview Press, 2013.
11. Abou El Fadl, Khaled. *Islam and the Challenge of Democracy*. Princeton University Press, 2004; Sachedina, Abdulaziz. *Islam and the Challenge of Human Rights*. Oxford University Press, 2009.
12. Piscatori, James and Saikal, Amin. *Islam Beyond Borders: The Umma in World Politics*. Cambridge University Press, 2019.
13. Yildirim, A. Kadir. "The New Guardians of Religion: Islam and Authority in the Middle East." *Baker Institute for Public Policy*, March 12, 2019, https://www.bakerinstitute.org/research/new-guardians-religion-islam-and-authority-middle-east; Eickelman, Dale and Piscatori, James. *Muslim Politics*. Princeton University Press, 1996.
14. Yildirim. "The New Guardians of Religion."
15. Mandaville, Peter. *Islam and Politics*. Routledge, 2020.
16. Brown, Nathan. *Arguing Islam after the Revival of Arab Politics*. Oxford University Press, 2016.
17. Ibid.
18. Baskan, Birol. *The Politics of Islam: The Muslim Brothers and the State in the Arab Gulf*. Edinburgh University Press, 2021.
19. Cesari, Jocelyn. *The Awakening of Muslim Democracy: Religion, Modernity, and the State*. Cambridge University Press, 2014; Cesari, Jocelyn. *What is Political Islam?* Lynne Rienner Publishers, Inc., 2018.
20. Brown, Nathan et al. "Roundtable on State Islam after the Arab Uprisings." *Jadaliyya*, November 23, 2020, https://www.jadaliyya.com/Details/41990/Roundtable-on-State-Islam-after-the-Arab-Uprisings.
21. Ibid.
22. Chalcraft, John. *Popular Politics in the Making of the Modern Middle East*. Cambridge University Press, 2016.
23. Bayat, Asef. *Post-Islamism: The Changing Faces of Political Islam*. Oxford University Press, 2013.
24. Mohammad Fadel. ""Islamic Law and Constitution-Making: The Authoritarian Temptation of the Arab Spring."" *Osgoode Hall Law Journal*, Vol. 53, No. 2, 2016, pp. 472–507.

25 Ebrahim Moosa. ""Political theology in the Aftermath of the Arab Spring: Returning to the Ethical."" In *The African Renaissance and the Afro-Arab Spring*, ed. Charles Villa-Vincencio, Erik Doxtader, and Ebrahim Moosa. Georgetown University Press, 2015, pp. 101–19.
26 Ahmet Kuru. *Islam, Authoritarianism, and Underdevelopment: A Global and Historical Comparison.* Cambridge University Press, 2019; Mustafa Akyol. *Reopening Muslim Minds: A Return to Reason, Freedom, and Tolerance.* St. Martin's Essentials, 2021.
27 Sachedina. *Islam and the Challenge of Human Rights.*
28 Abou El-Fadl, Khaled. *The Prophet's Pulpit: Commentaries on the State of Islam.* Usuli Press, 2022.
29 Ibid.
30 Nakissa, Aria. "The Fiqh of Revolution and the Arab Spring: Secondary Segmentation as a Trend in Islamic Legal Doctrine." *The Muslim World*, Vol. 105, No. 3, 2015, pp. 398–421.
31 Zulfiqar, Adnan. "Revolutionary Islamic Jurisprudence: A Restatement of the Arab Spring." *New York University Journal of International Law and Politics*, Vol. 49, 2017, pp. 443–97.
32 Adam Hanieh. "Ambitions of a Global Gulf: The Arab Uprisings, Yemen, and the Saudi-Emirati Alliance." *Middle East Report*, Vol. 289, 2018, pp. 21–6.
33 Hamid, Shadi and McCants, William. "Islamism after the Arab Spring: Between the Islamic State and the Nation-state." *Brookings Institution*, January 2017, https://www.brookings.edu/research/islamism-after-the-arab-spring-between-the-islamic-state-and-the-nation-state/.
34 Bank, Andre et al. "Authoritarianism Reconfigured: Evolving Forms of Political Control." In *The Political Science of the Middle East: Theory and Research since the Arab Uprisings*, ed. Marc Lynch et al. Oxford University Press, 2022, pp. 35–61.
35 Dawisha, Adeed. *Islam in Foreign Policy.* Cambridge University Press, 1983.
36 Ibid.
37 Abu Sulayman, Abdul Hamid. *Towards an Islamic Theory of International Relations: New Directions for Islamic Methodology and Thought.* The International Institute of Islamic Thought, 1993; Rizvi, Hasan-Askari. *Pakistan and the Geostrategic Environment: A Study of Foreign Policy.* Palgrave, 1993; Turner, John. "Uncovering an Islamic Paradigm of International Relations." In *Political and Cultural Representations of Muslims: Islam in the Plural*, ed. Christopher Flood. Brill, 2012; Mohammad Reza Saidabadi. ""Islam and Foreign Policy in the Contemporary Secular World: The Case of Post-Revolutionary Iran."" *Pacifica Review: Peace, Security & Global Change*, Vol. 8, No. 2, 1996, pp. 32–44.
38 Strakes, Jason. "Towards an Islamic Geopolitics: Reconciling the Ummah and Territoriality in Contemporary International Relations." In *Islam in*

International Relations: Politics and Paradigms, ed. Nassef Manabilang Adiong et al. Routledge, 2018, pp. 218–32.
39 Barnett, Michael and Telhami, Shibley. *Identity and Foreign Policy in the Middle East*. Cornell University Press, 2002; Shaffer, Brenda. *The Limits of Culture: Islam and Foreign Policy*. MIT Press, 2006; Louer, Laurence. *Transnational Shia Politics: Religious and Political Networks in the Gulf*. Oxford University Press, 2008; Abdo, Geneive. *The New Sectarianism: The Arab Uprisings and the Rebirth of the Sunni-Shia Divide*. Oxford University Press, 2016.
40 Salloukh, B. "Overlapping Contests and Middle East International Relations: The Return of the Weak Arab State." *American Political Science Association*, Vol. 50, No. 3, 2017, pp. 660–3.
41 Rubin, Lawrence. *Islam in the Balance: Ideational Threats in Arab Politics*. Stanford University Press, 2014.
42 Warren, David. *Rivals in the Gulf: Yusuf al-Qaradawi, Abdullah Bin Bayyah, and the Qatar-UAE Contest Over the Arab Spring and the Gulf Crisis*. Routledge, 2021.
43 Walt, Stephen. *The Origins of Alliances*. Cornell University Press, 1987.
44 Gengler, Justin. "Sectarianism from the Top Down or Bottom up? Explaining the Middle East's Unlikely De-sectarianization after the Arab Spring." *Review of Faith and International Affairs*, Vol. 18, No. 1, 2020, pp. 109–13.
45 Ryan, Curtis. *Inter-Arab Alliances: Regime Security and Jordanian Foreign Policy*. University Press of Florida, 2009.
46 Cavatorta, Francesco et. al. ""The Future of Political Islam in the Middle East and North Africa under the Changing Regional Order."" *Jadaliyya*, August 16, 2018, https://www.jadaliyya.com/Details/37864.
47 Mandaville, Peter. "Islam and International Relations in the Middle East: From Umma to Nation State." In *International Relations of the Middle East*, ed. Louise Fawcett. Oxford University Press, 2019, pp. 180–200.
48 Hoffman, Jonathan. "The Return of Great-Power Competition to the Middle East: A Two-Level Game." *Middle East Policy*, Vol. 28, No. 1, 2021a, pp. 87–104,
49 Ulrichsen, Kristian. *The United Arab Emirates: Power, Politics, and Policymaking*. Routledge, 2017b.
50 Akbarzadeh, Shahram. "The Burred Line Between State Identity and Realpolitik." In *Routledge Handbook of International Relations in the Middle East*, ed. Shahram Akbarzadeh. Routledge, 2019, pp. 1–7.
51 Lynch, Mark. "New Arab World Order." *Foreign Affairs*, August 16, 2018, https://carnegieendowment.org/2018/08/16/new-arab-world-order-pub-77056.
52 Hashemi, Nader and Postel, Danny. *Sectarianization: Mapping the New Politics of the Middle East*. Oxford University Press, 2017.
53 Nasr, Vali. *The Shia Revival: How Conflicts within Islam will Shape the Future*. W. W. Norton & Company, 2007.

54 Mason, Robert. (ed.). *Reassessing Order and Disorder in the Middle East: Regional Imbalance or Disintegration?* Rowman and Littlefield, 2017.
55 Louer, Laurence. *Sunnis and Shi'a: A Political History*. Princeton University Press, 2020.
56 Bianco, Cinzia and Stansfield, Gareth. "The Intra-GCC Crises: Mapping GCC Fragmentation after 2011." *International Affairs*, Vol. 94, No. 3, 2018, pp. 613–35.
57 Mandaville. "Islam and International Relations in the Middle East."
58 Amasha, Muhammad. "The UAE-sponsored 'Islams': Mapping the Terrain." *Maydan*, September 15, 2020, https://themaydan.com/2020/09/the-uae-sponsored-islams-mapping-the-terrain/.
59 Gause, Gregory. "What the Qatar Crisis Shows about the Middle East." *The Washington Post*, June 27, 2017, https://www.washingtonpost.com/news/monkey-cage/wp/2017/06/27/what-the-qatar-crisis-shows-about-the-middle-east/.
60 Josua, Maria. "What Drives Diffusion? Anti-Terrorism Legislation in the Arab Middle East and North Africa." *Journal of Global Security Studies*, Vol. 6, No. 3, 2021, pp. 1–15.
61 Savage, Charlie et al. "Trump Pushes to Designate Muslim Brotherhood as Terrorist Organization." *The New York Times*, April 30, 2019, https://www.nytimes.com/2019/04/30/us/politics/trump-muslim-brotherhood.html.
62 Mamdani, Mahmood. "Good Muslim, Bad Muslim: A Political Perspective on Culture and Terrorism." *American Anthropologist*, Vol. 104, No. 3, 2002, pp. 766–75.
63 Warren, David. "Interfaith Dialogue in the United Arab Emirates: Where International Relations Meets State-Branding." *Berkley Center for Religion, Peace, and World Affairs*, July 12, 2021, https://berkleycenter.georgetown.edu/posts/interfaith-dialogue-in-the-united-arab-emirates-where-international-relations-meets-state-branding.
64 Trenin, Dmitri. *What is Russia up to in the Middle East?* Polity Press, 2017; Markey, Daniel. *China's Western Horizon: Beijing and the New Geopolitics of Eurasia*. Oxford University Press, 2020.
65 Hoffman, Jonathan. "Moscow, Beijing, and the Crescent: Russian and Chinese Religious Soft Power in the Middle East." *Digest of Middle East Studies*, Vol. 30, No. 1, 2021b, pp. 1–11.
66 Tabaar, Mohammad Ayatollahi. *Religious Statecraft: The Politics of Islam in Iran*. Columbia University Press, 2018.
67 Volpi, Frederic. "Islam, Political Islam, and the State System." In *Routledge Handbook of International Relations in the Middle East*, ed. Shahram Akbarzadeh. Routledge, 2019, pp. 69–81.
68 Tabaar. *Religious Statecraft*.
69 Ibid.
70 Mandaville, Peter. *Islam and Politics*. Routledge, 2014.

Chapter 3

1. Lacroix, Stephane. *Awakening Islam: The Politics of Religious Dissent in Contemporary Saudi Arabia.* Harvard University Press, 2011.
2. Abou El Fadl, Khaled. "Islam and the Theology of Power: Wahhabism and Salafism." *Middle East Research and Information Project (MERIP),* Winter 2001, pp. 28–33.
3. Mandaville, Peter. *Islam and Politics.* Routledge, 2020.
4. Al-Rasheed, Madawi. *The Son King: Reform and Repression in Saudi Arabia.* Oxford University Press, 2021.
5. Ismail, Raihan. *Saudi Clerics and Shi'a Islam.* Oxford University Press, 2016.
6. Ibid.
7. Mandaville, Peter. *Wahhabism and the World: Understanding Saudi Arabia's Global Influence on Islam.* Oxford University Press, 2022.
8. Menoret, Pascal. "Saudi Arabia." In *The Middle East,* ed. Ellen Lust. CQ Press, 2017, pp. 737–54.
9. Lacroix. *Awakening Islam.*
10. Al-Rasheed. *The Son King.*
11. Varagur, Krithika. *The Call: Inside the Global Saudi Religious Project.* Columbia University Press, 2020.
12. Menoret. "Saudi Arabia."
13. Lacroix. *Awakening Islam.*
14. Al-Rasheed. *The Son King.*
15. Baskan, Birol. *The Politics of Islam: The Muslim Brothers and the State in the Arab Gulf.* Edinburgh University Press, 2021.
16. "Saudi Arabia: Royal Decree Limits Authority to Issue Fatwas." *Library of Congress,* August 25, 2010, https://www.loc.gov/item/global-legal-monitor/2010-08-25/saudi-arabia-royal-decree-limits-authority-to-issue-fatwas/.
17. Lacroix. *Awakening Islam.*
18. Matthiesen, Toby. "Renting the Casbah: Gulf States' Foreign Policy Towards North Africa Since the Arab Uprisings," in *The Changing Security Dynamics of the Persian Gulf,* ed. Kristian Ulrichsen. Oxford University Press, 2017a, pp. 43–60.
19. Al-Rasheed, Madawi. "Sectarianism as Counter-Revolution: Saudi Responses to the Arab Spring." In *Sectarianization: Mapping the New Politics of the Middle East,* ed. Nader Hashemi and Danny Postel. Oxford University Press, 2017, pp. 143–58.

20 "Demands of the Saudi Youth for the Future of the Nation." March 5, 2011, https://al-bab.com/albab-orig/albab/arab/docs/saudi/saudi_reform_documents_2011.htm#demands_of_saudi_youth.
21 "Towards a State of Rights and Institutions." *Ahewar.org*, February 23, 2011, https://www.ahewar.org/debat/show.art.asp?aid=247642.
22 "Demands of the Saudi Youth for the Future of the Nation." March 5, 2011, https://al-bab.com/albab-orig/albab/arab/docs/saudi/saudi_reform_documents_2011.htm#demands_of_saudi_youth
23 See "In Saudi Arabia, Reformers Intensify Calls for Change." *The Christian Science Monitor*, February 22, 2011, https://www.csmonitor.com/World/Middle-East/2011/0222/In-Saudi-Arabia-reformers-intensify-calls-for-change.
24 Al-Rasheed. "Sectarianism as Counter-Revolution."
25 Al-Awdah, Salman. *As'ilat al-Thawra*. Markaz Inma lil-Buhuth wa al-Dirasat, 2012.
26 Twitter post by Salman Al-Awdah, https://x.com/salman_alodah/status/36117670759763968.
27 Twitter post by Salman Al-Awdah, https://twitter.com/salman_alodah/status/205287399327150081.
28 See "Saudi Cleric Issues Rare Warning in Call for Reform." *Reuters*, March 16, 2013, https://www.reuters.com/article/us-saudi-cleric/saudi-cleric-issues-rare-warning-in-call-for-reform-idUSBRE92F0DI20130316.
29 Discussed in Lacroix, Stephane. "Saudi Islamists and the Arab Spring." *London School of Economics and Political Science: Kuwait Programme on Development, Governance, and Globalisation in the Gulf States*, May 2014, https://eprints.lse.ac.uk/56725/1/Lacroix_Saudi-Islamists-and-theArab-Spring_2014.pdf.
30 Al-Rasheed. "Sectarianism as Counter-Revolution."
31 Nasr, Vali. *The Shia Revival: How Conflicts Within Islam will Shape the Future*. W. W. Norton & Company, 2007.
32 Matthiesen, Toby. *Sectarian Gulf: Bahrain, Saudi Arabia, and the Arab Spring that Wasn't*. Stanford University Press, 2013.
33 Fuller, Graham and Francke, Rend. *Arab Shi'a: The Forgotten Muslims*. Palgrave, 1999.
34 For a comprehensive overview of such hate speech, see "They Are Not Our Brothers: Hate Speech by Saudi Officials." *Human Rights Watch*, 2017, https://www.hrw.org/sites/default/files/report_pdf/saudi0917_web.pdf.
35 Al-Rasheed. "Sectarianism as Counter-Revolution."
36 See "Saudi Arabia: Free Cleric Who Backs Change." *Human Rights Watch*, February 29, 2011, https://www.hrw.org/news/2011/02/28/saudi-arabia-free-cleric-who-backs-change.
37 Wehrey, Frederic. "The Forgotten Uprising in Eastern Saudi Arabia." *Carnegie Endowment for International Peace*, June 14, 2013, https://

carnegieendowment.org/2013/06/14/forgotten-uprising-in-eastern-saudi-arabia-pub-52093.
38 Matthiesen, Toby. *The Other Saudis: Shiism, Dissent, and Sectarianism.* Cambridge University Press, 2015.
39 A video of the full speech is available here: https://www.youtube.com/watch?v=8bRh_-CkBgE.
40 Ibid.
41 Dorsey, James. "Wahhabism vs. Wahhabism: Qatar Challenges Saudi Arabia." *Institute of Fan Culture, University of Wurzburg,* July 3, 2013, https://papers.ssrn.com/sol3/papers.cfm?abstract_id=2305485.
42 Matthiesen, Toby. "Saudi Arabia." In *Rethinking Political Islam,* ed. Shadi Hamid and William McCants. Oxford University Press, 2017b, pp. 118–31.
43 "Saudi King Expresses Support for Mubarak." *Reuters,* January 29, 2011, https://www.reuters.com/article/egypt-saudi-idAFLDE70S08V20110129.
44 Lister, Charles. *The Syrian Jihad: Al-Qaeda, The Islamic State, and the Evolution of an Insurgency.* Oxford University Press, 2015.
45 Bunzel, Cole. "The Kingdom and the Caliphate: Saudi Arabia and the Islamic State." In *Beyond Sunni and Shi'a: The Roots of Sectarianism in a Changing Middle East,* ed. Frederic Wehrey. Oxford University Press, 2017, pp. 239–64.
46 Discussed in Bunzel. "The Kingdom and the Caliphate: Saudi Arabia and the Islamic State."
47 "Islamic State Leader Urges Attacks in Saudi Arabia." *Reuters,* November 13, 2014, https://jp.reuters.com/article/us-mideast-crisis-baghdadi-idUSKCN0IX1Y120141114.
48 Discussed in Lacroix. "Saudi Islamists and the Arab Spring."
49 The full statement is available here: "A Fatwa from the Council of Senior Scholars in the Kingdom of Saudi Arabia Warning Against Mass Demonstrations." Islamopedia, March 10,2011, https://archive.ph/lGOhB.
50 Discussed in Lacroix, Stephane. "Comparing the Arab Revolts: Is Saudi Arabia Immune?" *Journal of Democracy,* Vol. 22, No. 4, 2011, pp. 48–59.
51 See "Saudi Arabia Imposes Ban on All Protests." *BBC News,* March 5, 2011, https://www.bbc.com/news/world-middle-east-12656744.
52 See "Saudi Arabia: Rights Activists, Bloggers Arrested." *Human Rights Watch,* May 3, 2011, https://www.hrw.org/news/2011/05/03/saudi-arabia-rights-activist-bloggers-arrested.
53 "Saudi Stocks Soar after King's Spending Spree." *AFP,* March 20, 2011, https://english.ahram.org.eg/NewsContent/3/12/8119/Business/Economy/Saudi-stocks-soar-after-kings-spending-spree.aspx.
54 See, respectively: Werr, Patrick. "UAE Offers Egypt $3 billion, Saudis $5 billion." *Reuters,* July 9, 2013, https://www.reuters.com/article/us-egypt-protests-loan/uae-offers-egypt-3-billion-support-saudis-5-billion-idUSBRE9680H020130709; Hedges, Matthew and Cafiero, Giorgio. "The

GCC and the Muslim Brotherhood: What Does the Future Hold?" *Middle East Policy*, Vol 24, No. 1, 2017, pp. 129–53.
55 "Saudi King Back Egypt's Military." *Aljazeera*, August 17, 2013, https://www.aljazeera.com/news/2013/8/17/saudi-king-backs-egypts-military.
56 Kirkpatrick, David. "Saudis Put Terrorist Label on Muslim Brotherhood." *The New York Times*, March 7, 2014, https://www.nytimes.com/2014/03/08/world/middleeast/saudis-put-terrorist-label-on-muslim-brotherhood.html.
57 Lacroix, Stephane. "Saudi Arabia's Muslim Brotherhood Predicament." *The Washington Post*, March 20, 2014, https://www.washingtonpost.com/news/monkey-cage/wp/2014/03/20/saudi-arabias-muslim-brotherhood-predicament/.
58 Full statement available at "Statement on the Events in Egypt." *Al-Moslim.net*, July 9, 2013, https://www.almoslim.net/node/186224?page=2.
59 Full statement available at "Statement on the Political Positions of the Nour Party." *Al-Moslim.net*, January 12, 2014, https://www.almoslim.net/node/198580?page=1.
60 Worth, Robert. "Leftward Shift by Conservative Cleric Leaves Saudis Perplexed." *The New York Times*, April 4, 2014, https://www.nytimes.com/2014/04/05/world/middleeast/conservative-saudi-cleric-salman-al-awda.html.
61 See Sciutto, Jim, and Herb, Jeremy. "Exclusive: The Secret Documents That Help Explain the Qatar Crisis." *CNN*, July 11, 2017, www.cnn.com/2017/07/10/politics/secret-documents-qatar-crisis-gulf-saudi/index.html.
62 Ibid.
63 "ISIS Is No. 1 Enemy of Islam, Says Saudi Grand Mufti." *Al-Arabiya News*, August 19, 2014, https://english.alarabiya.net/News/middle-east/2014/08/19/Saudi-mufti-ISIS-is-enemy-No-1-of-Islam-.
64 See "Council of Senior Scholars: ISIS is a conspiracy against Islam created by hidden hands." *Al-Riyadh News*, September 29, 2015, https://www.alriyadh.com/1086543.
65 Discussed in Bunzel., "The Kingdom and the Caliphate: Saudi Arabia and the Islamic State."
66 See "Saudi Arabia: New Terrorism Law in Effect." *Library of Congress*, February 2, 2014, https://www.loc.gov/item/global-legal-monitor/2014-02-04/saudi-arabia-new-terrorism-law-in-effect/#:~:text=4%2C%202014)%20Saudi%20Arabia%27s%20new,undermines%20the%20state%20or%20society.
67 "Official Source Issues Statement on Qatif Governorate Incident." *Saudi Press Agency*, October 4, 2011, https://www.spa.gov.sa/viewstory.php?newsid=931281.
68 Fur the full statement, see "Word of Sheikh Al-Barrak about the Demonstrations." *Saaid.org*, http://www.saaid.net/ahdath/90.htm.

69 "Who Was the Shiite Sheikh Executed by Saudi Arabia?" NPR, January 4, 2016, https://www.npr.org/sections/thetwo-way/2016/01/04/461912757/who-was-the-shiite-sheikh-executed-by-saudi-arabia.
70 "Sheikh Nimr al-Nimr: Saudi Arabia Executes Top Shia Cleric." *BBC News*, January 2, 2016, https://www.bbc.com/news/world-middle-east-35213244.
71 See "Saudi Arabia: Mass Execution of 81 Men Shows Urgent Need to Abolish the Death Penalty." Amnesty International, March 15, 2022, https://www.amnesty.org/en/latest/news/2022/03/saudi-arabia-mass-execution-of-81-men-shows-urgent-need-to-abolish-the-death-penalty/#:~:text=Saudi%20Arabia%20has%20previously%20carried,cleric%20Sheikh%20Nimr%20al%2DNimr.
72 Siegel, Alexandra. "Twitter Wars: Sunni-Shia Conflict and Cooperation in the Digital Age." In *Beyond Sunni and Shia: The Roots of Sectarianism in a Changing Middle East*, ed. Frederic Wehrey. Oxford University Press, 2017, pp. 157–80.
73 Gengler, Justin. "Bahrain's Sunni Awakening." *Middle East Research and Information Project (MERIP)*, January 17, 2012, https://merip.org/2012/01/bahrains-sunni-awakening/.
74 "Bahrain Unrest: King Hamad Says Foreign Plot Foiled." *BBC News*, March 21, 2011, https://www.bbc.com/news/world-middle-east-12802945.
75 Erdbrink, Thomas and Warrick, Joby. "Bahrain Crackdown Fueling Tensions Between Iran, Saudi Arabia." *The Washington Post*, April 22, 2011, https://www.washingtonpost.com/world/bahrain-crackdown-fueling-tensions-between-iran-saudi-arabia/2011/04/21/AFVe6WPE_story.html.
76 "A Talk with Peninsula Shield Force Commander Mutlaq Bin Salem al-Azima." *Asharq Al-Awsat*, March 28, 2011, https://eng-archive.aawsat.com/theaawsat/interviews/a-talk-with-peninsula-shield-force-commander-mutlaq-bin-salem-al-azima.
77 For the full interview, see "Sheikh Abdallah Al-Salafi's talk on the program Bahrain In Our Hearts." *Dd-sunnah.net,* March 3, 2011, https://www.dd-sunnah.net/records/view/action/view/id/3440/.
78 See "Top Saudi Cleric Slams Iran Intervention." *TradeArabia*, April 16, 2011, https://www.tradearabia.com/news/MISC_196990.html.
79 See https://www.alwatanvoice.com/arabic/content/print/170277.html.
80 Discussed in: Mabon, Simon. "Meeting the Trumpets of Sabotage: Saudi Arabia, the US, and the Quest to Securitize Iran." *British Journal of Middle East Studies*, Vol. 45, No. 5, 2018, pp. 742–59.
81 See "Islamic Alliance Stands by Bahrain." *UPI*, November 26, 2012, https://www.upi.com/Top_News/Special/2012/11/26/Islamic-alliance-stands-by-Bahrain/98931353938998/.
82 For the full statement, see "The Association of Muslim Scholars Warn the Sunnah of Bahrain Against their Emigration [from Bahrain] and the

Safavid Tide." *Al-Moslim.net,* March 23, 2011, https://almoslim.net/node
/143526.
83 Ibid.
84 See "Al-Awdah: I Regret that the Protests in Bahrain have Reached
Sectarian Tension." *Islamtoday.net,* March 20, 2011, https://www
.islamtoday.net/salman/artshow-78-147809.htm.
85 Twitter post by al-Islah Society, https://www.twitlonger.com/show
/9maf27.
86 Freer, Courtney. "Challenges to Sunni Islamism in Bahrain Since 2011."
Carnegie Endowment for International Peace, March 6, 2019, https://
carnegie-mec.org/2019/03/06/challenges-to-sunni-islamism-in-bahrain
-since-2011-pub-78510.
87 Phillips, Christopher. *The Battle for Syria: International Rivalry in the New
Middle East.* Yale University Press, 2016.
88 Lister. *The Syrian Jihad.*
89 Discussed in Lacroix, Stephane. "Saudi Islamists and the Arab Spring."
London School of Economics (LSE), 2014, https://eprints.lse.ac.uk/56725
/1/Lacroix_Saudi-Islamists-and-theArab-Spring_2014.pdf. Some of these
calls have since been deleted.
90 Discussed in Ismail, Raihan. *Saudi Clerics and Shi'a Islam.* Oxford
University Press, 2016.
91 See "Feature—Saudi Steers Citizens Away from Syrian 'Jihad.'" *Reuters,*
September 12, 2012, https://www.reuters.com/article/saudi-syria-jihad/
feature-saudi-steers-citizens-away-from-syrian-jihad-idUSL6E8J98BN20
120912.
92 For the full statement, see "Scholars and Preachers Issue a Statement of
Endorsement for the "Islamic Front" in the Levant and Call for Support."
Al-Moslim.net, December 5, 2013, https://almoslim.net/node/19514
93 See "Saudi Mufti Tells Young Saudis Not to Heed Call to Jihad." *Reuters,*
August 28, 2014, https://www.reuters.com/article/us-saudi-security/saudi
-mufti-tells-young-saudis-not-to-heed-call-to-jihad-idUSKBN0GS1
9M20140828.
94 Borger, Julian. "Saudi Strongman 'Encouraged' Russia Intervention in
Syria, Lawsuit Claims." *The Guardian,* August 16, 2020, https://www
.theguardian.com/world/2020/aug/16/saudi-strongman-encouraged
-russia-syria-intervention-lawsuit-claims.
95 Ibid.
96 "Saudi Crown Prince Says US Troops Should Stay in Syria." *TIME,* March
30, 2018, https://time.com/5222746/saudi-crown-prince-donald-trump
-syria/.
97 See "Fight or Flight? Saudi Cleric Heads to London After Call for Jihad
in Syria." *Al-Arabiya,* June 22, 2013, https://english.alarabiya.net/News/
middle-east/2013/06/22/Fight-or-flight-Saudi-cleric-heads-to-London
-after-calling-for-Jihad-in-Syria.

98 Facebook post by 4Shbab, https://www.facebook.com/4shbab.net/posts/416650288358282?stream_ref=5.
99 For the full letter, see "Statement from Saudi Scholars and Preachers about the Russian Aggression on Syria." *Al-Moslim.net*, October 3, 2015, https://www.almoslim.net/node/242652.
100 Spencer, James. "The GCC Needs a Successful Strategy for Yemen, Not Failed Tactics." *Middle East Research and Information Project (MERIP)*, September 11, 2015, https://merip.org/2015/09/the-gcc-needs-a-successful-strategy-for-yemen/.
101 Selim Gamal. "The United States and the Arab Spring: The Dynamics of Political Engineering." *Arab Studies Quarterly*, Vol. 35, No. 3, 2013, pp. 255–72.
102 Stein, Ewan. *International Relations in the Middle East: Hegemonic Strategies and Regional Order*. Cambridge University Press, 2021.
103 "Decisive Storm Gains Support from Scholars." *Arab News*, April 4, 2015, https://www.arabnews.com/node/727616/%7B%7B.
104 For the full statement, see "Council of Senior Scholars: Decisive Storm Supports Legitimacy in Yemen." *Al-Arabiya News*, March 26, 2015, https://www.alarabiya.net/saudi-today/2015/03/26/%D8%A8%D9%8A%D8%A7%D9%86-%D9%85%D9%86-%D9%87%D9%8A%D8%A6%D8%A9-%D9%83%D8%A8%D8%A7%D8%B1-%D8%A7%D9%84%D8%B9%D9%84%D9%85%D8%A7%D8%A1-%D8%B9%D9%86-%D8%B9%D8%A7%D8%B5%D9%81%D8%A9-%D8%A7%D9%84%D8%AD%D8%B2%D9%85
105 Aboudi, Sami. "Saudi Arabia's Top Cleric Urges Businessmen to Help Troops." *Reuters*, August 4, 2016, https://www.reuters.com/article/us-yemen-security-saudi/saudi-arabias-top-cleric-urges-businessmen-to-help-troops-idUSKCN10F1KN.
106 See "Islamic Affairs Concludes a Legal [Sharia] Course for Imams and Muezzins at the Southern Border in Jizan." *Al-Riyad News*, July 18, 2019, https://www.alriyadh.com/1766716.
107 See "Jihad Against the Houthis is a Duty..And Whoever Stands With Them Takes Their Ruling, Even if He Has a Qur'an Hung Around His Neck." *Akhbar 24*, September 22, 2014, https://akhbaar24.argaam.com/article/detail/186895.
108 See "Sheikh Al-Barrak: Fighting the Houthis is a jihad for Allah." *Al-Moslim.net*, December 4, 2011, https://almoslim.net/node/156792.
109 Ibid.
110 For the full interview, see https://www.youtube.com/watch?v=1R5K4eNV_ww#t=38.
111 See Twitter post by Mohamad Al-Arefe, https://twitter.com/MohamadAlarefe/status/581153870597873664.
112 See "'For you Salman' [...] New from Sheikh Dr. Ayed Al-Qarni." *Sabq Online Newspaper*, March 31, 2015, https://sabq.org/saudia/ye2gde#.VRrtxNrzwbU.twitter.

113 For an overview, see Byman, Daniel L. "Saudi Arabia and the United Arab Emirates Have a Disastrous Yemen Strategy." *Brookings Institution*, July 18, 2018, www.brookings.edu/blog/order-from-chaos/2018/07/17/saudi-arabia-and-the-united-arab-emirates-have-a-disastrous-yemen-strategy/
114 "Sold to an Ally, Lost to an Enemy." CNN, February 2019, https://www.cnn.com/interactive/2019/02/middleeast/yemen-lost-us-arms/.
115 Ulrichsen, Kristian. "Crown Prince of Disorder." *Foreign Policy*, March 21, 2018, https://foreignpolicy.com/2018/03/21/crown-prince-of-disorder/.
116 Bank, Andre et al. "Authoritarianism Reconfigured: Evolving Forms of Political Control." In *The Political Science of the Middle East: Theory and Research since the Arab Uprisings*, ed. Marc Lynch et al. Oxford University Press, 2022, pp. 35–61.
117 "Crown Prince Mohammed bin Salman Talks to TIME about the Middle East, Saudi Arabia's Plans, and President Trump." *TIME Magazine*, April 5, 2018, https://time.com/5228006/mohammed-bin-salman-interview-transcript-full/.
118 See Friedman, Thomas. "Saudi Arabia's Arab Spring, at Last." *The New York Times*, November 23, 2017, https://www.nytimes.com/2017/11/23/opinion/saudi-prince-mbs-arab-spring.html.
119 Sheline, Annelle and Ulrichsen, Kristian. "Mohammed bin Salman and Religious Authority and Reform in Saudi Arabia." *Rice University's Baker Institute for Public Policy*, September 19, 2019, https://scholarship.rice.edu/bitstream/handle/1911/108116/bi-report-092319-cme-mbs-saudi.pdf?sequence=1&isAllowed=y.
120 Alaoudh, Abdullah. "State-Sponsored Fatwas in Saudi Arabia." *Carnegie Endowment for International Peace*, April 3, 2018, https://carnegieendowment.org/sada/75971.
121 See "Reordering Saudi Religion: MBS Is Defanging Wahhabism, Not Dethroning It." *Maydan*, September 20, 2021, https://themaydan.com/2021/09/reordering-saudi-religion-mbs-is-defanging-wahhabism-not-dethroning-it/.
122 See Abou El Fadl, Khaled. "Saudi Arabia Is Misusing Mecca." *The New York Times*, November 12, 2018, https://www.nytimes.com/2018/11/12/opinion/saudi-arabia-mbs-grandmosque-mecca-politics.html.
123 See, respectively: "Senior Saudi Scholars Support King's Decision Allowing Women to Drive." *Gulf News*, September 27, 2017, https://gulfnews.com/world/gulf/saudi/senior-saudi-scholars-support-kings-decision-allowing-women-to-drive-1.2096797; Hubbard, Ben. "Saudi Prince, Asserting Power, Brings Clerics to Heel." *The New York Times*, November 5, 2017, https://www.nytimes.com/2017/11/05/world/middleeast/saudi-arabia-wahhabism-salafism-mohammed-bin-salman.html.

124 See "Saudi Senior Scholars Praise King's Decisions on Khashoggi Death." *Reuters*, October 20, 2018, https://www.reuters.com/article/us-saudi-khashoggi-clerics/saudi-senior-scholars-praise-kings-decisions-on-khashoggi-death-idUSKCN1MU0BO.

125 "Saudi Senior Scholars Council Rejects Report Provided to Congress About Killing of Saudi Citizen Jamal Khashoggi." *Saudi Press Agency*, February 28, 2021, https://www.spa.gov.sa/viewstory.php?lang=en&newsid=2195481.

126 Farouk, Yasmine and Brown, Nathan. "Saudi Arabia's Religious Reforms are Touching Nothing but Changing Everything." *Carnegie Endowment for International Peace*, June 7, 2021, https://carnegieendowment.org/2021/06/07/saudi-arabia-s-religious-reforms-are-touching-nothing-but-changing-everything-pub-84650.

127 "Saudi Arabia: New Counterterrorism Law Enables Abuse." *Human Rights Watch*, November 23, 2017, https://www.hrw.org/news/2017/11/23/saudi-arabia-new-counterterrorism-law-enables-abuse.

128 "Goldberg, Jeffrey. "Saudi Crown Prince: Iran's Supreme Leader 'Makes Hitler Look Good.'" *The Atlantic*, April 2, 2018, https://www.theatlantic.com/international/archive/2018/04/mohammed-bin-salman-iran-israel/557036/.

129 "Council of Senior Scholars: Muslim Brothers' Group Don't Represent Method of Islam, Rather Only Follows Its Partisan Objectives, Violating Our Graceful Religion." *Saudi Press Agency*, November 10, 2020, https://www.spa.gov.sa/viewfullstory.php?lang=en&newsid=2155594.

130 "Saudi Arabia's Heir to the Throne Talks to 60 Minutes." *CBS News*, March 19, 2018, https://www.cbsnews.com/news/saudi-crown-prince-talks-to-60-minutes/.

131 See "Vision 2030: Religious Education Reform in the Kingdom of Saudi Arabia." *King Faisal Center for Research and Islamic Studies*, September 2020, https://kfcris.com/pdf/cc53a3201f65554c400886325b5f715e5f577d35934f7.pdf.

132 Alhussein, Eman. "New Saudi Textbooks Put Nation First." *Arab Gulf States Institute in Washington*, October 17, 2019, https://agsiw.org/new-saudi-textbooks-put-nation-first/.

133 See Jones, Marc Owen. *Digital Authoritarianism in the Middle East: Deception, Disinformation, and Social Media*. Oxford University Press, 2022.

134 See Alhussein, Eman. "Saudi First: How Hyper-Nationalism is Transforming Saudi Arabia." *European Council on Foreign Relations*, June 19, 2019, https://ecfr.eu/publication/saudi_first_how_hyper_nationalism_is_transforming_saudi_arabia/.

135 Savage, Charlie et al. "Trump Pushes to Designate Muslim Brotherhood a Terrorist Group." *The New York Times*, April 30, 2019, https://www.nytimes.com/2019/04/30/us/politics/trump-muslim-brotherhood.html.

136 "Crown Prince Mohammed bin Salman Talks to TIME about the Middle East, Saudi Arabia's Plans, and President Trump." *TIME Magazine*, April 5, 2018, https://time.com/5228006/mohammed-bin-salman-interview-transcript-full/.
137 See McFarlane, Sarah et al. "Saudi Arabia Lines up Deal to Buy US Natural Gas." *The Wall Street Journal*, May 22, 2019, https://www.wsj.com/articles/saudi-arabia-strikes-deal-to-buy-u-s-natural-gas-11558487974.
138 See "Islamist Group Rejects Terrorism Charge by Sates Boycotting Qatar." *Reuters*, December 1, 2017, https://www.reuters.com/article/gulf-qatar/islamist-group-rejects-terrorism-charge-by-states-boycotting-qatar-idUSL8N1O12V8; Raghavan, Sudarsan and Warrick, Joby. "How a 91-year-old Imam Came to Symbolize the Feud between Qatar and Its Neighbors." *The Washington Post*, June 27, 2017, https://www.washingtonpost.com/world/middle_east/how-a-91-year-old-imam-came-to-symbolize-feud-between-qatar-and-its-neighbors/2017/06/26/601d41b4-5157-11e7-91eb-9611861a988f_story.html.
139 "Qatari MediaCalls Saudi Council of Scholars 'Hypocrites.'" *Egypt Today*, June 15, 2017, https://www.egypttoday.com/Article/1/7794/Qatari-media-calls-Saudi-Council-of-Scholars-%E2%80%9Chypocrites%E2%80%9D.
140 "Senior Scholars Council Warns of Al Jazeera as the Mouthpiece of Terrorist Groups." *Saudi Press Agency*, March 27, 2018, https://www.spa.gov.sa/1744840.
141 Hubbard. "Saudi Prince, Asserting Power, Brings Clerics to Heel."
142 "Saudi Ideological War Center Launches Initiatives to fight Terrorism." *Arab News*, May 2, 2017, https://www.arabnews.com/node/1093386/saudi-arabia.
143 "Counter-Extremism Center Etidal Calls for 'Proper Reading of Religious Text.'" *Arab News*, August 5, 2021, https://www.arabnews.com/node/1905826/saudi-arabia.
144 "Saudi Arabia to Stop Funding Mosques in Foreign Countries." *Middle East Monitor*, January 25, 2020, https://www.middleeastmonitor.com/20200125-saudi-arabia-to-stop-funding-mosques-in-foreign-countries/.
145 "Muslim World League Launches Global Forum for Moderate Islam." Arab News, May 27, 2019, https://www.arabnews.com/node/1502441/saudi-arabia.
146 Hoffman, Jonathan. "Israel and the Counterrevolutionaries: Gauging Tel Aviv's Evolving Regional Alliances." *Durham Middle East Papers*, No. 102, 2020.
147 Kazziha, Walid. "The Impact of Palestine on Arab Politics." *The International Spectator*, Vol. 20, No. 2, 1985, pp. 11–19; Labelle, Maurice Jr. "The Only Thorn: Early Saudi-American Relations and the Question of Palestine, 1945-1949." *Diplomatic History*, Vol. 35, No. 2, 2011, pp. 257–81.

148 "Saudi Arabia Hosts Rare Vvisit of US Evangelical Christian Figures." Reuters, November 1, 2018, https://www.reuters.com/article/us-saudi-christians/saudi-arabia-hosts-rare-visit-of-u-s-evangelical-christian-figures-idUSKCN1N6675.
149 "U.S. Christian Evangelical Delegation Meets Saudi Crown Prince." *Associated Press (AP)*, September 10, 2019, https://apnews.com/article/united-arab-emirates-religion-jiddah-jamal-khashoggi-dubai-e7f10269e60b46dabe31c455fa04017e.
150 "In First, US Jewish Umbrella Group Sends Delegation to Saudi Arabia." *The Times of Israel*, February 13, 2020, https://www.timesofisrael.com/in-first-us-jewish-umbrella-group-sends-delegation-to-saudi-arabia/.
151 "This Must Never Happen Again, Says Saudi Cleric as Muslim Group Tours Auschwitz." *The Times of Israel*, January 24, 2020, https://www.timesofisrael.com/this-must-never-happen-again-says-saudi-cleric-as-muslim-group-tours-auschwitz/.
152 See "Pope Francis received His Excellency Sheikh Dr. Mohammad bin Abdulkarim Al-Issa at the Vatican for important discussions on interfaith dialogue." August 13, 2021, https://mohammadalissa.com/en/news/meetings/1932.
153 Ratelle, J. "A Kadyrovization of Russian Foreign Policy in the Middle East: Autocrats in Track II Diplomacy and Other Humanitarian Activities." In *Russia's Islamic diplomacy*, ed. M. Laruelle. Institute for European, Russian, and Eurasian Studies, 2019.
154 Galeeva, D. "Balancing Adversaries: Russian Policy in the Gulf and the Role of Russian Muslims." *London School of Economics Blog*, January 2, 2020, https://blogs.lse.ac.uk/mec/2020/01/02/balancing-adversaries-russian-policy-in-the-gulf-and-the-role-of-russian-muslims/; Katz, Mark. "Always Looming: The Russian Muslim Factor in Moscow's Relations with Arab Gulf States." In *Russia's Islamic Diplomacy*, ed. M. Laruelle. Institute for European Russian, and Eurasian Studies, 2019.
155 Hassan, Hassan. "Moscow's Little Noticed Islamic Outreach Effort." *The Atlantic*, January 5, 2019, https://www.theatlantic.com/ideas/archive/2019/01/russia-promotes-politically-pacifist-islam/579394/.
156 Reported in Koo, Jamyan. "North-Caucasus as Russia's Springboard Toward the Muslim World." *Atlas Institute for International Affairs*, June 23, 2020, https://www.internationalaffairshouse.org/north-caucasus-as-russias-springboard-toward-the-muslim-world/.
157 "The Muslim World League Launches Its International Conference in Moscow with the Participation of 43 Countries." *Muslim World League*, March 30, 2019, https://themwl.org/en/node/36002.
158 Discussed in Koo, Jamyan. "North-Caucasus as Russia's Springboard Toward the Muslim World." *Atlas Institute for International Affairs*, June 23, 2020, https://www.internationalaffairshouse.org/north-caucasus-as-russias-springboard-toward-the-muslim-world/.

159 Samuel, S. "China is Treating Islam Like a Mental Illness." *The Atlantic*, August 28, 2018, https://www.theatlantic.com/international/archive/2018/08/china-pathologizing-uighur-muslims-mental-illness/568525/.
160 Al-Sudairi, M. T. "Hajis, Refugees, Salafi Preachers, and a Myriad of Others: An Examination of Islamic Connectivities in the Sino-Saudi Relationship." In *The Red Star & the Crescent: China and the Middle East*, ed. J. Reardon-Anderson. Oxford University Press, 2018, pp. 207–40.
161 Discussed in Al-Sudairi. "Hajis, Refugees, Salafi Preachers, and a Myriad of Others: An Examination of Islamic Connectivities in the Sino-Saudi Relationship."
162 Cummings-Bruce, Nick. "China's Retort over Its Mass Detentions: Praise from Russia and Saudi Arabia." *The New York Times*, July 12, 2019, https://www.nytimes.com/2019/07/12/world/asia/china-human-rights-united-nations.html.
163 Discussed in Guzansky, Yoel. "Either You Are with Us or You Are against Us: Gulf States Caught between America and China." *The National Interest*, June 14, 2020, https://nationalinterest.org/blog/buzz/either-you-are-us-or-against-us-gulf-states-caught-between-america-and-china-162741.
164 Deif, Farida. "A Missed Opportunity to Protect Muslims in China." *Human Rights Watch*, March 21, 2019, https://www.hrw.org/news/2019/03/21/missed-opportunity-protect-muslims-china.
165 See "Middle East Countries Deported Exiled Uighurs to China: Report." *Middle East Eye*, October 2, 2020, https://www.middleeasteye.net/news/uighur-china-middle-east-deport-beijing.
166 Discussed in "The Chinese Islamic Association in the Arab World: The Use of Islamic Soft Power in Promoting Silence in Xinjiang." *Middle East Institute*, July 14, 2020, https://www.mei.edu/publications/chinese-islamic-association-arab-world-use-islamic-soft-power-promoting-silence.

Chapter 4

1 Freer, Courtney. *Rentier Islamism: The Influence of the Muslim Brotherhood in Gulf Monarchies*. Oxford University Press, 2018.
2 Roberts, David. ""Qatar and the Muslim Brotherhood: Pragmatism or Preference?"" *Middle East Policy*, Vol. 21, No. 3, 2014, pp. 84–94.
3 Freer,. *Rentier Islamism*.
4 Baskan, Birol and Wright, Steven. "Seeds of Change: Comparing State-Religion Relations in Qatar and Saudi Arabia." *Arab Studies Quarterly*, Vol. 33, No. 2, 2011, pp. 96–111.
5 Freer. *Rentier Islamism*.
6 Warren, David. "Qatari Support for the Muslim Brotherhood Is More Than Just Realpolitik, It Has a Long, Personal History." *Maydan*, July

12, 2017, https://themaydan.com/2017/07/qatari-support-muslim-brotherhood-just-realpolitik-long-personal-history/.
7. See "Al-Qaradawi: I am part of Qatar and Qatar is part of me." *International Union of Muslim Scholars*, April 4, 2014, https://iumsonline.org/ar/ContentDetails.aspx?ID=498.
8. Cited in Al-Atawned, Muhammad. "Khuruj in Contemporary Islamic Thought: The Case of the 'Arab Spring.'" *Ilahiyat* Studies, Vol. 7, No. 1, 2016, pp. 27–52.
9. Diwan, Kristin. "Clerical Associations in Qatar and the United Arab Emirates: Soft Power Competition in Islamic Politics." *International Affairs*, Vol. 97, No. 4, 2021, pp. 945–63.
10. Kamrava, Mehran. *Qatar: Small State, Big Politics*. Cornell University Press, 2015.
11. See "Al-Qaradawi: The Arab Spring called for Islamic principles." *International Union of Muslim Scholars*, January 20, 2017, https://iumsonline.org/ar/ContentDetails.aspx?ID=6606.
12. Fromherz, Allen. *Qatar: A Modern History*. Georgetown University Press, 2012.
13. See Twitter post by Yusuf Al-Qaradawi, https://x.com/alqaradawy/status/126281478890983425.
14. Warren, David. ""Religion, Politics, and the Anxiety of Maslaha Reasoning: The Production of Fiqh Al-Thawra after the 2011 Egyptian Revolution."" In *Locating the Sharia: Legal Fluidity in Theory*, ed. S. Siddiqui. Brill, 2019, pp. 226–48.
15. Nakissa. "The Fiqh of Revolution and the Arab Spring."
16. See For the full video, see: https://www.aljazeera.net/news/arabic/2011/10/3/%D8%A7%D9%84%D9%82%D8%B1%D8%B6%D8%A7%D9%88%D9%8A-%D9%8A%D9%86%D8%AA%D9%82%D8%AF-%D9%81%D8%AA%D9%88%D9%89-%D8%B9%D9%84%D9%85%D8%A7%D8%A1-%D8%A8%D8%A7%D9%84%D9%8A%D9%85%D9%86.
17. Cherribi, Sam. *Fridays of Rage: Al Jazeera, The Arab Spring, and Political Islam*. Oxford University Press, 2017.
18. See For the full video, see: https://www.youtube.com/watch?v=PGpRu2nE2hA&t=1196s.
19. Roberts, David. *Qatar: Securing the Global Ambitions of a City-State*. Hurst, 2017a.
20. For the full sermon, see https://www.youtube.com/watch?v=336tK8gxjIk&t=1391s. Translation obtained from: Al-Azami, Usaama. *Islam and the Arab Revolutions: The Ulama between Democracy and Autocracy*. Oxford University Press, 2021.
21. Ulrichsen, Kristian. "Reflections on Mohammed bin Zayed's Preferences Regarding UAE Foreign Policy." *Arab Center Washington DC*, July 24, 2020a, https://arabcenterdc.org/resource/reflections-on-mohammed-bin-zayeds-preferences-regarding-uae-foreign-policy/.

22 For the full video, see: https://www.youtube.com/watch?v=PGpRu2nE2hA&t=84s; Translation obtained from: Al-Azami. *Islam and the Arab Revolutions.*
23 Baskan, Birol. *The Politics of Islam: The Muslim Brothers and the State in the Arab Gulf.* Edinburgh University Press, 2021.
24 See "Al-Qaradawi:Democracy is not infidelity as some claim but is repentance itself." *International Union of Muslim Scholars*, May 5, 2012, https://iumsonline.org/ar/ContentDetails.aspx?ID=2406.
25 Kamrava, Mehran. *Qatar: Small State, Big Politics.* Cornell University Press, 2015.
26 See "Al-Qaradawi:Democracy is not infidelity as some claim but is repentance itself."
27 Bianco, Cinzia and Stansfield, Gareth. "The Intra-GCC Crises: Mapping GCC Fragmentation after 2011." *International Affairs*, Vol. 94, No. 3, 2018, pp. 613–35.
28 Cited in Cherribi. *Fridays of Rage:.*
29 Cherribi. *Fridays of Rage.*
30 See "Al-Qaradawi confirms the Islamic movement is capable of leading Egypt." *International Union of Muslim Scholars*, December 2, 2011, https://iumsonline.org/ar/ContentDetails.aspx?ID=5125.
31 Nakissa, Aria. "The Fiqh of Revolution and the Arab Spring: Secondary Segmentation as a Trend in Islamic Legal Doctrine." *The Muslim World*, Vol. 105, No. 3, 2015, pp. 398–421.
32 Murphy, Dan. "Egyptian Revolution Unfinished, Qaradawi Tells Tahrir Masses." *The Christian Science Monitor*, February 18, 2011, https://www.csmonitor.com/World/Middle-East/2011/0218/Egypt-revolution-unfinished-Qaradawi-tells-Tahrir-masses.
33 See Twitter post by Yusuf Al-Qaradawi, https://x.com/alqaradawy/status/140449927338795008.
34 See Twitter post by Yusuf Al-Qaradawi, https://twitter.com/alqaradawy/status/140843997504614400.
35 Cited in Polka, Sagi. *Shaykh Yusuf al-Qaradawi: Spiritual Mentor of Wasati Salafism.* Syracuse University Press, 2019.
36 "Qatar: A Tiny Country Asserts Powerful Influence." *CBS News*, July 1, 2012, https://www.cbsnews.com/news/qatar-a-tiny-country-asserts-powerful-influence-01-07-2012/.
37 See https://iumsonline.org/ar/ContentDetails.aspx?ID=3378.
38 Cited in: Cherribi. *Fridays of Rage.*
39 See Amara, Tarek. "Qatar Bank Grants Tunisia $500 Mln to Support Currency. . ." *Reuters*, November 23, 2013, www.reuters.com/article/tunisia-economy/update-2-qatar-bank-grants-tunisia-500-mln-to-support-currency-reserve-idUSL5N0J808320131123.
40 See Cherif, Youssef. "Tunisia's Fledgling Gulf Relations." *Carnegie Endowment for International Peace*, January 17, 2017, https://www.carnegieendowment.org/sada/67703.

41 "Qatar to Proceed with $2 bln Refinery in Tunisia." *Reuters*, May 15, 2012, https://www.reuters.com/article/ozabs-tunisia-qatar-refinery-20120515-idAFJOE84E09Z20120515.
42 Osman, Mohammed. "Qatar Partner in Tunisia Democratic Transition, Says Rached Ghannouchi of Ennahda." *The Peninsula*, December 3, 2016, https://thepeninsulaqatar.com/article/03/12/2016/Qatar-partner-in-Tunisia-s-democratic-transition,-says-Rached-Ghannouchi-of-Ennahda.
43 See Doherty, Regan. "Qatar Hails New Egypt Leader in Apparent Policy Shift." *Reuters*, July 4, 2013, www.reuters.com/article/us-egypt-protests-qatar/qatar-hails-new-egypt-leader-in-apparent-policy-shift-idUSBRE96301220130704.
44 For an verview of pledged Qatari investments following the removal of Mubarak, see Awad, Marwa. "Qatar Says to Invest $18 Billion in Egypt Economy." *Reuters*, September 6, 2012, www.reuters.com/article/us-egypt-qatar-investment/qatar-says-to-invest-18-billion-in-egypt-economy-idUSBRE8850YK20120906.
45 For the full video, see: https://www.youtube.com/watch?v=QkWY0_yT0Bw.
46 See "The International Union of Muslim Scholars congratulate the revolutionaries of Libya." *International Union of Muslim Scholars*, August 28, 2011, https://iumsonline.org/ar/ContentDetails.aspx?ID=5108.
47 Black, Ian. "Qatar Admits Sending Hundreds of Troops to Support Libyan Rebels." *The Guardian*, October 26, 2011, https://www.theguardian.com/world/2011/oct/26/qatar-troops-libya-rebels-support.
48 Wehrey, Frederic. *The Burning Shores: Inside the Battle for the New Libya*. Farrar, Straus & Giroux (FSG), 2018.
49 See "Al-Qaradawi to Assad and his allies: Leave power, you have no place in it." *International Union of Muslim Scholars*, October 14, 2011, https://iumsonline.org/ar/ContentDetails.aspx?ID=5264.
50 Cited in Warren, David. "The Ulama and the Arab Uprisings 2011–13: Considering Yusuf al-Qaradawi, the 'Global Mufti,' between the Muslim Brotherhood, the Islamic Legal Tradition, and Qatari Foreign Policy." *New Middle Eastern Studies*, Vol. 4, 2014, pp. 2–32.
51 See "Al-Qaradawi calls for arming the Syrian opposition, praises valor of the revolution." *International Union of Muslim Scholars*, March 3, 2012, https://iumsonline.org/ar/ContentDetails.aspx?ID=2560.
52 See "Al-Qaradawi calls for Jihad in Syria." *International Union of Muslim Scholars*, June 1, 2013, https://iumsonline.org/ar/ContentDetails.aspx?ID=1208.
53 See "In an episode of Sharia and Life, Al-Qaradawi discusses what is happening in Egypt and Syria." *International Union of Muslim Scholars*, July 22, 2013, https://iumsonline.org/ar/ContentDetails.aspx?ID=1149.

54. "Top Cleric Qaradawi Calls for Jihad against Hezbollah, Assad in Syria." *Al-Arabiya*, June 2, 2013, https://english.alarabiya.net/News/middle-east/2013/06/02/Top-cleric-Qaradawi-calls-for-Jihad-against-Hezbollah-Assad-in-Syria.
55. See "Al-Qaradawi calls on Turkey and the Gulf to immediately intervene in Syria." *International Union of Muslim Scholars,* September 26, 2015 https://iumsonline.org/ar/ContentDetails.aspx?ID=7450.
56. "Qatar: A Tiny Country Asserts Powerful Influence."
57. Mazzetti, Mark et al. "Taking Outsize Role in Syria, Qatar Funnels Arms to Rebels." *The New York Times*, June 29, 2013, https://www.nytimes.com/2013/06/30/world/middleeast/sending-missiles-to-syrian-rebels-qatar-muscles-in.html.
58. For an overview, see Abouzeid, Rania. "Syria's Secular and Islamist Rebels: Who Are the Saudis and Qataris Arming?" *TIME*, September 18, 2012, https://world.time.com/2012/09/18/syrias-secular-and-islamist-rebels-who-are-the-saudis-and-the-qataris-arming/.
59. See "Al-Qaradawi Calls on the Sons of Bahrain to Confront the Sectarian Project." *International Union of Muslim Scholars,* May 24,2012, https://iumsonline.org/ar/ContentDetails.aspx?ID=2354.
60. Ibid.
61. "Qaradawi Says Bahrain's Revolution Sectarian." *Al-Arabiya*, March 19, 2011, https://english.alarabiya.net/articles/2011%2F03%2F19%2F142205.
62. For the interview, see Kepel, Giles. "The Arab Uprisings: How They Were Different and Why It Matters." *Chatham House*, November 21, 2012, https://www.chathamhouse.org/sites/default/files/public/Meetings/Meeting%20Transcripts/211112KepelQA.pdf.
63. See "Letter from Ayah Allah Al-Taskhiri to the Scholar Al-Qaradawi." *Rohma*, April 5, 2011, http://web.archive.org/web/20131012110809/www.rohama.org/ar/pages/?cid=5217.
64. "Qatar Has Sent Troops to Bahrain." *AFP*, March 18, 2011, https://english.ahram.org.eg/NewsContent/2/8/7988/World/Region/Qatar-has-sent-troops-to-Bahrain.aspx.
65. See "Al-Qaradawi Criticizes the Fatwa of Scholars in Yemen." *Al-Jazeera*, October 3, 2011, https://www.aljazeera.net/news/arabic/2011/10/3/%D8%A7%D9%84%D9%82%D8%B1%D8%B6%D8%A7%D9%88%D9%8A-%D9%8A%D9%86%D8%AA%D9%82%D8%AF-%D9%81%D8%AA%D9%88%D9%89-%D8%B9%D9%84%D9%85%D8%A7%D8%A1-%D8%A8%D8%A7%D9%84%D9%8A%D9%85%D9%86.
66. See "Qatar Sends 1,000 Ground Troops to Yemen Conflict." *Reuters*, September 7, 2015, https://www.reuters.com/article/us-yemen-security/qatar-sends-1000-ground-troops-to-yemen-conflict-al-jazeera-idUSKCN0R710W20150907.
67. See "Al-Qaradaghi Condemns Houthi Coup in Yemen." *International Union of Muslim Scholar,* January 21, 2015, https://iumsonline.org/

ar/ContentDetails.aspx?ID=7958;"The Union Condemns the Armed Houthi Coup Against Power and the People's Revolution in Yemen, and Condemns the Arab, Regional, and International Retreat Since the Beginning of the Crisis until the Situation Worsened." *International Union of Muslim Scholars*, January 22, 2015, https://iumsonline.org/ar/ContentDetails.aspx?ID=7957.

68 See "The Secretary-General of the Union Supports Operation "Decisive Storm" Led by 10 Countries Against the Houthi Coup in Yemen and Calls for the Protection of Civilians." *International Union of Muslim Scholars*, March 3, 2015, https://iumsonline.org/ar/ContentDetails.aspx?ID=7771;"Al-Qaradaghi Condoles the Arab Soldiers in Yemen, Praying to Allah to Accept Them and Martyrs and All Yemeni Martyrs and to Hasten Clear Victory, Stressing Support for the Will of the People in the Region." *International Union of Muslim Scholar*, September 6, 2015, https://iumsonline.org/ar/ContentDetails.aspx?ID=7432.

69 Gasim, Gamal. "The Qatari Crisis and Al Jazeera's Coverage of the War in Yemen." *Arab Media & Society*, February 15, 2018, www.arabmediasociety.com/the-qatari-crisis-and-al-jazeeras-coverage-of-the-war-in-yemen/.

70 Kirkpatrick, David. *Into the Hands of Soldiers: Freedom and Chaos in Egypt and the Middle East*. Viking, 2018.

71 Kirkpatrick, David and El Sheikh, Mayy. "Citing Deadlock, Egypt's Leader Seizes New Power and Plans Mubarak Retrial." *The New York Times*, November 22, 2012, https://www.nytimes.com/2012/11/23/world/middleeast/egypts-president-morsi-gives-himself-new-powers.html.

72 "Top Egyptian Cleric Sanctions Anti-Morsi Protests." *The Times of Israel*, June 19, 2013, https://www.timesofisrael.com/top-egyptian-cleric-sanctions-anti-morsi-protest/.

73 For the full video, see https://www.youtube.com/watch?v=nJrImaCkxo4&t=35s. Translation obtained from: Polka. *Shaykh Yusuf al-Qaradawi*.

74 For the full statement, see "International Union of Muslim Scholars Warns of Egypt Destabilization, Calls on Opposition to Follow Democratic Rules." *International Union of Muslim Scholars*, June 26, 2013, https://www.al-qaradawi.net/node/4788.

75 See "Al-Qaradawi: The Egyptian Coup is a War Against Islam." *International Union of Muslim Scholars*, September 14, 2013, https://iumsonline.org/ar/ContentDetails.aspx?ID=965.

76 See "The Scholar Al-Qaradawi: The Kharijites Are The Ones Who Rebelled Against President Morsi." *International Union of Muslim Scholars*, August 26, 2013, https://iumsonline.org/ar/ContentDetails.aspx?ID=100 For the full video, see: https://www.youtube.com/watch?v=V12zCzozumQ&t=1302s.

77 See "Al-Azhar Participation in the Coup. Efforts to Revoke Al-Qaradawi's Senior Membership." *International Union of Muslim Scholars*, July 31, 2013, https://iumsonline.org/ar/ContentDetails.aspx?ID=1134.

78 Facebook post by Yusuf Al-Qaradawi, https://www.facebook.com/alqaradawy/posts/598404810199587.
79 See "Al-Qaradawi Calls on Egyptians to Rally in the Face of Killers." *Al-Jazeera*, July 27, 2013, https://www.aljazeera.net/news/arabic/2013/7/27/%D8%A7%D9%84%D9%82%D8%B1%D8%B6%D8%A7%D9%88%D9%8A-%D9%8A%D8%AF%D8%B9%D9%88-%D8%A7%D9%84%D9%85%D8%B5%D8%B1%D9%8A%D9%8A%D9%86-%D9%84%D9%84%D8%A7%D8%AD%D8%AA%D8%B4%D8%A7%D8%AF.
80 Ibid.
81 See "Reply to the Military Mufti (Ali Goma'a)." *Al-Qaradawi.net*, November 10, 2013, https://www.al-qaradawi.net/node/2836.
82 "All According to Plan: The Rab'a Massacre and the Mass Killing of Protesters in Egypt." Human Rights Watch, August 12, 2014, https://www.hrw.org/report/2014/08/12/all-according-plan/raba-massacre-and-mass-killings-protesters-egypt.
83 Ibid.
84 See "Denounce the Criminal Killers: Al-Qaradawi Calls on Every Egyptian and their Families to go to Rabaa Al-Adawiya." *International Union of Muslim Scholars*, July 29,2013, https://iumsonline.org/ar/ContentDetails.aspx?ID=1137.
85 Ibid.
86 See "The Union Condemns the Heinous Massacres of Pro-Legitimacy Demonstrators." *International Union of Muslim Scholars*, July 26, 2013, https://iumsonline.org/ar/ContentDetails.aspx?ID=1143.
87 See "Al-Qaradawi: The Egyptian Military and "Tartur" are Terrorists and Murderers." *International Union of Muslim Scholars*, December 12, 2013, https://iumsonline.org/ar/ContentDetails.aspx?ID=750.
88 "Egypt Summons Qatari Envoy after Criticisms of Crackdown." *Reuters*, January 4, 2014, https://www.reuters.com/article/us-egypt-brotherhood-qatar/egypt-summons-qatari-envoy-after-criticisms-of-crackdown-idUKBREA0304W20140104.
89 Roberts, David. "Qatar and the UAE: Exploring Divergent Responses to the Arab Spring." *Middle East Journal*, Vol. 71, No. 4, 2017b, pp. 544–62.
90 Sciutto, Jim and Herb, Jeremy. "Exclusive: The Secret Documents That Help Explain the Qatar Crisis." *CNN*, July 11, 2017, https://www.cnn.com/2017/07/10/politics/secret-documents-qatar-crisis-gulf-saudi.
91 For the full video, see https://www.youtube.com/watch?v=7dMSK7YaNZg&t=406s. Translation obtained from: Al-Azami,. *Islam and the Arab Revolutions*.
92 Black, Ian. "Arab States Withdraw Ambassadors from Qatar in Protest at 'Interference.'" *The Guardian*, March 5, 2014, https://www.theguardian.com/world/2014/mar/05/arab-states-qatar-withdraw-ambassadors-protest.
93 DeYoung, Karen, and Ellen Nakashima. "UAE Orchestrated Hacking of Qatari Government Sites, Sparking Regional Upheaval, According to

U.S. Intelligence Officials." *The Washington Post*, WP Company, July 16, 2017, www.washingtonpost.com/world/national-security/uae-hacked-qatari-government-sites-sparking-regional-upheaval-according-to-us-intelligence-officials/2017/07/16/00c46e54-698f-11e7-8eb5-cbccc2e7bfbf_story.html.

94 "Islamist Group Reject Terrorism Charge by States Boycotting Qatar." *Reuters*, December 1, 2017, https://www.reuters.com/article/gulf-qatar/islamist-group-rejects-terrorism-charge-by-states-boycotting-qatar-idUSL8N1O12V8.

95 "List of Demands on Qatar by Saudi Arabia, Other Arab Nations." *Associated Press*, June 23, 2017, https://apnews.com/article/bahrain-qatar-iran-saudi-arabia-united-arab-emirates-3a58461737c44ad58047562e48f46e06.

96 See McFarlane, Sarah et al. "Saudi Arabia Lines Up Deal to Buy U.S. Natural Gas." *The Wall Street Journal*, May 22, 2019, https://www.wsj.com/articles/saudi-arabia-strikes-deal-to-buy-u-s-natural-gas-11558487974.

97 For an overview, see Greenwald, Glenn. "How Former Treasury Officials and the UAE are Manipulating American Journalists." *The Intercept*, September 25, 2014, https://theintercept.com/2014/09/25/uae-qatar-camstoll-group/.

98 Savage, Charlie et al. "Trump Pushes to Designate Muslim Brotherhood a Terrorist Organization." *The New York Times*, April 30, 2019, https://www.nytimes.com/2019/04/30/us/politics/trump-muslim-brotherhood.html.

99 "We Are Not Ready to Surrender," Qatar FM Says." *Doha News*, June 9, 2017, https://dohanews.co/we-are-not-ready-to-surrender-qatar-fm-says-2/.

100 "Islamic Institutions Divided over Qatar Blockade." *Middle East Monitor*, June 7, 2017, https://www.middleeastmonitor.com/20170607-islamic-institutions-divided-over-qatar-blockade/.

101 See "Al-Qaradaghi: the Siege on Qatar Separates a Man from His Wife and Completes the Tearing Apart of the Nation." *International Union of Muslim Scholars*, July 12, 2017, https://iumsonline.org/ar/ContentDetails.aspx?ID=7108.

102 See "Al Qaradaghi Calls for Dialogue Between Brothers, Hopes for Near Reconciliation, and Sees it as a Duty, as Estrangement is Forbidden in Islamic law." *International Union of Muslim Scholars*, June 7, 2017, https://iumsonline.org/ar/ContentDetails.aspx?ID=7015.

103 See "Al-Qaradaghi: Qatar is Being Punished for its Honorable Positions." *International Union of Muslim Scholars*, May 29, 2017, https://iumsonline.org/ar/ContentDetails.aspx?ID=6992.

104 "Islamist Group Reject Terrorism Charge by States Boycotting Qatar." *Reuters*, December 1, 2017, https://www.reuters.com/article/gulf-qatar/islamist-group-rejects-terrorism-charge-by-states-boycotting-qatar-idUSL8N1O12V8.

105 Cited in Polka. *Shaykh Yusuf al-Qaradawi.*
106 See "Al-Qaradaghi: They will Fail to Destroy Muslim scholars." *International Union of Muslim Scholars,* November 25, 2017, https://iumsonline.org/ar/ContentDetails.aspx?ID=8197.
107 See, respectively: "Al-Qaradaghi: Tyrannical Rulers and the Elimination of Legitimacy is the Cause of the Phenomenon of Terrorism." *International Union of Muslim Scholars,* March 2, 2015, https://iumsonline.org/ar/ContentDetails.aspx?ID=7793;"Al-Raissouni: The Current Violence is a Reaction to the Violence of the Counter-revolution." *International Union of Muslim Scholars,* April 20,2015, https://iumsonline.org/ar/ContentDetails.aspx?ID=1739.
108 See "Al-Qaradaghi: "Muslim Scholars Spread Peace. And Are Not Subject to the Desires of Rulers." *International Union of Muslim Scholars,* December 2, 2017, https://iumsonline.org/ar/ContentDetails.aspx?ID=8202.
109 See "Al-Raissouni: There is No Country that Can Interfere in the International Union of Muslim Scholars." *International Union of Muslim Scholars,* November 29, 2018, https://iumsonline.org/ar/ContentDetails.aspx?ID=8935.
110 See "Al-Raissouni: The Union is Not Controlled by the Muslim Brotherhood and No Country Determines Positions." *International Union of Muslim Scholars,* November 17, 2018, https://iumsonline.org/ar/ContentDetails.aspx?ID=8907.
111 See "Al-Raissouni: Scholars in Egypt and Saudi are Against Islamic Renewal." *International Union of Muslim Scholars,* August 26, 2014, https://iumsonline.org/ar/ContentDetails.aspx?ID=151.
112 See Finn, Tom. "Turkey to Set Up Qatar Military Base to Face 'Common Enemies.'" *Reuters,* December 16, 2015, www.reuters.com/article/us-qatar-turkey-military-idUSKBN0TZ17V20151216.
113 See "Erdogan Underlines Qatar's Support for Turkey." *Qatar Tribune,* July 31, 2016, www.qatar-tribune.com/Latest-News/ArtMID/423/ArticleID/4457/Erdogan-Underlines-Qatars-Support-for-Turkey.
114 Beaumont, Peter. "Turkey Demands an End to Qatar Blockade as Humanitarian Deepens." *The Guardian,* June 10, 2017, https://www.theguardian.com/world/2017/jun/10/turkey-erdogan-end-qatar-blockade.
115 Bora, Birce. "Analysis: Why Is Turkey Deploying Troops to Qatar?" *Aljazeera,* June 11, 2017, https://www.aljazeera.com/features/2017/6/11/analysis-why-is-turkey-deploying-troops-to-qatar.
116 See "Al-Qaradaghi in his Meeting with the Turkish Diplomat in Doha: The Tyrannical Leader is the One who Creates Terrorism Through his Tyranny." *International Union of Muslim Scholars,* December 20, 2014, https://iumsonline.org/ar/ContentDetails.aspx?ID=8098.
117 See "Al-Qaradawi Praises the Role of Qatar and Turkey in Uniting Muslims." *International Union of Muslim Scholars,* November 21,2016, https://iumsonline.org/ar/ContentDetails.aspx?ID=6428.

118 See "New Video of Al-Qaradawi. The Implications of Turkey's Failed Coup. Victory and Support from God." *International Union of Muslim Scholars,* August 17, 2016, https://iumsonline.org/ar/ContentDetails.aspx?ID=6117.
119 See "Al-Qaradawi Calls on the Governments of Arab and Islamic Countries to Rally Around Turkey." *International Union of Muslim Scholars,* July 22, 2016, https://iumsonline.org/ar/ContentDetails.aspx?ID=5947.
120 Diwan. "Clerical Associations in Qatar and the United Arab Emirates."
121 Mitchell, Jocelyn Sage and Al-Hammadi, Mariam Ibrahim. "Nationalism and Identity in Qatar after 2017: The Narrative of the New National Museum." *Journal of Arabian Studies,* Vol. 10, No. 2, 2020, pp. 256–77.
122 For a discussion of this nationalist turn in the Gulf monarchies, see Crystal, Jill. "Nationalism in the Persian Gulf's Oil Monarchies." In *Routledge Handbook of Persian Gulf Politics,* ed. Mehran Kamrava. Routledge, 2020, pp. 280–91.
123 Freer. *Rentier Islamism.*
124 See "Union of Ccholars: Qatar is the Oppressed Kaaba." *International Union of Muslim Scholars,* September 23, 2014, https://iumsonline.org/ar/ContentDetails.aspx?ID=120
125 See, for example, "Al-Qaradaghi Condemns Death Sentences and Life Imprisonment Against Those Who Reject the Coup in Egypt." *International Union of Muslim Scholars,* April 11, 2015, https://iumsonline.org/ar/ContentDetails.aspx?ID=7760; "Al-Qaradaghi: Release the UAE Detainees, Enough Injustice and Aggression. Activist Alaa Al-Siddiq tells the story of her detained father." *International Union of Muslim Scholars,* June 17, 2020, https://iumsonline.org/ar/ContentDetails.aspx?ID=11808;"International Union of Muslim Scholars Calls for Immediate Release of Sheikh Salman Al-Awda and his Companions." *International Union of Muslim Scholars,* September 11, 2017, https://iumsonline.org/ar/ContentDetails.aspx?ID=7227.
126 See "Al-Qaradaghi from Cape Town Praises the Steadfastness of the Martyr Morsi on the Truth and Patience and His Patience on the Affliction." *International Union of Muslim Scholars,* June 19, 2019, https://iumsonline.org/ar/ContentDetails.aspx?ID=9665.
127 "International Union of Muslim Scholars on Al-Ouda's Trail: 'Incarcerating the Righteous Is Harbinger of Doom.'" *Middle East Monitor,* September 6, 2018, https://www.middleeastmonitor.com/20180906-international-union-of-muslim-scholars-on-al-oudas-trial-incarcerating-the-righteous-is-harbinger-of-doom/.
128 See "Al-Qaradaghi Criticizes China's Decisions Against Muslims in Xinjiang." *International Union of Muslim Scholars,* May 10, 2015, https://iumsonline.org/ar/ContentDetails.aspx?ID=7703.

129 See "Al-Raissouni: China is Working Hard to Erase the Islam of the Uyghur People. Several Cities are Witnessing Demonstrations Condemning China." *International Union of Muslim Scholars,* December 31, 2019, https://iumsonline.org/ar/ContentDetails.aspx?ID =10746.

130 See "The Union Strongly Condemns the Chinese Authorities' Ban on Fasting During Ramadan for Uyghur Muslims in Xinjiang Province." *International Union of Muslim Scholars,* June 24, 2015, https://iumsonline.org/ar/ContentDetails.aspx?ID=7576.

131 See "International Union of Muslim Scholars Condemns the Repressive Arrests of Turkestan Students in Egypt and China." *International Union of Muslim Scholars,* July 8, 2017, https://iumsonline.org/ar/ContentDetails.aspx?ID=7100.

132 Younes, Ali. "Activists Hail Qatar Withdrawal from Pro-China Text over Uighurs." Aljazeera, August 21, 2019, https://www.aljazeera.com/news/2019/8/21/activists-hail-qatar-withdrawal-from-pro-china-text-over-uighurs.

133 Hassanein, Haisam. "Arab States Give China a Pass on Uyghur Crackdown." *Washington Institute for Near East Policy,* August 26, 2019, https://www.washingtoninstitute.org/policy-analysis/arab-states-give-china-pass-uyghur-crackdown.

134 "U.N. Body Rejects Debate on China's Treatment of Uyghur Muslims in Blow to West." *CNBC,* October 6, 2022, https://www.cnbc.com/2022/10/07/un-body-rejects-debate-on-chinas-treatment-of-uyghur-muslims-in-blow-to-west.html.

135 For an overview, see Ramani, Samuel. "China's Growing Security Relationship with Qatar." *The Diplomat,* November 16, 2017, https://thediplomat.com/2017/11/chinas-growing-security-relationship-with-qatar/.

136 D'Acunto, Federica. "The Brand of Peace: The Relations Between Qatar, Palestine, and Israel." *Università Ca' Foscari Venezia,* 2016, http://dspace.unive.it/handle/10579/9199.

137 Polka. *Shaykh Yusuf al-Qaradawi.*

138 Cherribi. *Fridays of Rage.*

139 See "Al-Qaradaghi: The Palestinian Issue is our Issue and the Al-Aqsa Mosque is Our Sanctity." *International Union of Muslim Scholars,* February 4, 2019, https://iumsonline.org/ar/ContentDetails.aspx?ID=9307.

140 See "Al-Qaradaghi Calls for an Islamic and Arab Uprising for Palestine." *International Union of Muslim Scholars,* July 6, 2014, https://iumsonline.org/ar/ContentDetails.aspx?ID=283.

141 See "The Union Strongly Condemns the Decision of an Egyptian Court to Designate Hamas as a Terrorist Organization." *International Union of Muslim Scholars,* March 2, 2015, https://iumsonline.org/ar/ContentDetails.aspx?ID=7791.

142 See, respectively: "Al-Qaradawi: We Do Not Accept a Concession on Jerusalem and Al-Aqsa Mosque." *International Union of Muslim Scholars*, December 7, 2017, https://iumsonline.org/ar/ContentDetails.aspx?ID=8208; "Al-Qaradaghi Participates in a Solidarity Protest in Istanbul to Reject the Deal of the Century." *International Union of Muslim Scholars*, January 2, 2020, https://iumsonline.org/ar/ContentDetails.aspx?ID=10891.

143 See "Muslim Scholars: Netanyahu-Bin Zayed Agreement is "High Treason" and Aboutrika: The Issue of Palestine is an Issue of Awareness of Peoples, Not Agreements of Rulers or Treaties of Countries." *International Union of Muslim Scholars*, August 14, 2020, https://iumsonline.org/ar/ContentDetails.aspx?ID=12194.

144 See "Statement of the Union of Scholars on the Normalization of Bahrain." *International Union of Muslim Scholars*, September 14, 2020, https://iumsonline.org/ar/ContentDetails.aspx?ID=12361.

145 See "The Union Condemns Bahraini Normalization with the Occupation and Stresses the Prohibition of Normalization with the Occupiers of Al-Aqsa, Jerusalem and Palestine and that it is High Treason." *International Union of Muslim Scholars*, September 13, 2020, https://iumsonline.org/ar/ContentDetails.aspx?ID=12358.

146 See "Al-Khalil: Do not Compromise on Al-Aqsa if You are Unable to Liberate it. And Al-Qaradaghi: "Congratulations to the Traitors on their Treason."" *International Union of Muslim Scholars*, August 15, 2020, https://iumsonline.org/ar/ContentDetails.aspx?ID=12203.

147 See "Al-Qaradawi: The Palestinian Cause is Our Cause and Defending it is Obligatory Upon Us." *International Union of Muslim Scholars,* September 27, 2020, https://iumsonline.org/ar/ContentDetails.aspx?ID=12422.

148 See "Al-Raissouni Calls on Muslim Scholars to "Break the Siege of Normalization."" *International Union of Muslim Scholars,* December 18, 2020, https://iumsonline.org/ar/ContentDetails.aspx?ID=12859.

149 See "Al-Raissouni: Palestine is Afflicted by the Oppression of Enemies and Wretched Brothers (Dialogue)." *International Union of Muslim Scholars,* December 18, 2020, https://iumsonline.org/ar/ContentDetails.aspx?ID=12860.

150 Jones, Clive and Guzansky, Yoel. *Fraternal Enemies: Israel and the Gulf Monarchies*. Oxford University Press, 2019.

151 "Israeli National Anthem Plays in Qatar." *The Jerusalem Post*, March 25, 2019, https://www.jpost.com/israel-news/israeli-national-anthem-plays-in-qatar-watch-584517.

152 Kingsley, Patrick and Nereim, Vivian. "Qatar Will Allow Israelis to Fly Directly to Doha for World Cup." *The New York Times*, November 10, 2022, https://www.nytimes.com/2022/11/10/world/middleeast/qatar-israelis-world-cup.html.

Chapter 5

1 Shahrour, Karam. "The Evolution of Emirati Foreign Policy (1971-2020): The Unexpected Rise of a Small State with Boundless Ambitions." *Sciences Po Kuwait Program*, 2020, https://www.sciencespo.fr/kuwait-program/wp-content/uploads/2021/02/Shahrour-Karam-The-evolution-of-Emirati-foreign-policy-1971-2020.pdf.
2 Christie, Kenneth. "Globalization, Religion, and State Formation in the United Arab Emirates and Pakistan." *Totalitarian Movements and Political Religions*, Vol. 11, No. 2, 2010, pp. 203–12.
3 Rubin, Barry. "Guide to Islamist Movements." M.E. Sharpe, 2010.
4 Al-Qassemi, Sultan. "The Brothers and the Gulf." *Foreign Policy*, December 14, 2012, https://foreignpolicy.com/2012/12/14/the-brothers-and-the-gulf/.
5 Hedges, Matthew, and Cafiero, Giorgio. "'The GCC and the Muslim Brotherhood: What Does the Future Hold?'" *Middle East Policy*, Vol. 21, No. 1, 2017, pp. 129–53.
6 Baskan, Birol. *The Politics of Islam: The Muslim Brothers and the State in the Arab Gulf*. Edinburgh University Press, 2021.
7 Freer, Courtney. *Rentier Islamism: The Influence of the Muslim Brotherhood in Gulf Monarchies*. Oxford University Press, 2018.
8 Fyfe, Ann. "Wealth and Power: Political and Economic Change in the United Arab Emirates." *Durham University Thesis*, 1989, http://etheses.dur.ac.uk/6505/1/6505_3805.PDF?UkUDh:CyT.
9 Roberts, David. "Mosque and State: The United Arab Emirates' Secular Foreign Policy." *Foreign Affairs*, March 18, 2016, https://www.foreignaffairs.com/united-arab-emirates/mosque-and-state.
10 Freer, Courtney. "Political Islam in the Arabian Peninsula." In *Routledge Handbook of Persian Gulf Politics*, ed. Mehran Kamrava. Routledge, 2020, pp. 308–26.
11 Baskan. *The Politics of Islam*.
12 Ulrichsen, Kristian. "Links Between Domestic and Regional Security." In *The Changing Security Dynamics of the Persian Gulf*, ed. Kristian Ulrichsen. Oxford University Press, 2017a, pp. 23–42.
13 Shahrour. "The Evolution of Emirati Foreign Policy (1971-2020)."
14 Almezaini, Khalid. "The Transformation of UAE Foreign Policy since 2011." In *The Changing Security Dynamics of the Persian Gulf*, ed. Kristian Ulrichsen. Oxford University Press, 2017, pp. 191–204.
15 Ulrichsen, Kristian. *The United Arab Emirates: Power, Politics, and Policymaking*. Routledge, 2017b.
16 Roberts, David. "Bucking the Trend: The UAE and the Development of Military Capabilities in the Arab World." *Security Studies*, Vol. 29, No. 2, 2020, pp. 301–34.
17 Ulrichsen, Kristian. *Qatar and the Gulf Crisis*. Oxford University Press, 2020b.

18 Shahrour. "The Evolution of Emirati Foreign Policy (1971-2020)."
19 Bianco, Cinzia and Stansfield, Gareth. "The Intra-GCC Crises: Mapping GCC Fragmentation after 2011." *International Affairs*, Vol. 94, No. 3, 2018, pp. 613–35.
20 Baskan. *The Politics of Islam*.
21 Davidson, Christopher. "The UAE, Qatar, and the Question of Political Islam." In *Divided Gulf: The Anatomy of a Crisis*, ed. Andreas Krieg. Palgrave, 2019, pp. 71–90.
22 Hightower, Victoria. "Assessing Historical Narratives of the UAE." *London School of Economics and Political Science Blog*, December 12, 2018, https://blogs.lse.ac.uk/mec/2018/12/12/assessing-historical-narratives-of-the-uae/.
23 Sabban, Rima. "State Building, State Branding, and Heritage in the UAE." *London School of Economics and Political Science Blog*, December 17, 2018, https://blogs.lse.ac.uk/mec/2018/12/17/state-building-state-branding-and-heritage-in-the-uae/.
24 Ozgen, Zeynep, and Hassan, Sharif Ibrahim El-Shishtawy. "Meaning of a Textbook: Religious Education, National Islam, and the Politics of Reform in the United Arab Emirates." *Nations and Nationalism*, Vol. 27, No. 4, 2021, pp. 1181–97.
25 "United Arab Emirates: International Religious Freedom Report 2007." *U.S. Department of State*, 2007, https://www.justice.gov/sites/default/files/eoir/legacy/2013/06/10/uae.pdf.
26 Ibid.
27 "The Strange Case of the UAE's WWW.UAEHEWAR.NET." *The Sigers*, November 15, 2010, http://thesigers.com/analysis/2010/11/15/the-strange-case-of-the-uaes-wwwuaehewarnet.html.
28 "Access to Independent Online Discussion Forum Blocked." *Reporters Without Borders*, February 24, 2010, https://rsf.org/en/access-independent-online-discussion-forum-blocked.
29 See Davidson, Christopher. "Fear and Loathing in the Emirates." *Carnegie Endowment for International Peace*, September 18, 2012, https://carnegieendowment.org/sada/49409.
30 For the full petition and a complete list of its signatories, see Emiratis send a message to the rulers of the Emirates demanding a complete reform of the parliamentary system. https://www.ipetitions.com/petition/uaepetition71/.
31 This joint letter has since been removed. This quote was obtained from Davidson. "Fear and Loathing in the Emirates."
32 See Twitter post by Mohammad Abdul Razzaq Al-Siddiq, https://twitter.com/malsiddiq/status/156814657175298048.
33 See Twitter post by Mohammad Abdul Razzaq Al-Siddiq, https://twitter.com/malsiddiq/status/156813070432342016.
34 See Twitter post by Mohammad Abdul; Razzaq Al-Siddiq, https://twitter.com/malsiddiq/status/168076271807508480.

35 See Twitter post by Mohammad Abdul; Razzaq Al-Siddiq, https://twitter.com/malsiddiq/status/168077577095872512.
36 See Twitter post by Mohammad Abdul; Razzaq Al-Siddiq, https://twitter.com/malsiddiq/status/171680455937110018.
37 Freer, Courtney. "Rentier Islamism in the Absence of Elections: The Political Role of Muslim Brotherhood Affiliates in Qatar and the United Arab Emirates." *International Journal of Middle East Studies*, Vol. 49, No. 3, 2017, pp. 479–500.
38 Davidson, Christopher. "Viewpoint: Wealthy and Stable UAE Keeps the Lid on Dissent." *BBC*, April 15, 2015a, https://www.bbc.com/news/world-middle-east-31986653.
39 See "UAE: Investigate Threats against 'UAE 5.'" *Human Rights Watch*, November 25, 2011, https://www.hrw.org/news/2011/11/25/uae-investigate-threats-against-uae-5; "UAE: Crackdown on Islamist Group Intensifies." *Human Rights Watch*, July 18, 2012, https://www.hrw.org/news/2012/07/18/uae-crackdown-islamist-group-intensifies.
40 "UAE Islamist Group Denies Reports it has an Armed Wing." *Reuters*, September 23, 2012, https://www.reuters.com/article/uk-emirates-islamists/uae-islamist-group-denies-reports-it-has-an-armed-wing-idUKBRE88M05X20120923.
41 "94 Emiratis Charged with Compromising UAE Security." *The National*, January 27, 2013, https://www.thenationalnews.com/uae/government/94-emiratis-charged-with-compromising-uae-security-1.458803.
42 "UAE Strips Citizenship from Family of Political Prisoner." *Middle East Eye*, March 10, 2016, https://www.middleeasteye.net/news/uae-strips-citizenship-family-political-prisoner.
43 See, respectively: "Ministry Dissolves Teachers' Association Board." *The National*, May 2, 2011, https://www.thenationalnews.com/uae/ministry-dissolves-teachers-association-board-1.377119; "UAE: Government Suspension of Jurist Association Board Part of Ongoing Crackdown on Civil Society." *Amnesty International*, January 6, 2012, https://www.amnesty.org/en/wp-content/uploads/2021/07/mde250032012en.pdf.
44 "UAE Uncovers Muslim Brotherhood Cell, Arrests its Members." *Gulf News*, January 1, 2013, https://gulfnews.com/uae/government/uae-uncovers-muslim-brotherhood-cell-arrests-its-members-1.1126560.
45 "UAE Jails 30 over 'Muslim Brotherhood Ties.'" *BBC*, January 21, 2014, https://www.bbc.com/news/world-middle-east-25824395.
46 "Dh5.7bn Allocated for New Water and Electricity Projects in Northern Emirates." *Emirates 24/7*, March 2, 2011, https://www.emirates247.com/news/government/dh5-7bn-allocated-for-new-water-and-electricity-projects-in-northern-emirates-2011-03-02-1.362966.
47 "UAE Boosts Military Pensions, Seen Pre-empting Unrest." *Al-Arabiya*, March 24, 2011, https://english.alarabiya.net/articles/2011%2F03%2F24%2F142832.

48 "President Issues National Day Resolutions." *Gulf News Report*, November 30, 2011, https://gulfnews.com/uae/president-issues-national-day-resolutions-1.940718.
49 Ibid.
50 Black, Ian. "Emirati Nerves Rattled by Islamists' Rise." *The Guardian*, October 12, 2012, https://www.theguardian.com/world/on-the-middle-east/2012/oct/12/uae-muslimbrotherhood-egypt-arabspring.
51 "UAE: Terrorism Law Threatens Lives, Liberty." *Human Rights Watch*, December 3, 2014, https://www.hrw.org/news/2014/12/04/uae-terrorism-law-threatens-lives-liberty#:~:text=(Beirut)%20%E2%80%93%20The%20United%20Arab,and%20sentence%20them%20to%20death..
52 "UAE Lists Muslim Brotherhood as Terrorist Group." *Reuters*, November 15, 2014, https://www.reuters.com/article/us-emirates-politics-brotherhood/uae-lists-muslim-brotherhood-as-terrorist-group-idUSKCN0IZ0OM20141115.
53 "UAE's Tolerance of Extremism is 'Quite Low.'" *The National*, November 21, 2014, https://www.thenationalnews.com/world/uae-s-tolerance-of-extremism-is-quite-low-1.588788.
54 "UAE Arrests: 41 Accused of Plotting 'Caliphate.'" *BBC*, August 2, 2015, https://www.bbc.com/news/world-middle-east-33751205.
55 Wintour, Patrick. "Donald Trump Hoping to Call Gulf States to Washington Summit." *The Guardian*, July 27, 2018, https://www.theguardian.com/world/2018/jul/27/donald-trump-hoping-to-call-gulf-states-to-washington-summit.
56 "Anwar Gargash: Six Pillars that Support Security in the UAE." *The National*, March 30, 2014, https://www.thenationalnews.com/uae/government/anwar-gargash-six-pillars-that-support-security-in-the-uae-1.592418.
57 For a comprehensive analysis of regional interventions following the uprisings, see Petti, Matthew, and Parsi, Trita. "No Clean Hands: The Interventions of Middle Eastern Powers, 2010-2020." *Quincy Institute for Responsible Statecraft*, July 19, 2021, https://quincyinst.org/report/no-clean-hands-the-interventions-of-middle-eastern-powers/.
58 See Cherif, Youssef. "Tunisia's Fledgling Gulf Relations." *Carnegie Endowment for International Peace*, January 17, 2017, https://www.carnegieendowment.org/sada/67703.
59 Matthiesen, Toby. "Renting the Casbah: Gulf States' Foreign Policy Toward North Africa Since the Arab Uprisings." In *The Changing Security Dynamics of the Persian Gulf*, ed. Kristian Ulrichsen. Oxford University Press, 2017, pp. 43–60.
60 Ibid.
61 See "UAE Expresses Full Confidence and Support for Tunisia—Statement." *Reuters*, July 28, 2021, https://www.reuters.com/world/middle-east/uae-expresses-full-confidence-support-tunisia-statement

-2021-07-28/; "Tunisia Coup: UAE Supports President Saied's 'Positive Agenda,' says Official." *Middle East Eye*, August 7, 2021, https://www.middleeasteye.net/news/tunisia-coup-uae-supports-president-saieds-positive-agenda-says-official.

62 See "Egypt's Mubarak Meets UAE Foreign Minister Amid Ongoing Unrest." *Trend News Agency*, February 8, 2011, https://en.trend.az/world/arab/1825736.html.

63 Kirkpatrick, David. "Recordings Suggest Emirates and Egyptian Military Pushed Ousting of Morsi." *The New York Times*, March 1, 2015, https://www.nytimes.com/2015/03/02/world/middleeast/recordings-suggest-emirates-and-egyptian-military-pushed-ousting-of-morsi.html.

64 See, respectively: "UAE Signs $4.9 Billion Aid Package to Egypt." *Reuters*, October 26, 2013, https://www.reuters.com/article/uk-uae-egypt/uae-signs-4-9-billion-aid-package-to-egypt-idUKBRE99P08620131026; "Dubai's Emaar Says Not Part of Egypt's Capital City Project." *Reuters*, March 16, 2015, https://www.reuters.com/article/emaar-properties-egypt/dubais-emaar-says-not-part-of-egypts-capital-city-project-idUKL6N0WI07P20150316.

65 "UAE Says Sent 500 Police Officers into Bahrain." *Reuters*, March 14, 2011, https://www.reuters.com/article/us-g8-bahrain-uae/uae-says-sent-500-police-officers-into-bahrain-idUSTRE72D6DE20110314.

66 "UAE Fighter Jets on the Way to Libya." *The National*, March 25, 2011, https://www.thenationalnews.com/uae/uae-fighter-jets-on-the-way-to-libya-1.574666.

67 See, respectively: Malsin, Jared. "U.A.E. Boosted Arms Transfers to Libya to Salvage Warlord's Campaign, U.N. Panel Finds." *The Wall Street Journal*, September 29, 2020, https://www.wsj.com/articles/u-a-e-boosted-arms-transfers-tolibyato-salvage-warlords-campaign-u-n-panel-finds-11601412059; Bazzi, Mohamed. "Biden is Doubling Down on Trump's Mistake of Arms Deals with this Rogue Regime." *The Washington Post*, September 21, 2021, https://www.washingtonpost.com/opinions/2021/09/21/biden-is-doubling-down-trumps-mistakes-arms-deals-with-this-rogue-regime/; Mackinnon, Amy and Detsch, Jack. "Pentagon Says UAE Possibly Funding Russia's Shadowy Mercenaries in Libya." *Foreign Policy*, November 30, 2020, https://foreignpolicy.com/2020/11/30/pentagon-trump-russia-libya-uae/.

68 "Madkhalism Well-rooted in Libya to Help Pass Saudi Agenda by UAE Funding." *Libyan Express*, April 7, 2018, https://www.libyanexpress.com/madkhalism-well-rooted-in-libya-to-help-pass-saudi-agenda-by-uae-funding/.

69 Freer, Courtney. "Is the UAE's Fear of the Muslim Brotherhood Driving Its Yemen Strategy?" *Middle East Centre, London School of Economics and Political Science*, June 28, 2016, www.blogs.lse.ac.uk/mec/2016/06/28/is-the-uaes-fear-of-the-muslim-brotherhood-driving-its-yemen-strategy/.

70 See, respectively: Elbagir, Nima et al. "Sold to an Ally, Lost to an Enemy." *CNN*, March 28, 2019, https://www.cnn.com/interactive/2019/02/middleeast/yemen-lost-us-arms/; Roston, Aram. "American Mercenaries." *Buzzfeed News*, October 16, 2018, https://www.buzzfeednews.com/article/aramroston/mercenaries-assassination-us-yemen-uae-spear-golan-dahlan.

71 Worth, Robert. "Mohammed bin Zayed's Dark Vision of the Middle East's Future." *The New York Times*, January 9, 2020, https://www.nytimes.com/2020/01/09/magazine/united-arab-emirates-mohammed-bin-zayed.html.

72 See, respectively: Cafiero, Giorgio. "UAE Boosts Assad as Part of Anti-Turkey Strategy." *Responsible Statecraft*, April 16, 2020, https://responsiblestatecraft.org/2020/04/16/uae-boosts-assad/; Ramani, Samuel. "Why the Relationship Between Russia and the United Arab Emirates is Strengthening." *Responsible Statecraft*, January 24, 2020, https://responsiblestatecraft.org/2020/01/24/why-the-relationship-between-russia-and-the-united-arab-emirates-is-strengthening/; "UAE Reopens Syria Embassy in Boost for Assad." *Reuters*, December 27, 2018, https://www.reuters.com/article/us-mideast-crisis-syria-emirates/uae-reopens-syria-embassy-in-boost-for-assad-idUSKCN1OQ0QV; "US Sanctions Challenge Syria's Arab League Return: UAE." *Aljazeera*, March 9, 2021, https://www.aljazeera.com/news/2021/3/9/us-sanctions-challenge-syrias-return-to-arab-fold-says-uae; "UAE Praises Syria's Assad for 'Wise Leadership,' Cementing Ties." *Reuters*, December 3, 2019, https://www.reuters.com/article/us-syria-emirates-relations/uae-praises-syrias-assad-for-wise-leadership-cementing-ties-idUSKBN1Y71O0.

73 "Syria's Assad Visits UAE, First Trip to Arab State since War Began." *Reuters*, March 18, 2022, https://www.reuters.com/world/middle-east/syrian-president-assad-met-dubai-ruler-syrian-presidency-2022-03-18/.

74 See Greenwald, Glen. "How Former Treasury Officials and the UAE Are Manipulating American Journalists." *The Intercept*, September 25, 2014, https://theintercept.com/2014/09/25/uae-qatar-camstoll-group/; Pecquet, Julian. "Washington Lobbyists Continue to Cash in on Dispute between Qatar and UAE." *Middle East Eye*, September 16, 2020, https://www.middleeasteye.net/news/qatar-uae-continue-lobbying-washington.

75 Hoffman, Jon. "'Bots' and Bans: Social Media and Regime Propaganda in the Middle East." *Open Democracy*, March 12, 2020, https://www.opendemocracy.net/en/north-africa-west-asia/bots-and-bans-social-media-and-regime-propaganda-in-the-middle-east/.

76 For the full investigation, see Schectman, Joel and Bing, Christopher. "White House Veterans Helped Gulf Monarchy Build Secret Surveillance Unit." *Reuters*, December 10, 2019, https://www.reuters.com/investigates/special-report/usa-raven-whitehouse/.

77 Ibid.

78 See "UAE Leader Returns after Lengthy Unexplained Absence." *Middle East Eye*, September 8, 2016, https://www.middleeasteye.net/news/uae-leader-returns-after-lengthy-unexplained-absence.
79 See Al-Rasheed, Madawi. "How United is the GCC?" *Al-Monitor*, April 1, 2016, https://www.al-monitor.com/originals/2016/04/gulf-nationalism-regime-survivial-saudi-qatar-uae.html.
80 For a comprehensive overview of the increase in Emirati weapons purchases from Russia and China, see Hoffman, Jonathan. "The Return of Great-Power Competition to the Middle East: A Two-Level Game." *Middle East Policy*, Vol. 28, No. 1, 2021a, pp. 87-104.
81 See Mustafa, Awad. "Saudi, UAE Influence Grows with Purchases." *Defense News*, March 22, 2015, https://www.defensenews.com/2015/03/22/saudi-uae-influence-grows-with-purchases/; Jo, Haena. "Can the UAE Emerge as a Leading Global Defense Supplier?" *Defense News*, February 15, 2021, https://www.defensenews.com/digital-show-dailies/idex/2021/02/15/can-the-uae-emerge-as-a-leading-global-defense-supplier/.
82 "UAE Announces Martyr's Day, but Why November 30?" *Al-Arabiya*, August 20, 2015, https://english.alarabiya.net/News/middle-east/2015/08/20/UAE-announces-Martyr-s-day-but-why-November-30-.
83 Al-Hussein, Mira. "UAE: National Identity and the Social Contract." *Carnegie Endowment for International Peace*, November 10, 2022, https://carnegieendowment.org/sada/88371.
84 See, respectively: "Khalifa Stresses National Identity." *The National*, December 1, 2008, https://www.thenationalnews.com/uae/khalifa-stresses-national-identity-1.562584; "2018 declared 'Year of Zayed.'" *The National*, August 5, 2017, https://www.thenationalnews.com/uae/2018-declared-year-of-zayed-1.617122; "Qasr Al Watan Opens to the Public: First-person Account of a Visit." *Gulf News*, March 11, 2019, https://gulfnews.com/uae/qasr-al-watan-opens-to-the-public-first-person-account-of-a-visit-1.1552311396753; "As the Museum of the Future Opens, Here Are Five other UAE Museums to See." *The National*, February 21, 2022, https://www.thenationalnews.com/arts-culture/art/2022/02/22/as-the-museum-of-the-future-opens-here-are-five-other-uae-museums-to-see/; "When Is UAE's National Day 2022 and Why Is It Celebrated?" *The National*, November 24, 2022, https://www.thenationalnews.com/uae/2022/11/24/when-is-national-day-2022/.
85 Ozgen, Zeynep, and Hassan, Sharif Ibrahim El-Shishtawy. "Meaning of a Textbook: Religious Education, National Islam, and the Politics of Reform in the United Arab Emirates." *Nations and Nationalism*, Vol. 27, No. 4, 2021, pp. 1181-97.
86 Ibid.
87 Warren, David. "The Modernist Roots of Islamic Autocracy: Shaykh Abdullah Bin Bayyah and the UAE-Israel Peace Deal." *Maydan*, August

27, 2020, https://themaydan.com/2020/08/the-modernist-roots-of-islamic-autocracy-shaykh-abdullah-bin-bayyah-and-the-uae-israel-peace-deal/.
88 O'Sullivan, Jack. "'If You Hate the West, Emigrate to a Muslim Country.'" *The Guardian*, October 8, 2001, https://www.theguardian.com/world/2001/oct/08/religion.uk.
89 Al-Azami, Usaama. *Islam and the Arab Revolutionaries: The Ulama between Democracy and Autocracy*. Oxford University Press, 2021.
90 For the full interview, see https://www.youtube.com/watch?v=9Mba1RLzaWU.
91 Ibid. For an article discussing the interview, see "Letter of Resignation of the Scholar Abdullah bin Bayyah from the International Union of Muslim Scholars." *BinBayyah.net*, https://binbayyah.net/arabic/archives/1454.
92 Ibid. Translation obtained from: Al-Azami. *Islam and the Arab Revolutionaries*.
93 For the full resignation letter, see https://binbayyah.net/arabic/archives/1454.
94 For the full blog post on Tunisia, see Yusuf, Hamza. "Deferred Dreams, Self-Destruction, and Suicide Bombings."
95 Ibid.
96 For the full blog post on Egypt, see Yusuf, Hamza. "When the Social Contract is Breached, It's Breached on Both Sides." https://sandala.org/blogs/uncategorized/when-the-social-contract-is-breached-on-one-side-its-breached-on-both-sides.
97 Ibid.
98 Ibid.
99 Ibid.
100 For the full blog post on Libya, see Yusuf, Hamza. "on Libya." https://sandala.org/blogs/uncategorized/on-libya
101 Ibid.
102 For the full interview, see https://www.youtube.com/watch?v=WhV791UyT0o&t=961s. Translation obtained from: Al-Azami. *Islam and the Arab Revolutionaries*.
103 Amasha, Muhammad. "The UAE-Sponsored 'Islams': Mapping the Terrain." *Maydan*, September 15, 2020, https://themaydan.com/2020/09/the-uae-sponsored-islams-mapping-the-terrain/.
104 See *Muslim Council of Elders English Website*, see: https://www.muslim-elders.com/en.
105 See https://peacems.com/ar/about-us/brief/message/.
106 See https://peacems.com/about-us/sponsor-message/.
107 See "Mohamed bin Zayed: Great Challenges Facing Muslim Scholars Confronting Sedition Advocates." *Al-Bayan.net*, March 11, 2014, https://www.albayan.ae/across-the-uae/news-and-reports/2014-03-11-1.2078376.

108 "UAE Cabinet forms Emirates Fatwa Council." *The National*, June 25, 2018, https://www.thenationalnews.com/uae/government/uae-cabinet-forms-emirates-fatwa-council-1.743799.
109 See "Summary of the Answers of the Scholar Abdullah bin Bayyah in the First Press Conference of the Emirates Council for Sharia Ifta." *BinBayyah.net*,https://binbayyah.net/arabic/archives/4014.
110 See http://www.tolerance.gov.ae/en/tolerance.aspx.
111 Ibid.
112 See, respectively: "Sheikh of Al-Azhar Wins Dubai International Holy Quran Award." *Akhbar El-Yom*, July 22, 2013, https://akhbarelyom.com/news/newdetails/247542/0/0.html; "Cultural Personality of the Year 2013: Dr. Sheikh Ahmad Muhammad Al Tayyeb." https://www.zayedaward.ae/en/previous.editions/winners/dr.sheikh.ahmad.muhammad.al.tayyeb.aspx
113 "Mohamed bin Zayed Visits Al Azhar, Meets Grand Imam—UPDATE." *Emirates News Agency*, September 18, 2014, http://wam.ae/en/details/1395269811015.
114 See "UAE to Fund Projects Undertaken by Al Azhar in Egypt." *Gulf News*, July 5, 2012, https://gulfnews.com/uae/government/uae-to-fund-projects-undertaken-by-al-azhar-in-egypt-1.1044934; "Call for College in UAE Affiliated to Al Azhar." *Khaleej Times*, August 6, 2015, https://www.khaleejtimes.com/mena/call-for-college-in-uae-affiliated-to-al-azhar.
115 Quisay, Walaa, and Parker, Thomas. "On the Theology of Obedience: An Analysis of Shaykh Bin Bayyah and Shaykh Hamza Yusuf's Political Thought." *Maydan*, January 8, 2019, https://themaydan.com/2019/01/theology-obedience-analysis-shaykh-bin-bayyah-shaykh-hamza-yusufs-political-thought/.
116 Helmy, Yomna. "From Islamic Modernism to Theorizing Authoritarianism: Bin Bayyah and the Politicization of Maqasid Discourse." *American Journal of Islam and Society*, Vol. 38, No. 3–4, 2021, pp. 36–70.
117 Warren, David. *Rivals in the Gulf: Yusuf al-Qaradawi, Abdullah Bin Bayyah, and the Qatar-UAE Contest Over the Arab Spring and the Gulf Crisis*. Routledge, 2021a.
118 See "Scholar Ibn Bin Bayyah Calls for "Institutionalization" of Fatwa Systems in Islamic Countries." *BinBayyah.net*, https://binbayyah.net/arabic/archives/4025.
119 Warren, David. "Interfaith Dialogue in the United Arab Emirates: Where International Relations Meets State-Branding." *Berkley Center for Religion, Peace, and World Affairs*, July 12, 2021b, https://berkleycenter.georgetown.edu/posts/interfaith-dialogue-in-the-united-arab-emirates-where-international-relations-meets-state-branding.
120 See "Scholar Ibn Bin Bayyah Calls for "Institutionalization" of Fatwa Systems in Islamic Countries." *BinBayyah.net*, https://binbayyah.net/arabic/archives/4025.

121 See "In Pursuit of Peace: 2014 Forum for Promoting Peace in Muslim Societies." https://en.calameo.com/read/0047058449063e53d072e.
122 "We Want to Be No. 1, Says Sheikh Mohammed." *Arabian Business*, December 30, 2011, https://www.arabianbusiness.com/politics-economics/we-want-be-no-1-says-sheikh-mohammed-437622.
123 See "The Marrakesh Declaration: On the Rights of Religious Minorities in Muslim-Majority Lands." https://www.abc-usa.org/wp-content/uploads/2021/05/Marrakesh-Final-04-12-18.pdf.
124 For the full interview panel, see "A Conversation with Sheikh Abdallah bin Bayyah." *Council on Foreign Relations*, June 4, 2015, https://www.cfr.org/event/conversation-shaykh-abdallah-bin-bayyah.
125 Cited in Warren, David. *Rivals in the Gulf: Yusuf al-Qaradawi, Abdullah Bin Bayyah, and the Qatar-UAE Contest Over the Arab Spring and the Gulf Crisis*. Routledge, 2021.
126 See Twitter post by 5Pillars, https://x.com/5pillarsuk/status/1307667568325521408.
127 See "In Pursuit of Peace: 2014 Forum for Promoting Peace in Muslim Societies." https://en.calameo.com/read/0047058449063e53d072e.
128 Cited in Quisay, Walaa, and Parker, Thomas. "On the Theology of Obedience: An Analysis of Shaykh Bin Bayyah and Shaykh Hamza Yusuf's Political Thought." *Maydan*, January 8, 2019, https://themaydan.com/2019/01/theology-obedience-analysis-shaykh-bin-bayyah-shaykh-hamza-yusufs-political-thought/.
129 "Outrage as Hamza Yusuf Releases Video Mocking Syrian Refugees." *The New Arab*, September 10, 2019, https://www.newarab.com/news/outrage-hamza-yusuf-releases-video-mocking-syrian-refugees.
130 See "In Pursuit of Peace: 2014 Forum for Promoting Peace in Muslim Societies." https://en.calameo.com/read/0047058449063e53d072e.
131 Roberts. "Mosque and State."
132 Mamdani, Mahmood. "Good Muslim, Bad Muslim: A Political Perspective on Culture and Terrorism." *American Anthropologist*, Vol. 104, No. 3, 2002, pp. 766–75.
133 Warren, David et al. "Roundtable on State Islam after the Arab Uprisings." *Jadaliyya*, November 23, 2020, https://www.jadaliyya.com/Details/41990/Roundtable-on-State-Islam-after-the-Arab-Uprisings.
134 See "Embassy of the United Arab Emirates, Washington, DC—Religious Inclusion." https://www.uae-embassy.org/discover-uae/society/religious-inclusion.
135 Ibid.
136 "UAE Names 2019 the Year of Tolerance to Reflect Zayed's Vision." *The National*, January 23, 2019, https://www.thenationalnews.com/uae/government/uae-names-2019-the-year-of-tolerance-to-reflect-zayed-s-vision-1.802853.

137 "Muslim Brotherhood Terrorist Organization, Affirms UAE Fatwa Council." *Emirates New Agency*, November 23, 2020, https://wam.ae/en/details/1395302889318.
138 "Muslim Council of Elders Calls on Qatari Regime to Review Its Stances." *Emirates New Agency*, June 6, 2017, http://wam.ae/en/details/1395302617880.
139 For both the Arabic and English versions of this statement, see "A Call to the Qatari Government to Change its Ways and Correct its Mistakes." Forum for Promoting Peace in Muslim Societies, June 7, 2017, https://www.academia.edu/34099420/Translation_of_the_statement_from_the_Forum_Promoting_Peace_in_Muslim_Societies_regarding_the_Blockade_of_Qatar_Issued_on_June_7th_2017.
140 Ratelle, J. "A Kadyrovization of Russian Foreign Policy in the Middle East: Autocrats in Track II Diplomacy and Other Humanitarian Activities." In *Russia's Islamic diplomacy*, ed. M. Laruelle. Institute for European, Russian, and Eurasian Studies, 2019.
141 Dorsey, James. "Fighting for the Soul of Islam: A Battle of the Paymasters." *Huffpost*, September 30, 2016, https://www.huffpost.com/entry/fighting-for-the-soul-of_b_12259312.
142 Ramani, Samuel. "Russia and the UAE: An Ideational Partnership." *Middle East Policy*, Vol. 27, No. 1, 2020, pp. 125–40.
143 See "The Marrakesh Declaration: On the Rights of Religious Minorities in Muslim-Majority Lands." https://www.abc-usa.org/wp-content/uploads/2021/05/Marrakesh-Final-04-12-18.pdf.
144 Ibid.
145 Ibid.
146 Ibid.
147 See, for example, https://www.peacems.com/media-center/news/2019-10-30/; "Influential Muslim Scholar Criticized for Calling the UAE a 'Tolerant Country.'" *Middle East Eye*, December 7, 2018, https://www.middleeasteye.net/fr/news/hamza-yusuf-criticised-calling-uae-tolerant-country-47964647.
148 For former US president Barack Obama's comment on bin Bayyah, see "Full Text of President Obama's 2014 Address to the United Nations General Assembly." *The Washington Post*, September 24, 2014, https://www.washingtonpost.com/politics/full-text-of-president-obamas-2014-address-to-the-united-nations-general-assembly/2014/09/24/88889e46-43f4-11e4-b437-1a7368204804_story.html. On Hamza Yusuf's role in Trump administration, see "Muslim Scholar Appointed as Human Rights Adviser to Trump Administration." *Middle East Eye*, July 9, 2019, https://www.middleeasteye.net/news/muslim-scholar-appointed-human-rights-adviser-trump-administration.

149 See "UAE Fatwa Council Member Among Experts of US 'Commission on Unalienable Rights.'" *Emirates New Agency*, July 9, 2019, http://www.wam.ae/en/details/1395302773134.
150 See "A Document on Human Fraternity for World Peace and Living Together." https://www.vatican.va/content/francesco/en/travels/2019/outside/documents/papa-francesco_20190204_documento-fratellanza-umana.html.
151 "NYU chaplain to be the first chief rabbi of the UAE Jewish community." *The Jerusalem Post*, May 22, 2019, https://www.jpost.com/Diaspora/NYU-chaplain-to-be-first-chief-rabbi-in-the-United-Arab-Emirates-589715.
152 For the full document, see "A Document on Human Fraternity for World Peace and Living Together." https://www.vatican.va/content/francesco/en/travels/2019/outside/documents/papa-francesco_20190204_documento-fratellanza-umana.html.
153 See "Abrahamic Family House." https://www.forhumanfraternity.org/abrahamic-family-house/.
154 See "Embassy of the United Arab Emirates, Washington, DC—Religious Inclusion." https://www.uae-embassy.org/discover-uae/society/religious-inclusion
155 See "The Abraham Accords Declaration." https://www.state.gov/the-abraham-accords/.
156 See "Embassy of the United Arab Emirates, Washington, DC – The Abraham Accords: Unlocking Sustainable and Inclusive Growth Across the Middle East." https://www.uae-embassy.org/abraham-accords-sustainable-inclusive-growth.
157 "Kushner in Knesset: We All Have a Role in Advancing Abraham Accords." *The Jerusalem Post*, October 11, 2021, https://www.jpost.com/israel-news/kushner-in-knesset-we-all-have-a-role-in-advancing-abraham-accords-681668.
158 See Hoffman, Jon. "The Abraham Accords and the Imposed Middle East Order." *The National Interest*, October 3, 2022, https://nationalinterest.org/blog/middle-east-watch/abraham-accords-and-imposed-middle-east-order-205136.
159 For the full video, see Twitter post by 5Pillars, https://x.com/5pillarsuk/status/1307667568325521408.
160 "International Treatise, Relations Rightful Authority of Sovereign Ruler: Emirates Fatwa Council." *Emirates News Agency*, August 14, 2020, http://wam.ae/en/details/1395302862343.
161 See "The Board of Trustees of the Forum for the Promotion of Peace will hold its seventh meeting in Abu Dhabi next December." *Emirates News Agency-WAM*, August 16, 2020,

Conclusion

1. Bolling, Landrum. "Religion and Politics in the Middle East Conflicts." *Middle East Journal*, Vol. 45, No. 1, 1991, pp. 125–30; Huntington, Samuel. *The Clash of Civilizations and the Remaking of World Order*. Simon and Schuster, 1996; Hamid, Shadi. *Islamic Exceptionalism: How the Struggle Over Islam Is Reshaping the World*. St. Martin's Press, 2016.
2. Esposito, John and Voll, John. *Islam and Democracy*. Oxford University Press, 1996; Mernissi, Fatema and Lakeland, Mary Jo. *Islam and Democracy: Fear of the Modern World*. Basic Books, 2002.
3. "Islamic Scholars Issue Fatwa Saying Arab Regimes Must Intervene to Save Gaza." *5Pillars*, November 1, 2023, https://5pillarsuk.com/2023/11/01/islamic-scholars-issue-fatwa-saying-arab-regimes-must-intervene-to-save-gaza/.
4. El Yaakoubi, Aziz and Abdallah, Nayera. "Arab and Muslim Leaders Demand Immediate End to Gaza War." *Reuters*, November 11, 2023, https://www.reuters.com/world/middle-east/saudi-arabia-host-extraordinary-joint-islamic-arab-summit-riyadh-saturday-2023-11-10/.
5. Al Omran, Ahmed. "Saudi Arabia's Israel Strategy Upended by Anger over Gaza War." *Financial Times*, March 31, 2024, https://www.ft.com/content/821b67bd-5736-4ffd-b66f-3bb1830560d2.
6. "Chairman of UAE Fatwa Council: 'UAE at Forefront of Helping Those in Need, in General, and People in Palestine, in Particular.'" *Emirates News Agency—WAM*, October 16, 2023, https://www.wam.ae/en/details/1395303209518.

REFERENCES

Abdo, Geneive. *The New Sectarianism: The Arab Uprisings and the Rebirth of the Sunni-Shia Divide*. Oxford University Press, 2016.

Abou El Fadl, Khaled. "Islam and the Theology of Power: Wahhabism and Salafism." *Middle East Research and Information Project (MERIP)*, Winter 2001, pp. 28–33.

Abou El Fadl, Khaled. *Islam and the Challenge of Democracy*. Princeton University Press, 2004.

Abou El Fadl, Khaled. *The Prophet's Pulpit: Commentaries on the State of Islam*. Usuli Press, 2022.

Abu Sulayman, Abdul Hamid. *Towards an Islamic Theory of International Relations: New Directions for Islamic Methodology and Thought*. The International Institute of Islamic Thought, 1993.

Acharya, Amitav. *The End of American World Order*. Polity, 2018.

Adiong, Nassef Manabilang, et al. *Islam in International Relations: Politics and Paradigms*. Routledge, 2018.

Ahmed, Shahab. *What is Islam? The Importance of Being Islamic*. Princeton University Press, 2016.

Akbarzadeh, Shahram. "The Burred Line Between State Identity and Realpolitik." In *Routledge Handbook of International Relations in the Middle East*, edited by Shahram Akbarzadeh. Routledge, 2019, pp. 1–7.

Akyol, Mustafa. Reopening Muslim Minds: A Return to Reason, Freedom, and Tolerance. St. Martin's Essentials, 2021.

Al-Anani, Khalil. *Inside the Muslim Brotherhood: Religion, Identity, and Politics*. Oxford University Press, 2016.

Almezaini, Khalid. "The Transformation of UAE Foreign Policy since 2011." In *The Changing Security Dynamics of the Persian Gulf*, edited by Kristian Ulrichsen. Oxford University Press, 2017, pp. 191–204.

Al-Nakib, Farah. "Modernity and the Arab Gulf States: The Politics of Heritage, Memory, and Forgetting." In *Routledge Handbook of Persian Gulf Politics*, edited by Mehran Kamrava. Routledge, 2020, pp. 57–82.

Al-Qassemi, Sultan. "The Brothers and the Gulf." *Foreign Policy*, December 14, 2012, https://foreignpolicy.com/2012/12/14/the-brothers-and-the-gulf/.

Al-Rasheed, Madawi. "Sectarianism as Counter-Revolution: Saudi Responses to the Arab Spring-." In *Sectarianization: Mapping the New Politics of the Middle East*, edited by Nader Hashemi and Danny Postel. Oxford University Press, 2017, pp. 143–58.

Al-Rasheed, Madawi. *The Son King: Reform and Repression in Saudi Arabia*. Oxford University Press, 2021.

Al-Sudairi, M. T. "Hajis, Refugees, Salafi Preachers, and a Myriad of Others: An Examination of Islamic Connectivities in the Sino-Saudi Relationship." In *The Red Star & the Crescent: China and the Middle East*, edited by J. Reardon-Anderson. Oxford University Press, 2018, pp. 207–40.

Amasha, Muhammad. "The UAE-sponsored 'Islams': Mapping the Terrain." *Maydan*, September 15, 2020, https://themaydan.com/2020/09/the-uae-sponsored-islams-mapping-the-terrain/.

Asad, Talal. *The Idea of an Anthropology of Islam*. Georgetown University Press, 1986.

Aydin, Cemil. *The Idea of the Muslim World: A Global Intellectual History*. Harvard University Press, 2019.

Ayoob, Mohammed. "Political Islam: Image and Reality." *World Policy Journal*, Vol. 21, No. 3, 2004, pp. 1–14.

Bank, Andre et al. "Authoritarianism Reconfigured: Evolving Forms of Political Control." In *The Political Science of the Middle East: Theory and Research since the Arab Uprisings*, edited by Marc Lynch et al. Oxford University Press, 2022, pp. 35–61.

Barbato, Mariano and Kratochwil, Frederic. "Towards a Post-Secular Political Order?" *European Political Science Review*, Vol. 1, No. 3, 2009, pp. 317–40.

Barnett, Michael. *Dialogues in Arab Publics: Negotiations in Regional Order*. Columbia University Press, 2019.

Barnett, Michael and Telhami, Shibley. *Identity and Foreign Policy in the Middle East*. Cornell University Press, 2002.

Baskan, Birol. *The Politics of Islam: The Muslim Brothers and the State in the Arab Gulf*. Edinburgh University Press, 2021.

Baskan, Birol and Wright, Steven. "Seeds of Change: Comparing State-Religion Relations in Qatar and Saudi Arabia." *Arab Studies Quarterly*, Vol. 33, No. 2, 2011, pp. 96–111.

Bayat, Asef. *Post-Islamism: The Changing Faces of Political Islam*. Oxford University Press, 2013.

Beach, Derek. "Process-Tracing Methods in Social Science." *Oxford Research Encyclopedias*, 2017.

Bianco, Cinzia and Stansfield, Gareth. "The Intra-GCC Crises: Mapping GCC Fragmentation after 2011." *International Affairs*, Vol. 94, No. 3, 2018, pp. 613–35.

Berger, Maurits. *Religion and Islam in Contemporary International Relations*. Netherlands Institute of International Relations, 2010.

Bettiza, Gregorio. "States, Religions, and Power: Highlighting the Role of Sacred Capital in World Politics." *Berkley Center for Religion, Peace, and World Affairs*, March 30, 2020, https://berkleycenter.georgetown.edu/publications/states-religions-and-power-highlighting-the-role-of-sacred-capital-in-world-politics.

Bolling, Landrum. "Religion and Politics in the Middle East Conflicts." *Middle East Journal*, Vol. 45, No. 1, 1991, pp. 125–30.

Brands, Hal. "Democracy vs. Authoritarianism: How Ideology Shapes Great-Power Conflict." *Survival*, Vol. 60, No. 1, 2018, pp. 61–114.

Brown, Nathan. *Arguing Islam after the Revival of Arab Politics*. Oxford University Press, 2016.

Brown, Nathan et al. "Roundtable on State Islam after the Arab Uprisings." *Jadaliyya*, November 23, 2020, https://www.jadaliyya.com/Details/41990/Roundtable-on-State-Islam-after-the-Arab-Uprisings.

Bunzel, Cole. "The Kingdom and the Caliphate: Saudi Arabia and the Islamic State." In *Beyond Sunni and Shi'a: The Roots of Sectarianism in a Changing Middle East*, edited by Frederic Wehrey. Oxford University Press, 2017, pp. 239–64.

Cammett, Melani, et al. *A Political Economy of the Middle East*. Routledge, 2013.

Cavatorta, Francesco et. al. "The Future of Political Islam in the Middle East and North Africa under the Changing Regional Order." Jadaliyya, August 16, 2018, https://www.jadaliyya.com/Details/3786

Cesari, Jocelyn. *The Awakening of Muslim Democracy: Religion, Modernity, and the State*. Cambridge University Press, 2014.

Cesari, Jocelyn. *What is Political Islam?* Lynne Rienner Publishers, Inc., 2018.

Chafetz, Glenn, et al. "Introduction: Tracing the Influence of Identity on Foreign Policy." *Security Studies*, Vol. 8, No. 2–3, 1998, pp. 7–22.

Chalcraft, John. *Popular Politics in the Making of the Modern Middle East*. Cambridge University Press, 2016.

Chen, Jian. *Mao's China and the Cold War*. The University of North Carolina Press, 2001.

Christie, Kenneth. "Globalization, Religion, and State Formation in the United Arab Emirates and Pakistan." *Totalitarian Movements and Political Religions*, Vol. 11, No. 2, 2010, pp. 203–12.

Collier, David. "Understanding Process Tracing." *Political Science and Politics*, Vol. 44, No. 4, 2011, pp. 823–30.

Conner, Walker. *Ethnonationalism*. Princeton University Press, 1993.

Cook, Michael. *Ancient Religion, Modern Politics: The Islamic Case in Comparative Perspective*. Princeton University Press, 2016.

D'Acunto, Federica. "The Brand of Peace: The Relations Between Qatar, Palestine, and Israel." *Università Ca' Foscari Venezia*, 2016, http://dspace.unive.it/handle/10579/9199.

Dahl, Robert. *Who Governs?* Yale University Press, 1963.

Darwich, May. "The Challenge of Bridging IR and Area Studies in Middle East International Relations Teaching." *LSE Middle East Center Blog*, August 15, 2018, https://blogs.lse.ac.uk/mec/2015/08/18/the-challenge-of-bridging-ir-and-area-studies-in-middle-east-international-relations-teaching/.

David, Steven. "Explaining Third World Alignment." *World Politics*, Vol. 43, No. 1, 1991, pp. 233–56.

Davidson, Christopher. "Viewpoint: Wealthy and Stable UAE Keeps the Lid on Dissent." *BBC*, April 15, 2015a, https://www.bbc.com/news/world-middle-east-31986653.

Davidson, Christopher. *After the Sheikhs: The Coming Collapse of the Gulf Monarchies*. Oxford University Press, 2015b.

Davidson, Christopher. "The UAE, Qatar, and the Question of Political Islam." In *Divided Gulf: The Anatomy of a Crisis*, edited by Andreas Krieg. Palgrave, 2019, pp. 71–90.

Davis, James. *Threats and Promises: The Pursuit of International Influence*. Johns Hopkins University Press, 2000.

Dawisha, Adeed. *Islam in Foreign Policy*. Cambridge University Press, 1983.

Diwan, Kristin. "Clerical Associations in Qatar and the United Arab Emirates: Soft Power Competition in Islamic Politics." *International Affairs*, Vol. 97, No. 4, 2021, pp. 945–63.

Dorsey, James. "Wahhabism vs. Wahhabism: Qatar Challenges Saudi Arabia." *Institute of Fan Culture, University of Wurzburg*, July 3, 2013, https://papers.ssrn.com/sol3/papers.cfm?abstract_id=2305485.

Ebrahim, Moosa. "Political theology in the Aftermath of the Arab Spring: Returning to the Ethical," in *The African Renaissance and the Afro-Arab Spring*, ed. by Charles Villa-Vincencio, Erik Doxtader, and Ebrahim Moosa. Georgetown University Press, 2015, 101–119.

Eickelman, Dale and Piscatori, James. *Muslim Politics*. Princeton University Press, 1996.

Esposito, John. *The Future of Islam*. Oxford University Press, 2010.

Esposito, John and Voll, John. *Islam and Democracy*. Oxford University Press, 1996.

Fan, Ying. "Branding the Nation: Towards a Better Understanding." *Place Branding and Diplomacy*, Vol. 6, No. 1, 2010, pp. 97–103.

Fadel, Mohammed. "Islamic Law and Constitution-Making: The Authoritarian Temptation of the Arab Spring. Osgoode Hall Law Journal, Vol 53, No. 2, 2016, pp. 472–500

Farouk, Yasmine and Brown, Nathan. "Saudi Arabia's Religious Reforms are Touching Nothing but Changing Everything." *Carnegie Endowment for International Peace*, June 7, 2021, https://carnegieendowment.org/2021/06/07/saudi-arabia-s-religious-reforms-are-touching-nothing-but-changing-everything-pub-84650.

Fearon, James. "Domestic Politics, Foreign Policy, and Theories of International Relations." *Annual Review of Political Science*, Vol. 1, No. 1, 1998, pp. 289–313.

Finnemore, Martha. *Defining State Interests: National Interests in International Society*. Cornell University Press, 1996.

Fischer, Markus. "Culture and Foreign Politics." In *The Limits of Culture: Islam and Foreign Policy*, edited by Brenda Shaffer. MIT Press, 2006, pp. 27–64.

Flockhart, Trine. "Constructivism and Foreign Policy." In *Foreign Policy: Theories, Actors, Cases*, edited by Steve Smith et al. Oxford University Press, 2016, pp. 79–94.

Fox, Jonathan and Sandal, Nukhet. "Toward Integrating Religion into International Relations Theory." *Zeitschrift für internationale Beziehungen*, Vol. 17, No. 1, 2010, pp. 149–59.

Fox, Jonathan and Sandal, Nukhet. "Integrating Religion into International Affairs." In *Routledge Handbook of Religion and Politics*, edited by Jeffrey Haynes. Routledge, 2016, pp. 270–83.

Fox, Jonathan and Sandler, Shmuel. *Brining Religion into International Relations*. Palgrave Macmillan, 2004.

Freeden, Michael. *Ideologies and Political Theory: A Conceptual Approach*. Oxford University Press, 1996.

Freer, Courtney. "Rentier Islamism in the Absence of Elections: The Political Role of Muslim Brotherhood Affiliates in Qatar and the United Arab Emirates." *International Journal of Middle East Studies*, Vol. 49, No. 3, 2017, pp. 479–500.

Freer, Courtney. *Rentier Islamism: The Influence of the Muslim Brotherhood in Gulf Monarchies*. Oxford University Press, 2018.

Freer, Courtney. "Challenges to Sunni Islamism in Bahrain since 2011." *Carnegie Endowment for International Peace*, March 6, 2019, https://carnegie-mec.org/2019/03/06/challenges-to-sunni-islamism-in-bahrain-since-2011-pub-78510.

Freer, Courtney. "Political Islam in the Arabian Peninsula." In *Routledge Handbook of Persian Gulf Politics*, edited by Mehran Kamrava. Routledge, 2020, pp. 308–26.

Freer, Courtney, et al. "The Future of Political Islam in the Middle East and North Africa under the Changing Regional Order." *Jadaliyya - جدلية*, Arab Studies Institute, 2018, http://www.jadaliyya.com/Details/37864/The-Future-of-Political-Islam-in-the-MENA-under-the-Changing-Regional-Order.

Fromherz, Allen. *Qatar: A Modern History*. Georgetown University Press, 2012.

Fuller, Graham and Francke, Rend. *Arab Shi'a: The Forgotten Muslims*. Palgrave, 1999.

Fyfe, Ann. "Wealth and Power: Political and Economic Change in the United Arab Emirates." *Durham University Thesis*, 1989, http://etheses.dur.ac.uk/6505/1/6505_3805.PDF?UkUDh:CyT.

Galeeva, D. "Balancing Adversaries: Russian Policy in the Gulf and the Role of Russian Muslims." *London School of Economics Blog*, January 2, 2020, https://blogs.lse.ac.uk/mec/2020/01/02/balancing-adversaries-russian-policy-in-the-gulf-and-the-role-of-russian-muslims/.

Gasim, Gamal. "The Qatari Crisis and Al Jazeera's Coverage of the War in Yemen." *Arab Media & Society*, February 15, 2018, www.arabmediasociety.com/the-qatari-crisis-and-al-jazeeras-coverage-of-the-war-in-yemen/.

Gause, Gregory. "Balancing What? Threat Perception and Alliance Choice in the Gulf." *Security Studies*, Vol. 13, No. 2, 2003/4, pp. 273–305.

Gause, Gregory. "What the Qatar Crisis Shows about the Middle East." *The Washington Post*, June 27, 2017, https://www.washingtonpost.com/news/monkey-cage/wp/2017/06/27/what-the-qatar-crisis-shows-about-the-middle-east/.

Geddes, Barbara. "How the Cases You Choose Affect the Answers You Get: Selection Bias in Comparative Politics." *Political Analysis*, Vol. 2, 1990, pp. 131–50.

Geertz, Clifford. *Islam Observed: Religious Development in Morocco and Indonesia*. University of Chicago Press, 1971.

Gengler, Justin. "Bahrain's Sunni Awakening." *Middle East Research and Information Project (MERIP)*, January 17, 2012, https://merip.org/2012/01/bahrains-sunni-awakening/.

Gengler, Justin. *Group Conflict and Political Mobilization in Bahrain and the Arab Gulf: Rethinking the Rentier State*. Indiana University Press, 2015.

Gengler, Justin. "Sectarianism from the Top Down or Bottom Up? Explaining the Middle East's unlikely de-sectarianization after the Arab Spring." *Review of Faith and International Affairs*, Vol. 18, No. 1, 2020, pp. 109–13.

George, Alexander and Bennett, Andrew. *Case Studies and Theory Development in the Social Sciences*. MIT Press, 2005.

Gerring, John. "What Is a Case Study and What Is It Good for?" *The American Political Science Review*, Vol. 98, No. 2, 2004, pp. 341–54.

Goldstone, Jack. "Comparative Historical Analysis and Knowledge Accumulation in the Study of Revolutions." In *Comparative Historical Analysis in the Social Sciences*, edited by James Mahoney and Dietrich Rueschemeyer. Cambridge University Press, 2003, pp. 41–90.

Gould-Davies, Nigel. "Rethinking the Role of Ideology in International Politics During the Cold War." *Journal of Cold War Studies*, Vol. 1, No. 1, 1999, pp. 90–109.

Gries, Peter, Chun Yam, and Paton Pak. "Ideology and International Relations." *Current Opinion in Behavioral Sciences*, Vol. 34, No. 1, 2020, pp. 135–41.

Haas, Mark. *The Ideological Origins of Great Power Politics, 1789-1989*. Cornell University Press, 2005.

Haas, Mark. "Ideological Polarity and Balancing in Great Power Politics." *Security Studies*, Vol. 23, No. 4, 2014, pp. 715–53.

Habermas, Jürgen. "Religion in the Public Sphere." *European Journal of Philosophy*, Vol. 14, No. 1, 2006, pp. 1–25.

Hagan, Joe. "Domestic Political Explanations in the Analysis of Foreign Policy." In *Foreign Policy Analysis: Continuity and Change in its Second Generation*, edited by Laura Neack, et al. Pearson, 1995, pp. 117–44.

Hamid, Shadi. *Islamic Exceptionalism: How the Struggle Over Islam Is Reshaping the World*. St. Martin's Press, 2016.

Hamid, Shadi and McCants, William. "Islamism after the Arab Spring: Between the Islamic State and the Nation-state." *Brookings Institution*, January 2017, https://www.brookings.edu/research/islamism-after-the-arab-spring-between-the-islamic-state-and-the-nation-state/.

Hanieh, Adam. "Ambitions of a Global Gulf: The Arab Uprisings, Yemen, and the Saudi-Emirati Alliance." Middle East Report, 289, 2018, No. pp. 21–26.

Harknett, Richard and Vandenberg, Jeffrey. "Alignment Theory and Interrelated Threats: Jordan and the Persian Gulf Crisis." *Security Studies*, Vol. 6, No. 3, 1997, pp. 112–53.

Hashemi, Nader and Postel, Danny. *Sectarianization: Mapping the New Politics of the Middle East*. Oxford University Press, 2017.

Haynes, Jeffrey. "Religion and Foreign Policy Making in the USA, India, and Iran: Towards a Research Agenda." *Third World Quarterly*, Vol. 29, No. 1, 2008, pp. 143–65.

Haynes, Jeffrey. *Religious Transnational Actors and Soft Power*. Routledge, 2012.

Haynes, Jeffrey. "Religion in Foreign Policy." In *The Oxford Encyclopedia of Foreign Policy Analysis*, edited by Cameron G. Thies. Oxford University Press, 2017.

Haynes, Jeffrey. "Religion and International Relations: What Do We Know and How Do We Know It?" *Religions*, Vol. 12, No. 5, 2021, pp. 1–14

Helmy, Yomna. "From Islamic Modernism to Theorizing Authoritarianism: Bin Bayyah and the Politicization of Maqasid Discourse." *American Journal of Islam and Society*, Vol. 38, No. 3–4, 2021, pp. 36–70.

Henne, Peter. *Religious Appeals in Power Politics*. Cornell University Press, 2023.

Hightower, Victoria. "Assessing Historical Narratives of the UAE." *London School of Economics and Political Science Blog*, December 12, 2018, https://blogs.lse.ac.uk/mec/2018/12/12/assessing-historical-narratives-of-the-uae/.

Hill, Christopher. *The Changing Politics of Foreign Policy*. Palgrave, 2003.

Hinnebusch, Raymond. *The International Politics of the Middle East*. Manchester University Press, 2015.

Hinnebusch, Raymond. "The Politics of Identity in Middle East International Relations." In *International Relations of the Middle East*, edited by Louise Fawcett. Oxford University Press, 2019, pp. 158–79.

Hinnebusch, Raymond and Ehteshami, Anoushiravan. "Foreign Policymaking in the Middle East: Complex Realism." In *International Relations of the Middle East*, edited by Louise Fawcett. Oxford University Press, 2019, pp. 249–70.

Hodgson, Marshall. *The Venture of Islam*. University of Chicago Press, 1974.

Hoffman, Jonathan. "The Strategic Convergence of Sectarianism and Geopolitics: The Case of Bahrain." *Cornell International Affairs Review*, Vol. 12, No. 1, 2018, pp. 54–81.

Hoffman, Jonathan. "Religion, the State, and Politics in Saudi Arabia." *Middle East Policy*, Vol. 26, No. 3, 2019, pp. 113–29.

Hoffman, Jonathan. "Israel and the Counterrevolutionaries: Gauging Tel Aviv's Evolving Regional Alliances." *Durham Middle East Papers*, No. 102, 2020.

Hoffman, Jonathan. "The Return of Great-Power Competition to the Middle East: A Two-Level Game." *Middle East Policy*, Vol. 28, No. 1, 2021a, pp. 87–104,

Hoffman, Jonathan. "Moscow, Beijing, and the Crescent: Russian and Chinese Religious Soft Power in the Middle East." *Digest of Middle East Studies*, Vol. 30, No. 1, 2021b, pp. 1–11.

Holtsi, Kal. "National Role Conceptions in the Study of Foreign Policy." *International Studies Quarterly*, Vol. 14, No. 1, 1970, pp. 233–309.

Hopf, Ted. "The Promise of Constructivism in International Relations Theory." *International Security*, Vol. 23, No. 1, 1998, pp. 171–200.

Houghton, David. "Reinvigorating the Study of Foreign Policy Decision Making: Toward a Constructivist Approach." *Foreign Policy Analysis*, Vol. 3, No. 1, 2007, pp. 24–45.

Huang, Reyko. "Religious Instrumentalism in Violent Conflict." *Ethnopolitics*, Vol. 19, No. 2, 2020, pp. 150–61.

Hunt, Michael. *Ideology and U.S. Foreign Policy*. Yale University Press, 1987.

Huntington, Samuel. *The Clash of Civilizations and the Remaking of World Order*. Simon and Schuster, 1996.

Hurd, Ian. "Legitimacy and Authority in International Politics." *International Organization*, Vol. 53, No. 2, 1999, pp. 379–408.

Isaacs, Harold. *Idols of the Tribe: Group Identity and Political Change*. Harvard University Press, 1989.

Ismail, Raihan. *Saudi Clerics and Shi'a Islam*. Oxford University Press, 2016.

Jervis, Robert. *Perception and Misperception in International Politics*. Princeton University Press, 1976.

Jones, Clive and Guzansky, Yoel. Fraternal Enemies: Israel and the Gulf Monarchies. Oxford University Press, 2019.

Josua, Maria. "What Drives Diffusion? Anti-Terrorism Legislation in the Arab Middle East and North Africa." *Journal of Global Security Studies*, Vol. 6, No. 3, 2021, pp. 1–15.

Kahl, Colin. "Constructing a Separate Peace: Constructivism, Collective Liberal Identity, and Democratic Peace." *Security Studies*, Vol. 8, No. 2–3, 1998, pp. 94–144.

Kamrava, Mehran. *Qatar: Small State, Big Politics*. Cornell University Press, 2015.

Kaneva, Nadia. "Nation Branding: Toward an Agenda for Critical Research." *International Journal of Communication*, Vol. 5, No. 1, 2011, pp. 117–41.

Kaplan, Robert. *The Coming Anarchy: Shattering the Dreams of the Post-Cold War*. Vintage, 2001.

Katz, Mark. "Always Looming: The Russian Muslim Factor in Moscow's Relations with Arab Gulf States." In *Russia's Islamic Diplomacy*, edited by M. Laruelle. Institute for European Russian, and Eurasian Studies, 2019.

Kaufman, Stuart. *Modern Hatreds: The Symbolic Politics of Ethnic War*. Cornell University Press, 2001.
Kazziha, Walid. "The Impact of Palestine on Arab Politics." *The International Spectator*, Vol. 20, No. 2, 1985, pp. 11–19.
Keohane, Robert and Goldstein, Judith. *Ideas and Foreign Policy: Beliefs, Institutions, and Political Change*. Cornell University Press, 1993.
King, Keohane, and Verba. *Designing Social Inquiry: Scientific Inference in Qualitative Research*. Princeton University Press, 1994.
Kroenig, Matthew. *The Return of Great Power Rivalry: Democracy versus Autocracy from the Ancient World to the U.S. and China*. Oxford University Press, 2020.
Kuru, Ahmet. Islam, Authoritarianism, and Underdevelopment: A Global and Historical Comparison. Cambridge University Press, 2019.
Labelle, Maurice Jr. "The Only Thorn: Early Saudi-American Relations and the Question of Palestine, 1945-1949." *Diplomatic History*, Vol. 35, No. 2, 2011, pp. 257–81.
Lacroix, Stephane. *Awakening Islam: The Politics of Religious Dissent in Contemporary Saudi Arabia*. Harvard University Press, 2011.
Lee, Robert. *Religion and Politics in the Middle East: Identity, Ideology, Institutions, and Attitudes*. Routledge, 2014.
Lefevre, Raphael. "Syria." In *Rethinking Political Islam*, edited by Shadi Hamid and William McCants. Oxford University Press, 2017, pp. 73–87.
Levi, Werner. "Ideology, Interests, and Foreign Policy." *International Studies Quarterly*, Vol. 14, No. 1, 1970, pp. 1–31.
Levy, Jack. "Domestic Politics and War." *The Journal of Interdisciplinary History*, Vol. 18, No. 4, 1988, pp. 653–73.
Lewis, Bernard. "The Roots of Muslim Rage." *The Atlantic*, September 1990, https://www.theatlantic.com/magazine/archive/1990/09/the-roots-of-muslim-rage/304643/.
Lister, Charles. *The Syrian Jihad: Al-Qaeda, The Islamic State, and the Evolution of an Insurgency*. Oxford University Press, 2015.
Louer, Laurence. *Transnational Shia Politics: Religious and Political Networks in the Gulf*. Oxford University Press, 2008.
Louer, Laurence. *Sunnis and Shi'a: A Political History*. Princeton University Press, 2020.
Lynch, Mark. "Jordan's Identity and Interests." In *Identity and Foreign Policy in the Middle East*, edited by Shibley Telhami and Michael Barnett. Cornell University Press, 2002, pp. 26–57.
Lynch, Mark. *The New Arab Wars: Uprisings and Anarchy in the Middle East*. Public Affairs, 2017.
Lynch, Mark. "New Arab World Order." *Foreign Affairs*, August 16, 2018, https://carnegieendowment.org/2018/08/16/new-arab-world-order-pub-77056.
Mamdani, Mahmood. "Good Muslim, Bad Muslim: A Political Perspective on Culture and Terrorism." *American Anthropologist*, Vol. 104, No. 3, 2002, pp. 766–75.

Mandaville, Peter. *Islam and Politics*. Routledge, 2014.
Mandaville, Peter, and Hamid, Shadi. "Islam as Statecraft: How Governments Use Religion in Foreign Policy." *Brooking Institution*, 2018.
Mandaville, Peter. "Islam and International Relations in the Middle East: From Umma to Nation State." In *International Relations of the Middle East*, edited by Louise Fawcett. Oxford University Press, 2019, pp. 180–200.
Mandaville, Peter. *Islam and Politics*. Routledge, 2020.
Mandaville, Peter. *Wahhabism and the World: Understanding Saudi Arabia's Global Influence on Islam*. Oxford University Press, 2022.
Mandaville, Peter. *The Geopolitics of Religious Soft Power: How States Use Religion in Foreign Policy*. Oxford University Press, 2023.
Maoz, Zeev, and Henderson, Errol. *Scriptures, Shrines, Scapegoats, and World Politics*. University of Michigan Press, 2020.
Markey, Daniel. *China's Western Horizon: Beijing and the New Geopolitics of Eurasia*. Oxford University Press, 2020.
Mason, Robert, ed. *Reassessing Order and Disorder in the Middle East: Regional Imbalance or Disintegration?* Rowman and Littlefield, 2017.
Masoud, Tarek. *Counting Islam: Religion, Class, and Elections in Egypt*. Cambridge University Press, 2014.
Matthiesen, Toby. *Sectarian Gulf: Bahrain, Saudi Arabia, and the Arab Spring That Wasn't*. Stanford University Press, 2013.
Matthiesen, Toby. *The Other Saudis: Shiism, Dissent, and Sectarianism*. Cambridge University Press, 2015.
Matthiesen, Toby. "Renting the Casbah: Gulf States' Foreign Policy Towards North Africa Since the Arab Uprisings." In *The Changing Security Dynamics of the Persian Gulf*, edited by Kristian Ulrichsen. Oxford University Press, 2017a, pp. 43–60.
Matthiesen, Toby. "Saudi Arabia." In *Rethinking Political Islam*, edited by Shadi Hamid and William McCants. Oxford University Press, 2017b, pp. 118–31.
Mayer, Ann Elizabeth. *Islam and Human Rights: Tradition and Politics."* Westview Press, 2013.
Meibauer, Gustav. "Interests, Ideas, and the Study of State Behaviour in Neoclassical Realism." *Review of International Studies*, Vol. 46, No. 1, 2019, pp. 20–36
Meibauer, Gustav. "Interests, Ideas, and the Study of State Behavior in Neoclassical Realism." *Review of International Studies*, Vol. 46, No. 1, 2020, pp. 20–36.
Menoret, Pascal. "Saudi Arabia-." In *The Middle East*, edited by Ellen Lust. CQ Press, 2017, pp. 737–54.
Mernissi, Fatema and Lakeland, Mary Jo. *Islam and Democracy: Fear of the Modern World*. Basic Books, 2002.
Mitchell, Jocelyn Sage and Al-Hammadi, Mariam Ibrahim. "Nationalism and Identity in Qatar after 2017: The Narrative of the New National Museum." *Journal of Arabian Studies*, Vol. 10, No. 2, 2020, pp. 256–77.

Moravcsik, Andrew. "Taking Preferences Seriously: A Liberal Theory of International Relations." *International Organization*, Vol. 51, No. 4, 1997, pp. 513–53.

Nakissa, Aria. "The Fiqh of Revolution and the Arab Spring: Secondary Segmentation as a Trend in Islamic Legal Doctrine." *The Muslim World*, Vol. 105, No. 3, 2015, pp. 398–421.

Nasr, Vali. "The Rise of Muslim Democracy." *Journal of Democracy*, Vol. 16, No. 2, 2005, pp. 13–27.

Nasr, Vali. *The Shia Revival: How Conflicts within Islam will Shape the Future*. W. W. Norton & Company, 2007.

Neack, Laura. *The New Foreign Policy: Complex Interactions, Competing Interests*. Rowman and Littlefield, 2014.

Nexon, Daniel. "Religion and International Relations: No Leap of Faith Required." In *religion and International Relations Theory*, edited by Jack Snyder, 2011, pp. 141–67.

Nye, Joseph. "Soft Power." *Foreign Policy*, 1990.

Nye, Joseph. *Soft Power: The Means to Success in World Politics*. Public Affairs, 2004.

Ozgen, Zeynep and Hassan, Sharif Ibrahim El Shishtawy. "Meaning of a Textbook: Religious Education, National Islam, and the Politics of Reform in the United Arab Emirates." *Nations and Nationalism*, Vol. 27, No. 4, 2021, pp. 1181–97.

Pahwa, Sumita. "Pathways of Islamist Adaptation: The Egyptian Muslim Brothers' Lessons for Inclusion Moderation Theory." *Democratization*, Vol. 24, No. 6, 2017, pp. 1066–84.

Phillips, Christopher. *The Battle for Syria: International Rivalry in the New Middle East*. Yale University Press, 2016.

Piscatori, James. *Islam in the Political Process*. Cambridge University Press, 1993.

Piscatori, James and Saikal, Amin. *Islam Beyond Borders: The Umma in World Politics*. Cambridge University Press, 2019.

Przeworski, Adam and Teune, Henry. *The Logic of Comparative Social Inquiry*. John Wiley and Sons, 1970.

Putnam, Robert. "Diplomacy and Domestic Politics: The Logic of Two-Level Games." *International Organization*, Vol. 42, No. 3, 1998, pp. 427–69.

Quisay, Walaa and Parker, Thomas. "On the Theology of Obedience: An Analysis of Shaykh Bin Bayyah and Shaykh Hamza Yusuf's Political Thought." *Maydan*, January 8, 2019, https://themaydan.com/2019/01/theology-obedience-analysis-shaykh-bin-bayyah-shaykh-hamza-yusufs-political-thought/.

Ratelle, J. "A Kadyrovization of Russian Foreign Policy in the Middle East: Autocrats in Track II Diplomacy and Other Humanitarian Activities." In *Russia's Islamic Diplomacy*, edited by M. Laruelle. Institute for European, Russian, and Eurasian Studies, 2019.

Risen, Clay. "Branding Nations." New York Times, December 11, 2005. https://www.nytimes.com/2005/12/11/magazine/branding-nations.html

Risse-Kappen, Thomas. "Public Opinion, Domestic Structure, and Foreign Policy in Liberal Democracies." *World Politics*, Vol. 43, No. 1, 1991, pp. 479–512.

Rizvi, Hasan-Askari. *Pakistan and the Geostrategic Environment: A Study of Foreign Policy*. Palgrave, 1993.

Roberts, David. "Qatar and the Muslim Brotherhood: Pragmatism or Preference?" Middle East Policy, Vol. 21, No. 3, 2014, 84–94

Roberts, David. "Mosque and State: The United Arab Emirates' Secular Foreign Policy." *Foreign Affairs*, March 18, 2016, https://www.foreignaffairs.com/united-arab-emirates/mosque-and-state.

Roberts, David. *Qatar: Securing the Global Ambitions of a City-State*. Hurst, 2017a.

Roberts, David. "Qatar and the UAE: Exploring Divergent Responses to the Arab Spring." *Middle East Journal*, Vol. 71, No. 4, 2017b, pp. 544–62.

Roberts, David. "Bucking the Trend: The UAE and the Development of Military Capabilities in the Arab World." *Security Studies*, Vol. 29, No. 2, 2020, pp. 301–34.

Rousseau, David and Garcia-Retamero, Rocio. "Identity, Power, and Threat Perception." *Journal of Conflict Resolution*, Vol. 51, No. 5, 2007, pp. 744–71.

Rubin, Barry. *Guide to Islamist Movements*. M.E. Sharpe, 2010.

Rubin, Lawrence. *Islam in the Balance: Ideational Threats in Arab Politics*. Stanford University Press, 2014.

Ruggie, John. *Constructing the World Polity: Essays on International Institutionalization*. Routledge, 1998.

Russett, Bruce, et al. "The Democratic Peace." *International Security*, Vol. 19, No. 4, 1995, pp. 164–84.

Ryan, Curtis. *Inter-Arab Alliances: Regime Security and Jordanian Foreign Policy*. University Press of Florida, 2009.

Sabban, Rima. "State Building, State Branding, and Heritage in the UAE." *London School of Economics and Political Science Blog*, December 17, 2018, https://blogs.lse.ac.uk/mec/2018/12/17/state-building-state-branding-and-heritage-in-the-uae/.

Sachedina, Abdulaziz. *Islam and the Challenge of Human Rights*. Oxford University Press, 2009.

Sadowski, Yahya. "The Evolution of Political Identity in Syria." In *Identity and Foreign Policy in the Middle East*, edited by Shibley Telhami and Michael Barnett. Cornell University Press, 2002, pp. 137–54.

Said, Edward. *Orientalism*. Pantheon Books, 1978.

Saidabadi, Mohammad Reza. "Islam and Foreign Policy in the Contemporary Secular World: The Case of Post-Revolutionary Iran." *Pacifica Review: Peace, Security & Global Change*, Vol. 8, No. 2, 1996, pp. 32–44.

Salloukh, B. "Overlapping Contests and Middle East International Relations: The Return of the Weak Arab State." *American Political Science Association*, Vol. 50, No. 3, 2017, pp. 660–3.

Samuel, S. "China Is Treating Islam Like a Mental Illness." *The Atlantic*, August 28, 2018, https://www.theatlantic.com/international/archive/2018/08/china-pathologizing-uighur-muslims-mental-illness/568525/.

Sandal, Nukhet. *Religion in International Relations: Interactions and Possibilities*. Routledge, 2015.

Sandal, Nukhet and James, Patrick. "Religion and International Relations Theory: Towards a Mutual Understanding." *European Journal of International Relations*, Vol. 17, No. 1, 2010, pp. 3–25.

Savage, Charlie, et al. "Trump Pushes to Designate Muslim Brotherhood as Terrorist Organization." *The New York Times*, April 30, 2019, https://www.nytimes.com/2019/04/30/us/politics/trump-muslim-brotherhood.html.

Schwedler, Jillian. *Faith in Moderation: Islamist Parties in Jordan and Yemen*. Cambridge University Press, 2007.

Selim Gamal. "The United States and the Arab Spring: The Dynamics of Political Engineering." *Arab Studies Quarterly*, Vol. 35, No. 3, 2013, pp. 255–72.

Shaffer, Brenda. *The Limits of Culture: Islam and Foreign Policy*. MIT Press, 2006.

Shahrour, Karam. "The Evolution of Emirati Foreign Policy (1971-2020): The Unexpected Rise of a Small State with Boundless Ambitions." *Sciences Po Kuwait Program*, 2020, https://www.sciencespo.fr/kuwait-program/wp-content/uploads/2021/02/Shahrour-Karam-The-evolution-of-Emirati-foreign-policy-1971-2020.pdf.

Sheikh, Mona Kanwal. "How Does Religion Matter? Pathways to Religion in International Relations." *Review of International Studies*, Vol. 38, No. 1, 2012, pp. 365–92.

Sheline, Annelle and Ulrichsen, Kristian. "Mohammed bin Salman and Religious Authority and Reform in Saudi Arabia." *Rice University's Baker Institute for Public Policy*, September 19, 2019, https://scholarship.rice.edu/bitstream/handle/1911/108116/bi-report-092319-cme-mbs-saudi.pdf?sequence=1&isAllowed=y.

Sheline, Annelle. "Shifting Reputations for 'Moderation': Evidence from Qatar, Jordan, and Morocco." Middle East Law and Governance, Vol 12, No. 1, 2020, pp. 109–129

Siegel, Alexandra. "Twitter Wars: Sunni-Shia Conflict and Cooperation in the Digital Age." In *Beyond Sunni and Shia: The Roots of Sectarianism in a Changing Middle East*, edited by Frederic Wehrey. Oxford University Press, 2017, pp. 157–80.

Snyder, Jack. *Myths of Empire: Domestic Politics and International Ambition*. Cornell University Press, 1991.

Snyder, Jack. *Religion and International Relations*. Columbia University Press, 2011.

Spencer, James. "The GCC Needs a Successful Strategy for Yemen, Not Failed Tactics." *Middle East Research and Information Project (MERIP)*, September 11, 2015, https://merip.org/2015/09/the-gcc-needs-a-successful-strategy-for-yemen/.

Stein, Ewan. *International Relations in the Middle East: Hegemonic Strategies and Regional Order*. Cambridge University Press, 2021.

Stein, Sabina. "Competing Political Science Perspectives on the Role of Religion in Conflict." *Center for Security Studies*, ZTH Zurich, 2011, https://css.ethz.ch/content/dam/ethz/special-interest/gess/cis/center-for-securities-studies/pdfs/Politorbis-52-21-26.pdf.

Strakes, Jason. "Towards an Islamic Geopolitics: Reconciling the Ummah and Territoriality in Contemporary International Relations." In *Islam in International Relations: Politics and Paradigms*, edited by Nassef Manabilang Adiong et. al. Routledge, 2018, pp. 218–32.

Tabaar, Mohammad Ayatollahi. *Religious Statecraft: The Politics of Islam in Iran*. Columbia University Press, 2018.

Tambiah, S. J. *Buddhism Betrayed? Religion, Politics, and Violence in Sri Lanka*. University of Chicago Press, 1992.

Tayfur, Fatih M. "Systemic-Structural Approaches, World-System Analysis, and the Study of Foreign Policy." *METU Studies in Development*, Vol. 27, No. 3–4, 2000, pp. 265–99.

Tir, J. and Jasinski, M. "Domestic-Level Diversionary Theory of War: Targeting Ethnic Minorities." *Journal of Conflict Resolution*, Vol. 52, No. 5, 2008, pp. 641–64.

Trenin, Dmitri. *What Is Russia up to in the Middle East?* Polity Press, 2017.

Turner, John. "Uncovering an Islamic Paradigm of International Relations." In *Political and Cultural Representations of Muslims: Islam in the Plural*, edited by Christopher Flood. Brill, 2012.

Ugarriza, Juan and Craig, Matthew. "The Relevance of Ideology to Contemporary Armed Conflicts: A Quantitative Analysis of Former Combatants in Columbia." *Journal of Conflict Resolution*, Vol. 57, No. 3, 2013, pp. 445–77.

Ulrichsen, Kristian. "Links Between Domestic and Regional Security." In *The Changing Security Dynamics of the Persian Gulf*, edited by Kristian Ulrichsen. Oxford University Press, 2017a, pp. 23–42.

Ulrichsen, Kristian. *The United Arab Emirates: Power, Politics, and Policymaking*. Routledge, 2017b.

Ulrichsen, Kristian. "Crown Prince of Disorder." *Foreign Policy*, March 21, 2018, https://foreignpolicy.com/2018/03/21/crown-prince-of-disorder/.

Ulrichsen, Kristian. "Reflections on Mohammed bin Zayed's Preferences Regarding UAE Foreign Policy." *Arab Center Washington DC*, July 24, 2020a, https://arabcenterdc.org/resource/reflections-on-mohammed-bin-zayeds-preferences-regarding-uae-foreign-policy/.

Ulrichsen, Kristian. *Qatar and the Gulf Crisis*. Oxford University Press, 2020b.

Van Ham, Peter. "The Rise of the Brand State: The Postmodern Politics of Image and Reputation." *Foreign Affairs*, Vol. 80, No. 5, 2001, pp. 2–6.

Varagur, Krithika. *The Call: Inside the Global Saudi Religious Project*. Columbia University Press, 2020.

Volpi, Frederic. "Islam, Political Islam, and the State System." In *Routledge Handbook of International Relations in the Middle East*, edited by Shahram Akbarzadeh. Routledge, 2019, pp. 69–81.

Walker, Stephen. "Symbolic Interactionism and International Politics: Role Theory's Contribution to International Organization." In *Contending Dramas: A Cognitive Approach to International Organizations*, edited by Martha Cottam and Zhiyu Shi. Praeger, 1992.

Walt, Stephen. *The Origins of Alliances*. Cornell University Press, 1987.

Waltz, Kenneth. *Theory of International Politics*. Addison-Wesley Publishing Co., 1979.

Walzer, Michael. "The New Tribalism." *Dissent Magazine*, Spring 1992, https://www.dissentmagazine.org/article/the-new-tribalism.

Warner, Carolyn. "Christian Democracy in Italy: An Alternative Path to Religious Party Moderation." *Party Politics*, Vol. 19, No. 2, 2013, pp. 256–76.

Warner, Carolyn and Walker, Stephen. "Thinking About the Role of Religion in Foreign Policy: A Framework for Analysis." *Foreign Policy Analysis*, Vol. 7, No. 1, 2011, pp. 113–35.

Warren, David. "Qatari Support for the Muslim Brotherhood is More Than Just Realpolitik, It Has a Long, Personal History." *Maydan*, July 12, 2017, https://themaydan.com/2017/07/qatari-support-muslim-brotherhood-just-realpolitik-long-personal-history/.

Warren, David. "Religion, Politics, and the Anxiety of Maslaha Reasoning: the Production of Fiqh Al-Thawra after the 2011 Egyptian Revolution," in Locating the Sharia: Legal Fluidity in Theory, ed. by S. Siddiqui. Brill, 2019, 226–248.

Warren, David. *Rivals in the Gulf: Yusuf al-Qaradawi, Abdullah Bin Bayyah, and the Qatar-UAE Contest Over the Arab Spring and the Gulf Crisis*. Routledge, 2021.

Warren, David. "Interfaith Dialogue in the United Arab Emirates: Where International Relations Meets State-Branding." *Berkley Center for Religion, Peace, and World Affairs*, July 12, 2021, https://berkleycenter.georgetown.edu/posts/interfaith-dialogue-in-the-united-arab-emirates-where-international-relations-meets-state-branding.

Warren, David, et al. "Roundtable on State Islam after the Arab Uprisings." *Jadaliyya*, November 23, 2020, https://www.jadaliyya.com/Details/41990/Roundtable-on-State-Islam-after-the-Arab-Uprisings.

Wastnidge, Edward and Mabon, Simon. *Saudi Arabia and Iran: The Struggle to Shape the Middle East*. Manchester University Press, 2022.

Wehrey, Frederic. "The Forgotten Uprising in Eastern Saudi Arabia." *Carnegie Endowment for International Peace*, June 14, 2013, https://carnegieendowment.org/2013/06/14/forgotten-uprising-in-eastern-saudi-arabia-pub-52093.

Wehrey, Frederic. *Beyond Sunni and Shia: The Roots of Sectarianism in a Changing Middle East*. Oxford University Press, 2018.

Wendt, Alexander. "Anarchy Is What States Make of It." *International Organization*, Vol. 46, No. 3, 1992, pp. 391–425.

Wendt, Alexander. *Social Theory of International Politics*. Cambridge University Press, 1999.

Wilhelmsen, J. "Between a Rock and a Hard Place: The Islamization of the Chechen Separatist Movement." *Europe-Asia Studies*, Vol. 57, No. 1, 2005, pp. 35–59.

Yadav, Stacey. "Understanding What Islamists Want: Public Debate and Contestation in Lebanon and Yemen." *Middle East Journal*, Vol. 64, No. 2, 2010, pp. 199–213.

Yildirim, A. Kadir. "The New Guardians of Religion: Islam and Authority in the Middle East." *Baker Institute for Public Policy*, March 12, 2019, https://www.bakerinstitute.org/research/new-guardians-religion-islam-and-authority-middle-east.

Zachariades, Alexandros. "Identity and Turkish Foreign Policy in the AK Parti Era." *E-International Relations*, March 21, 2018, https://www.e-ir.info/2018/03/21/identity-and-turkish-foreign-policy-in-the-ak-parti-era/.

Zulfiqar, Adnan. "Revolutionary Islamic Jurisprudence: A Restatement of the Arab Spring." *New York University Journal of International Law and Politics*, Vol. 49, 2017, pp. 443–97.

INDEX

9/11 terrorist attacks 48, 71
1991 Gulf War 10

Abou El Fadl, Khaled 51
Abraham Accords 60, 144, 190, 191, 210
"Abrahamic Family House" 1, 190
absolute obedience 101, 170
Abu Dhabi 1, 15, 151, 152, 154, 155, 157–60, 162, 164, 165, 167–9, 172, 175–7, 186, 189, 191–5, 199, 201–3, 210
Al-Ahmad, Sheikh Yusuf 89
Aljazeera 80, 86, 94, 102, 118, 120, 121, 125, 129, 135, 140, 143
al-Qaeda 2, 48, 71, 88, 95
American Jewish Committee 104
Al-'Amir, Tawfiq 78
Ankara 58, 138, 139, 141
anti-Shi'ism 78, 101, 108
anti-terror quartet 102, 136, 137, 139
Arab Cold War 68
Arab uprisings 8–10, 12, 14, 15, 32, 46, 47, 49, 51, 52, 57, 64, 65, 72–4, 78, 82, 87, 91, 102, 106–10, 113, 119–21, 131, 139, 140, 146, 147, 149, 158, 166, 171, 178, 180, 193, 195, 197, 198, 202, 209
Al-Arefe, Sheikh Mohamad 92, 94
Al-Assad, Bashar 57, 59, 72, 91, 92, 108, 127, 168, 200
Al-Attiyah, Sheikh Mohammed 88
Al-Awdah, Sheikh Salman 75–7, 85, 90, 99, 141
Al-Azhar 124, 125, 132, 133, 177, 187
Al-Baghdadi, Abu Bakr 81, 82

Bahrain 57, 58, 69, 78, 80, 88–90, 92, 95, 107, 129, 130, 141, 167, 199
Barnett, Michael 26
Al-Barrak, Sheikh Abul Rahman 94
Al-Barrak, Sheikh Nasir 87
Beijing 61, 105, 106, 141–3
Ben Ali, Zine El Abidine 123, 173
Bin Bayyah, Sheikh Abdullah 171–8, 180–2, 184, 188–90, 196
Bin Laden, Osama 70, 71
Bin Nayef, Muhammad 95

China 105, 106, 141, 142, 147, 201
Chinese Islamic Association 106
constructivism 3, 6, 13, 17, 19, 25–8, 43, 45, 46, 53, 54
The Council of Senior Scholars 67, 72, 78, 82–4, 86, 93, 98, 99, 102
Council on American-Islamic Relations (CAIR) 165
counterrevolutionaries 131, 135, 139, 140

democracy 50, 58, 76, 93, 122, 162, 178–80, 196, 208
Doha 10, 14, 58, 85, 102, 108, 113, 116, 118–20, 127, 129–31, 135, 137–43, 146–9, 168, 199–201, 203

Eastern Province (Saudi Arabia) 77–9, 88, 89, 108
Egypt 50, 52, 68, 76, 81, 85, 124, 126, 131, 132, 135, 136, 166, 175, 177
Erdogan, Recep Tayyip 138, 139

fiqh al-thawra (the jurisprudence of revolution)   51, 113, 123, 125, 129, 130, 148, 203
foreign policy   2, 3, 18, 19, 26, 31–3, 35–7, 41, 43, 56, 69, 73, 117, 154, 197, 204
Forum for Promoting Peace in Muslim Societies (FPPMS)   175, 176, 186, 191
Fox, Jonathan   18, 26
Francis, Pope   189, 190

Gaddafi, Muammar   126, 127, 167, 174
Gargash, Anwar   165
Gaza   143, 145, 209, 210
Al-Ghannouchi, Rashid   123, 126
Grand Mosque in Mecca   69, 70, 98, 105, 209
Gulf Cooperation Council (GCC)   89, 130, 187
Gulf crisis   102, 130, 135–9, 148, 201

Hadi, Abd Rabu Mansour   93, 130, 167
Haftar, Khalifa   127, 167
Hamad, Emir   117, 125, 128
Hamas   143, 156, 209
hermeneutical hegemony   39, 48, 50, 56, 111
Hezbollah   128, 156
Houthi movement   93, 167
Hussein, Saddam   70

Ibn al-Uthaymeen, Muhammad   71
Ibn Baz, Sheikh Abd al-Aziz   71
Ibn Saud   66
identity   34–7, 39
ideology   7, 22, 24, 26, 28, 37–9, 42
instrumentalism   6, 13, 19, 22–4, 45, 46, 53–4
international relations (IR)   2, 13, 17, 18, 23, 43

International Union of Muslim Scholars (IUMS)   102, 113, 116, 117, 123, 127–30, 134, 137–9, 141–3, 172, 173, 209
Iran   38, 57, 72, 73, 78, 87–9, 91, 94, 111, 128
Islah   94, 153, 154, 156–8, 160, 161, 163, 164, 167
Islam   5, 9–12, 45–7, 51, 53, 55, 59, 60, 63, 66, 82, 97, 98, 100, 104, 109, 185, 205
Islamic State (ISIS)   2, 50, 81, 86, 92
Islamism   11, 15, 50, 58, 60, 66, 69, 99, 151, 152, 186
Islamophobia   208
Israel   60, 103, 143–5, 190, 209, 210
Al-Issa, Mohammed bin Abdul-Karim   103, 104

jihad   69, 70, 91, 128
jurisprudence of peace   178, 184

Kadyrov, Ramzan   104, 105
Al-Khalifa, Hamad bin Isa   88–90, 167
Al-Khalifa monarchy   57, 58, 78, 79, 167
Khashoggi, Jamal   98

"Liberal World Order"   2, 18
Libya   80, 126–8, 167, 174
Libyan National Army (LNA)   127, 167

Al-Majid, Sheikh Fahad bin Saad   93, 94
Al-Maktoum, Sheikh Rashid bin Sa'id   153, 180
Middle East   1, 4, 5, 8–10, 12, 26, 32, 45, 49, 50, 52–5, 57, 59, 61, 71, 72, 80, 101, 113, 115, 117, 119, 131, 139, 140, 148, 149, 153, 156, 158, 166, 171, 178, 189, 191, 192, 199, 206–8

moderate Islam 15, 59, 60, 97, 102–4, 106, 109, 152, 176, 185, 193, 202, 207
Mohammed bin Salman (MbS) 14, 66, 87, 92, 95–100, 103, 104, 110, 111, 169
Mohammed bin Zayed Al-Nahyan (MbZ) 15, 155–8, 160, 168–70, 195
Morsi, Mohamed 52, 76, 81, 84, 85, 125, 131, 132, 141, 166
Moscow 61, 105, 168
Mubarak, Hosni 76, 81, 124, 133, 166
mujahideen 69
Muslim Brotherhood (MB) 14, 49, 50, 58–60, 67, 68, 72, 74, 76, 80, 81, 84–6, 90, 91, 94, 96, 98, 99, 101, 108, 113, 115, 118, 120, 123–5, 127, 128, 131, 132, 134, 135, 138, 139, 141, 146, 153, 154, 156, 159, 164, 167, 168, 170, 186, 188, 192, 195, 200
Muslim Council of Elders (MCE) 175, 176
Muslim World League (MWL) 68, 103, 105

Al-Nahyan, Sheikh Khalifa bin Zayed 155, 189
Nasser, Gamal Abdel 68
Nidaa Tounes 166
Al-Nimr, Sheikh Nimr 78, 79, 87

Operation Decisive Storm 93, 94, 130
Organization of Islamic Cooperation (OIC) 89, 105–6
Al-Otaybi, Juhayman 69

Palestine 103, 143, 147, 201
politics of Islam 62, 63
post-Islamism 50

post-Islamists 206
primordialism 13, 19–22, 45
primordialist approach 20–2, 45
Putin, Vladimir 61

Al-Qaradaghi, Ali 130, 137–9, 141, 143, 144
Al-Qaradawi, Sheikh Yusuf 76, 102, 113, 116–18, 120–36, 139, 143, 144, 148, 170, 172, 173
Al-Qarni, Sheikh A'id 94
Al-Qarni, Sheikh Awad 92
Al-Qasimi, Sheikh Saqr bin Muhammad 154, 156, 158
Al-Qassemi, Sultan 153
Qatar 10, 14, 58–60, 73, 85, 86, 91, 102, 104, 108, 113–50, 152, 154, 159, 161, 168, 170, 186, 192, 195, 198–202, 209
Questions of Revolution (As'ilat al-Thawra) (Al-Awdah) 76
Quran 47, 80, 94, 123, 181

Rabaa Massacre 84, 134, 135
radicalism 60, 103, 185
Raissouni, Ahmed 138, 141, 144
Ras al-Khaimah 152–4, 156, 158, 163
regime Islam 49
religion 1–8, 11–15, 17–29, 31, 33, 34, 36, 39–43, 46, 48–50, 53, 54, 56, 61, 65, 67, 69, 72, 73, 97, 100, 101, 104, 109–11, 113, 149, 151, 163, 164, 194, 197, 204, 208
religious resources 3, 6, 9, 41, 42, 64, 197
religious soft power 1, 4, 6–9, 11–14, 19, 20, 28, 40–4, 46, 47, 63–5, 87, 101, 104, 106, 107, 110, 111, 113, 121, 140, 145–51, 159, 171, 174, 177, 178, 185, 189, 190, 192, 193, 195, 197–201, 204–9

Index

Riyadh 9, 11, 14, 65, 68–70, 72, 73, 78, 80, 82, 84–6, 89, 91–6, 101–7, 109–11, 116, 117, 130, 141, 167, 199, 200, 202, 204
Russia 2, 61, 92, 104, 105, 188

sacred capital 3, 41, 42, 64, 115, 120, 171, 176, 177
"Safavids" 89, 92
sahwa; *sahwa al-islamiyyah* (Islamic awakening) movement 67, 69–72, 74, 75, 85, 92, 98
Al-Salafi, Saudi Sheikh Abdullah 89
Salafism 67
Saleh, Ali Abdullah 92, 93, 130, 167
Salman, Mohammed bin 92, 95–7, 99–101, 105, 109, 111, 202
Al-Saud, Abdulaziz bin Abdul Rahman 66
Al-Saud, Abdullah bin Abdulaziz 81, 84, 95, 98, 100
Al-Saud, Fahd bin Abdulaziz 70, 89, 199
Al-Saud, Faisal bin Abdulaziz 68
Al-Saud, Salman bin Abdulaziz 95
Saudi Arabia 9, 12, 38, 57, 59, 65–111, 114–17, 127, 129, 130, 140, 154, 158, 159, 162, 167, 197, 202, 204, 209
Saudi Ministry of Islamic Affairs 94
Saudi-UAE-Egypt axis 59–61
sectarianism 57, 58, 77, 78, 84, 87, 88, 95, 108, 110, 175, 204
Al-Sheikh, Abd al-Latif 86
Al-Sheikh, Abdulaziz Abdullah 66, 82, 89, 91, 94, 95, 98
Shi'ism 57, 87
Al-Siddiq, Mohammad Abdul Razzaq 161, 162, 164

El-Sisi, Abdel Fattah 52, 132–5, 167
statecraft 1, 3, 5, 6, 8, 12, 15, 27, 29, 42, 47, 59, 64, 65, 110, 113, 114, 151, 194, 197, 204–8
state Islam 49
Al-Sudais, Abdul-Rahman 98, 209
Sunnism 51, 59
Syria 57, 59, 91, 92, 127, 128, 168, 200, 204

Tabaar, Mohammad Ayatollahi 27, 28, 62
Tahrir Square 76, 124
Tamarod movement 167
Al-Tarifi, Sheikh Abdulaziz 94
Al-Taskhiri, Muhammad 'Ali 130
El-Tayeb, Ahmed 175, 177, 190
Tehran 57, 88, 200
terrorism 59, 60, 84, 86, 102, 103, 137, 156, 164
Al-Thani, Emir Ahmad bin 'Ali 116, 117, 119, 120, 125, 130, 199, 200
Al-Thani, Mohammed bin Abdulrahman 137
Al-Thani, Tamim bin Hamad 135
Trump, Donald 137, 144, 168, 190
Tunisia 80, 90, 123, 124, 126, 173
Turkey 58, 59, 128, 138, 139, 141
Twelver Shi'ism 93, 94

UAE Fatwa Council 176, 178, 186, 191
United Arab Emirates (UAE) 1, 10, 15, 101, 113, 127, 151–96, 201–4, 210
United States 2, 10, 18, 38, 55, 60, 61, 69–71, 102, 117, 137, 155–8, 168, 170, 172, 174, 185, 186, 192, 193, 204, 207

Vision 2030 96, 100

Al-Wahhab, Muhammad Ibn
    Abd   66, 67, 82, 86
Wahhabism   38, 67, 78, 81, 96,
    115, 152
wilayat al-faqih   76

Xi Jinping   61

Yemen   80, 92–5, 101, 108, 110,
    129, 130, 137, 167, 204
Yusuf, Hamza   171, 172, 174–6,
    182, 184, 188, 189

Al-Zayd, Sheikh Umar   91
Zayed, Abdullah bin   175